5?

THE PENGUIN CLASSICS

FOUNDER EDITOR (1944–64) E. V. RIEU

Editor: Betty Radice

PLATO (*c.* 427–347 B.C.) stands with Socrates and Aristotle as one of the shapers of the whole intellectual tradition of the West. He came from a family that had long played a prominent part in Athenian politics, and it would have been natural for him to follow the same course. He declined to do so, however, disgusted by the violence and corruption of Athenian political life, and sickened especially by the execution in 399 of his friend and teacher, Socrates. Inspired by Socrates' inquiries into the nature of ethical standards, Plato sought a cure for the ills of society not in politics but philosophy, and arrived at his fundamental and lasting conviction that those ills would never cease until philosophers became rulers or rulers philosophers. At an uncertain date in the early fourth century B.C. he founded in Athens the Academy, the first permanent institution devoted to philosophical research and teaching, and the prototype of all western universities. He travelled extensively, notably to Sicily as political adviser to Dionysius II, ruler of Syracuse.

Plato wrote over twenty philosophical dialogues, of which the *Laws* – in which he depicts a *practical* 'Utopia' – is probably the last and certainly the longest; there are also extant under his name thirteen letters, whose genuineness is keenly disputed. His literary activity extended over perhaps half a century; few other writers have exploited so effectively the grace and ███████ flexibility and power, of Greek prose.

TREVOR J. SAUN██████████████████████████ and was educated at Chi██████████████████████████ London, and Emmanuel ██████████████████████████ ersities of London and H██████████████████████ ersity of Newcastle upon T██████████████████ ne Institute for Advanced Study, F████████████ is in Greek philosophy, especially political, ██████████ ory, on which he has published numerous works, in█████ revision and representation of T. A. Sinclair's translation of Aristotle's *Politics* in Penguin Classics. His recreations include railway history and the cinema.

PLATO
THE LAWS

———————— * ————————

TRANSLATED
WITH AN INTRODUCTION BY
TREVOR J. SAUNDERS

PENGUIN BOOKS

Penguin Books Ltd, Harmondsworth, Middlesex, England
Penguin Books, 40 West 23rd Street, New York, New York 10010, U.S.A.
Penguin Books Australia Ltd, Ringwood, Victoria, Australia
Penguin Books Canada Ltd, 2801 John Street, Markham, Ontario, Canada L3R 1B4
Penguin Books (N.Z.) Ltd, 182–190 Wairau Road, Auckland 10, New Zealand

—

First published in this translation 1970
Reprinted 1972
Reprinted with minor revisions 1975
Reprinted 1976, 1978, 1980, 1982, 1984

—

—

Made and printed in Great Britain by
Hazell Watson & Viney Limited,
Member of the BPCC Group,
Aylesbury, Bucks
Set in Monotype Garamond

CONTENTS

CONTENTS

BK
V

7

CONTENTS

CONTENTS

CONTENTS

CONTENTS

CONTENTS

13

CONTENTS

Map of Central Crete

Iraklion

Anóyia

Cnossós

Korfais•

Mt. I D A

Cave of Zeus
Plain of Nida

Mt. Koudhouni

M E S S A R A

R.Hieropotamos

•Gortyn

Phaistos

Asterousian Mts.

0 Miles 10

The probable site of Plato's Magnesia is somewhere in the shaded area at the western end of the plain of Messara. For the evidence, see G. R. Morrow, *Plato's Cretan City*, 31 and 95; see also 27–8 for a reconstruction of the probable route taken by the Athenian and his companions from Cnossos to the Cave of Zeus.

INTRODUCTION

If you control the way children play, and the same children always play the same games under the same rules and in the same conditions, and get pleasure from the same toys, you'll find that the conventions of adult life too are left in peace without alteration. . . . Change, we shall find, except in something evil, is extremely dangerous.

PLATO, *Laws*, 797

In a higher world it is otherwise; but here below to live is to change, and to be perfect is to have changed often.

JOHN HENRY NEWMAN, *An Essay on the Development of Christian Doctrine*, Chapter 1, Section 1

UTOPIANISM

The *Laws* describes, in rich and fascinating detail, a Utopia to be founded in Crete in the middle of the fourth century B.C. It is to be a small agricultural state, governed by a virtually unalterable code of laws and insulated from almost all day-to-day contact with the rest of the world. The fundamental conviction which inspires the whole project is that, given care and effort, it is possible to achieve a society that is at once excellent and unchanging. At a popular level, this optimistic belief has never lost its influence: it is still the unformulated assumption behind political programmes of widely varying complexions. The procedure sounds straightforward enough: simply decide on your model, your perfect society; then mould your existing society to it, and behold! the millennium has arrived. But the millennium seems constantly to elude us; and our fellow-men often display an unaccountable reluctance to be moulded. Should we then *force* them to conform? After all, it will surely be for their own good. Now at this point the utopian risks dangerous conflict with society,[1] and for these and other reasons both philosophers and laymen in recent years have waxed hot against utopianism, particularly Plato's, so that today it may fairly be said to be discredited. It is generally held that 'piecemeal' reform is as much as we should ever attempt; constant change in the structure of society, and versatility and adaptability in its members, are looked on with approval. Newman's aphorism has become the conventional wisdom.

But does this mean that the *Laws*, as a utopian work, deserves the full measure of our censure? A brief review of Plato's life and thought will enable us to understand the origins and nature of his book.

PLATO'S LIFE AND WORK

Plato was born in 427 B.C. into an aristocratic and well-connected Athenian family. His father's name was Ariston, his mother's Perictione; he had two brothers and one sister. When he was no more than a boy his father died, and his mother married Pyrilampes, who had been on friendly terms with Pericles (died 429), the leader of the Athenian democracy. Plato himself never married; of his appearance, habits and character we know little. He was probably wealthy, and after a long career devoted largely to philosophy and politics, died in 347.

In the half-century before his birth Athens had reached the peak of her wealth, influence and renown. With Sparta, she had taken the leading part in the repulse of the Persian invasions in 490 and 480–79; she had become the dominating power in the Delian League, which the Greek states formed in 478–7 to protect themselves against further Persian attacks; and by the late fifth century the richness and variety of her political, commercial and especially cultural life entitled her to be called, in the striking expression put into Pericles' mouth

1. As H. D. P. Lee puts it, 'You have only to be sufficiently determined to realize heaven on earth to be sure of raising hell' (Introduction to the Penguin *Republic*, p. 46; revised edn, 1974, p. 55).

by Thucydides,[2] the 'school of Greece'. But her highly democratic constitution and increasingly aggressive and arrogantly imperialist policies brought her into inevitable conflict with Sparta. Sparta was the antithesis of Athens – oligarchic, conservative, deriving her wealth from a rigidly repressed class of serfs, and hostile to experiment, especially in the arts: she preferred to cultivate the narrow excellences of military efficiency. Each state sensed the other as a dangerous rival, and eventually, in 431, the Peloponnesian War broke out between them and their respective allies. The course of the war we need not trace: suffice it to say that after long and bitter years of fighting Athens went down to final defeat in 404. Plato himself probably saw military service when he reached the age of 18 in 409.

The Peloponnesian War was one of the two major formative influences on Plato in his youth and early manhood. He can hardly have failed to sense and share the bitterness and despair felt in Athens at the collapse and defeat of so many high ideals. Yet he was never an admirer of the Athenian democracy, and the policies and actions of the democratic leaders during the war certainly offered a handle for plenty of criticism, especially to a man probably predisposed by upbringing to anti-democratic sympathies. In his later political writings he gives qualified approval to democracy in principle,[3] but he seems never to have had much time for the democracy he actually experienced in Athens during the war and later; like many other Athenians, he felt that Athens' defeat was the defeat of laxity and incompetence by Spartan discipline and good order. Yet the Thirty Tyrants, installed at Athens in 404 at Spartan instigation, disgusted him equally by their reign of terror against the democrats.[4] After various sanguinary episodes the democracy was restored in 403; and

2. II, 41.

3. *Statesman* 303; *Laws* 693, 756. 'Democracy', however, is a protean term, and we should beware of thinking that Plato meant by it exactly the same range of social and political features as we do. See p. 154, and cf. G. R. Morrow, *Plato's Cretan City* (Princeton, 1960), pp. 528–30. In the *Republic* (555 ff.), however, only tyranny is worse than democracy.

4. *Letter* VII, 324–5.

four years later there followed an episode that seems to have confirmed Plato in his dislike and even hatred of the Athenian democracy – the execution of Socrates.[5]

Socrates (born 470) was one of the leading personalities of the day, and the second major formative influence on Plato. For our knowledge of Socrates, who wrote nothing, we depend on the memoirs of Xenophon, the comedies of Aristophanes, occasional remarks by Aristotle, and the dialogues of Plato himself. The reports of these writers differ widely in many ways for many reasons, and the credibility of each is a matter of dispute. But we can safely say that Socrates impressed Plato as a man of deep piety and seriousness, strong courage and prodigious intellectual acumen. According at any rate to Plato, his intellectual achievement was twofold:

(i) He put ordinary practical knowledge – of politics, rhetoric, ship-building, architecture, physics, astronomy – firmly in its proper place by insisting that 'true' knowledge was moral knowledge, the knowledge of how to be virtuous. This brought him into conflict with the Sophists, a heterogeneous body of freelance teachers ranging from charlatans to serious and formidable intellects, who met the rising demand for education, particularly in oratory, politics, ethics and philosophy. Socrates considered that the Sophists were superficial thinkers who merely adopted and reflected the prejudices of society at large. This in turn brought him at odds with democratic opinion, for he made no secret of his view that the democratic leaders were influenced more by popular pressures and prejudices than by true political wisdom.[6]

(ii) He perfected the tool of verbal cross-examination. He subjected his interlocutors to a razor-sharp series of questions which invariably revealed the shaky and ill-thought-out foundations of their opinions. He reduced his opponents to a state of *aporia* (a state of 'not knowing where to turn next'); he never claimed to know the answer himself, but showed the importance of thorough analyses of concepts and definitions of

5. *Letter* VII, 325.   6. See for example *Gorgias* 521–2.

terms. How Plato developed this side of Socrates' teaching will be described below.

In 399, Socrates was tried on a charge of impiety and of corrupting the youth of Athens. His accusers were certain democratic politicians acting from motives of political spite: the real point at issue was his propagation, especially among the young, of views unflattering to democracy. At his trial, Socrates was absolutely unrepentant and refused to be bullied into a promise to 'behave himself'; he was found guilty and sentenced to death. It would probably have been easy for him to escape from prison and to flee from Athens, but he preferred to die (as Plato saw it) a martyr to philosophy.

In the early years of the fourth century Plato founded in Athens the Academy, a philosophical school-cum-research-institute. We do not know much about its internal organization; contact was maintained with philosophers all over Greece, and Plato himself probably travelled widely, notably to Egypt. The Academy gained a considerable reputation for expertise in political, legal and constitutional studies, and its members were retained as advisers to a number of communities existing and projected.[7]

When visiting Southern Italy in 388 Plato was invited to the court of Dionysius I of Syracuse in Sicily. The moving spirit behind the invitation was Dionysius' brother-in-law, Dion, a young and intelligent aristocrat of somewhat haughty demeanour. Dion was no liberal, but he seems to have been attracted to Plato's teaching, and anxious to mitigate the harsh absolutism of Dionysius' rule and to reform his court and kingdom. Plato advised the abandonment of political intrigue, the adoption of constitutional government and observance of a code of laws. His advice had virtually no effect on Dionysius, but he left Sicily having struck up a lasting friendship with Dion, who still awaited an opportunity of putting Plato's political principles into practice in Sicily.

In 367, Dionysius I died and his successor, Dionysius II,

---

7. The evidence is assembled in G. R. Morrow, *Plato's Cretan City* (Princeton, 1960), pp. 8-9; cf. P.-M. Schuhl in *Revue des Études Grecques*, 59 (1946), 46-53.

seemed to Dion likely to prove amenable to Plato's teaching, and with considerable misgivings Plato was persuaded by them both to visit Sicily again. Dionysius, however, did not prove a good learner; he was of an autocratic and jealous temperament, and certain suspicions he entertained of Dion's loyalty soon extended to Plato. Dion was then forced to leave Syracuse, and Plato returned to Athens. In 361, however, he was persuaded to return to Syracuse yet again on the strength of Dionysius' promise to consult Plato's wishes in regard to Dion, but Dionysius neither kept his promise nor progressed in his studies. Eventually Plato, under Dionysius' severe displeasure, managed with difficulty to return to Athens. In 357 Dion attacked Syracuse and expelled Dionysius, only to be assassinated in 354 by his political enemies. Plato's *Letter* VII was written by way of advice to Dion's party in Syracuse a year or two later.[8] Much of it is taken up with a history of Plato's political philosophy and a justification of his attempts to influence Dionysius.

Plato reached a wider public by means of his dialogues, all of which have come down to us. They vary widely in subject-matter and treatment. The question of their chronology and the development of Plato's thought is a mine-field, and here I can do no more than indicate the three major classes into which the dialogues are customarily divided.[9] First we have the early 'Socratic' dialogues, in which Socrates is typically portrayed subjecting an individual to cross-examination on some opinion or concept; the individual is discomfited, but no positive conclusion is reached. Next there are the dramatic and exciting dialogues of the 'middle' period; Socrates is still commonly the leading character, and propounds doctrines that go beyond anything the historical Socrates is likely to have taught. Finally came the late dialogues, written in roughly the last twenty years of Plato's life; usually someone other than Socrates is the main speaker. In these late productions philosophical analysis and exposition far outweigh

8. See Appendix.

9. A fuller summary may be read in I. M. Crombie, *An Examination of Plato's Doctrines* (London, 1962), vol. I, pp. 9 ff.

dramatic interest. The *Laws*, the longest dialogue of all, belongs to this period; I describe its contents, style and structure later in this introduction (p. 37ff).

PLATO'S POLITICAL THOUGHT

We have already seen that Plato was no lover of the Athenian democracy and sympathized with Socrates' impatience with it. But this is a somewhat negative point, and it is time we turned to Plato's distinctive contribution to political theory. The essence of his view is this: that society can never be reformed by gradual and conventional means, but *only if it is governed according to philosophic principles*. To understand what these principles were, we shall have to examine Socrates' philosophical method more closely.

Socrates was concerned to discover the essential common element present in all members of a particular class of actions. He would ask 'What is piety?', or 'What is justice?', and insist that the proper answer lay not in an enumeration of a list of individual just or pious actions, but in a statement of the general 'piety' or 'justice' that permeated each particular action and accounted for its being pious or just. His interlocutors, he discovered, were invariably unable to give an answer that would stand up to cross-examination: in other words, they did not *know* what piety or justice (or whatever) was.[10] Socrates' general suspicion of democracy was thus confirmed: many people claimed to know the good in politics, but as their *opinions* never stood up to examination, their *actions* were likely to be wrong, being based on ignorance. In effect, Socrates turned questions of morality and politics into questions of knowledge; he was convinced that if only we knew the answers to his questions we could avoid moral confusion and error, because no man who *really knew* what piety was would ever, in the nature of the case, voluntarily commit an impious action; impiety stems from ignorance. This approach to moral problems also accounts for the two

10. See for example, *Euthyphro*, especially 5–6, *Meno* 70 ff., and the first book of the *Republic*.

paradoxes attributed to Socrates by Plato: 'Virtue is knowledge', and 'No one does wrong willingly'.[11] Further than
this the historical Socrates probably did not go (if indeed he
went so far), and it was left to Plato to adopt and develop his
teaching. Plato believed that the moral definitions Socrates
was asking for had, in some sense, a real and independent
existence of their own; he called them ἰδέαι, 'Ideas' or
'Forms'. He held that an individual moral action was never
perfectly 'moral' but always 'fell short' of absolute morality,
and was moral only in so far as it 'partook' of that norm;[12]
and that the central problem of politics and government was
therefore to ensure that society was organized and controlled
by persons who really knew what the norms were, so that the
moral standards of the state reflected the absolute values to
the greatest possible degree. In short, he thought the only
salvation for society lay in removing government from the
untutored hands of the ordinary man in order that the state
could be directed according to the findings of philosophy.[13]

THE *REPUBLIC*

A society governed by philosophers is described in the
Republic (written probably in the 380s and/or 370s). The
population is divided into three classes: the Perfect Guardians,
the Auxiliary Guardians, and (for the want of a better term)
the 'Third Class'.[14] The Perfect Guardians undergo a long
and rigorous training in philosophy; they, if anyone, really
know the moral norms that society must obey.[15] They have

11. *Meno* 77–8; *Protagoras* 352, 357–8; *Gorgias* 466–8, 509; *Laws* 860 ff.
For an analysis of these paradoxes, see N. Gulley, *The Philosophy of
Socrates* (London, 1968), 75–164.

12. *Phaedo* 74–5, 100. Plato's 'Theory of Ideas' embraced not only
moral concepts but the whole of reality: for instance, 'tableness' was
thought to be a kind of perfect examplar to which individual tables
approximated.

13. *Republic* 473, 487, 499, 501, 540; *Letter* VII, 325–6.

14. *Republic* 412 ff., 440–41.

15. Their training is described in Books V–VII of the *Republic*,
especially 473 ff.

absolute and untrammelled power over the rest of the state; in their hands lies the making of such rules and regulations as are necessary.[16] The Auxiliary Guardians assist their superior colleagues in administration and keeping order, and undertake the defence of the state.[17] Their education is more limited than that of the Perfect Guardians; they have only a partial understanding of the reasons for the laws they administer, and do not appreciate their metaphysical basis.[18] The Third Class consists of the rest of the state – farmers, traders, artisans and so forth; their education is confined to the instruction they need in order to perform their own individual tasks efficiently. The essential features of such a state are that the few who really know the absolute moral standards rule the many who do not, and that such control is willingly exercised and willingly accepted.[19]

In the *Republic* Plato is hardly concerned with the detailed structure of society or with the minutiae of laws and regulations: he assumes that such details can be formulated easily enough by anyone with knowledge of the eternal moral verities.[20] In fact, he gives us not so much the description of a particular utopia as an *analysis* of those general features of society that will ensure its moral salvation. The *Republic* is thus the extreme statement of Plato's central ideas about moral and political problems.

THE *STATESMAN* ('POLITICUS')

The *Statesman*, which probably belongs to the middle or late 360s, forms a bridge between the *Republic* and the *Laws*. Although Plato reaffirms the ideal of the absolute ruler entitled to govern unhampered by law, he expresses strong doubts about the possibility of such a paragon ever appearing. Accordingly he attaches vastly increased importance to a code

16. *Republic* 484, 519–20, 540.   17. *Republic* 414 ff., 440–41.
18. *Republic* 428, 430, 537 ff.   19. *Republic* 431–2, 442.
20. *Republic* 425, 484 ff. But does a metaphysical insight into moral values necessarily confer a *technical* ability to frame or administer laws embodying them in specialized fields? Plato seems to assume that it does.

of law as an instrument of government. (Perhaps 'code of conduct' would be a better term: the Greeks thought of 'law' as something which affected all aspects of life, not merely as a list of crimes and punishments.) The ideal instrument, in Plato's view, is the ruler with knowledge of moral truths, who can react to every situation in the proper way and deal with it as it ought to be dealt with, using laws if he must; but in his absence the best instrument available is a good code of laws – the *best* instrument, but a *blunt* instrument nevertheless, because no law can be so precise as to provide for all possible contingencies: it can only lay down general rules that may prove inadequate or unfair in a given situation. (Hence the philosopher-ruler should never be bound by his own laws if they prove to encumber him.) However, Plato's lack of confidence in the possibility of an ideal ruler was not accompanied by any great trust in the political abilities of the man in the street; the existing laws of actual states he regarded as no more than the crude blunderings of laymen without the required expert knowledge of true morality.[21] His order of preference in the *Statesman* has been well summed up as follows:[22]

'Thus a free operation of the art of government is best; legal prescription by the expert statesman, variable at his discretion, is admirable; but where there is no such statesman, the best legal codes are those which preserve the "traces" (*Statesman* 301e) of a philosophical statesman's insight, and *any* established code is to be upheld as giving a better hope of sound government than no code at all.'

THE *LAWS*

We now come to the *Laws*, Plato's last and longest sermon to the world. It was written in the 350s and early 340s, though some passages may conceivably be earlier. Here the importance of law overshadows all, and the ideal ruler with his expert knowledge of moral values is barely mentioned. Plato now

21. *Statesman* 293–300 contains the substance of this paragraph.
22. J. B. Skemp, *Plato's Statesman* (London, 1952), 49.

sees law as the supreme, though essentially imperfect, instrument for the moral salvation of society: he calls it the 'dispensation of reason' (714), and the entire life of the community must accordingly be governed by a detailed code of laws which will express as far as possible the philosopher's vision of the true good. But in so far as the true good never changes, and the code's expression of the philosopher's vision will be the best attainable, any change in the laws can only be for the worse. And that brings us back to the first of the two quotations with which we opened: the impassioned advice never to change the laws of the state in the minutest particular, even as regards something so apparently trivial as children's games. Change the games and you change the children; they will grow up with a taste for novelty, and will then wish to change the laws and customs of the state. That is the way to moral relativism and the abandonment of the absolute standards to which Socrates' questioning had, for Plato, pointed the way.[23]

THE RELATIONSHIP BETWEEN THE *REPUBLIC*
AND THE *LAWS*

The reader of the *Republic* who picks up the *Laws* is likely to have difficulty in believing that the same person wrote both. The obvious explanation of the apparent vast difference of approach between the two works is that as Plato grew older and wiser his optimism turned to pessimism, and his idealism into realism; and that in the *Statesman* we can see in him the act of changing horses. What makes this explanation so irresistible is of course the way in which the alleged doctrinal development matches the chronological sequence of the dialogues concerned: we feel in our bones that realism must come later than idealism. But this charmingly simple account of the development of Plato's political theory really will not do, because it confuses *attainable* ideals with *unattainable* ideals. Only if we take the *Republic* as an attainable ideal does it make sense to argue that Plato abandoned it in favour of something more realistic; but to suppose that Plato ever

23. Cf. *Republic* 424–5.

thought that the *Republic* was attainable would be to suppose him capable not merely of optimism or idealism but of sheer political *naïveté*. It makes much better sense to think of the *Republic* as an extreme statement, designed to shock, of the consequences of an uncompromising application of certain political principles – in fact, as an *un*attainable ideal – and to suppose that even when Plato wrote the *Republic*, he had some realistic practical programme, which may well have been more or less what we find in the *Laws*.[24] (I grant, however, that Plato's advancing years and political disappointments probably stimulated him to commit his political programme to writing for the benefit of his successors.) In short, Plato could perfectly well have written the *Laws* when he wrote the *Republic* and the *Republic* when he wrote the *Laws*, for they are the opposite sides of the same coin. The *Republic* presents merely the *theoretical* ideal, and – a point which is often ignored – explicitly and emphatically allows for some diminution in rigour if it were to be put into practice.[25] The *Laws* describes, in effect, the *Republic* modified and realized in the conditions of this world. It is therefore both true and not true to say, as H. D. P. Lee does, [26] that 'those who have read the *Republic* have read all the essential things Plato has to say on the subject' (politics). It is true that he will have read the basic principles, but he will not have read the methods by which Plato, if he had had the chance, would have put those principles into practice by abating their rigour. Yet it would be equally one-sided to say, with T. D. Weldon, that 'those who want to know what Plato thought about politics would do well to study the *Laws* rather than the *Republic*'.[27] I should prefer to plead that the one should not be read without the other.

MAGNESIA: THE NEW UTOPIA

Plato's new utopia is to be named Magnesia. As we have seen, its guiding principles will be:

24. See further on this topic, pp. 546–7.
25. *Republic* 472–3.
26. Penguin *Republic*, p. 18 (modified in revised edn, 1974, p. 21).
27. *The Vocabulary of Politics* (London, 1953), p. 15.

(a) That certain absolute moral standards exist.

(b) That such standards can be, however imperfectly, embodied in a code of law.

(c) That most of the inhabitants of the state, being innocent of philosophy, must never presume to act on their own initiative in modifying *either* their moral ideal *or* the code of laws which expresses it: they must live in total and unconditional obedience to the unchanging rules and regulations laid down for them by the legislator.

How do these principles dictate the structure and organization of the new state?[28]

(a) *Size and Situation.* Magnesia is to be a small state, nine or ten miles from the sea, in country which will afford a decent, but not a luxurious, standard of living. Its relatively small size will encourage intimacy and friendship among its inhabitants; its modest living standards will ensure sobriety and moderation, and discourage excess and debauchery; and its remote situation will deter visitors from abroad, such as sailors and traders, who are potential sources of innovation and discord.

(b) *Population and Occupations.* There are to be precisely 5,040 citizens,[29] of whom some, at least, will own slaves. There will in addition be a class of resident aliens, each restricted to a sojourn of twenty years. Every citizen will own a farm capable of providing himself and his family (and slaves, if any) with a livelihood. Extreme wealth and extreme poverty must be avoided, so as to prevent civil strife. The wealthier citizens could probably expect to see most of their manual work performed by slaves; certainly all trades and handicrafts – occupations which debase the soul by encouraging a desire for excessive profit – are to be in the hands of the resident aliens, whose moral corruption is of little moment; a citizen has enough to do in pursuing a life of virtue by caring

28. A glance at the list of contents will readily show the sections of the *Laws* on which the following paragraphs are based.

29. The number 5,040 is chosen because it is divisible by any number from 1 to 12, except 11, and is therefore highly convenient for purposes of administration. Cf. p. 218.

for his own farm and family and by playing his proper part in the running of the state. Each farm is inalienable from the holder's family, and on his death must be handed on to one of his sons; this prevents the enrichment of some citizens at the expense of impoverishing others.

(c) *Education.* There is to be a comprehensive programme of state education, both physical and cultural; it is to start in a child's earliest years, and its overriding purpose is to train him in the correct moral standards and in obedience to the laws. The whole curriculum is closely supervised by a Minister of Education assisted by a corps of subordinate officials; their duties are to maintain standards and exercise a strict control over the literary, musical and artistic works put before the young, to prevent the infiltration of undesirable ideas and standards. All young men (and to some extent women too) must also undertake a programme of military training – not for purposes of aggression, but simply to ensure the defence of the state.

(d) *Religion.* Plato treats religion as a bulwark of morality. He goes to great lengths to refute certain contemporary theories about the status of the gods and nature of the world, which in his view lead to moral relativism; he proves to his own satisfaction that the gods exist and are the cosmic guarantors of the eternal moral standards expressed in the law of Magnesia. All Magnesians are therefore required to subscribe to the three 'articles' of the state religion: (i) that the gods exist, (ii) that they are concerned for our welfare, (iii) that they are incapable of being persuaded by our prayers and sacrifices to ignore our misdeeds. The converse theses constitute three 'heresies', which Plato deals with by some of the most scrupulous and rigorous provisions of his penal code. Traditional pieties and religious practices are encouraged, but all worship must be at public shrines; private shrines are forbidden, because of the way in which private devotions can encourage incorrect religious beliefs – notably the belief that sacrifices and prayers can influence the gods.

(e) *Law.* When Magnesia has been founded, it will doubtless be necessary to modify its laws slightly in the light of experience; but thereafter, Plato seems to think, they will remain virtually unaltered for ever. Nevertheless he allows, but does not explain in detail, a procedure for improving them as a result of the inquiries and researches of the 'Nocturnal Council'.

Much as Plato believes that each citizen must give the laws wholehearted and unconditional obedience, he sees that Magnesia will founder if that obedience is not given willingly. Thus each section of laws is prefaced by a persuasive 'preamble' whose avowed purpose is in effect to make the positive prescriptions of the law redundant: far better to be convinced of the wrongness of a crime and to refrain from it than to commit it and need to be punished.

The detailed provisions of the laws are in general based on those of contemporary Athenian law,[30] though other codes too, now almost completely unknown to us, may have exercised some influence. Naturally, Plato has to adapt contemporary law to suit the special conditions of the new utopia. The same is true of the legal procedure: many of the institutions and forms of Athenian law are found in Magnesia, suitably modified and in some respects fundamentally reformed – as for instance in the provision for a supreme appeal court to review the verdicts of the popular courts. I cannot do better than quote Morrow's[31] admirable summing-up: 'The pattern he lays down is in the main the procedure of Athenian law, with its freedom of prosecution and its rich variety of actions and remedies; but it is Athenian law modified at many points in directions, we may say, that are suggested by that law itself. In giving to the presiding magistrates power to control the pleading and prevent the introduction of irrelevant and misleading matter, in introducing something like inquisition of witnesses and principals, in excluding the opportunities for rhetorical jousting afforded by the archaic challenge to the oath and the challenge to the torture, in enlarging the range of competent witnesses and enforcing a litigant's right to compel their assistance, in eliminating the

30. There are innumerable specialized studies; the fullest general account is G. R. Morrow, *Plato's Cretan City* (Princeton, 1960).
31. *Op. cit.* 295–6.

oath of witnesses and principals, in relying at all stages upon written documents, and in invoking the power of the state to assist a litigant in enforcing a judgment obtained in court –in all these provisions Plato's law, while still essentially Attic in character, embodies a conception of the judicial process broader and more enlightened than ever characterized Athenian practice at its best.'

The penology underlying the legal code shows Plato, at first sight, in his most radical and reforming mood. He upholds the Socratic paradox 'No one does wrong willingly', and asserts that all crime is involuntary, in the sense that the criminal has been 'conquered' against his 'real' wishes, by ignorance or anger or bad education or pernicious environment: 'cure' rather than punishment is therefore indicated. In fact only rarely do the penalties Plato lays down differ in kind (flogging, fines, etc.) from those of contemporary law. However, it remains true that their purpose is reform, not vengeance, and to that extent Plato achieves some advance on contemporary ideas about the nature and purpose of punishment. On the other hand, he provides for the death penalty, particularly where the security and fundamental assumptions of the state are concerned, with revolting frequency (on the grounds that the criminal is 'incurable').

(f) *Government and Administration.* The constitution is to be mixed, in the sense that it should combine authority and freedom, oligarchy and democracy. There is a vast range of officials elected by the whole citizen body, and the day-to-day administration of the state is to a considerable degree in the hands of the citizens themselves. The stultifying effects of rigid control from the top are to be avoided; the ordinary citizen must feel that he has a 'stake in the country'. His discretion, however, is far from unlimited: the general lines of policy he must observe are laid down by higher authority, notably the board of Guardians of the Laws. The Guardians, whose tenure and powers make them tolerably independent of popular pressures, should themselves obey the laws in all things, and interpret them when necessary in the spirit in which they were framed. Yet even they are not exempt from the general rule that every official must be accountable for his conduct: to scrutinize their record and that of all other officials, there is a powerful board of Scrutineers – who can themselves be called to account if occasion arises. One authority must check another; firm government must not be allowed to degenerate into tyranny.

Over and above all the other authorities stands the Nocturnal Council, composed in part of the most senior and distinguished officials of the state, each with a younger protégé; it is not an elected body, except in so far as some of its members belong to it by virtue of having been previously elected to some high office. The Council's duties will be (i) to pursue philosophical studies to the highest level of which its members are capable, so that they gain some understanding of the real reasons for the laws they observe and the policies they administer; (ii) to carry on research – partly by contact with philosophers abroad – with the aim of improving the institutions and laws of Magnesia; (iii) to make sure, through those of its members who hold office, that its insights into philosophy and law are understood and put into practice by the state at large. In so far as the members of the Nocturnal Council will come nearest to knowledge of the real immutable moral standards, as distinct from their inevitably imperfect expression in the legal code, they will be Magnesia's nearest approach to the Perfect Guardians of the *Republic*.

PLATO AND TOTALITARIANISM

Plato offers a very easy target to modern political philosophers and in recent years three fundamental and related aspects of his political ideas have come under heavy and repeated bombardment: (i) his *basic assumption*, (ii) his *method*, and (iii) his *programme*.

(i) Plato assumes that politics is an exact science. The shepherd or shoemaker has a clearly defined sphere in which he operates (looking after sheep, shoemaking), an obvious set of objects on which he exercises his skill (sheep, leather, etc.), and specified results at which he aims (healthy sheep, good shoes). A statesman, Plato believes, proceeds or should proceed similarly. In his own field of operation (the state), the statesman has a definite result (virtue) to produce in the objects of his skill (the citizens). Now the chief objection to this idea centres on the question of results: whereas in the case of the shoemaker there is, within limits, a universally known set of criteria by which his work can be assessed, there is no such set of universally known aims in the case of statesmanship, because the term 'political virtue' has different meanings for different people. For these and other reasons the analogy between statesmanship and (say) shoemaking is attacked as illegitimate.

(ii) Plato's method is to set up a blueprint of an ideal society and then put it into effect by whatever means lie to hand; in other words, his methods are utopian. The obvious objection is that this method, if it is to succeed, will usually call for an unpalatable degree of coercion.

(iii) Plato's programme envisages a 'closed' society largely cut off from the outside world and fundamentally hostile to freedom of thought and inquiry. An illiberal orthodoxy is laid down from above, and heterodoxy is suppressed by brutal measures which convict Plato of a total lack of humanitarian feeling.

Clearly (i) is crucial: once you believe that you can isolate some sort of 'absolute' moral aim, your great temptation will be to make a root-and-branch reform of society whatever opposition you encounter, and refuse to tolerate other views, which, *ex hypothesi*, are wrong. And even from my necessarily very summary account of Plato's political thought it will be obvious that the three accusations have a great deal of truth in them. Although we have to discount some of the more extreme of the detailed charges brought against Plato, which have been shown to depend on fevered misinterpretations of what he actually said, the modern liberal attack on him has, in my view, a solid core of justification.[32]

32. See especially R. H. S. Crossman, *Plato Today* (second edition, London, 1959); K. R. Popper, *The Open Society and its Enemies*, vol. 1, *The Spell of Plato* (fifth edition, London, 1966). The most detailed and penetrating reply is by R. B. Levinson, *In Defense of Plato* (Cambridge, Mass., 1953).

THE MODERN REACTION TO PLATO

Yet however censorious we feel, it is important to be clear just what it is we really want to censure. Do we wish to blame Plato for accepting and approving certain institutions and customs of his day, simply because we find them repellent? Slavery, which is fundamental to the whole structure of Magnesia, is a case in point. We reject it utterly; yet it was as completely taken for granted in the ancient world as the employer–employee relationship today (which may itself in time come to be regarded with as much distaste as slavery is regarded now). Plato simply never questioned the legitimacy of the institution, though he had strong views on contemporary abuses of it: he saw its value in the kind of state he wanted, and built it into Magnesia's social and economic structure with a number of hard-headed but sensible and even humane recommendations.[33] Let us by all means censure Plato for accepting slavery: but let us also condemn the entire ancient world, and not single out Plato for special mention. 'Now that is all very well,' I can hear an objector saying, 'but is it not the case that in some ways Plato goes out of his way to *emphasize* the status of the slave, and gratuitously treats him more severely – as for instance when punishing him – than the free man?' We have to agree that this is so,[34] and a partial answer is of course that the ancients were less squeamish than we and held life cheaper: by the standards of his own time Plato has done nothing very shocking. But with the word 'gratuitously' we come to the heart of the controversy. This rough treatment of slaves, as well as Plato's approval of slavery itself and of many other institutions we find objectionable, spring from passionately held and carefully argued philosophical tenets (or, less formally, a certain characteristic way of looking at reality) – tenets that in them-

33. See pp. 258–9.
34. E.g. law no. 47ABDF. Sometimes, however, it is the free man who comes off worse than the slave; but I cannot here go into the fascinating complexities of Plato's penology.

selves are morally neutral. The fundamental one – that the
world and society are imperfect expressions of some sort of
order and structure in the 'ideas', a grand system of subordination in which reason strives to control unreason – is
clearly not the kind of belief that leads its holder to question
slavery: he will see a slave as a menial and unthinking person
who needs firm rational control from above and a correspondingly greater degree of brute force in his punishments.[35] Yet
that same tenet is at bottom responsible for Plato's hatred of
anarchy and his insistence on law and order in society, as well
as many other related points in his political thought that we
should wish to approve. A critic of Plato should therefore
concentrate his attention on the validity of the philosophical
assumptions that led Plato to his particular political institutions, and the cogency of the reasoning by which the latter
are derived from and supported by the former.[36] Of course, it
would be absurd to suggest that when Plato proposes
something to which we object, he can be defended by the
simple argument that he had reasons; I merely point out that
an attack on his reasons is an attack at the roots of his political
ideas, and that is the only really effective place to strike.[37]
Merely to disapprove of particular doctrines often means only
'Thank Heaven we don't live in the fourth century B.C., in
Magnesia'. With this I should be in general agreement, and it
is a valid and important level of response; but as an answer to
Plato's *arguments* it will not do.

I have laboured these none-too-original points because it
seems to me that modern criticism of Plato all too often
moves on a quite superficial level: 'Plato proposed x, x does
not measure up to twentieth-century standards, therefore
Plato is a pernicious political philosopher.' Yet we think we

35. Cf. *Republic* 431; *Letter* VII, 331, and Aristotle, *Politics* I, 3–7. The
classic book on Plato and slavery is G. R. Morrow, *Plato's Law of Slavery
in its Relation to Greek Law* (Urbana, Illinois, 1939).

36. Which is another way of putting the point I have made before,
that the *Republic* and the *Laws* should be read side by side: neither is fully
intelligible without the other.

37. The best of the modern controversialists have in fact done precisely
this. (See p. 34, note 32.)

do well to examine the reasons for our political choices – and that means we have to continue to examine both the reasons and the choices of political philosophers of the past, including Plato.

But even if we are content merely to consider particular institutions, the case against Plato is by no means an 'open and shut' one. In particular, we must not ignore (i) the important role the utopian can play in the long-term erosion of accepted political programmes and the influence he can exert on subsequent political thought,[38] and (ii) the vast amount of what is in effect 'piecemeal' reform contained in the *Laws*. The concrete proposals Plato makes for the reform of the institutions of his day frequently contain political wisdom of a high order for which he is rarely given credit. Some of these insights and proposals I have already mentioned: the complex arrangements for a 'mixed' constitution, the reforms of legal procedure, the enlightened theory of punishment, the persuasive legal preambles, and the provision for a continuing review of the legal code by a specially trained body, the Nocturnal Council. Not all these proposals are wholly original to Plato; but taken together with countless measures of lesser moment they constitute an impressive programme for the reform of society by the rule of law, informed by the insights of research and philosophy.

COMPOSITION AND STRUCTURE OF THE *LAWS*: SUMMARY

The *Laws* is traditionally supposed to have been Plato's last work, left unrevised on his death in 347. Precisely what it owes to Philip of Opus, who is said to have 'revised' or 'copied' the work, is not very clear, but he probably confined himself to stitching it together in accordance with Plato's wishes, known or inferred. It is not likely that he altered the actual text much, if at all: it contains inconsistencies of detail and irregularities of syntax which an editor bent on rewriting

38. See the references to Partridge, Horsburgh, Welles, Ferguson, Gouldner (pp. 294–6) and von Fritz in the bibliography, pp. 534–5.

would hardly have allowed. The argument lurches from topic to topic, and Wilamowitz had some justification for his description of the *Laws* as a '*wunderliches Chaos*'. Nevertheless, taken as a whole, the work is a unity with a fairly clear structure.

Books One and Two contain a preliminary review of two famous legal codes, the Cretan and the Spartan, and some elementary lessons on the nature of education and how it is affected by the arts. Book Three considers what history has to teach us about legislation and government. The description of Magnesia gets under way in Book Four; first we hear of its site and population, then the correct method of composing its legal code. After some miscellaneous moral lessons, Book Five describes the procedure for founding the new state and distributing the land. Book Six deals in detail with administration and the election of the various officials, and then discusses the question of marriage. This topic naturally leads in Book Seven to a long discussion of education, which in turn leads in Book Eight to a treatment of sport and military training; then after an examination of problems of sex, we pass to economics and trade. Book Nine introduces the criminal law, and contains an important digression on questions of legal responsibility. A discussion of various crimes of impiety leads to a long excursus on religion, which occupies most of Book Ten. Book Eleven resumes the criminal code, which continues into Book Twelve; we read a long series of miscellaneous offences, in the middle of which we find two digressions, one on the law of the family, the other on the Scrutineers. The last topic discussed is, appropriately enough, the Nocturnal Council, the 'anchor' of the state.

There is thus a clear overall plan in spite of detailed confusion. It is Plato's habit to let one topic launch him into a discussion of another, even when he has not finished the first, which then has to be resumed later. Some digressions are better organized, as for instance the discussion of responsibility in Book Nine, which is clearly relevant to its context.

The *Laws* lacks the dramatic power of some of the earlier Platonic dialogues. Three old gentlemen – an Athenian

Stranger (in effect Plato himself), Cleinias a Cretan, and Megillus a Spartan – meet at Cnossos in Crete and walk to the cave and sanctuary of Zeus on Mount Ida.[39] They address each other with grave courtesy; the Athenian is authoritative and loquacious, his companions naïve and slightly overawed. Much of the *Laws* resembles a formal lecture by the Athenian rather than dialogue, and even what conversation there is, is rather wooden.[40] There is a great deal of 'As I said before', and 'Now let's examine the next point', and similar humming and hawing and clearing the throat. However, as dialogue it is no worse than many other works of Plato (even the *Republic* consists largely of Socrates' exposition peppered with formal expressions of assent from his interlocutors), and there are several flashes of life and humour, as well as a lot of elephantine punning and other kinds of word-play, usually impossible to reproduce in English.

THE TRANSLATION

Plato's Greek in the *Laws* is difficult: emphatic yet imprecise, elaborate yet careless, prolix yet curiously elliptical; the meaning is often obscure and the translator is forced to turn interpreter. How should such an extraordinary text be rendered into English? Any translation which preserved every note of the original would be doomed to failure more surely in the case of the *Laws* than of almost any other classical text: it would be quite unreadable. Or, to go to the other extreme, should the translator shoo the refractory nuances out of the text and produce a version in racy and idiomatic English? I think not: it would be out of keeping with the tone and subject-matter of the work. Every translator is plagued by this problem of reconciling accuracy with readability, and the translator of the *Laws* is plagued to an unusual degree. Here I can only record my attempted solution. My aim has been a simple plain clarity, and I have stuck as closely to the Greek as

39. See map, p. 15.
40. In Lucian's *Icaromenippus* (24), Zeus grumbles that he is so neglected by mankind that his altars are 'colder than the *Laws* of Plato'.

seemed consistent with this ideal. A number of colloquial-isms have been admitted as a spice, but I have not gone out of my way to seek them. E. B. England's superb commentary on the dialogue has been constantly at my side; it remains our best guide to Plato's labyrinthine prose.

Different readers will turn to the *Laws* for different pur-poses, and the division of the translation into sections and subsections will enable a reader whose particular interest is (say) education, by skimming through the table of contents, to pick out rapidly those parts of the text likely to be relevant to him; for other references, he should consult the index of names (which has been made as detailed and comprehensive as possible), and the list of crimes on pp. 539–44. At the head of each section, and occasionally elsewhere, there is a 'signpost' (printed in italics), in which I attempt to summarise and elucidate the argument, with brief comment on points of interest and difficulty.

My biggest headache has been the presentation of the legal code. Simply to translate it as it stands, as a plain lecture by the Athenian, entails printing long paragraphs of complex detail in which the salient points and overall organization are difficult to grasp; on the other hand, to articulate the entire code by a comprehensive use of 1, 2, 3, (a), (b), (c), etc., would be equally confusing, because the material is far too complicated to be organized consistently according to any single method. Yet the modern reader expects clarity and tidiness in a penal code, and I have therefore evolved a compromise, inevitably imperfect, between organizing everything and organizing nothing. I have assumed that in any given set of regulations the central point or climax – in however much exhortation, incidental comment, ritual and administrative detail it may be embedded – is the statement of the offence and its penalty or other consequence. Now when the Athenian makes such a statement, he typically uses the formula 'If a man does so-and-so, let him be punished in such-and-such a way'. It is these items that I have attempted to isolate and articulate, by the use of indented type, consecutive numeration, and a liberal sprinkling of (a), (b), (c), etc. – devices which I hope will facilitate reference to the penal code in future.[41] But in some unusually tangled parts of the code (mainly in the long discussions of homicide, wounding and assault), a rigidly consistent application of these devices would have confused rather than clarified the text, and I have had to print in indented type a certain amount of other material too.[42] The reader may be assured that if I had done otherwise, I should have taxed his eye and his brain severely.

The crimes and the punishments defy alphabetical arrangement, and the index to them therefore takes the form of a numerical list with page references. The indented type has also been used for such preambles as can be easily and clearly isolated in their context.

The translation has been made from the text in the Budé series (editors É. des Places and A. Diès, Paris, 1951–6); a list of the points at which I have departed from it will be found at the end of the volume. I discuss the text, translation and interpretation of these and many other passages of the *Laws* in *Notes on the Laws of Plato* (Supplement 28 of the *Bulletin of the Institute of Classical Studies*, University of London, 1972, with *Addenda et Corrigenda*, 1976).

The traditional mode of detailed reference to Plato is by the numbers of the pages in the edition of Stephanus (1578): these are printed in the margin.[43] The 'books' into which the *Laws* is customarily divided are shown in the table of contents, and in the margin of the translation at the point where each begins.

---

41. When Plato's references from one part of the code to another are not immediately obvious, I have inserted the appropriate details in *square* brackets.

42. This is not entirely a drawback, as the various regulations by no means fall into watertight categories. For instance, in the homicide law there are several measures which could be treated *either* as penalties *or* as mere religious observances.

43. The letters a, b, c, d, and e that are often found after these numbers are subsections: 'a' refers to approximately the first fifth of the relevant Stephanus page, and so on. The numbers that follow these letters refer to individual lines of the subsections in a Greek text, not to the lines in any translation.

ACKNOWLEDGEMENTS

It is a pleasant duty to express my thanks to those whose brains I have ruthlessly plundered on points of translation and technical difficulty: Dr E. K. Borthwick, Professor D. E. Eichholz, Professor B. Einarson, Professor D. J. Furley, Professor H. A. Harris, Mr J. F. Lazenby, Dr J. G. Landels, Mr G. E. M. de Ste Croix, Professor J. B. Skemp, Professor R. P. Winnington-Ingram, and Professor W. J. Verdenius. Mr G. E. Benfield has had the fortitude to read and criticize the entire translation in draft, an invaluable service for which I am very grateful. My wife, Teresa, has nobly performed the back-breaking task of checking the proofs. I am particularly indebted to Mrs Betty Radice, the Editor of the series, for her wise advice and friendly encouragement over a long period.

Kingston upon Hull   **T. J. SAUNDERS**
Newcastle upon Tyne
1965–9

In the 1982 reprint, as in several of the earlier ones, the bibliographies have been brought up to date.

May 1981   T. J. S.

THE LAWS

*A summer day in Crete
in the middle of the fourth century* B.C.
Participants in the discussion:

An Athenian Stranger

CLEINIAS, *a Cretan*

MEGILLUS, *a Spartan*

§1. THE INADEQUACY OF SPARTAN AND CRETAN LEGISLATION

The main purpose of this first section is to put Spartan and Cretan laws into proper perspective. The Athenian, while politely deferential about the divine origin claimed for them, makes two criticisms: they over-develop one side of virtue (courage), and are useless for the internal government of a country. When Cleinias and Megillus have been thus brought to see the deficiencies of the laws of their own states, they will be more ready to accept the Athenian's later suggestions about the nature and purpose of legislation.

Part of the Athenian's argument hinges on the ambiguity of the Greek words kreittôn *and* hêttôn, *which were ordinarily used to denote both physical and moral superiority and inferiority – 'stronger/ weaker', 'better/worse'. The Athenian's point is that the first pair of terms does not necessarily imply the second: we may be physically stronger than our enemies, but inferior morally; we should strive to be 'stronger' than ourselves, i.e. our base instincts and desires, to achieve self-control. This is one of the central moral themes of the dialogue.*

INTRODUCTORY CONVERSATION

ATHENIAN: Tell me, gentlemen, to whom do you give the credit for establishing your codes of law? Is it a god, or a man?

CLEINIAS: A god, sir, a god – and that's the honest truth. Among us Cretans it is Zeus; in Sparta – which is where our friend here hails from – they say it is Apollo, I believe. Isn't that right?

MEGILLUS: Yes, that's right.

ATHENIAN: You follow Homer, presumably, and say that every ninth year Minos used to go to a consultation with his father Zeus,[1] and laid down laws for your cities on the basis of the god's pronouncements?

CLEINIAS: Yes, that's our Cretan version, and we add that

1. *Odyssey* XIX, 178–9.

45

Minos' brother, Rhadamanthus – doubtless you know the
625 name – was an absolute paragon of justice. We Cretans would
say that he won this reputation because of the scrupulously
fair way in which he settled the judicial problems of his day.

ATHENIAN: A distinguished reputation indeed, and one
particularly appropriate for a son of Zeus. Well then, since
you and your companion have been raised under laws with
such a splendid ancestry, I expect you will be quite happy
if we spend our time together today in a discussion about
constitutions and laws, and occupy our journey in a mutual
exchange of views. I've heard it said that from Cnossos to
Zeus' cave and shrine is quite a long way, and the tall trees
along the route provide shady resting-places which will be
more than welcome in this stiflingly hot weather. At our age,
there is every excuse for having frequent rests in them, so
as to refresh ourselves by conversation. In this way we shall
come to the end of the whole journey without having tired ourselves out.

CLEINIAS: And as you go on, sir, you find tremendously
tall and graceful cypress trees in the sacred groves; there are
also meadows in which we can pause and rest.

ATHENIAN: That sounds a good idea.

CLEINIAS: It is indeed, and it'll sound even better when
we see them. Well then, shall we wish ourselves *bon voyage*,
and be off?

THE AIM OF SPARTAN AND CRETAN LAWS

ATHENIAN: Certainly. Now, answer me this. You have
meals which you eat communally; you have a system of
physical training, and a special type of military equipment.
Why is it that you give all this the force of law?

CLEINIAS: Well, sir, I think that these customs are quite
easy for anyone to understand, at any rate in our case. You
see the Cretan terrain in general does not have the flatness of
Thessaly: hence we usually train by running (whereas the
Thessalians mostly use horses), because our land is hilly and
more suited to exercise by racing on foot. In this sort of

country we have to keep our armour light so that we can run without being weighed down, and bows and arrows seem appropriate because of their lightness. All these Cretan practices have been developed for fighting wars, and that's precisely the purpose I think the legislator intended them to serve when he instituted them. Likely enough, this is why he organized the common meals, too: he observed that when men are on military service they are all obliged by the pressure of events, for their own protection, to eat together throughout the campaign. In this, I think, he censured the stupidity of ordinary men, who do not understand that they are all engaged in a never-ending lifelong war against all other states. So, if you grant the necessity of eating together for self-protection in war-time, and of appointing officers and men in turn to act as guards, the same thing should be done in peace-time too. The legislator's position would be that what most men call 'peace' is really only a fiction, and that in cold fact all states are by nature fighting an undeclared war against every other state. If you see things in this light, you are pretty sure to find that the Cretan legislator established all these institutions of ours, both in the public sphere and the private, with an eye on war, and that this was the spirit in which he gave us his laws for us to keep up. He was convinced that if we don't come out on top in war, nothing that we possess or do in peace-time is of the slightest use, because all the goods of the conquered fall into the possession of the victors.

ATHENIAN: You certainly have had a splendid training, sir! It has, I think, enabled you to make a most penetrating analysis of Cretan institutions. But explain this point to me rather more precisely: the definition you gave of a well-run state seems to me to demand that its organization and administration should be such as to ensure victory in war over other states. Correct?

CLEINIAS: Of course, and I think our companion supports my definition.

MEGILLUS: My dear sir, what other answer could one possibly make, if one is a Spartan?

ATHENIAN: But if this is the right criterion as between

states, what about as between villages? Is the criterion different?

CLEINIAS: Certainly not.

ATHENIAN: It is the same, then?

CLEINIAS: Yes.

ATHENIAN: Well now, what about relations between the village's separate households? And between individual and individual? Is the same true?

CLEINIAS: The same is true.

ATHENIAN: What of a man's relations with himself – should he think of *himself* as his own enemy? What's our answer now?

CLEINIAS: Well done, my Athenian friend! (I'd rather not call you 'Attic', because I think it is better to call you after the goddess,[2] as you deserve.) You have made the argument clearer by expressing it in its most elementary form. Now you will find it that much easier to realize that the position we took up a moment ago is correct: not only is everyone an enemy of everyone else in the public sphere, but each man fights a private war against himself.

ATHENIAN: You *do* surprise me, my friend. What do you mean?

CLEINIAS: This, sir, is where a man wins the first and best of victories – over himself. Conversely, to fall a victim to oneself is the worst and most shocking thing that can be imagined. This way of speaking points to a war against ourselves within each one of us.

ATHENIAN: Now let's reverse the argument. You hold that each one of us is either 'conqueror of' or 'conquered by' himself: are we to say that the same holds good of household, village and state? Or not?

CLEINIAS: You mean that they are individually either 'conquerors of' or 'conquered by' themselves?

ATHENIAN: Yes.

CLEINIAS: This again is a good question to have asked. Your suggestion is most emphatically true, particularly in the

2. I.e. Athena, goddess of wisdom and 'patron saint' of Athens in Attica.

48

Miss us Praiseworthiness or Success

case of states. Wherever the better people subdue their inferiors, the state may rightly be said to be 'conqueror of' itself, and we should be entirely justified in praising it for its victory. Where the opposite happens, we must give the opposite verdict.

ATHENIAN: It would take too long a discussion to decide whether in fact there *is* a sense in which the worse element could be superior to the better, so let's leave that aside. For the moment, I understand your position to amount to this: sometimes evil citizens will come together in large numbers and forcibly try to enslave the virtuous minority, although both sides are members of the same race and the same state. When they prevail, the state may properly be said to be 'inferior to' itself and to be an evil one; but when they are defeated, we can say it is 'superior to' itself and that it is a good state.

CLEINIAS: That's a paradoxical way of putting it, sir, but it is impossible to disagree.[3]

ATHENIAN: But now wait a minute. Let's look at this point again: suppose a father and mother had several sons – should we be surprised if the majority of these brothers were unjust, and the minority just? — *Metaphor*

CLEINIAS: By no means.

ATHENIAN: We could say that if the wicked brothers prevail the whole household and family may be called 'inferior to' itself, and 'superior to' itself if they are subdued – but it would be irrelevant to our purpose to labour the point. The reason why we're now examining the usage of the common man is not to pass judgement on whether he uses language properly or improperly, but to determine what is essentially right and wrong in a given law.

CLEINIAS: Very true, sir.

MEGILLUS: I agree – it's been nicely put, so far.

ATHENIAN: Let's look at the next point. Those brothers I've just mentioned – they'd have a judge, I suppose?

---

3. Cleinias is struck by the paradox that when 'inferior' numbers conquer, the state is morally 'superior', and when 'superior' numbers conquer, it is morally 'inferior'. See introductory note, p. 45.

CLEINIAS: Of course.

ATHENIAN: Which of these judges would be the better, the one who put all the bad brothers to death and told the better ones to run their own lives, or the one who put the virtuous brothers in command, but let the scoundrels go on living in willing obedience to them? And we can probably add a third and even better judge – the one who will take this single quarrelling family in hand and (reconcile) its members, 628 without killing any of them; by laying down regulations to guide them in the future, he will be able to ensure that they remain on friendly terms with each other.

CLEINIAS: Yes, this judge – the legislator – would be incomparably better.

ATHENIAN: But in framing these regulations he would have his eye on the exact opposite of war.

CLEINIAS: True enough.

ATHENIAN: But what about the man who brings harmony to the (state)? In regulating its life, will he pay more attention to external war, or internal? This 'civil' war, as we call it, does break out on occasion, and is the last thing a man would want to see in his own country; but if it did flare up, he would wish to have it over and done with as quickly as possible.

CLEINIAS: He'll obviously pay more attention to the second kind.

ATHENIAN: One side might be destroyed through the victory of the other, and then peace would follow the civil war; or, alternatively, peace and friendship might be the result of reconciliation. Now, which of these results would you prefer, supposing the city then had to turn its attention to a foreign enemy?

CLEINIAS: Everybody would prefer the second situation to the first, so far as his own state was concerned.

ATHENIAN: And wouldn't a legislator have the same preference?

CLEINIAS: He certainly would.

ATHENIAN: Now surely, every legislator will enact his every law with the aim of achieving the greatest good?

CLEINIAS: Of course.

ATHENIAN: The greatest good, however, is neither war nor civil war (God forbid we should ever need to resort to either of them), but peace and goodwill among men. And so the victory of a state over itself, it seems, does not after all come into the category of ideals; it is just one of those things in which we've no choice. You might just as well suppose that the sick body which has been purged by the doctor was therefore in the pink of condition, and disregard the body that never had any such need. Similarly, anyone who takes this sort of view of the happiness of a state or even an individual will never make a true statesman in the true sense – if, that is, he adopts foreign warfare as his first and only concern; he'll become a *genuine* lawgiver only if he designs his legislation about war as a tool for peace, rather than his legislation for peace as an instrument of war.

CLEINIAS: What you say, sir, has the air of having been correctly argued. Even so, I shall be surprised if our Cretan institutions, and the Spartan ones as well, have not been wholly orientated towards warfare.

ATHENIAN: Well, that's as may be. At the moment, how- 629 ever, there's no call for a stubborn dispute on the point. What we need to do is to conduct our inquiry into these institutions dispassionately, seeing that we share this common interest with their authors. So keep me company in the conversation I'm going to have. Let's put up Tyrtaeus,[4] for example, an Athenian by birth who became a citizen of Sparta. He, of all men, was particularly concerned with what we are discussing. He said:

'I'd not mention a man, I'd take no account of him,

no matter' (he goes on) 'if he were the richest of men, no matter if he had a huge number of good things' (he enumer-

4. Tyrtaeus composed about the middle of the seventh century, and was noted for his poems in praise of courage in war. The Athenian quotes the first line of the poem verbatim and then summarizes the next nine; on p. 52 he gives a somewhat adapted quotation of lines 11 and 12. For the text and a translation of the whole poem see J. M. Edmonds, *Elegy and Iambus* (London and New York, 1931; Loeb edition), vol. I, pp. 74-7.

ated pretty nearly all of them) 'unless his prowess in war were beyond compare.' Doubtless you too have heard the lines; Megillus here knows them backwards, I expect.

MEGILLUS: I certainly do.

CLEINIAS: And they have certainly got as far as Crete: they were brought across from Sparta.

ATHENIAN: Now then, let's jointly ask our poet some such question as this: 'Tyrtaeus, you are a poet, and divinely inspired. We are quite sure of your wisdom and virtue, from the special commendation you have bestowed on those who have particularly distinguished themselves in active service. On this point we – Megillus here, Cleinias of Cnossos and I – find ourselves, we think, emphatically in agreement with you; but we want to be quite clear that we are talking about the same people. Tell us: do you clearly distinguish, as we do, two sorts of war? Or what?' I fancy that in reply to this even a man far less gifted than Tyrtaeus would state the facts of the case and say 'Two'. The first would be what we all call 'civil' war, and as we were saying just now, this is the most bitterly fought of all; and we shall all agree, I think, in making the other type of war the one we fight when we quarrel with our foreign enemies from outside the state, which is a much less vicious sort of war than the other.

CLEINIAS: I agree.

ATHENIAN: 'Well now, Tyrtaeus, which category of soldiers did you shower with your praises and which did you censure? Which was the type of war they were fighting, that led you to speak so highly of them? The war fought against foreign enemies, it would seem – at any rate, you have told us in your verses that you have no time for men who cannot "stand the sight of bloody butchery

and do not attack in close combat with the foe".'

So here is the next thing we'd say: 'It looks as if you reserve your special praise, Tyrtaeus, for those who fight with conspicuous gallantry in external war against a foreign enemy.' I suppose he'd agree to this, and say 'Yes'?

CLEINIAS: Surely.

ATHENIAN: However, while not denying the courage of those soldiers, we still maintain that those who display conspicuous gallantry in *total* war[5] are very much more courageous. 630 We have a poet to bear witness to this, Theognis,[6] a citizen of Megara in Sicily, who says:

> 'Cyrnus, find a man you can trust in deadly feuding:
> He is worth his weight in silver and gold.'

Such a man, in our view, who fights in a tougher war, is far superior to the other – to just about the same degree as the combination of justice, self-control and good judgement, reinforced by courage, is superior to courage alone. In civil war a man will never prove sound and loyal unless he has every virtue; but in the war Tyrtaeus mentions there are hordes of mercenaries who are ready to dig their heels in and die fighting,[7] most of whom, apart from a very small minority, are reckless and insolent rogues, and just about the most witless people you could find. Now, what conclusion does my argument lead to? What is the point I am trying to make clear in saying all this? Simply that in laying down his laws every legislator who is any use at all – and especially your legislator here in Crete, duly instructed by Zeus – will never have anything in view except the highest virtue. This means, in Theognis' terms, 'loyalty in a crisis'; one might call it 'complete justice'. The virtue that Tyrtaeus praised so highly is indeed a noble one, and has been appropriately celebrated by the poet, but strictly speaking, in order of merit it comes only fourth.

5. I.e. in civil war.

6. Theognis lived about the end of the sixth century, and was a member of the landed gentry of Megara (probably the Megara near Athens, in spite of what is said here). He wrote lively, indignant poems from a conservative point of view about the social and political changes of his day. Some 1400 lines of his work survive: see J. M. Edmonds, *Elegy and Iambus* (London and New York, 1931; Loeb edition), vol. I, pp. 216–401. The Athenian quotes lines 77–8.

7. A glancing reference to lines 16–18 of Tyrtaeus' poem (see note on p. 51).

CLEINIAS: And that, sir, is to reduce our Cretan legislator to the status of a failure.

ATHENIAN: No, my dear fellow, it is not. The failure was entirely on our part. We were quite wrong to imagine that when Lycurgus[8] and Minos established the institutions of Sparta and this country the primary end they had in view was invariably warfare.

CLEINIAS: But what ought we to have said?

ATHENIAN: We had no particular axes to grind in our discussion, and I think we ought to have told the honest truth. We ought not to have said that the legislator laid down his rules with an eye on only a part of virtue, and the most trivial part at that. We should have said that he aimed at virtue in its entirety, and that the various separate headings under which he tried to frame the laws of his time were quite different from those employed by modern legal draftsmen.[9] Each of these invents any category he feels he wants, and adds it to his code. For instance, one will come up with a category on 'Inheritances and Heiresses', another with 'Assault', and others will suggest other categories *ad infinitum*. But we insist that the correct procedure for framing laws, which is followed by those who do the job properly, is precisely the one we have just embarked upon. I am delighted at the way you set about explaining your laws: you rightly started with *virtue*, and explained that this was the aim of the laws the legislator laid down. However, you did say that he legislated entirely by reference to only one part of virtue, and the most inconsiderable part at that. Now there I thought you were wrong: hence all these additional remarks. So what is this distinction I could have wished to hear you draw in your argument? Shall I tell you?

CLEINIAS: Certainly.

ATHENIAN: 'Now, Sir,' you ought to have said, 'it is no accident that the laws of the Cretans have such a high repu-

___

8. Traditional founder of the Spartan constitution.

9. The Athenian's point is that modern legislators group laws according to subject-matter, whereas the proper classification is a more philosophical one – presumably the particular virtue or virtues promoted by each law.

tation in the entire Greek world. They are sound laws, and
achieve the happiness of those who observe them, by producing for them a great number of benefits. These benefits fall
into two classes, "human" and "divine". The former depend
on the latter, and if a city receives the one sort, it wins the
other too – the greater include the lesser; if not, it goes without
both. Health heads the list of the lesser benefits, followed by
beauty; third comes strength, for racing and other physical
exercises. Wealth is fourth – not "blind" wealth,[10] but the
clear-sighted kind whose companion is good judgement – and
good judgement itself is the leading "divine" benefit; second
comes the habitual self-control of a soul that uses reason. If
you combine these two with courage, you get (thirdly)
justice; courage itself lies in fourth place. All these take a
natural precedence over the others, and the lawgiver must of
course rank them in the same order. Then he must inform the
citizens that the other instructions they receive have these
benefits in view: the "human" benefits have the "divine" in
view, and all these in turn look towards reason, which is
supreme. The citizens join in marriage; then children, male
and female, are born and reared; they pass through childhood
and later life, and finally reach old age. At every stage the
lawgiver should supervise his people, and confer suitable
marks of honour or disgrace. Whenever they associate with
each other, he should observe their pains, pleasures and
desires, and watch their passions in all their intensity; he
must use the laws themselves as instruments for the proper
distribution of praise and blame. Again, the citizens are
angry or afraid; they suffer from emotional disturbances
brought on by misfortune, and recover from them when life
is going well; they have all the feelings that men usually
experience in illness, war, poverty or their opposites. In all
these instances the lawgiver's duty is to isolate and explain
what is good and what is bad in the way each individual
reacts. Next, the lawgiver must supervise the way the citizens
acquire money and spend it; he must keep a sharp eye on the

10. Plutus, the god of wealth, was traditionally represented as blind.

various methods they all employ to make and dissolve (voluntarily or under duress) their associations[11] with one another, noting which methods are proper and which are not; honours should be conferred upon those who comply with the laws, and specified penalties imposed on the disobedient. When the lawgiver comes to the final stages of organizing the entire life of the state, he must decide what honours should be accorded the dead and how the manner of burial should be varied.[12] His survey completed, the author of the legal code will appoint guardians (some of whom will have rational grounds for their actions, while others rely on "true opinion"),[13] so that all these regulations may be welded into a rational whole, demonstrably inspired by considerations of justice and self-restraint, not of wealth and ambition.' That is the sort of explanation, gentlemen, that I should have liked you to give, and still want now – an explanation of how all these conditions are met in the laws attributed to Zeus and the Pythian Apollo, which Minos and Lycurgus laid down. I wish you could have told me why the system on which they are arranged is obvious to someone with an expert technical – or even empirical – knowledge of law, while to laymen like ourselves it is entirely obscure.

CLEINIAS: Well then, sir, where do we go from here?

COURAGE AND PLEASURE

ATHENIAN: I think we ought to go back and start again. As before, we should consider first the activities that promote courage; then, if you like, we'll work through the other kinds of virtue, one by one. We'll take the way we deal with the first as a model, and try to while away the journey by discussing the others in the same way. Then after dealing with virtue

11. Social and political clubs of various kinds seem to be meant: see pp. 359–60, 453.

12. I.e. according to property-class: see p. 513.

13. A man with 'true opinion' cannot justify his (perfectly correct) actions on philosophical grounds. To do this a man needs 'knowledge' or 'wisdom' or 'reason'.

as a whole, we shall show, God willing, that the regulations we have just listed had this in view.

MEGILLUS: A splendid idea! Our friend here is an admirer 633 of Zeus, so try examining him, to start with.

ATHENIAN: I'll try to examine not only him, but you and myself as well – we all have a stake in the discussion. Tell me, then, you two: do we maintain that the common meals and gymnastic exercises have been invented by your legislator for the purpose of war?

MEGILLUS: Yes.

ATHENIAN: What about a third such institution, and a fourth? To make a full list like this will probably be the right procedure in the case of the other 'parts'[14] of virtue, too (or whatever the right terminology is: no matter, so long as one's meaning is clear).

MEGILLUS: I – and any Spartan, for that matter – would mention the legislator's invention of hunting as the third item.

ATHENIAN: Let's have a shot at adding a fourth, and a fifth too, if we can.

MEGILLUS: Well, I might try to add a fourth: the endurance of pain. This is a very conspicuous feature of Spartan life. You find it in our boxing matches, and also in our 'raids', which invariably lead to a severe whipping. There is also the 'Secret Service',[15] as it is called, which involves a great deal of hard work, and is a splendid exercise in endurance. In winter, its members go barefoot and sleep without bedclothes. They dispense with orderlies and look after themselves, ranging night and day over the whole country. Next, in the 'Naked Games', men display fantastic endurance, contending as they do with the full heat of summer. There are a great many other practices of the same kind, but if you produced a detailed list it would go on pretty well for ever.

ATHENIAN: You've put it all very well, my Spartan friend. But what is to be our *definition* of courage? Are we to define it simply in terms of a fight against fears and pains only, or

14. I.e. self-control, justice, good judgement.

15. An official organization of young Spartans, who had the job of keeping the Spartan slave class (helots) in subjection.

do we include desires and pleasures, which cajole and seduce us so effectively? They mould the heart like wax – even the hearts of those who loftily believe themselves superior to such influences.

MEGILLUS: Yes, I think so – the fight is against all these feelings.

ATHENIAN: Now, if we remember aright what was said earlier on, our friend from Cnossos spoke of a city and an individual as 'conquered by' themselves. Isn't that right?

CLEINIAS: Surely.

ATHENIAN: Well, shall we call 'bad' only the man who is 'conquered by' pains, or shall we include the victim of pleasures as well?

CLEINIAS: The term 'bad' we apply, I think, to the victim of pleasures even more than to the other. When we say that a man has been shamefully 'conquered by' himself, we are all, I fancy, much more likely to mean someone defeated by pleasures than by pains.

634 ATHENIAN: But the legal code of those lawgivers (inspired as they are by Zeus and Apollo) certainly did not envisage a courage with one hand tied behind its back, able to hit out on the left, but powerless in face of the cunning and seductive blandishments from the right. Surely it was supposed to resist in both directions?

CLEINIAS: Yes, both, I think.

ATHENIAN: We ought to mention next what practices exist in your two cities that give a man a taste of pleasure rather than teach him how to avoid it – you remember how a man could not avoid pains, but was surrounded by them, and then forced, or persuaded by awards of honour, to get the better of them.[16] Now where in your codes of law is the institution that does the same for pleasure? Could you say, please, what institution you have that makes one and the same body of citizens courageous in face of pains and of pleasures alike, so that they conquer where they ought to

16. I.e. in the Spartan 'Secret Service', 'Naked Games', etc. – see p. 57.

conquer and never fall victims to these their most intimate and dangerous enemies?

MEGILLUS: I was certainly able to point to a good many laws that were designed to counteract pains, stranger, but I doubt if I should find it so easy to give striking and clear examples in the case of pleasures. I might have some success, perhaps, in finding minor cases.

CLEINIAS: No more would I be able to find an obvious illustration of this sort of thing in the laws of Crete.

ATHENIAN: My dear sirs, this should not surprise us. (I hope, by the way, that if in his desire to discover goodness and truth any of us is led to criticize some legal detail in the homeland of either of his companions, we shall receive such criticism from each other tolerantly and without truculence.)

CLEINIAS: You have put it quite fairly, my Athenian friend. We must do as you say.

ATHENIAN: Truculence, Cleinias, would be hardly the thing for men of our age.

CLEINIAS: No indeed.

ATHENIAN: The criticisms people bring against the way Sparta and Crete are run may be right or wrong: that is another issue. At any rate, I am probably better able than either of you to report what most people generally say. However, granted that your codes of law have been composed with reasonable success, as indeed they have been, one of the best regulations you have is the one which forbids any young man to inquire into the relative merits of the laws; everyone has to agree, with one heart and voice, that they are all excellent and exist by divine *fiat*; if anyone says differently, the citizens must absolutely refuse to listen to him. If an old man has some point to make about your institutions, he must make such remarks to an official, or someone of his own age when no young man is present.

CLEINIAS: That's absolutely right, sir – you must be a wizard! You are far removed in time from the legislator who laid down these laws, but I think you have hit on his intentions 635 very nicely, and state them with perfect accuracy.

ATHENIAN: Well, there are no young men here now. In

view of our age, the legislator surely grants us the indulgence of having a private discussion on these topics without giving offence.

CLEINIAS: So be it: don't hesitate to criticize our laws. There is no disgrace in being told of some blemish – indeed, if one takes criticism in good part, without being ruffled by it, it commonly leads one to a remedy.

ATHENIAN: Splendid. But criticism of your laws is not what I propose: that can wait until we have scrutinized them exhaustively. I shall simply mention my difficulties. Among all the Greek and foreign peoples who have come to my knowledge, you are unique in that you have been instructed by your lawgiver to keep away from the most attractive entertainments and pleasures, and to refrain from tasting them. Yet when it came to pains and fears, your legislator reckoned that if a man ran away from them on every occasion from his earliest years and was then faced with hardships, pains and fears he could not avoid, he would likewise run away from any enemies who *had* received such a training, and become their slaves. I think this same lawgiver ought to have taken this same line in the case of pleasures too. He ought to have said to himself: 'If our citizens grow up without any experience of the keenest pleasures, and if they are not trained to stand firm when they encounter them, and to refuse to be pushed into any disgraceful action, their fondness for pleasure will bring them to the same bad end as those who capitulate to fear. Their slavery will be of a different kind, but it will be more humiliating: they will become the slaves of those who are able to stand firm against the onslaughts of pleasure and who are past-masters in the art of temptation – utter scoundrels, sometimes. Spiritually, our citizens will be part slave, part free, and only in a limited sense will they deserve to be called courageous and free.' Just consider this argument: do you think it has any relevance at all?

CLEINIAS: Yes, I think it has, at first blush. But it is a weighty business, and to jump to confident conclusions so quickly may well be childish and naïve.

ATHENIAN: Well then, Cleinias and our friend from Sparta,

let's turn to the next item we put on the agenda: after courage, let's discuss self-control. We found, in the case of war, that your two political systems were superior to those of states with a more haphazard mode of government. Where's the superiority in the case of self-control?

636

MEGILLUS: That's rather a difficult question. Still, I should think the common meals and the gymnastic exercises are institutions well calculated to promote both virtues.

ATHENIAN: Well, my friends, I should think the real difficulty is to make political systems reflect in practice the trouble-free perfection of theory. (The human body is probably a parallel. One cannot rigidly prescribe a given regimen for a given body, because any regimen will invariably turn out, in some respects, to injure our bodies at the same time as it helps them in others.) For instance, these gymnastic exercises and common meals, useful though they are to a state in many ways, are a danger in their encouragement of revolution – witness the example of the youth of Miletus, Boeotia and Thurii.[17] More especially, the very antiquity of these practices seems to have corrupted the natural pleasures of sex, which are common to man and beast. For these perversions, your two states may well be the first to be blamed, as well as any others that make a particular point of gymnastic exercises. Circumstances may make you treat this subject either light-heartedly or seriously; in either case you ought to bear in mind that when male and female come together in order to have a child, the pleasure they experience seems to arise entirely naturally. But homosexual intercourse and lesbianism seem to be unnatural crimes of the first rank, and are committed because men and women cannot control their desire for pleasure. It is the Cretans we all hold to blame for making up the story of Ganymede:[18] they were so firmly

17. The vagueness of this remark makes it difficult to tell whether the Athenian is in fact referring to the few episodes known to us which would fit this description: see Aristotle, *Politics*, V 7 (1307b6 ff.) and Plutarch, *On the Sign of Socrates*, 594c.

18. A handsome boy carried off to be Zeus' companion and cupbearer: see Homer, *Iliad* XX, 231 ff.

convinced that their laws came from Zeus that they saddled him with this fable, in order to have a divine 'precedent' when enjoying that particular pleasure. That story, however, we may dismiss, but not the fact that when men investigate legislation, they investigate almost exclusively pleasures and pains as they affect society and the character of the individual. Pleasure and pain, you see, flow like two springs released by nature. If a man draws the right amount from the right one at the right time, he lives a happy life; but if he draws unintelligently at the wrong time, his life will be rather different. State and individual and every living being are on the same footing here.

§2. DRINKING PARTIES AS AN EDUCATIONAL DEVICE

Spartan and Cretan laws, then, excel in making a man resist fear, but they fail when it comes to resisting the temptations of pleasure; they give a man courage, but not self-control. The smug remark of Megillus, that Sparta does not tolerate drunkenness, now gives the Athenian the opportunity to suggest – to the scandalized amazement of his companions – that a degree of inebriation may in fact be a valuable educational tool, in two ways: (1) a man reveals his true character under the influence of wine; (2) just as Sparta and Crete trained their young men to be fearless by encouraging them to resist their fears in conditions in which they would be likely to be moderately afraid (e.g. various athletic and military exercises), so a man can be made to acquire self-control by being exposed to conditions in which he is likely to be particularly licentious – the drinking party. Being taught by encouragement and threats to resist temptation when mildly drunk is a valuable exercise in self-control. Drinking parties are therefore eminently 'educational', because education is essentially a training in virtue *(not simply in a given trade or vocation), as the digression on the nature and purpose of education makes clear.*

The theme that Spartan and Cretan institutions are inadequate is not dropped, but develops into something more positive. Courage (the resistance to fear), besides being harmful when overstressed, is not the only virtue necessary; self-control, which the Spartans and Cretans achieved, if at all, only by a total *repression of the desire for pleasure, is more effectively cultivated by moderate indulgence.*

TEETOTALLERS MISGUIDED

MEGILLUS: Well, sir, I suppose that what you say is more or less right; at any rate, we're baffled to find an argument against it. But in spite of that I still think the legislator of Sparta is right to recommend a policy of avoiding pleasure (our friend here will come to the rescue of the laws of Cnossos,

1. Spartan law gits rid of symposia.   2. Symposia promote vice

Symposium?

if he wants to). The Spartan law relating to pleasures seems
637 to me the (best) you could find anywhere. It has completely
eliminated from our country the thing which particularly
prompts men to indulge in the keenest pleasures, so that they
become unmanageable and make every kind of a fool of
themselves: drinking parties, with all their violent incitements
to every sort of pleasure, are not a sight you'll see anywhere
in Sparta, either in the countryside or in the towns under her
control. None of us would fail to inflict there and then the
heaviest punishment on any tipsy merrymaker he happened to
meet; he would not let the man off even if he had the festival
of Dionysus as his excuse. Once, I saw men in that condition
on wagons in your country,[1] and at Tarentum, among our
colonials, I saw the entire city drunk at the festival of Dionysus. *We* don't have anything like that.

ATHENIAN: My Spartan friend, all this sort of thing is
perfectly laudable in men with a certain strength of character;
it is when they cannot stop themselves that it becomes rather
silly. A countryman of mine could soon come back at you tit
for tat by pointing to the easy virtue of your women. There is
one answer, however, which in Tarentum and Athens and
Sparta too is apparently thought to excuse and justify all such
practices. When a foreigner is taken aback at seeing some
unfamiliar custom there, the reply he gets on all hands is this:
'There is no need to be surprised, stranger: this is what we
do here; probably you handle these things differently.' Still,
my friends, the subject of this conversation is not mankind in
general but only the merits and faults of legislators. In fact,
there is a great deal more we ought to say on the whole subject
of drinking: it is a custom of some little importance, and needs
a legislator of some little skill to understand it properly. I
am not talking about merely drinking wine or totally abstaining from it: I mean *drunkenness*. How should we deal with it?
One policy is that adopted by the Scythians and Persians, as
well as by the Carthaginians, Celts, Iberians and Thracians –
belligerent races, all of them. Or should we adopt your policy?

1. At the festival of Dionysus, drunken revellers on wagons shouted
ribald jokes at the crowd.

This, as you say, is one of complete abstention, whereas the Scythians and Thracians (the women as well as the men) take their wine neat, and tip it down all over their clothes; in this they reckon to be following a glorious and splendid custom. And the Persians indulge on a grand scale (though with more decorum) in these and other luxuries which you reject.

MEGILLUS: Oh, but my fine sir, when we get weapons in our hands we rout the lot of them.

ATHENIAN: Oh, but my *dear* sir, you must not say that. Many a time an army has been defeated and routed in the past, and will be in the future, without any very obvious reason. Merely to point to victory or defeat in battle is hardly to advance a clear and indisputable criterion of the merits or demerits of a given practice. Larger states, you see, defeat smaller ones in battle, and the Syracusans enslave the Locrians, the very people who are supposed to be governed by the best laws you could find in those parts; the Athenians enslave the Ceians, and we could find plenty of other similar instances. It is by discussing the individual practice itself that we should try to convince ourselves of its qualities: for the moment, we ought to leave defeats and victories out of account, and simply say that such-and-such a practice is good and such-and-such is bad. First, though, listen to my explanation of the correct way to judge the relative value of these practices.

MEGILLUS: Well then, let's have the explanation.

ATHENIAN: I think that everyone who sets out to discuss a practice with the intention of censuring it or singing its praises as soon as it is mentioned is employing quite the wrong procedure. You might as well condemn cheese out of hand when you heard somebody praising its merits as a food, without stopping to ask about what effect it has and how it is taken (by which I mean such questions as how it should be given, who should take it, what should go with it, in what condition it should be served, and the state of health required of those who eat it). But this is just what I think we are doing in our discussion. We have only to hear the word 'drunkenness', and one side immediately disparages it while the other praises it – a pointless procedure if there ever was one. Each puts up enthusiastic witnesses to endorse its recommendations: one side thinks that the number of its witnesses clinches the matter, the other points to the sight of the teetotallers conquering in battle – not that the facts of the case are beyond dispute even here. Now, if this is the way we are going to work one by one through the other customs, I for one shall find it goes against the grain. I want to discuss our present subject, drunkenness, by following a different – and, I think, correct – procedure, to see if I can demonstrate the right way to conduct an inquiry into such matters as these in general. Thousands and thousands of states, you see, differ from your pair of states in their view of these things, and would be prepared to fight it out in discussion.

MEGILLUS: Certainly, if a correct method of inquiry into 639 such matters is available, we ought not to shy away from hearing what it is.

ATHENIAN: Let us conduct the inquiry more or less like this: suppose somebody were to praise goat-keeping, and commended the goat as a valuable article of possession; suppose somebody else were to disparage goats because he had seen some doing damage to cultivated land by grazing on it without a goatherd, and were to find similar fault with every animal he saw under incompetent control or none at all. What do we think of the censure of someone like that? Does it carry any weight at all?

MEGILLUS: Hardly.

ATHENIAN: If a man possesses only the science of navigation, can we say that he will be a useful captain on board a ship, and ignore the question whether he suffers from sea-sickness or not? Can we say that, or can't we?

MEGILLUS: Certainly not, at any rate if, for all his skill, he's prone to the complaint you mention.

ATHENIAN: What about the commander of an army? Is he capable of taking command just by virtue of military skill, in spite of being a coward in face of danger? The 'sea-sickness' in this case is produced by being, as it were, drunk with terror.

MEGILLUS: Hardly a capable commander, that.

ATHENIAN: And what if he combines cowardice with incompetence?

66

MEGILLUS: You are describing a downright useless fellow – a commander of the daintiest of dainty women, not of men at all.

ATHENIAN: Take any social gathering you like, which functions naturally under a leader and serves a useful purpose under his guidance: what are we to think of the observer who praises or censures it although he has never seen it gathered together and running properly under its leader, but always with bad leaders or none at all? Given that kind of observer and that kind of gathering, do we reckon that his blame or praise will have any value?

MEGILLUS: How could it, when he has never seen or joined any of these gatherings run in the proper way?

ATHENIAN: Hold on a moment. There are many kinds of gatherings, and presumably we'd say drinkers and drinking-parties were one?

MEGILLUS: Of course.

ATHENIAN: Has anyone *ever* seen such a gathering run in the proper way? You two, of course, find the answer easy: 'Never, absolutely never'; drinking-parties are just not held in your countries, besides being illegal. But I have come across a great many, in different places, and I have investigated pretty nearly all of them. However, I have never seen or heard of one that was properly conducted throughout; one could approve of a few insignificant details, but most of them were mismanaged virtually all the time.

CLEINIAS: What are you getting at, sir? Be a little more explicit. As you said, we have no experience of such events, so that even if we did find ourselves at one we would probably be unable to tell off-hand which features were correct and which not.

ATHENIAN: Very likely. But you can try to understand from my explanation. You appreciate that each and every assembly and gathering for any purpose whatever should invariably have a leader?

CLEINIAS: Of course.

ATHENIAN: We said a moment ago that if it is a case of men fighting, their leader must be brave.

CLEINIAS: Yes, indeed.

ATHENIAN: And a brave man, surely, is less thrown off balance by fears than cowards are.

CLEINIAS: That too is true enough.

ATHENIAN: If there were some device by which we could put in charge of an army a commander who was completely fearless and imperturbable, this is what we should make every effort to do, surely?

CLEINIAS: It certainly is.

ATHENIAN: But the man we are discussing now is not going to take the lead in hostile encounters as between enemies, but in the peaceful meetings of friends with friends, gathering to foster mutual goodwill.

CLEINIAS: Exactly.

ATHENIAN: But we can assume that this sort of assembly will get rather drunk, so it won't be free of a certain amount of disturbance, I suppose.

CLEINIAS: Of course not – I imagine precisely the opposite.

ATHENIAN: To start with, then, the members of the gathering will need a leader?

CLEINIAS: Of course they will, more than anybody else.

ATHENIAN: Presumably we should if possible equip them with a leader who can keep his head?

CLEINIAS: Naturally.

ATHENIAN: And he should also, presumably, be a man who knows how to handle a social gathering, because his duty is not only to preserve the existing friendliness among its members, but to see that it is strengthened as a result of the party.

CLEINIAS: Quite true.

ATHENIAN: So, when men become merry with drink, don't they need someone put in charge of them who is sober and discreet rather than the opposite? If the man in charge of the revellers were himself a drinker, or young and indiscreet, he ought to thank his lucky stars if he managed to avoid starting some serious trouble.

CLEINIAS: Lucky? I'll say so!

ATHENIAN: Consequently, an attack on such gatherings in cities where they are conducted impeccably might not in itself amount to unjustified criticism, provided the critic were attacking the institution itself. But if he abuses the institution simply because he sees every possible mistake being made in running it, he clearly does not realize, first, that this is a case of mismanagement, and secondly that any and every practice will appear in the same light if it is carried on without a sober leader to control it. Surely you appreciate that a drunken steersman, or any commander of anything, will always make 641 a total wreck of his ship or chariot or army, or whatever else he may be directing?

CAN DRINKING PARTIES BE EDUCATIONAL?

CLEINIAS: Yes, sir, there's truth in *that*, certainly. But the next step is for you to tell us what conceivable benefit this custom of drinking parties would be to us, given proper management. For instance, to take our example of a moment ago, if an army were properly controlled, its soldiers would win the war and this would be a considerable benefit, and the same reasoning applies to our other instances. But what solid benefit would it be to individuals or the state to instruct a drinking party how to behave itself?

ATHENIAN: Well, what solid benefit are we to say it is to the state when just one lad or just one chorus[2] of them has been properly instructed? If the question were put like that, we should say that the state gets very little benefit from just one; but ask in general what great benefit the state derives from the training by which it educates its citizens, and the reply will be perfectly straightforward. The good education they have received will make them good men, and being good they will achieve success in other ways, and even conquer their enemies in battle. Education leads to victory; but victory, on occasions, results in the *loss* of education, because men often swell with pride when they have won a victory in war, and this pride fills them with a million other vices. Men have won many 'Cadmeian victories', and will win many

2. See pp. 84–5.

more, but there has never been such a thing as 'Cadmeian education'.[3]

CLEINIAS: It looks to us, my friend, as if you mean to imply that passing the time with friends over a drink – provided we behave ourselves – is a considerable contribution to education.

ATHENIAN: Most certainly.

CLEINIAS: Well then, could you now produce some justification for this view?

ATHENIAN: Justification? Only a god, sir, would be entitled to insist that this view is correct – there are so many conflicting opinions. But if necessary I am quite prepared to give my own, now that we have launched into a discussion of laws and political organizations.

CLEINIAS: This is precisely what we are trying to discover – your own opinion of the business we are now debating.

INTERLUDE: THE ATHENIAN PRESSED
FOR AN ANSWER

ATHENIAN: Well then, let that be our agenda: you have to direct your efforts to understanding the argument, while I direct mine to expounding it as clearly as I can. But first listen to this, by way of preface: you'll find every Greek takes it for granted that my city likes talking and does a great deal of it, whereas Sparta is a city of few words and Crete cultivates the intellect rather than the tongue. I don't want 642 to make you feel that I am saying an awful lot about a triviality, if I deal exhaustively and at length with such a limited topic as drinking. In fact, the genuinely correct way to regulate drinking can hardly be explained adequately and clearly except in the context of a correct theory of culture; and it is impossible to explain this without considering the whole subject of education. That calls for a very long discus-

3. Compare our expression 'Pyrrhic victory', i.e. one which is more disastrous for the victors than the vanquished. Cadmus, founder of Thebes, *sowed* the teeth of a dragon; armed men sprang up and killed each other. For 'seeds' of character, see pp. 258 and 277.

sion indeed. So what do you think we ought to do now? What about skipping all this for the moment, and passing on to some other legal topic?

MEGILLUS: As it happens, sir – perhaps you haven't heard – my family represents the interests of your state, Athens, in Sparta. I dare say all children, when they learn they are *proxeni*[4] of a state, conceive a liking for it from their earliest years; each of us thinks of the state he represents as a fatherland, second only to his own country. This is exactly my own experience now. When the Spartans were criticizing or praising the Athenians, I used to hear the little children say, 'Megillus, your state has done the dirty on us,' or, 'it has done us proud.' By listening to all this and constantly resisting on your behalf the charges of Athens' detractors, I acquired a whole-hearted affection for her, so that to this day I very much enjoy the sound of your accent. It is commonly said that when an Athenian is good, he is 'very very good', and I'm sure that's right. They are unique in that they are good not because of any compulsion, but spontaneously, by grace of heaven; it is all so genuine and unfeigned. So you're welcome to speak as long as you like, so far as I'm concerned.

CLEINIAS: I endorse your freedom to say as much as you like, sir: you'll see that when you've heard what I have to say, too. You have probably heard that Epimenides, a man who was divinely inspired, was born hereabouts. He was connected with my family, and ten years before the Persian attack he obeyed the command of the oracle to go to Athens,[5] where he performed certain sacrifices which the god had ordered. He told the Athenians, who were apprehensive at the preparations the Persians were making, that the Persians would not come for ten years, and that when they did, they would go back with all their intentions frustrated, after sustaining greater losses than they had inflicted. That was when

4. A *proxenos* looked after the interests of a foreign state in his own country.

5. Cleinias' chronology is a trifle confused. He thinks that Epimenides, a seer and wonder-worker, lived about 500 B.C., which is 100 years later than his actual date.

my ancestors formed ties of friendship with you Athenians, and ever since then my forebears and I have held you in 643 affection.

THE NATURE AND PURPOSE OF EDUCATION (1)

ATHENIAN: Well then, on your part you are prepared to listen, apparently; on my side, I am ready and willing to go ahead, but the job will certainly tax my abilities. Still, the effort must be made. To assist the argument, we ought to take the preliminary step of defining education and its potentialities, because we have ventured on a discussion which is intended to lead us to the god of wine, and we are agreed that education is as it were the route we have to take.

CLEINIAS: Certainly let's do that, if you like.

ATHENIAN: I am going to explain how one should describe education: see if you approve of my account.

CLEINIAS: Your explanation, then, please.

ATHENIAN: It is this: I insist that a man who intends to be good at a particular occupation must practise it from childhood: both at work and at play he must be surrounded by the special 'tools of the trade'. For instance, the man who intends to be a good farmer must play at farming, and the man who is to be a good builder must spend his playtime building toy houses; and in each case the teacher must provide miniature tools that copy the real thing. In particular, in this elementary stage they must learn the essential elementary skills. For example, the carpenter must learn in his play how to handle a rule and plumb-line, and the soldier must learn to ride a horse (either by actually doing it, in play, or by some similar activity).[6] We should try to use the children's games to channel their pleasures and desires towards the activities in which they will have to engage when they are adult. To sum up, we say that the correct way to bring up and educate a child is to use his playtime to imbue his soul with the greatest

6. That is, as I understand the Greek, *either* by actually riding horses (miniature ones: ponies, donkeys?), *or* by riding a rocking-horse or his teacher, who would go on hands and knees in imitation of a horse.

possible liking for the occupation in which he will have to be absolutely perfect when he grows up. Now, as I suggested, consider the argument so far: do you approve of my account?

CLEINIAS: Of course.

ATHENIAN: But let's not leave our description of education in the air. When we abuse or commend the upbringing of individual people and say that one of us is educated and the other uneducated, we sometimes use this latter term of men who have in fact had a thorough education – one directed towards petty trade or the merchant-shipping business, or something like that. But I take it that for the purpose of the present discussion we are not going to treat this sort of thing as 'education'; what we have in mind is education from childhood in *virtue,* a training which produces a keen desire *EMOTION* to become a perfect citizen who knows how to rule and be ruled as justice demands. I suppose we should want to mark 644 off this sort of training from others and reserve the title 'education' for it alone. A training directed to acquiring money or a robust physique, or even to some intellectual facility not guided by reason and justice, we should want to call coarse and illiberal, and say that it had no claim whatever to be called education. Still, let's not quibble over a name; let's stick to the proposition we agreed on just now: as a rule, men with a correct education become good, and nowhere in the world should education be despised, for when combined with great virtue, it is an asset of incalculable value. If it ever becomes corrupt, but can be put right again, this is a lifelong task which everyone should undertake to the limit of his strength.

CLEINIAS: True. We agree with your description.

ATHENIAN: Here is a further point on which we agreed some time ago:[7] those who can control themselves are good, those who cannot are bad.   *FRONTAL CORTEX*

CLEINIAS: Perfectly correct.

ATHENIAN: Let's take up this point again and consider even more closely just what we mean. Perhaps you'll let me try to clarify the issue by means of an illustration.

7. See p. 48.

CLEINIAS: By all means.

ATHENIAN: Are we to assume, then, that each of us is a single individual?

CLEINIAS: Yes.

ATHENIAN: But that he possesses within himself a pair of witless and mutually antagonistic advisers, which we call pleasure and pain?

CLEINIAS: That is so.

ATHENIAN: In addition to these two, he has opinions about the future, whose general name is 'expectations'. Specifically, the anticipation of pain is called 'fear', and the anticipation of the opposite is called 'confidence'. Over and against all these we have 'calculation', by which we judge the relative merits of pleasure and pain, and when this is expressed as a public decision of a state, it receives the title 'law'.

CLEINIAS: I can scarcely follow you; but assume I do, and carry on with what comes next.

MEGILLUS: Yes, I'm in the same difficulty.

ATHENIAN: I suggest we look at the problem in this way: let's imagine that each of us living beings is a puppet of the gods. Whether we have been constructed to serve as their plaything, or for some serious reason, is something beyond our ken, but what we certainly do know is this: we have these emotions in us, which act like cords or strings and tug us about; they work in opposition, and tug against each other to make us perform actions that are opposed correspondingly; back and forth we go across the boundary line where vice and virtue meet. One of these dragging forces, according to our argument, demands our constant obedience, and this is the one we have to hang on to, come what may; the pull of the other cords we must resist. This cord, which is golden and holy, transmits the power of 'calculation', a power which in a state is called the public law; being golden, it is pliant, while the others, whose composition resembles a variety of other substances, are tough and inflexible. The force exerted by law is excellent, and one should always co-operate with it, because although 'calculation' is a noble thing, it is gentle, not violent, and its efforts need assistants, so that the gold in us may prevail over the other substances. If we do give our help, the moral point of this fable, in which we appear as puppets, will have been well and truly made; the meaning of the terms 'self-superior' and 'self-inferior'[8] will somehow become clearer, and the duties of state and individual will be better appreciated. The latter must digest the truth about these forces that pull him, and act on it in his life; the state must get an account of it either from one of the gods or from the human expert we've mentioned, and incorporate it in the form of a law to govern both its internal affairs and its relations with other states. A further result will be a clearer distinction between virtue and vice; the light cast on that problem will perhaps in turn help to clarify the subject of education and the various other practices, particularly the business of drinking parties. It may well be thought that this is a triviality on which a great deal too much has been said, but equally it may turn out that the topic really does deserve this extended discussion.

THE EDUCATIONAL EFFECT OF
DRINKING PARTIES (I)

CLEINIAS: You are quite right; we certainly ought to give full consideration to anything that deserves our attention in the 'symposium' we are having now.

ATHENIAN: Well then, tell me: if we give drink to this puppet of ours, what effect do we have on it?

CLEINIAS: What's your purpose in harking back to that question?

ATHENIAN: No particular purpose, for the moment. I'm just asking, in a general way, what effect is had on something when it is associated with something else. I'll try to explain my meaning even more clearly. This is what I'm asking; does drinking wine make pleasures and pains, anger and love, more intense?

CLEINIAS: Very much so.

ATHENIAN: What about sensations, memory, opinions and thought? Do these too become more intense? Or rather,

8. Cf. pp. 48 ff.

don't they entirely desert a man if he fills himself with drink?

CLEINIAS: Yes, they desert him entirely.

ATHENIAN: So he reverts to the mental state he was in as a young child?

CLEINIAS: Indeed.

ATHENIAN: And it's then that his self-control would be at its lowest?

646 CLEINIAS: Yes, at its lowest.

ATHENIAN: A man in that condition, we agree, is very bad indeed.[9]

CLEINIAS: Very.

ATHENIAN: So it looks as if it's not only an old man who will go through a second childhood, but the drunkard too.

CLEINIAS: That's well said, sir.

ATHENIAN: Now, is there any argument that could even begin to persuade us that we ought to venture on this practice, rather than make every possible effort to avoid it?

CLEINIAS: Apparently there is; at any rate, this is what you say, and a minute ago you were ready to produce it.

ATHENIAN: A correct reminder; I'm ready still, now that you have both said you would be glad to listen to me.

CLEINIAS: We'll be all ears, sir, if only because of your amazing paradox that a man should, on occasions, voluntarily abandon himself to extreme depravity.

ATHENIAN: You mean spiritual depravity, don't you?

CLEINIAS: Yes.

ATHENIAN: And what about degradation of the body, my friend – emaciation, disfigurement, ugliness, impotence? Shouldn't we be startled to find a man voluntarily reducing himself to such a state?

CLEINIAS: Of course we should.

ATHENIAN: We don't suppose, do we, that those who voluntarily take themselves off to the surgery in order to drink down medicines are unaware of the fact that very soon after, for days on end, their condition will be such that, if it were to be anything more than temporary, it would make life insupportable? We know, surely, that those who resort to

9. See p. 73.

gymnasia for vigorous exercises become temporarily enfeebled?

CLEINIAS: Yes, we are aware of all this.

ATHENIAN: And of the fact that they go there of their own accord, for the sake of the benefit they will receive after the initial stages?

CLEINIAS: Most certainly.

ATHENIAN: So shouldn't we look at the other practices in the same light?

CLEINIAS: Yes indeed.

ATHENIAN: So the same view should be taken of time spent in one's cups – if, that is, we may think of it as a legitimate parallel.

CLEINIAS: Of course.

ATHENIAN: Now if time so spent turned out to benefit us no less than time devoted to the body, it would have the initial advantage over physical exercises in that, unlike them, it is painless.

CLEINIAS: You're right enough in that, but I'd be surprised if we could discover any such benefit in this case.

ATHENIAN: Then this is the point it looks as if we ought to be trying to explain. Tell me: can we conceive of two roughly opposite kinds of fear?

CLEINIAS: Which?

ATHENIAN: These: when we expect evils to occur, we are in fear of them, I suppose?

CLEINIAS: Yes.

ATHENIAN: And we often fear for our reputation, when we imagine we are going to get a bad name for doing or saying something disgraceful. This is the fear which we, and I 647 fancy everyone else, call 'shame'.

CLEINIAS: Surely.

ATHENIAN: These are the two fears I meant. The second resists pains and the other things we dread, as well as our keenest and most frequent pleasures.[10]

---

10. I.e. the fear that is 'shame', the fear of disgrace, makes us put up with pain we might otherwise flee, and resist temptations to which we might otherwise succumb.

CLEINIAS: Very true.

ATHENIAN: The legislator, then, and anybody of the slightest merit, values this fear very highly, and gives it the name 'modesty'. The feeling of confidence that is its opposite he calls 'insolence', and reckons it to be the biggest curse anyone could suffer, whether in his private or his public life.

CLEINIAS: True.

ATHENIAN: So this fear not only safeguards us in a lot of other crucial areas of conduct but contributes more than anything else, if we take one thing with another, to the security that follows victory in war. Two things, then, contribute to victory: fearlessness in face of the enemy, and fear of ill-repute among one's friends.

CLEINIAS: Exactly.

ATHENIAN: Every individual should therefore become both afraid and unafraid, for the reasons we have distinguished in each case.

CLEINIAS: Certainly.

ATHENIAN: Moreover, if we want to make an individual proof against all sorts of fears, it is by exposing him to fear, in a way sanctioned by the law, that we make him unafraid.

CLEINIAS: Evidently we do.

ATHENIAN: But what about our attempts to make a man *afraid*, in a way consistent with justice? Shouldn't we see that he enters the lists against impudence, and give him training to resist it, so as to make him conquer in the struggle with his pleasures? A man has to fight and conquer his feelings of cowardice before he can achieve perfect courage; if he has no experience and training in that kind of struggle, he will never more than half realize his potentialities for virtue. Isn't the same true of self-control? Will he ever achieve a perfect mastery here without having fought and conquered, with all the skills of speech and action both in work and play, the crowd of pleasures and desires that stimulate him to act shamelessly and unjustly? Can he afford *not* to have the experience of all these struggles?

CLEINIAS: It would seem hardly likely.

ATHENIAN: Well then, has any god given men a drug to

produce fear, so that the more a man agrees to drink of it, the more the impression grows on him, after every draught, that he is assailed by misfortune? The effect would be to make him apprehensive about his present and future prospects, until finally even the boldest of men would be reduced to absolute 648 terror; but when he had recovered from the drink and slept it off, he would invariably be himself again.

CLEINIAS: And what drink does that, sir? There's hardly an example we could point to anywhere in the world.

ATHENIAN: No. But if one had cropped up, would a legislator have been able to make any use of it to promote courage? This is the sort of point we might well have put to him about it: 'Legislator – whether your laws are to apply to Cretans or to any other people – tell us this: wouldn't you be particularly glad to have a criterion of the courage and cowardice of your citizens?'

CLEINIAS: Obviously, every legislator would say 'Yes'.

ATHENIAN: 'Well, you'd like a safe test without any serious risks, wouldn't you? Or do you prefer one full of risks?'

CLEINIAS: They will all agree to this as well: safety is essential.

ATHENIAN: 'Your procedure would be to test these people's reactions when they had been put into a state of alarm, and by encouraging, rebuking and rewarding individuals you would compel them to become fearless. You would inflict disgrace on anyone who disobeyed and refused to become in every respect the kind of man you wanted; you would discharge without penalty anyone who had displayed the proper courage and finished his training satisfactorily; and the failures you would punish. Or would you refuse point-blank to apply the test, even though you had nothing against the drink in other respects?'

CLEINIAS: Of course he would apply it, sir.

ATHENIAN: Anyway, my friend, compared with current practice, this training would be remarkably straightforward, and would suit individuals, small groups, and any larger numbers you may want. Now if a man retreated into some decent obscurity, out of embarrassment at the thought of being seen before he is in good shape, and trained against his fears alone and in privacy, equipped with just this drink instead of all the usual paraphernalia, he would be entirely justified. But he would be no less justified if, confident that he was already well equipped by birth and breeding, he were to plunge into training with several fellow-drinkers. While inevitably roused by the wine, he would show himself strong enough to escape its other effects: his virtue would prevent him from committing even one serious improper act, and from becoming a different kind of person. Before getting to the last round he would leave off, fearing the way in which drink invariably gets the better of a man.

CLEINIAS: Yes, sir, even he would be prudent enough to do that.

ATHENIAN: Let's repeat the point we were making to the 649 legislator: 'Agreed then: there is probably no such thing as a drug to produce fear, either by divine gift or human contrivance (I leave quacks out of account: they're beyond the pale). But is there a drink that will banish fear and stimulate over-confidence about the wrong thing at the wrong moment? What do we say to this?'

CLEINIAS: I suppose he'll say 'There is', and mention wine.

ATHENIAN: And doesn't this do just the opposite of what we described a moment ago?[11] When a man drinks it, it immediately makes him more cheerful than he was before; the more he takes, the more it fills him with boundless optimism: he thinks he can do anything. Finally, bursting with self-esteem and imposing no restraint on his speech and actions, the fellow loses all his inhibitions and becomes completely fearless: he'll say and do anything, without a qualm. Everybody, I think, would agree with us about this.

CLEINIAS: Certainly.

ATHENIAN: Now let's think back again to this point: we said that there were two elements in our souls that should be cultivated, one of them in order to make ourselves supremely confident, its opposite to make ourselves supremely fearful.

11. See pp. 78–9.

CLEINIAS: The latter being modesty, I suppose.

ATHENIAN: Well remembered! But in view of the fact that one has to learn to be courageous and intrepid when assailed by fears, the question arises whether the opposite quality will have to be cultivated in opposite circumstances.[12]

CLEINIAS: Probably so.

ATHENIAN: So the conditions in which we naturally become unusually bold and daring seem to be precisely those required for practice in reducing our shamelessness and audacity to the lowest possible level, so that we become terrified of ever venturing to say, suffer, or do anything disgraceful.

CLEINIAS: Apparently.

ATHENIAN: Now aren't we affected in this way[13] by all the following conditions – anger, love, pride, ignorance and cowardice? We can add wealth, beauty, strength and everything else that turns us into fools and makes us drunk with pleasure. However, we are looking for an inexpensive and less harmful test we can apply to people, which will also give us a chance to train them, and this we have in the scrutiny we can make of them when they are relaxed over a drink. Can we point to a more suitable pleasure than this – provided some appropriate precautions are taken? Let's look at it in this way. Suppose you have a man with an irritable and savage temper (this is the source of a huge number of crimes). Surely, to make contracts with him, and run the risk that he may default, is a more dangerous way to test him than to keep him company during a festival of Dionysus? Or again, 650 if a man's whole being is dominated by sexual pleasures, it is dangerous to try him out by putting him in charge of your wife and sons and daughters; this is to scrutinize the character of his soul at the price of exposing to risk those whom you hold most dear. You could cite dozens of other instances, and

12. I.e. caution/shame must be cultivated 'in a state of over-confidence and exhilaration' (England).

13. I.e. we become particularly bold and daring. The inclusion of 'cowardice' in the list seems odd: possibly it is meant to suggest the boldness born of desperation.

still not do justice to the superiority of this wholly innocuous 'examination by recreation'. In fact, I think neither the Cretans nor any other people would disagree if we summed it all up like this: we have here a pretty fair test of each other, which for cheapness, safety and speed is absolutely unrivalled.

CLEINIAS: True so far.

ATHENIAN: So this insight into the nature and disposition of a man's soul will rank as one of the most useful aids available to the art which is concerned to foster a good character – the art of *statesmanship*, I take it?

CLEINIAS: Certainly.

The Athenian has established drinking parties as a respectable educational device; he now goes further, and suggests they are in fact the 'safeguard' of education, provided they are properly run. How this can be so appears only at the end of the section, and meanwhile the Athenian launches into a discussion of the role of the arts in education.

He first describes education as the correct discipline of the feelings of pleasure and pain; this is the route by which virtue first enters the soul of a child. The arts are important because they reinforce this discipline in adult life. The assumption here – a very prominent one in Plato – is that when we enjoy the representation of men and their actions in the various art forms (whether we compose or perform ourselves, or see others performing), we are fired with the desire to imitate them. It is therefore vital that art should portray 'good' men attractively and 'bad' men unattractively, and if a poem or a play does this it is conforming to 'good' and 'correct' artistic standards. The assumption that the arts affect our moral character is not the only view it is possible to take of them, and indeed it would be widely challenged today. Even if we grant the assumption, we are faced with the further difficulty of deciding who the 'good' man is; but the Athenian only suggests that it will be the job of elderly, virtuous and well-educated citizens to decide canons of artistic merit, and his companions are (naturally) only too ready to agree. Plato is not in favour of allowing free choice in the adoption of artistic and moral standards; he is firmly on the side of censorship.

Once we grant the educational purpose of the arts, the conclusions of the central part of this section follow without much difficulty. (1) Obviously pleasure tout court will not be the only proper criterion of artistic merit (a view that roused Plato's particular loathing), but the pleasure felt by the virtuous. (2) Proper artistic forms and standards, once discovered, should be finalized and consecrated, as they have been in Egypt, and the constant search for novelty abandoned. (3) The arts should never teach that an unjust man can be happy. This is a point on which Cleinias and Megillus feel very doubtful – after all, rogues do seem, in fact, to live happy enough lives. The Athenian attempts no real refutation, but merely points to the paradox of supposing that the gods make the unjust man happier and more blessed than the just. (4) The lawgiver's job is to find the most effective means of persuading his entire community, especially children, to believe that injustice can never lead to happiness, and of embodying this doctrine in the art forms of the state.

The subject of drinking, which seemed to have been dropped, is now resumed in a rather surprising way. To show how drinking parties can 'safeguard' education, the Athenian introduces his 'third chorus'. In addition to the other choruses in a state, there should be a special one composed of older men, who will sing the 'best' songs. If we take the hints in 666-7, we can see that this is a picturesque way of saying that the old men will lay down the artistic standards to be observed by the state at large. But the old, though wise and virtuous, tend to be unduly austere; a sober intoxication, so to speak, will ensure that they are suitably mellowed. The qualifications of this 'third chorus' are discussed in somewhat technical detail: its members must have an accurate knowledge of (1) what is being represented in the arts (here their age and experience will count); (2) how well it is represented – the fidelity of copy to original and the suitability of the artistic style used to represent it; (3) the moral effect of the representation. Plato's language seems at times to imply that fidelity of copy to original is a major criterion of a work of art; in fact, he is much more concerned that it should imitate beauty and goodness itself (p. 109) by displaying the correct proportions and rhythms etc. Under (2) and (3) comes a strong attack on various contemporary artistic trends, notably the desire for striking novelties and the increasing separation of the component parts of Greek 'music', i.e. song, dance and accompaniment.

Finally, the Athenian sums up and tantalizes Cleinias and Megillus with the prospect of a discussion of gymnastics. But it is soon apparent that he has no intention of meeting their wishes, and in §4 he takes up an entirely fresh topic, the origins of civilization.

NOTE ON THE MUSICAL TERMINOLOGY. The kind of Greek 'music' in which Plato was particularly interested consisted of a *combination of singing and dancing, performed by 'choruses' to instrumental accompaniment; it is a difficult topic, and many of the technical details remain obscure. The Athenian analyses 'music' into two basic constituents, movement and sound. In the case of the body, 'postures' and 'gestures' seem too narrow to translate* schēmata *and I prefer the flat but comprehensive term 'movements'. 'Harmony' is described by the Athenian (p. 103) as 'order in the vocal sounds, the combination of high and low notes'. The word* harmonia *was often used to mean 'style' or 'mode' (e.g. Lydian or Doric), and the various modes were commonly associated with particular kinds of theme and treatment, but as the Athenian is concerned to isolate and analyse the various elements in music, the technical term 'harmony' seems more appropriate than 'mode'. 'Rhythm' is called 'order in movement', and is of course shared by both the movements of the body and the vocal sounds that accompany them (p. 114). For Plato's views on music in general, see* W. D. Anderson, Ethos and Education in Greek Music *(Cambridge, Mass., 1966).*

THE NATURE AND PURPOSE OF
EDUCATION (2)

ATHENIAN: It looks as if the next question we have to ask is this: is the insight we somehow get into men's natural temperaments the *only* thing in favour of drinking parties? Or does a properly run drinking party confer some other substantial benefit that we ought to consider very seriously? What do we say to this? We need to be careful here: as far as I can see, our argument does tend to point to the answer 'Yes', but when we try to discover how and in what sense, we may get tripped up by it.

CLEINIAS: Tell us why, then.

ATHENIAN: I want to think back over our definition of correct education, and to hazard the suggestion now that drinking parties are actually its *safeguard,* provided they are properly established and conducted on the right lines.

CLEINIAS: That's a large claim!

ATHENIAN: I maintain that the earliest sensations that a child feels in infancy are of pleasure and pain, and this is the route by which virtue and vice first enter the soul. (But for a man to acquire good judgement, and unshakeable correct opinions, however late in life, is a matter of good luck: a man who possesses them, and all the benefits they entail, is perfect.) I call 'education' the initial acquisition of virtue by the child, when the feelings of pleasure and affection, pain and hatred, that well up in his soul are channelled in the right courses before he can understand the reason why. Then when he does understand, his reason and his emotions agree in telling him that he has been properly trained by inculcation of appropriate habits. Virtue is this general concord of reason and emotion. But there is one element you could isolate in any account you give, and this is the correct formation of our feelings of pleasure and pain, which makes us hate what we ought to hate from first to last, and love what we ought to love. Call this 'education', and I, at any rate, think you would be giving it its proper name.

CLEINIAS: Yes, sir, we entirely approve of what you have just said about education and that goes for your previous account, too.[1]

HOW THE ARTS SHOULD REINFORCE EDUCATION

ATHENIAN: Splendid. Education, then, is a matter of correctly disciplined feelings of pleasure and pain. But in the course of a man's life the effect wears off, and in many respects it is lost altogether. The gods, however, took pity on the human race, born to suffer as it was, and gave it relief in the form of religious festivals to serve as periods of rest from its labours. They gave us the Muses, with Apollo their leader, and Dionysus; by having these gods to share their holidays, men were to be made whole again, and thanks to them, we find refreshment in the celebration of these festivals. Now, there is a theory which we are always having dinned into our ears: let's see if it squares with the facts or not. It runs like this: virtually all young things find it impossible to keep their

1. See pp. 72 ff.

bodies still and their tongues quiet. They are always trying to move around and cry out; some jump and skip and do a kind of gleeful dance as they play with each other, while others produce all sorts of noises. And whereas animals have no sense of order and disorder in movement ('rhythm' and 'harmony', as we call it), we human beings have been made sensitive to both and can enjoy them. This is the gift of the same gods whom we said were given to us as companions in dancing: it is the device which enables them to be our chorus-leaders and stimulate us to movement, making us combine to sing and dance – and as this naturally 'charms' us, they invented the word 'chorus'.[2] So shall we take it that this point is established? Can we assume that education comes originally from Apollo and the Muses, or not?

CLEINIAS: Yes.

ATHENIAN: So by an 'uneducated' man we shall mean a man who has not been trained to take part in a chorus; and we must say that if a man *has* been sufficiently trained, he is 'educated'.

CLEINIAS: Naturally.

ATHENIAN: And of course a performance by a chorus is a combination of dancing and singing?

CLEINIAS: Of course.

ATHENIAN: And this means that the well-educated man will be able both to sing and dance *well*?

CLEINIAS: So it seems.

ATHENIAN: Now let's see just what that word implies.

CLEINIAS: What word?

ATHENIAN: We say 'he sings *well*' or 'he dances *well*'. But should we expand this and say 'provided he sings *good* songs and dances *good* dances'? Or not?

CLEINIAS: Yes, we should expand it.

ATHENIAN: Now then, take a man whose opinion about what is good is correct (it really *is* good), and likewise in the case of the bad (it really *is* bad), and follows this judgement

2. A playful etymology, hardly reproducible in English: *choros* (chorus) is derived from *chara* (charm, joy, delight).

87

in practice. He may be able to represent, by word and gesture, and with invariable success, his intellectual conception of what is good, even though he gets no pleasure from it and feels no hatred for what is bad. Another man may not be very good at keeping on the right lines when he uses his body and his voice to represent the good, or at trying to form some intellectual conception of it; but he may be very much on the right lines in his feelings of pleasure and pain, because he welcomes what is good and loathes what is bad. Which of these two will be the better educated musically, and the more effective member of a chorus?

CLEINIAS: As far as education is concerned, sir, the second is infinitely superior.

ATHENIAN: So if the three of us grasp what 'goodness' is in singing and dancing, we have also a sound criterion for distinguishing the educated man from the uneducated. If we fail to grasp it, we'll never be able to make up our minds whether a safeguard for education exists, or where we ought to look for it. Isn't that so?

CLEINIAS: Yes, it is.

ATHENIAN: The next quarry we have to track down, like hounds at a hunt, will be what constitutes a 'good' bodily movement, tune, song and dance. But if all these notions give us the slip and get away, it will be pointless utterly to prolong our discussion of correct education, Greek or foreign.

CLEINIAS: Quite.

ATHENIAN: Good. Now, what is to be our definition of a good tune or bodily movement? Tell me – imagine a courageous soul and a cowardly soul beset by one and the 655 same set of troubles: do similar sounds and movements of the body result in each case?

CLEINIAS: Of course not. The complexion is different, to start with.

ATHENIAN: You are absolutely right, my friend. But music is a matter of rhythm and harmony, and involves tunes and movements of the body; this means that while it is legitimate to speak of a 'rhythmical' or a 'harmonious' movement or tune, we cannot properly apply to either of them the chorus-masters' metaphor 'brilliantly coloured'.[3] But what *is* the appropriate language to describe the movement and melody used to portray the brave man and the coward? The correct procedure is to call those of brave men 'good' and those of cowards 'disgraceful'. But let's not have an inordinately long discussion about the details; can we say, without beating about the bush, that all movements and tunes associated with spiritual or bodily excellence (the real thing or a representation) are good? And conversely bad if they have to do with vice?

CLEINIAS: Yes, that's a reasonable proposal. You may assume we agree.

IS PLEASURE THE PROPER CRITERION
IN THE ARTS?

ATHENIAN: Here's a further point: do we all enjoy every type of performance by a chorus to the same degree? Or is that far from being true?

CLEINIAS: As far as it could be!

ATHENIAN: But can we put our finger on the cause of our confusion? Is it that 'good' varies from person to person? Or that it is *thought* to vary, although in point of fact it does not? No one, I fancy, will be prepared to say that dances portraying evil are better than those portraying virtue, or that although other people enjoy the virtuous Muse, his own personal liking is for movements expressing depravity. Yet most men do maintain that the power of music to give pleasure to the soul is the standard by which it should be judged. But this is an insupportable doctrine, and it is absolute blasphemy to speak like that. More likely, though, it's something else that's misleading us.

CLEINIAS: What?

3. The point seems to be that adjectives applying to the *means* of representation ought to apply also to *what* is represented, e.g. a 'bad' tune is used to portray a bad man. The term 'brilliantly-coloured' tune is illegitimate because it misleadingly suggests that it portrays men who are (literally) brilliantly coloured.

ATHENIAN: Performances given by choruses are representations of character, and deal with every variety of action and incident. The individual performers enact their roles partly by expressing their own characters, partly by imitating those of others. That is why, when they find that the speaking or singing or any other element in the performance of a chorus appeals to their natural character or acquired habits, or both, they can't help applauding with delight and using the term 'good'. But sometimes they find these performances going against the grain of their natural character or their disposition or habits, in which case they are unable to take any pleasure in them and applaud them, and in this case the word they use is 'shocking'. When a man's natural character is as it should be, but he has acquired bad habits, or conversely when his habits are correct but his natural character is vicious, his pleasure and his approval fail to coincide: he calls the performances 'pleasant, but depraved'. Such performers, in the company of others whose judgement they respect, are ashamed to make this kind of movement with their bodies, and to sing such songs as though they genuinely approved of them. But in their heart of hearts, they enjoy themselves.

CLEINIAS: You are quite right.

ATHENIAN: Now, does a man's enjoyment of bad bodily movements or bad tunes do him any harm? And does it do him any good to take pleasure in the opposite kind?

CLEINIAS: Probably.

ATHENIAN: 'Probably'? Is that all? Surely there *must* be a precise analogy here with the man who comes into contact with depraved characters and wicked people, and who does not react with disgust, but welcomes them with pleasure, censuring them half-heartedly because he only half-realizes, as in a dream, how perverted such a state is: he just cannot escape taking on the character of what he enjoys, whether good or bad – even if he is ashamed to go so far as to applaud it. In fact we could hardly point to a greater force for good – or evil – than this inevitable assimilation of character.

CLEINIAS: No, I don't think we could.

ARTISTIC CENSORSHIP IN EGYPT

ATHENIAN: So, in a society where the laws relating to culture, education and recreation are, or will be in future, properly established, do we imagine that authors will be given a free hand? The choruses will be composed of the young children of law-abiding citizens: will the composer be free to teach them *anything* by way of rhythm, tune and words that amuses him when he composes, without bothering what effect he may have on them as regards virtue and vice?

CLEINIAS: That's certainly not sensible; how could it be?

ATHENIAN: But it is precisely this that they are allowed to do in virtually all states – except in Egypt.

CLEINIAS: Egypt! Well then, you'd better tell us what legislation has been enacted there.

ATHENIAN: Merely to hear about it is startling enough.[4] Long ago, apparently, they realized the truth of the principle we are putting forward only now, that the movements and tunes which the children of the state are to practise in their rehearsals must be good ones. They compiled a list of them according to style, and displayed it in their temples. Painters and everyone else who represent movements of the body of any kind were restricted to these forms; modification and innovation outside this traditional framework were prohibited, and are prohibited even today, both in this field and the arts in general. If you examine their art on the spot, you will find that ten thousand years ago (and I'm not speaking loosely: I mean literally ten thousand), paintings and reliefs were produced that are no better and no worse than those of today, 657 because the same artistic rules were applied in making them.

CLEINIAS: Fantastic! ← WHAT ABOUT SELF-EXPRESSION?

ATHENIAN: No: simply a supreme achievement of legislators and statesmen. You might, even so, find some other things to criticize there, but in the matter of music this inescapable fact deserves our attention: it has in fact proved

4. We have little but the Athenian's word for what follows. See G. R. Morrow, *Plato's Cretan City* (Princeton, 1960), p. 355.

feasible to take the kind of music that shows a natural correctness and put it on a firm footing by legislation. But it is the task of a god, or a man of god-like stature; in fact, the Egyptians do say that the tunes that have been preserved for so long are compositions of Isis. Consequently, as I said, if one could get even a rough idea of what constitutes 'correctness' in matters musical, one ought to have no qualms about giving the whole subject systematic expression in the form of a law. It is true that the craving for pleasure and the desire to avoid tedium lead us to a constant search for novelty in music, and choral performances that have been thus consecrated may be stigmatized as out-of-date; but this does not have very much power to corrupt them. In Egypt, at any rate, it does not seem to have had a corrupting effect at all: quite the contrary.

CLEINIAS: So it would seem, to judge from your account.

PROPER AND IMPROPER PLEASURES

ATHENIAN: So, equally without qualms, we can surely describe the proper conditions for festive music and performances of choruses more or less like this. When we think things are going well for us, we feel delight; and to put it the other way round, when we feel delight, we come to think that things are going well. Isn't that so?

CLEINIAS: It is.

ATHENIAN: In addition, when we are in that state – I mean 'delight' – we can't keep still.

CLEINIAS: That's true.

ATHENIAN: Our youngsters are keen to join the dancing and singing themselves, but we old men think the proper thing is to pass the time as spectators. The delight we feel comes from their relaxation and merry-making. Our agility is deserting us, and as we feel its loss we are only too pleased to provide competitions for the young, because they can best stir in us the memory of our youth and re-awaken the instincts of our younger days.

CLEINIAS: Very true.

ATHENIAN: So we'd better face the fact that there is a grain of truth in contemporary thought on the subject of holiday-makers. Most people say that the man who delights us most and gives us most pleasure should be highly esteemed for his skill, and deserves to be awarded first prize, because the fact that we are allowed to relax on such occasions means that we ought to lionize the man who gives most people most pleasure, so that, as I said just now, he deserves to carry off the prize. In theory that's right, isn't it? And wouldn't it be equally right in practice?

658

CLEINIAS: Maybe.

ATHENIAN: Ah, my fine fellow, such a conclusion 'may be' rash! We must make some distinctions, and examine the question rather like this: suppose somebody were to arrange a competition, and were to leave its character entirely open, not specifying whether it was to be gymnastic, artistic or equestrian. Assume that he gathers together all the inhabitants of the state, and offers a prize: anyone who wishes should come and compete in giving pleasure, and this is to be the sole criterion; the competitor who gives the audience most pleasure will win; he has an entirely free hand as to what method he employs, but provided he excels in this one respect he will be judged the most pleasing of the competitors and win the prize. What effect do we think such an announcement would have?

CLEINIAS: In what way do you mean?

ATHENIAN: Likely enough, I suppose, one competitor will play the Homer and present epic poetry, another will sing lyric songs to music, another will put on a tragedy, and another a comedy; and it will be no surprise if somebody even reckons his best chance of winning lies in putting on a puppet-show. Now, with all these competitors and thousands of others entering, can we say which would *really* deserve to win?

CLEINIAS: That's an odd question! Who could answer it for you with authority before hearing the contestants, and listening to them individually on the spot?

ATHENIAN: Well then, do you want me to give you an equally odd answer?

93

CLEINIAS: Naturally.

ATHENIAN: Suppose the decision rests with the smallest infant children. They'll decide for the exhibitor of puppets, won't they?

CLEINIAS: Of course.

ATHENIAN: If it rests with the older children, they will choose the producer of comedies. Young men, ladies of cultivated taste, and I dare say pretty nearly the entire populace, will choose the tragedy.

CLEINIAS: Yes, I dare say.

ATHENIAN: We old men would probably be most gratified to listen to a reciter doing justice to the *Iliad* or *Odyssey*, or an extract from Hesiod: we'd say he was the winner by a clear margin. Who, then, would be the *proper* winner? That's the next question, isn't it?

CLEINIAS: Yes.

ATHENIAN: Clearly you and I are forced to say that the proper winners would be those chosen by men of our vintage. To us, from among all the customs followed in every city all over the world today, this looks like the best.[5]

CLEINIAS: Surely.

ATHENIAN: I am, then, in limited agreement with the man in the street. Pleasure is indeed a proper criterion in the arts, but not the pleasure experienced by anybody and everybody. The productions of the Muse are at their finest when they delight men of high calibre and adequate education – but particularly if they succeed in pleasing the single individual whose education and moral standards reach heights attained by no one else. This is the reason why we maintain that judges in these matters need high moral standards: they have to possess not only a discerning taste, but courage too. A judge won't be doing his job properly if he reaches his verdict by listening to the audience and lets himself be thrown off balance by the yelling of the mob and his own lack of training; nor must he shrug his shoulders and let cowardice and indolence persuade him into a false verdict against his

5. The point is obscurely put: the custom referred to seems to be that of deferring to age in matters of artistic judgement. Cf. pp. 59 and 96–7.

better judgement, so that he lies with the very lips with which he called upon the gods when he undertook office.[6] The truth is that he sits in judgement as a teacher of the audience, rather than as its pupil; his function (and under the ancient law[7] of the Greeks he used to be allowed to perform it) is to throw his weight *against* them, if the pleasure they show has been aroused improperly and illegitimately. For instance, the law[7] now in force in Sicily and Italy, by truckling to the majority of the audience and deciding the winner by a show of hands, has had a disastrous effect on the authors themselves, who compose to gratify the depraved tastes of their judges; the result is that in effect *they* are taught by the audience. It has been equally disastrous for the quality of the pleasure felt by the spectators: they ought to come to experience more elevated pleasures from listening to the portrayal of characters invariably better than their own, but in fact just the opposite happens, and they have no one to thank but themselves. Well, then, now that we have finished talking about that, what conclusion is indicated? Let's see if it isn't this –

CLEINIAS: What?

ATHENIAN: For the third or fourth time, I think, our discussion has come full circle. Once again, education has proved to be a process of attraction, of leading children to accept right principles as enunciated by the law and endorsed as genuinely correct by men who have high moral standards and are full of years and experience. The soul of the child has to be prevented from getting into the habit of feeling pleasure and pain in ways not sanctioned by the law and those who have been persuaded to obey it; he should follow in their footsteps and find pleasure and pain in the same things as the old. That is why we have what we call songs, which are really 'charms' for the soul. These are in fact deadly serious devices for producing this concord[8] we are talking about; but the

6. Judges in artistic and athletic competitions swore to reach their verdicts without fear or favour.

7. Or perhaps 'custom'. Nothing is known of it except what can be inferred from this passage.

8. See p. 86: the concord between reason and emotion is meant. (The

souls of the young cannot bear to be serious, so we use the terms 'recreation' and 'song' for the charms, and children treat them in that spirit. We have an analogy in the sick and ailing; those in charge of feeding them try to administer the
660 proper diet in tasty foods and drinks, and offer them unwholesome items in revolting foods, so that the patients may get into the desirable habit of welcoming the one kind and loathing the other. This is just what the true legislator will persuade (or, failing persuasion, compel) the man with a creative flair to do with his grand and marvellous language: to compose correctly by portraying, with appropriate choreography and musical setting, men who are moderate, courageous and good in every way.

CLEINIAS: Good Heavens, sir, do you really think that's how they compose nowadays in other cities? My experience is limited, but I know of no such proceeding as you describe, except among us Cretans or in Sparta. In dancing and all the other arts one novelty follows another; the changes are made not by law but are prompted by wildly changing fancies that are very far from being permanent and stable like the Egyptian tastes you're explaining: on the contrary, they are never the same from minute to minute.

ATHENIAN: Well said, Cleinias. But if I gave you the impression that I was speaking of the present day when I referred to the procedure you mention, I expect it was my own lack of clarity in expressing my thoughts that led you astray and caused me to be misunderstood. I was only saying what I want to see happen in the arts, but perhaps I used expressions that made you think I was referring to facts. It always goes against the grain to pillory habits that are irretrievably on the wrong lines, but sometimes one has to. So, seeing that we are agreed in approving this custom,[9] tell me this, if you will: is it more prevalent among you Cretans and the Spartans than among the other Greeks?

---

pun here on *ôdai* [songs] and *epôdai* [charms] is only one of many plays on words in the *Laws* which it is either impossible or undesirable to reproduce in English.)

9. Of deferring to age — see note on p. 94.

CLEINIAS: Certainly.

ATHENIAN: And what if it became prevalent among the others as well? Presumably we'd say that that was an improvement on present practice?

CLEINIAS: Yes, I suppose it would be a tremendous improvement if they adopted the procedure of Crete and Sparta – which is also in accordance with the recommendations you made just now.

JUSTICE AND HAPPINESS GO TOGETHER

ATHENIAN: Now then, let's make sure we understand each other in this business. The essence of the entire cultural education of your countries is surely this: you oblige your poets to say that the good man, because he is temperate and just, enjoys good fortune and is happy, no matter whether he is big and strong, or small and weak, or rich, or poor; and that even if he is 'richer than Midas or Cinyras', and has not justice, he is a wretch, and lives a life of misery. 'I'd not mention a man', says your poet,[10] and how right he is, and 'I'd take no account of him', even if all his actions and possessions were what people commonly call 'good', if he were without justice, nor even if, with a character like that, he 661 'attacked in close combat with the foe'. If he is unjust, I wouldn't want him to 'stand the sight of bloody butchery' nor 'outdo in speed the north wind of Thrace', nor ever achieve any of the things that are generally said to be 'good'. You see, these things men usually call 'good' are misnamed. It is commonly said that health comes first, beauty second, and wealth third. The list goes on indefinitely: keen sight and hearing, and acute perception of all the objects of sensation; being a dictator and doing whatever you like; and the seventh heaven is supposed to be reached when one has achieved all this and is made immortal without further ado. You and I, presumably, hold that all these things are possessions of great

10. Tyrtaeus: see p. 51 and note. The Athenian makes further brief quotations from the same poem. Midas and Cinyras, kings of Phrygia and Cyprus respectively, were notorious for extreme wealth.

value to the just and pious, but that to the unjust they are a curse, every one of them, from health all the way down the list. Seeing, hearing, sensation, and simply being alive, are great evils, if in spite of having all these so-called good things a man gains immortality without justice and virtue in general; but if he survives for only the briefest possible time, the evil is less. I imagine you will persuade or compel the authors in your states to embody this doctrine of mine in the words, rhythms and 'harmonies' they produce for the education of your youth. Isn't that right? Look here, now: my position is quite clear. Although so-called evils are in fact evil for the just, they are good for the unjust; and so-called 'goods', while genuinely good for the good, are evils for the wicked. Let me ask the same question as before: are you and I in agreement, or not?

CLEINIAS: In some ways I think we are, but certainly not in others.

ATHENIAN: I expect this is where I sound implausible: suppose a man were to enjoy health and wealth and permanent absolute power – and, if you like, I'll give him enormous strength and courage as well, and exempt him from death and all the other 'evils', as people call them. But suppose he had in him nothing but injustice and insolence. It is obvious, I maintain, that his life is wretchedly *un*happy.

CLEINIAS: True, that's precisely where you fail to convince.

ATHENIAN: Very well, then. How should we put it now? If a man is brave, strong, handsome, and rich, and enjoys a 662 life-long freedom to do just what he wants to, don't you think – if he is unjust and insolent – that his life will inevitably be a disgrace? Perhaps at any rate you'd allow the term 'disgrace'?

CLEINIAS: Certainly.

ATHENIAN: Will you go further, and say he will live 'badly'?[11]

CLEINIAS: No, we'd not be so ready to admit that.

11. The expression is ambiguous: it may mean 'miserably' or 'wickedly'. In his reply, Cleinias is thinking of the first meaning.

ATHENIAN: What about going further still, and saying he will live 'unpleasantly and unprofitably'?

CLEINIAS: How could we possibly be prepared to go as far as that?

ATHENIAN: 'How'? My friend, it looks as if it would be a miracle if we ever harmonized on this point: at the moment your tune and mine are scarcely in the same key. To me, these conclusions are inescapably true – in fact, my dear Cleinias, rather more true and obvious than that Crete is an island. If I were a lawgiver, I should try to compel the authors and every inhabitant of the state to take this line; and if anybody in the land said that there are men who live a pleasant life in spite of being scoundrels, or that while this or that is useful and profitable, something else is more just, I should impose pretty nearly the extreme penalty. There are many other things I should persuade my citizens to say, which would flatly contradict what Cretans and Spartans maintain nowadays, apparently – to say nothing of the rest of the world. Zeus and Apollo! Just you imagine, my fine fellows, asking these gods who inspired your laws, 'Is the life of supreme justice also the life that gives most pleasure? Or are there two kinds of life, one being "the supremely just", the other "the most pleasurable"?' Suppose they replied 'There are two.' If we knew the right question to ask, we might perhaps pursue the point: 'Which category of men should we call the most blessed by heaven? Those who live the supremely just life, or the most pleasurable?' If they said 'Those who live the most pleasurable life', then that would be, for them, a curious thing to say.[12] However, I am unwilling to associate the gods with such a statement; I prefer to think of it in connexion with forefathers and lawgivers. So let's suppose those first questions have been put to a forefather and lawgiver, and that he has replied that the man who lives the life of greatest pleasure enjoys the greatest happiness. This is what I'd say then: 'Father, didn't you want me to receive as many of the blessings of heaven as I could? Yet in spite of that you never tired

12. Because the gods would appear to be denying happiness to the virtuous.

of telling me to order my life as *justly* as possible'. In taking up that kind of position our forefather or lawgiver will, I think, appear in rather an odd light: it will look as if he cannot speak without contradicting himself. However, if he declared that the life of supreme justice was the most blessed, I imagine that everybody who heard him would want to know what splendid benefit, superior to pleasure, was to be found in this kind of life. What was there in it that deserved the commendation of the law? Surely, any benefit a just man got out of it would be *inseparable* from pleasure? Look: are we to suppose that fame and praise from gods and men are fine and good, but unpleasant (and vice versa in the case of notoriety)? ('My dear legislator,' we'd say, 'of course not'.)[13] Or, if you neither injure another nor are injured yourself by someone else, is that unpleasant, in spite of being fine and good? Is the opposite pleasant, but disgraceful and wicked?[14]

CLEINIAS: Certainly not.

ATHENIAN: So the argument that does not drive a wedge between 'pleasant' on the one hand and 'just' and 'fine' and 'good' on the other, even if it achieves nothing else, will do something to persuade a man to live a just and pious life. This means that any teaching which denies the truth of all this is, from the lawgiver's standpoint, a complete disgrace and his worst enemy. (Nobody would willingly agree to do something which would not bring him more pleasure than pain.)

Looking at a thing from a distance makes nearly everyone feel dizzy, especially children; but the lawgiver will alter that for us, and lift the fog that clouds our judgement: somehow or other – by habituation, praise, or argument – he will persuade us that our ideas of justice and injustice are like

13. Apparently the legislator has been speaking, but it is not easy to see where his remarks began. 'Surely . . . pleasure' would, according to interpretation, be equally appropriate in either his mouth or his opponents'.

14. The Athenian wishes to combat the view that *if* a thing is pleasant, it is therefore good. He wants to avoid giving the impression that he believes '*if* good, then not pleasant', or '*if* pleasant, then not good'. His own view is, '*if* good, then pleasant'. It is in this sense that 'good' and 'pleasant' are inseparable.

pictures drawn in perspective. Injustice looks pleasant to the enemy of justice, because he regards it from his own personal standpoint, which is unjust and evil; justice, on the other hand, looks *un*pleasant to him. But from the standpoint of the just man the view gained of justice and injustice is always the opposite. ← RELATIVISM OF MORAL VIEWS

CLEINIAS: So it seems.

ATHENIAN: And which of these judgements are we to say has a better claim to be the correct one? The judgement of the worse soul or the better?

CLEINIAS: That of the better, certainly.

ATHENIAN: Then it is equally certain that the unjust life is not only more shocking and disgraceful, but also in fact less pleasant, than the just and holy.

CLEINIAS: On this argument, my friends, it certainly looks like it.

CHILDREN ARE EASILY PERSUADED

ATHENIAN: But just suppose that the truth had been different from what the argument has now shown it to be, and that a lawgiver, even a mediocre one, had been sufficiently bold, in the interests of the young, to tell them a lie. Could he have told a more useful lie than this, or one more effective in making everyone practise justice in everything they do, willingly and without pressure?

CLEINIAS: Truth is a fine thing, sir, and it is sure to prevail, but to persuade men of it certainly seems no easy task.

ATHENIAN: Yes, but what about that fairy story about the Sidonian?[15] That was well-nigh incredible, but it was easy enough to convince men of it, and of thousands of other similar stories.

CLEINIAS: What sort of stories?

ATHENIAN: The sowing of the teeth and the birth of armed men from them. This remarkable example shows the legislator that the souls of the young can be persuaded of 664 anything; he has only to try. The only thing he must consider

15. Cadmus. See note on p. 70.

and discover is what conviction would do the state most good; in that connexion, he must think up every possible device to ensure that as far as possible the entire community preserves in its songs and stories and doctrines an absolute and lifelong unanimity. But if you see the matter in any other light, have no hesitation in disputing my view.

CLEINIAS: No, I don't think either of us would be able to dispute that.

THE THREE CHORUSES

ATHENIAN: Then it will be up to me to introduce the next point. I maintain that our choruses – all three of them – should charm the souls of the children while still young and tender, and uphold all the admirable doctrines we have already formulated, and any we may formulate in the future. We must insist, as the central point of these doctrines, that the gods say the best life does in fact bring most pleasure. If we do that, we shall be telling the plain truth, and we shall convince those whom we have to convince more effectively than if we advanced any other doctrine.

CLEINIAS: Yes, one has to agree with what you say.

ATHENIAN: To start with, it will be only right and proper if the children's chorus (which will be dedicated to the Muses) comes on first to sing these doctrines with all its might and main before the entire city. Second will come the chorus of those under thirty, which will call upon Apollo Paean[16] to bear witness that what they say is true, and pray that he will vouchsafe to convince the young. Thirdly, there must be the songs of those between thirty and sixty. That leaves the men who are older than this, who are, of course, no longer up to singing; but they will be inspired to tell stories in which the same characters will appear.[17]

CLEINIAS: You mention these three choruses, sir: what are they? We are not very clear what you mean to say about them.

16. The god of healing.
17. I.e. virtuous characters who featured in the songs of the choruses.

ATHENIAN: But the greater part of the discussion we have had so far has been precisely for their sake!

CLEINIAS: We still haven't seen the point. Could you try to elucidate still further?

ATHENIAN: If we remember, we said at the beginning of our discussion[18] that all young things, being fiery and mettlesome by nature, are unable to keep their bodies or their tongues still – they are always making unco-ordinated noises and jumping about. No other animal, we said, ever develops a sense of order in either respect; man alone has a natural ability to do this. Order in movement is called 'rhythm', and order in the vocal sounds – the combination of high and low notes – is called 'harmony'; and the union of the two is called 'a performance by a chorus'. We said that the gods took pity on us and gave us Apollo and the Muses as companions and leaders of our choruses; and if we can cast our minds back, we said that their third gift to us was Dionysus.

665

CLEINIAS: Yes, of course we remember.

ATHENIAN: Well, we've mentioned the choruses of Apollo and the Muses; the remaining one, the third, must be identified as belonging to Dionysus.

CLEINIAS: What! You had better explain yourself: a chorus of elderly men dedicated to Dionysus sounds a weird and wonderful idea, at any rate at first hearing. Are men of more than thirty and even fifty, up to sixty, really going to dance in honour of Dionysus?

ATHENIAN: You are absolutely right – to show how this could be reasonable in practice does need, I think, some explanation.

CLEINIAS: It certainly does.

ATHENIAN: Are we agreed on the conclusions we have reached so far?

CLEINIAS: Conclusions about what?

ATHENIAN: About this – that every man and child, freeman and slave, male and female – in fact, the whole state – is in duty bound never to stop repeating to each other the charms[19] we have described. Somehow or other, we must see

18. See pp. 86 ff.   19. See p. 95, note 8.

that these charms constantly change their form; at all costs they must be continually varied, so that the performers always long to sing the songs, and find perpetual pleasure in them.

CLEINIAS: Agreed: that's exactly the arrangement we want.

ATHENIAN: This last chorus is the noblest element in our state; it carries more conviction than any other group, because of the age and discernment of its members. Where, then, should it sing its splendid songs, if it is to do most good? Surely we are not going to be silly enough to leave this question undecided? After all, this chorus may well prove to be consummate masters of the noblest and most useful songs.

CLEINIAS: No; if that's really the way the argument is going, we certainly can't leave this undecided.

ATHENIAN: So what would be a suitable method of procedure? See if this will do.

CLEINIAS: What, then?

ATHENIAN: As he grows old, a man becomes apprehensive about singing; it gives him less pleasure, and if it should happen that he cannot avoid it, it causes him an embarrassment which grows with the increasingly sober tastes of his advancing years. Isn't that so?

CLEINIAS: Indeed it is.

ATHENIAN: So naturally he will be even more acutely embarrassed at standing up and singing in front of the varied audience in a theatre. And if men of that age were forced to sing in the same condition as members of choruses competing for a prize – lean and on a diet after a course of voice-training – then of course they would find the performance positively unpleasant and humiliating, and would lose every spark of enthusiasm.

666 CLEINIAS: Yes, that would be the inevitable result.

ATHENIAN: So how shall we encourage them to be enthusiastic about singing? The first law we shall pass, surely, is this: children under the age of eighteen are to keep off wine entirely. We shall teach them that they must treat the violent tendencies of youth with due caution, and not pour fire on the

fire already in their souls and bodies until they come to undertake the real work of life. Our second law will permit the
young man under thirty to take wine in moderation, but he
must stop short of drunkenness and bibulous excesses. When
he reaches his thirties, he should regale himself at the common
meals, and invoke the gods; in particular, he should summon
Dionysus to what is at once the play-time and the prayer-time
of the old, which the god gave to mankind to help cure the
crabbiness of age. This is the gift he gave us to make us young
again: we forget our peevishness, and our hard cast of mind
becomes softer and grows more malleable, just like iron thrust
in a fire. Surely any man who is brought into that frame of
mind would be ready to sing his songs (that is, 'charms', as
we've called them often enough) with more enthusiasm and
less embarrassment? I don't mean in a large gathering of
strangers, but in a comparatively small circle of friends.

CLEINIAS: Certainly.

ATHENIAN: As a method of inducing them to join us in
our singing, there wouldn't be anything you could particularly object to in this.

CLEINIAS: By no means.

ATHENIAN: But what sort of philosophy of music will
inspire their songs? Obviously, it will have to be one appropriate to the performers.

CLEINIAS: Of course.

ATHENIAN: And the performers are men of almost divine
distinction. What notes would be appropriate for them?
Those produced by the choruses?

CLEINIAS: Well, sir, we Cretans, at any rate – and the same
goes for the Spartans – would hardly be up to singing any
song except those we learned to sing by growing familiar
with them in our choruses.

ATHENIAN: Naturally enough. In cold fact, you have
failed to achieve the finest kind of song. You organize your
state as though it were a military camp rather than a society of
people who have settled in towns, and you keep your young
fellows together like a herd of colts at grass. Not a man among
you takes his own colt and drags him, furiously protesting,

away from the rest of the herd; you never put him in the hands of a private groom, and train him by combing him down and stroking him. You entirely fail to lavish proper care on an education which will turn him out not merely a good soldier but a capable administrator of a state and its 667 towns. Such a man is, as we said early on, a better fighter than those of Tyrtaeus, precisely because he does not value courage as the principal element in virtue: he consistently relegates it to *fourth* place wherever he finds it, whether in the individual or the state.

CLEINIAS: I suspect, sir, you are being rather rude about our legislators again.

ATHENIAN: If I am, my dear fellow, it is entirely unintentionally. But if you don't mind, we ought to follow where the argument leads us. If we know of any music that is of finer quality than the music of choruses and the public theatres, we ought to try to allocate it to these older people. They are, as we said, embarrassed at the other kind; but music of the highest quality is just what they are keen to take part in.

CLEINIAS: Yes, indeed.

QUALIFICATIONS OF THE THIRD CHORUS, AND AN ATTACK ON CONTEMPORARY TRENDS IN THE ARTS

ATHENIAN: The most important point about everything that has some inherent attractive quality must be *either* this very quality *or* some kind of 'correctness' *or* (thirdly) its usefulness. For instance, I maintain that eating and drinking and taking nourishment in general are accompanied by the particular attractive quality that we might call pleasure; as for their usefulness and 'correctness', we invariably speak of the 'wholesomeness' of the foods we serve, and in their case the most 'correct' thing in them is precisely this.

CLEINIAS: Quite.

ATHENIAN: An element of attractiveness – the pleasure we feel – goes with the process of learning, too. But what gives rise to its 'correctness' and usefulness, its excellence and nobility, is its accuracy.

CLEINIAS: Exactly.

ATHENIAN: What about the arts of imitation, whose function is to produce likenesses? When they succeed in doing this, it will be quite proper to say that the pleasure – if any – that arises out of and accompanies that success constitutes the attractive quality of these arts.

CLEINIAS: Yes.

ATHENIAN: Generally speaking, I suppose, the 'correctness' in such cases would depend not so much on the pleasure given, as on the accurate representation of the size and qualities of the original?

CLEINIAS: Well put.

ATHENIAN: So pleasure would be the proper criterion in one case only. A work of art may be produced with nothing to offer by way of usefulness or truth or accuracy of representation (or harm, of course). It may be produced solely for the sake of this element that normally accompanies the others, the attractive one. (In fact, it is when this element is associated with none of the others that it most genuinely deserves the name 'pleasure'.)

CLEINIAS: You mean only harmless pleasure?

ATHENIAN: Yes, and it is precisely this that I call 'play', when it has no particular good or bad effect that deserves serious discussion.

CLEINIAS: Quite right.

ATHENIAN: And we could conclude from all this that no imitation at all should be judged by reference to incorrect opinions about it or by the criterion of the pleasure it gives. This is particularly so in the case of representational equality. What is equal is equal and what is proportional is proportional, 668 and this does not depend on anyone's opinion that it is so, nor does it cease to be true if someone is displeased at the fact.[20] Accuracy, and nothing else whatever, is the only permissible criterion.

20. That is, a work of art – a statue or a portrait, say – may preserve the size and shape of its original either by reproducing it life-size or by

CLEINIAS: Yes, that is emphatically true.

ATHENIAN: So do we hold that all music is a matter of representation and imitation?

CLEINIAS: Of course.

ATHENIAN: So when someone says that music is judged by the criterion of pleasure, we should reject his argument out of hand, and absolutely refuse to go in for such music (if any were ever produced) as a serious *genre*. The music we ought to cultivate is the kind that bears a resemblance to its model, beauty.

CLEINIAS: Very true.

ATHENIAN: These people,[21] then, who are anxious to take part in the finest possible singing, should, apparently, look not for a music which is sweet, but one which is correct; and correctness, as we said, lies in the imitation and successful reproduction of the proportions and characteristics of the model.

CLEINIAS: It does indeed.

ATHENIAN: This is certainly so in the case of music: everyone would admit that all musical compositions are matters of imitation and representation. In fact, composers, audiences and actors would register universal agreement on this point, wouldn't they?

CLEINIAS: Certainly.

ATHENIAN: So it looks as if a man who is not to go wrong about a given composition must appreciate what it is, because failure to understand its nature – what it is trying to do and what in fact it is a representation of – will mean that he gets virtually no conception of whether the author has achieved his aim correctly or not.

CLEINIAS: No, virtually none, naturally.

ATHENIAN: And if he cannot gauge the correctness of the composition, surely he won't be able to judge its moral

keeping the same relative proportions on a larger or smaller scale. But whether it does or not is a matter of objective fact, not of opinion. We have here a (rather rudimentary) objective and measurable criterion of excellence in art. See, however, pp. 84 and 109.

21. The third chorus – cf. p. 106.

goodness or badness? But this is all rather obscure. Perhaps this would be a clearer way of putting it.

CLEINIAS: What?

ATHENIAN: There are, of course, thousands of representations that strike the eye?

CLEINIAS: Yes.

ATHENIAN: Now, imagine someone who didn't know the character of each of the objects that are imitated and represented. Would he ever be able to estimate the correctness of the finished article? This is the sort of point I have in mind: does it preserve the overall proportions of the body and the position of each of its various parts? Does it hit off the proportions exactly and keep the parts in their proper positions relative to one another? And what of their colours and contours? Have all these features been reproduced higgledy-piggledy? Do you think that if a man did not know the character of the creature represented he would ever be able to assess these points?

CLEINIAS: Of course not.

ATHENIAN: What if we knew that the thing moulded or painted is a man, and that all his parts with their colours and contours have been caught by the artist's skill? Suppose a man knows all that; is he without further ado necessarily ready to judge whether the work is beautiful or falls short of beauty in some respect?

CLEINIAS: In that case, sir, pretty well all of us would be judges of the quality of a representation.

ATHENIAN: You have hit the nail on the head. So anyone who is going to be a sensible judge of any representation – in painting and music and every other field – should be able to assess three points: he must know, first, what has been represented; second, how correctly it has been copied; and then, third, the moral value of this or that representation, so far as language, tunes and rhythms are concerned.

CLEINIAS: Apparently so.

ATHENIAN: We ought not to fail to mention the peculiar difficulty about music, which is discussed much more than any other kind of artistic representation and needs much more careful handling than all the others. A man who goes wrong on this subject will suffer a good deal of harm because he feels attracted to evil dispositions; and his mistake is very difficult to detect, because the authors hardly have the same degree of creative ability as the actual Muses. The Muses would never make the ghastly mistake of composing the speech of men to a musical idiom suitable for women, or of fitting rhythms appropriate to the portrayal of slaves and slave-like people to the tune and bodily movements used to represent free men (or again of making rhythms and movements appropriate to free men accompany a combination of tune and words that conflicted with those rhythms). Nor would they ever mix up together into one production the din of wild animals and men and musical instruments and all kinds of other noises and still claim to be representing a unified theme. But human authors, in their silly way, jumble all these things together into complicated combinations; in Orpheus' words, anyone 'whose delight in life is in its springtime', will find them a rich source of amusement. And in the midst of all this confusion, he will find that the authors also divorce rhythm and movement from the tune by putting unaccompanied words into metre, and rob tune and rhythm of words by using stringed instruments and pipes on their own without singers. When this is done, it is extraordinarily difficult to know what the rhythm and harmony without speech are supposed to signify and what worth-while object they imitate and represent. The conclusion is inevitable: such practices appeal to the taste of the village idiot. It is this fondness for speed and dexterity (as in reproducing the noises of wild 670 animals) which prompts the use of pipes and lyre otherwise than as an accompaniment to dancing and singing. Using either instrument on its own is in fact sheer showmanship that has nothing to do with art. But enough of theory: what we are considering is not what sort of music our citizens over thirty and fifty should avoid, but what sort they should go in for. I think our argument so far seems to point to the conclusion that the fifty-year-olds who have the duty of singing must have enjoyed an education that reached a higher standard than the music of choruses. They must, of course, have a nice appreciation of rhythms and harmonies and be able to understand them. Otherwise how could a man assess the correctness of the tunes, and tell whether the Dorian mode was appropriate or not in a given case, or judge whether the author has set the tunes to the right rhythm or not?

CLEINIAS: Clearly he couldn't.

ATHENIAN: The belief of the general public, that they can form an adequate judgement of merit and demerit in matters of harmony and rhythm, is laughable: they have only been drilled into singing to the pipes and marching in step, and they never stop to think that they do all this without the smallest understanding of it. In fact, every tune with the right elements is correct, but if it has the wrong ones, it is faulty.

CLEINIAS: Inevitably.

ATHENIAN: What about the man who doesn't even understand what the elements are? As we said, will he ever be able to decide that any aspect of the piece is correct?

CLEINIAS: No, how could he?

ATHENIAN: So it looks as if once again we are discovering that it is virtually indispensable for these singers of ours (who are not only being encouraged to sing but *compelled* to do it in a willing spirit, if I may put it like that), to have been educated up to at least this point: they should each be able to follow the notes of the tunes and the basic units of rhythm, so that they may examine the harmonies and rhythms and select those that men of their age and character could appropriately sing. If that is how they sing, they will give themselves harmless pleasure, and at the same time stimulate the younger generation to adopt virtuous customs with the proper enthusiasm. Assuming the education of these singers reaches that level, they will have pursued a more advanced course of training than will be given to ordinary men, or even the authors themselves. The author is more or less obliged to have a knowledge of rhythm and harmony, but there is no necessity for him to be able to assess the third point – whether the imitation is a good one or not. The men we are talking about, however, must be equally competent in all three

fields,[22] so that they can isolate the primary and secondary
671 degrees of goodness; otherwise they will never prove capable
of charming the young in the direction of virtue.

THE EDUCATIONAL EFFECTS OF
DRINKING PARTIES (2)

ATHENIAN: Our argument has done its level best: we have to
consider whether it has succeeded in its original intention of
showing that our defence of Dionysus' chorus was justified.
A gathering like that, of course, inevitably gets increasingly
rowdier as the wine flows more freely. (In fact, our initial
assumption in the present discussion of this business was that
such a tendency is unavoidable.)

CLEINIAS: Yes, it is unavoidable.

ATHENIAN: Everyone is taken out of himself and has a
splendid time; the exuberance of his conversation is matched
only by his reluctance to listen to his companions, and he
thinks himself entitled to run their lives as well as his own.

CLEINIAS: He certainly does.

ATHENIAN: And didn't we say that when this happens the
souls of the drinkers get hot and, like iron in a fire, grow
younger and softer, so that anyone who has the ability and
skill to mould and educate them, finds them as easy to handle
as when they were young? The man to do the moulding is the
same one as before – the good lawgiver. When our drinker
grows cheerful and confident and unduly shameless and
unwilling to speak and keep quiet, to drink and sing, at the
proper times, the lawgiver's job will be to lay down drinking
laws which will be able to make this fellow willing to mend
his ways; and to do battle with this disgraceful over-
confidence as soon as it appears, they will be able to send
into the arena, with the blessing of justice, this divine and
splendid fear we have called 'modesty' and 'shame'.[23]

CLEINIAS: Exactly.

ATHENIAN: The cool-headed and sober should guard and
co-operate with these laws by taking command of those who
are not sober; fighting the enemy without cool-headed

22. Cf. p. 109.   23. See pp. 77–8.

leaders is actually *less* dangerous than fighting drink without such help as this. If a man cannot show a willing spirit and obey these commanders and the officials of Dionysus (who are upwards of sixty years of age), the dishonour he incurs must equal or even exceed that incurred by the man who disobeys the officials of the god of war.

CLEINIAS: Precisely.

ATHENIAN: So, if they drank and made merry like that, the revellers who took part in the proceedings would surely benefit? They would go their way on better terms with each other than they were before, instead of loathing each other, which is what happens nowadays; and this would be because they had rules to regulate the whole of their intercourse and 672 had followed every instruction given by the sober to the tipsy.

CLEINIAS: Precisely – if indeed the party were to go as you describe.

ATHENIAN: So let's not abuse the gift of Dionysus any longer in the old unqualified terms, saying that it is bad and does not deserve to be received into the state. One could, indeed, enlarge on its benefits even more. But in front of the general public I would be chary of mentioning the *main* benefit conferred by the gift, because people misconstrue and misunderstand the explanation.

CLEINIAS: What is the benefit?

ATHENIAN: There is a little-known current of story and tradition[24] which says that Dionysus was robbed of his wits by his stepmother Hera, and that he gets his revenge by stimulating us to Bacchic frenzies and all the mad dancing that results; and this was precisely the reason why he made us a present of wine. This sort of story, however, I leave to those who see no danger in speaking of the gods in such terms. But I am quite certain of this: no animal that enjoys the use of reason in its maturity is ever born with that faculty, or at any rate with it fully developed. During the time in which it has not yet attained its characteristic level of intelligence, it is completely mad: it bawls uncontrollably, and as soon as it can get on its feet it jumps about with equal abandon. Let's

24. Cf. Euripides, *Cyclops*, 3.

think back: we said that this situation gave rise to music and gymnastics.

CLEINIAS: We remember, of course.

ATHENIAN: And also that this was the source of man's appreciation of rhythm and harmony, and Apollo and the Muses and Dionysus were the gods who co-operated to implant it in us.

CLEINIAS: Yes, indeed.

ATHENIAN: In particular, it seems that according to the common story wine was given to men as a means of taking vengeance on us – it was intended to drive us insane. But our interpretation is entirely the opposite: the gift was intended to be a medicine and to produce reverence in the soul, and health and strength in the body.

CLEINIAS: Yes, sir, that's a splendid recapitulation of the argument.

SUMMING-UP ON THE USES OF DRINK

ATHENIAN: We are now half-way through our examination of singing and dancing. Shall we carry on with the other half in whatever way recommends itself, or shall we pass it over?

CLEINIAS: What halves do you mean? Where do you put your dividing-line?

ATHENIAN: We found that singing and dancing, taken together, amounted, in a sense, to education as a whole. One part of it – the vocal part – was concerned with rhythms and 'harmonies'.

CLEINIAS: Yes.

ATHENIAN: The second part concerned the movement of the body. Here too we had rhythm, a feature shared with the movement of the voice; but the body's movements were its 673 own particular concern, just as in the other half the tune was the special job of the vocal movements.

CLEINIAS: True enough.

ATHENIAN: When the sound of the voice penetrates the soul, we took that to be an education in virtue, and we hazarded the term 'music' to describe it.

CLEINIAS: And quite rightly.

ATHENIAN: When the movements of the body, which we described as 'dancing in delight', are such as to result in a fine state of physical fitness, we ought to call the systematic training which does this 'gymnastics'.

CLEINIAS: Exactly.

ATHENIAN: So much, then, for music, which is roughly the half of the subject of choruses that we said we had examined and finished with; so that's that. Shall we discuss the other half? Or what method should we follow now?

CLEINIAS: Really, my dear fellow! You are having a conversation with Cretans and Spartans, and we have discussed music thoroughly – leaving gymnastics still to come. What sort of answer do you think you'll get to that question, from either of us?

ATHENIAN: I should say that question was a pretty unambiguous answer. I take it that your question, as I said, amounts in fact to a reply, an order even, to finish off our examination of gymnastics.

CLEINIAS: You understand me perfectly: do just that.

ATHENIAN: Yes, I must. Of course, discussing a subject so familiar to you both is not very difficult. You see, you have had much more experience of this particular skill than of the other.

CLEINIAS: True enough.

ATHENIAN: Again, the origin of this form of recreation too lies in the fact that every animal has the natural habit of jumping about. The human animal, as we said, acquired a sense of rhythm, and that led to the birth of dancing. The tune suggested rhythm and awakened the memory of it, and out of the union of the two was born choral singing and dancing as a recreation.[25]

CLEINIAS: Exactly.

ATHENIAN: We have already discussed one of these two; now we are going to set about the discussion of the other.

CLEINIAS: Yes, indeed.

ATHENIAN: However, if you are agreeable, let's give our discussion of the use of drink its final flourish.

25. That is, as both singing and dancing involve rhythm, it seemed a good idea to combine both activities into one art form.

CLEINIAS: What flourish do you mean?

ATHENIAN: Suppose a state takes this practice we are now discussing sufficiently seriously to control it by a set of rules and use it to cultivate moderate habits; suppose it permits a similar enjoyment of other pleasures on the same principle, seeing it simply as a device for mastering them. In each and every case, our method will be the one that must be followed.[26] But if the state treats a drink as recreation pure and simple, and anybody who wants to can go drinking and please himself when and with whom he does it, and do whatever else he likes at the same time, then my vote would be in favour of never allowing this state or individual to take wine at all. I would go further than Cretan and Spartan practice: I would support the law of the Carthaginians,[27] which forbids anyone on military service to take a drink of wine, and makes water the only permissible beverage during the entire campaign. As for civilians, it forbids slaves, male and female, ever to touch wine; it forbids magistrates during their year of office; steersmen and jurymen on duty are absolutely prohibited from touching it, and so too is any councillor who is going to take part in an important discussion; nobody at all is permitted to drink wine during the day, except for reasons of training or health, nor at night if they intend to procreate children (this prohibition applying to men and women alike); and one could point to a great many other situations in which any sensible person with a respect for the law would find it proper not to drink wine. This kind of approach would mean that no state would need many vines and as part of the regulations covering agriculture in general and the whole question of diet, the production of wine in particular would be restricted to the most modest quantities. With your permission, gentlemen, let's take that as the final flourish to our discussion of wine.

CLEINIAS: Splendid! Permission granted.

26. That is, the procedure used in the case of wine-parties must be applied to other pleasurable activities.

27. Nothing more is known of this law. Cf. p. 64: did Carthage, at some point in its history, attempt to enforce semi-'Prohibition'?

§§1–3 *dealt with the education and moral training of the individual;* §§4–5 *discuss the correct constitution of the state. In order to illustrate his points, the Athenian undertakes a history of mankind, starting in the remote past with the few survivors of the Flood and finishing in his own lifetime. He is extremely cavalier in his handling of events, and 'bends' history a good deal to suit his own purposes; by modern standards – even if we grant that absolute objectivity and impartiality in history is a mirage – the Athenian hardly begins to rate as a historian at all. Yet it could be argued in his defence that ancient standards of historiography were less rigorous than ours today: the tradition of exact and detailed research was much less well established and historians were* expected *to draw edifying moral lessons from their material. And in the earlier part of his account the Athenian does not in fact profess to do more than paint a plausible picture – witness the frequency of the expressions 'it is likely', 'probably', 'it looks as if', and the like. His history is imaginative and didactic, and it is pointless to insist on criteria and standards which he was not trying to observe. (For an appraisal of Plato as a historian, and a commentary on §§4–5, the reader should consult R. Weil, L' 'Archéologie' de Platon (Paris, 1959).)*

The essence of the Athenian's method is to isolate the desirable features of a political system by examining the reasons for successful constitutions in the past, and the undesirable features by examining the causes of the failures.

§ 4. THE LESSONS OF HISTORY (1): LEGISLATION AND THE BALANCE OF POWERS

The main points of this section are (1) the necessity of law as a means of reconciling conflicting interests, (2) the dangers of unchecked power concentrated in one person, and conversely (3) the need of a balance of power in a state between the various ruling elements – in the case of Sparta, between kings, ephors and elders. We may also note the belief, common in the ancient world, that primitive man, being untouched by civilization, was morally 'better'.

LIFE AFTER THE FLOOD

BK III 676 ATHENIAN: We can take that as settled, then. But what about political systems? How are we to suppose they first came into existence? I feel sure that the best and easiest way to see their origins is this.

CLEINIAS: What?

ATHENIAN: To use the same method that we always have to adopt when we look into a state's moral progress or decline.

CLEINIAS: What method have you in mind?

ATHENIAN: We take an indefinitely long period of time and study the changes that occur in it.

CLEINIAS: How do you mean?

ATHENIAN: Look, do you think you could ever grasp how long it is that states have existed and men have lived under some sort of political organization?

CLEINIAS: No, not very easily.

ATHENIAN: But at any rate you realize it must be an enormously long time?

CLEINIAS: Yes, I see *that*, of course.

ATHENIAN: So surely, during this period, thousands upon thousands of states have come into being, while at least as many, in equally vast numbers, have been destroyed? Time and again each one of them has adopted every type of political system. And sometimes small states have become bigger, and big ones have grown smaller; superior states have deteriorated and bad ones have improved.

CLEINIAS: Inevitably.

ATHENIAN: Let's try to pin down just why these changes took place, if we can; then perhaps we shall discover how the various systems took root and developed.

CLEINIAS: Admirable! Let's get down to it. You must do your best to explain your views, and we must try to follow you.

ATHENIAN: Do you think there is any truth in tradition? 677

CLEINIAS: What sort of tradition do you mean?

ATHENIAN: This: that the human race has been repeatedly annihilated by floods and plagues and many other causes, so that only a small fraction of it survived.

CLEINIAS: Yes, of course, all that sort of thing strikes everyone as entirely credible.

ATHENIAN: Now then, let's picture just one of this series of annihilations – I mean the effect of the flood.

CLEINIAS: What special point are we to notice about it?

ATHENIAN: That those who escaped the disaster must have been pretty nearly all hill-shepherds – a few embers of mankind preserved, I imagine, on the tops of mountains.

CLEINIAS: Obviously.

ATHENIAN: Here's a further point: such men must have been in general unskilled and unsophisticated. In particular, they must have been quite innocent of the crafty devices that city-dwellers use in the rat-race to do each other down; and all the other dirty tricks that men play against one another must have been unknown.

CLEINIAS: Quite likely.

ATHENIAN: And we can take it, can't we, that the cities that had been built on the plains and near the sea were destroyed root-and-branch?

CLEINIAS: Yes, we can.

ATHENIAN: So all their tools were destroyed, and any worth-while discovery they had made in politics or any other field was entirely lost? You see, my friend, if their discoveries had survived throughout at the same level of development as they have attained today, it is difficult to see what room there can ever have been for any new invention.[1]

CLEINIAS: The upshot of all this, I suppose, is that for millions of years these techniques remained unknown to primitive man. Then, a thousand or two thousand years ago, Daedalus and Orpheus and Palamedes made their various discoveries, Marsyas and Olympus pioneered the art of music, Amphion invented the lyre, and many other discoveries were made by other people. All this happened only yesterday or the day before, so to speak.

ATHENIAN: How tactful of you, Cleinias, to leave out your friend, who really was born 'yesterday'!

CLEINIAS: I suppose you mean Epimenides?

ATHENIAN: Yes, that's the man. His discovery, my dear fellow, put him streets ahead of all the other inventors. Hesiod had foreshadowed it in his poetry long before, but it was Epimenides who achieved it in practice, so you Cretans claim.[2]

CLEINIAS: We certainly do claim that.

ATHENIAN: Perhaps we can describe the state of mankind after the cataclysm like this: in spite of a vast and terrifying desolation, plenty of fertile land was available, and although animals in general had perished it happened that some cattle still survived, together with perhaps a small stock of goats. They were few enough, but sufficient to maintain the correspondingly few herdsmen of this early period.

678

CLEINIAS: Agreed.

ATHENIAN: But at the moment we are talking about the state, and the business of legislation and political organization. Is it conceivable that any trace at all of such things survived – even, so to speak, in the memory?

1. The Greek is less than clear: apparently the Athenian means that the discoveries of our era must have been made in a 'vacuum' left by a disaster such as the flood.

2. Epimenides' 'magic brew' was believed to have been inspired by Hesiod's mention (*Works and Days*, 40–41) of the virtue of mallow and asphodel. For Epimenides, see p. 71.

CLEINIAS: Of course not.

ATHENIAN: So out of those conditions all the features of our present-day life developed: states, political systems, technical skills, laws, rampant vice and frequent virtue.

CLEINIAS: What do you mean?

ATHENIAN: My dear sir, can we really suppose that the men of that period, who had had no experience of city life in all its splendour and squalor, ever became totally wicked or totally virtuous?

CLEINIAS: A good point. We see what you mean.

ATHENIAN: So it was only as time went on, and the numbers of the human race increased, that civilization advanced and reached its present stage of development?

CLEINIAS: Exactly.

ATHENIAN: The process was probably not sudden, but gradual, and took a considerable time.

CLEINIAS: Yes, that's perfectly plausible.

ATHENIAN: I imagine men were all numbed with fear at the prospect of descending from the hills to the plains.

CLEINIAS: Naturally enough.

ATHENIAN: And what a pleasure it must have been to see each other, there being so few of them at that time! However, pretty well all vehicles they might have used to visit each other by land or sea had been destroyed, and the techniques used to construct them had been lost, so that I suppose they found getting together none too easy. They suffered from a scarcity of timber, because iron, copper and mineral workings in general had been overlaid with sludge and had been lost to sight, so that it was virtually impossible to refine fresh supplies of metal. Even if there was the odd tool left somewhere on the mountains, it was quickly worn down to nothing by use. Replacements could not be made until the technique of mining sprang up again among men.

CLEINIAS: True.

ATHENIAN: And how many generations later did that happen, on our calculation?

CLEINIAS: A good many, obviously.

ATHENIAN: Well then, during that period, or even longer,

all techniques that depend on a supply of copper and iron and so on must have gone out of use?

CLEINIAS: Of course.

ATHENIAN: For several reasons, then, war and civil war alike came to an end.

CLEINIAS: How so?

ATHENIAN: In the first place, men's isolation prompted them to cherish and love one another. Second, their food 679 supply was nothing they needed to quarrel about. Except perhaps for a few people in the very early stages, there was no shortage of flocks and herds, which is what men mostly lived on in that age. They always had a supply of milk and meat, and could always add to it plenty of good food to be got by hunting. They also had an abundance of clothes, bedding, houses, and equipment for cooking and other purposes. (Moulding pottery and weaving, skills that have no need of iron, were a gift from God to men – his way, in fact, of supplying them with all that kind of equipment. His intention was that whenever the human race was reduced to such a desperate condition it could still take root and develop.) Because of all this, they were not intolerably poor, nor driven by poverty to quarrel with each other; but presumably they did not grow rich either, in view of the prevailing lack of gold and silver. Now the community in which neither wealth nor poverty exists will generally produce the finest characters, because tendencies to violence and crime, and feelings of jealousy and envy, simply do not arise. So these men were *good*, partly for that very reason, partly because of what we might call their 'naïveté'. When they heard things labelled 'good' or 'bad', they were so artless as to think it a statement of the literal truth and believe it. This lack of sophistication precluded the cynicism you find today: they accepted as the truth the doctrine they heard about gods and men, and lived their lives in accordance with it. That is why they were the sort of people we have described.

CLEINIAS: Megillus and I, at least, agree with your account.

ATHENIAN: If we compare them with the era before the flood and with the modern world, we shall have to say that the many generations which lived in that way were inevitably unskilled and ignorant of techniques in general, and particularly of the military devices used on land and sea nowadays. They must also have been innocent of the techniques of warfare peculiar to city-life – generally called 'lawsuits' and 'party-strife' – in which men concoct every possible device to damage and hurt each other by word and deed. Weren't our primitive men simpler and manlier and at the same time more restrained and upright in every way? We have already explained why.

CLEINIAS: Yes, you're quite right.

AUTOCRACY

ATHENIAN: Let's remind ourselves that this reconstruction, and the conclusions we shall draw from it, are supposed to make us appreciate how early man came to feel the need of laws, and who their lawgiver was. 680

CLEINIAS: Well reminded!

ATHENIAN: Presumably they felt no need for legislators, and in that era law was not yet a common phenomenon. Men born at that stage of the world cycle[3] did not yet have any written records, but lived in obedience to accepted usage and 'ancestral' law, as we call it.

CLEINIAS: Quite likely.

ATHENIAN: But this is already a political system, of a sort.

CLEINIAS: What sort?

ATHENIAN: Autocracy – the name which everyone, I believe, uses for the political system of that age. You can still find it in many parts of the world today, both among Greeks and non-Greeks. I suppose this is what Homer is describing in his account of the household of the Cyclopes:[4]

'No laws, no councils for debate have they:
They live on the tips of lofty mountains
In hollow caves; each man lays down the law
To wife and children, with no regard for neighbour.'

3. A 'cycle' is apparently thought of as the interval between one cosmic upheaval (e.g. the flood) and the next.
4. *Odyssey* IX, 112 ff.

CLEINIAS: That poet of yours sounds as if he was a charming fellow. I have gone through other verses of his, and very polished they were too. Not that I know his work to any great extent – we Cretans don't go in for foreign poetry very much.

MEGILLUS: But we at Sparta do, and we think Homer is the prince of epic poets, even though the way of life he describes is invariably Ionian rather than Spartan. In this instance he certainly seems to bear you out when he points in his stories to the wild life of the Cyclopes as an explanation of their primitive customs.

ATHENIAN: Yes, he does testify in my favour. So let's take him as our evidence that political systems of this kind do sometimes develop.

CLEINIAS: Very well.

ATHENIAN: And they arise among these people who live scattered in separate households and individual families in the confusion that follows the cataclysms. In such a system the eldest member rules by virtue of having inherited power from his father or mother; the others follow his lead and make one flock like birds. The authority to which they bow is that of their patriarch: they are governed, in effect, by the most justifiable of all forms of kingship.

CLEINIAS: Yes, of course.

THE PRIMITIVE CITY AND THE ORIGIN
OF LEGISLATION

ATHENIAN: The next stage is when several families amalgamate and form larger communities. They turn their attention to agriculture, initially in the foot-hills, and build rings of dry stones to serve as walls to protect themselves against wild animals. The result now is a single large unit, a common homestead.

CLEINIAS: I suppose that's quite probable.

ATHENIAN: Well then, isn't this probable too?

CLEINIAS: What?

ATHENIAN: As these original relatively tiny communities

grew bigger, each of the small constituent families lived under its own ruler – the eldest member – and followed its own particular customs which had arisen because of its isolation from the others. The various social and religious standards to which people had grown accustomed reflected the bias of their ancestors and teachers: the more restrained or adventurous the ancestor, the more restrained or adventurous would be the character of his descendants. Consequently, as I say, the members of each group entered the larger community with laws peculiar to themselves, and were ready to impress their own inclinations on their children and their children's children.

CLEINIAS: Naturally.

ATHENIAN: And of course each group inevitably approved of its own laws and looked on those of other people with rather less favour.

CLEINIAS: Exactly.

ATHENIAN: So it looks as if we have unwittingly stumbled on the origin of legislation.

CLEINIAS: We certainly have.

ATHENIAN: At any rate the next and necessary step in this amalgamation is to choose some representatives to review the rules of all the families, and to propose openly to the leaders and heads of the people – the 'kings', so to speak – the adoption of those rules that particularly recommend themselves for common use. These representatives will be known as lawgivers, and by appointing the leaders as officials they will create out of the separate autocracies a sort of aristocracy, or perhaps kingship. And while the political system passes through this transitional stage they will administer the state themselves.

CLEINIAS: Yes, that sort of change would certainly come about by stages.

TROY

ATHENIAN: So we can now go on to describe the birth of a third type of political system, one which in fact admits *all* systems and all their modifications and exhibits equal variety and change in the actual states as well.

CLEINIAS: What type is this?

ATHENIAN: The one which Homer too listed as the successor of the second. This is how he describes the origin of the third:[5] 'He founded Dardania' – I think this is how it goes – 'when holy Ilium,

A town upon the plain for mortal men, had not been built:
For still they lived upon the lower slopes of many-fount-
ained Ida.'

682 He composed these lines, as well as those about the Cyclopes, under some sort of inspiration from God. And how true to life they are! This is because poets as a class are divinely gifted and are inspired when they sing, so that with the help of Graces and Muses they frequently hit on how things really happen.

CLEINIAS: They do indeed.

ATHENIAN: Let's carry on with the story we are telling: it may suggest something to our purpose. I take it this is what we ought to do?

CLEINIAS: Of course.

ATHENIAN: Ilium was founded, according to us, when men had descended from the hills to a wide and beautiful plain. They built their city on a hill of moderate height near several rivers which poured down from Ida above.

CLEINIAS: So the story goes.

ATHENIAN: I suppose we may assume that this descent of theirs took place many ages after the flood?

CLEINIAS: Yes, naturally, many ages later.

ATHENIAN: I mean that apparently the disaster we've just described must have been forgotten to a quite remarkable degree if they founded their city on the lower reaches of several rivers flowing down from the mountains, and put their trust in hills that were none too high.

CLEINIAS: Yes, a clear proof that they were far removed in time from any such experience.

ATHENIAN: With the increase in the human population

5. *Iliad* XX, 216 ff. 'He' is Dardanus; Ilium is Troy.

many other cities, one supposes, were already being founded.

CLEINIAS: Naturally.

ATHENIAN: These cities also mounted an expedition against Ilium, probably by sea as well, because by then all mankind had overcome its fear and had taken to ships.

CLEINIAS: So it seems.

ATHENIAN: And after a siege of about ten years the Achaeans sacked Troy.

CLEINIAS: Indeed they did.

ATHENIAN: They besieged Ilium for ten years, and during this period the domestic affairs of the individual attackers took a turn for the worse. The younger generation revolted, and the ugly and criminal reception they gave the troops when they returned to their own cities and homes led to murder, massacre and expulsion on a large scale. When the exiles came back again they adopted a new name, and were now known as Dorians instead of Achaeans, in honour of Dorieus, who had rallied them while they were in exile. A full and exhaustive account of subsequent events can be found in your traditional Spartan stories.

MEGILLUS: Of course.

THE DORIAN LEAGUE

ATHENIAN: When we were starting to discuss legislation, the question of the arts and drinking cropped up, and we made a digression.[6] But now we really do have a chance to come to grips with our subject. As if God himself were guiding us, we've come back to the very point from which we digressed: the actual foundation of Sparta. You maintained 683 that Sparta was established on the right lines,[7] and you said the same of Crete, because it has laws that bear a family resemblance to Sparta's. We have had a rather random discussion about various foundations and political systems, but we have achieved at least this much: we have watched the first, second and third type of state being founded in succession over a vast period of time, and now we discover this fourth

6. See pp. 63 ff.   7. See p. 64.

state (or 'nation', if you like) whose historical foundation and development we are tracing down to its maturity today.[8] After all this, perhaps we can get some idea of what was right and wrong in the way these foundations were established. Can we see what kind of laws are responsible for continued preservation of the features that survive and the ruin of those that collapse? What detailed alterations will produce happiness in a state? If we can understand all this, Cleinias and Megillus, we shall have to discuss the whole business all over again: it will be like making a fresh start.[9] However, we may be able to find some fault in our account so far.

MEGILLUS: Well, sir, if some god were to give us his word that if we do make a second attempt to look at the problem of legislation, we shall hear an account of at least the quality and length of the one we have just had, I for one would willingly extend our journey, and the present day would seem not a moment too long – though it is in fact pretty well the longest day of summer.

ATHENIAN: So it looks as if we must press on with the investigation.

MEGILLUS: Certainly.

ATHENIAN: Let's imagine that we are living at the time when the territory of Sparta, Argos and Messene, and the districts nearby, had in effect come under the control of your ancestors, Megillus. Their next decision, or so the story goes, was to split their forces into three and establish three states – Argos, Messene and Sparta.

MEGILLUS: That's quite right.

ATHENIAN: Temenos became king of Argos, Cresphontes of Messene, and Procles and Eurysthenes of Sparta.

MEGILLUS: True.

8. The four are: (1) single families under autocratic rule, (2) collections of families under aristocratic rule, (3) the cities of the plains (e.g. Troy) with various constitutions, (4) a league of such cities, now to be discussed.

9. The Athenian expresses himself vaguely. He seems to mean that the historical review has suggested certain lessons about the origins and effects of law, and that the Spartan and Cretan constitutions must now be reconsidered from this point of view. That will be more illuminating than the superficial and somewhat partisan judgements on them in §§1-3.

ATHENIAN: And all their contemporaries swore to them that they would go to their help if anybody tried to subvert their thrones.

MEGILLUS: Precisely.

ATHENIAN: Now when a monarchy is overthrown (and indeed when any other type of authority has been destroyed at any time) surely no one but the rulers themselves are to blame? That was the line we took when the subject cropped up a little time ago[10] – or have we forgotten by now?

MEGILLUS: No, of course not.

ATHENIAN: So now we can put our thesis on a firmer footing, because it looks as if our study of history has led us to the same conclusion as before. This means we shall carry on our investigation on the basis of the actual facts rather than conjecture. The facts are, of course, as follows: each of the three royal families, and each of the three royal states they ruled, exchanged oaths in accordance with mutually binding laws which they had adopted to regulate the exercise of authority and obedience to it. The kings swore never to stiffen their rule as the nation continued down the years; the others undertook, provided the rulers kept to their side of the bargain, never themselves to overthrow the kingships nor tolerate an attempt to do so by others. The kings would help the kings and peoples if they were wronged, and the peoples would help the peoples and the kings likewise. That's right, isn't it?

MEGILLUS: Certainly.

ATHENIAN: Now whether it was the kings or someone else who laid down laws for this political system thus established in the three states, the crucial provision, surely, was this –

MEGILLUS: What?

ATHENIAN: Whenever a given state broke the established laws, an alliance of the other two would always be there to take the field against it.

MEGILLUS: Obviously.

10. The reference is not clear: p. 48 may be meant, or possibly p. 128.

ATHENIAN: Of course, most people only ask their legislators to enact the kind of laws that the population in general will accept without objection. But just imagine asking your trainer or doctor to give you pleasure when he trains or cures your body!

MEGILLUS: Exactly.

ATHENIAN: In fact, you often have to be satisfied if you can restore your body to health and vigour without undue pain.

MEGILLUS: True.

ATHENIAN: In another respect too the people of that time were particularly well placed to make legislation a painless process.

MEGILLUS: What respect?

ATHENIAN: Their legislators' efforts to establish a certain equality of property among them were not open to one particularly damaging accusation which is frequently made in other states. Suppose a legal code is being framed and someone adopts the policy of a change in the ownership of land and a cancellation of debts, because he sees that this is the only way in which equality can be satisfactorily achieved. 'Hands off fundamentals' is the slogan everybody uses to attack a legislator who tries to bring in that kind of reform, and his policy of land-redistribution and remission of debts earns him only curses. It's enough to make any man despair. So here is another tremendous advantage the Dorians enjoyed: the absence of resentment. No one could object to the way the land was parcelled out, and large long-standing debts did not exist.

MEGILLUS: True.

ATHENIAN: Then why on earth, my friends, did this foundation and its legislation turn out such a dismal failure?

685 MEGILLUS: What do you mean by that? What's your objection?

ATHENIAN: Three states were founded but in two of them the political system and the legal code were quickly corrupted. Only the third settlement survived – that of your state, Sparta.

MEGILLUS: A pretty difficult problem you're posing!

ATHENIAN: Nevertheless, it demands our attention. So now let's look into it, and while away the journey, as we said when we set out, by amusing ourselves with laws – it's a dignified game and it suits our time of life.

MEGILLUS: Of course. We must do as you say.

ATHENIAN: No laws could form a better subject for our investigation than those by which these states have been administered. Or are there any bigger or more famous states whose foundation we might examine?

MEGILLUS: No, it's not easy to think of alternatives.

ATHENIAN: Well then, it's pretty obvious that they intended the arrangements they made to protect adequately not only the Peloponnese but the Greeks in general against any possible attack by non-Greeks – as for example occurred when those who then lived in the territory of Ilium trusted to the power of the Assyrian empire, which Ninos had founded, and provoked the war against Troy by their arrogance. You see, a good deal of the splendour of the Assyrian empire still remained, and the dread of its united organization was the counterpart in that age of our fear of the Great King of Persia today. The Assyrians had a tremendous grudge against the Greeks: Troy, which was part of the Assyrian empire, had been captured for a second time.[11] To meet such dangers the Dorian army formed a single unified body, although at that period it was distributed among the three states under the command of the kings (who were brothers, being sons of Hercules). It seemed to be excellently conceived and equipped – better even than the army which sailed against Troy. For a start, people thought the sons of Hercules were, as commanders, a cut above the grandsons of Pelops;[12] secondly, they rated the prowess of the army itself higher than that of the expedition which went to Troy. After all, they calculated, *that* had consisted of Achaeans, the very people the Dorians had defeated. So may we take it that this was the nature and purpose of the arrangements they made?

MEGILLUS: Certainly.

11. For the first capture, see Homer, *Iliad* V, 640.
12. Agamemnon and Menelaus, who led the expedition against Troy.

ATHENIAN: And for various reasons they probably ex-
686 pected these arrangements would be permanent and last a
long time. They had been comrades in a great many toils and
dangers in the past, and now they had been brought under
the control of a single family (the kings being brothers); and
they had also consulted a large number of prophets, notably
Apollo's at Delphi.

MEGILLUS: Yes, that's probable enough, of course.

WHY DID THE LEAGUE FAIL?

ATHENIAN: But apparently these large expectations evap-
orated pretty quickly, except, as we said a minute ago, in
the case of just one small part of the alliance – your state,
Sparta. And right up to the present day Sparta has never
stopped fighting the other two members. But if they had done
as they intended and had agreed on a common policy, their
power would have been irresistible, militarily speaking.

MEGILLUS: It certainly would.

ATHENIAN: So just how did their plans misfire? This is
surely a problem we ought to look into: why was such a vast
and tremendous organization unlucky enough to be destroyed?

MEGILLUS: True: this is the right direction to look.
Neglect these, and you'll never find any other laws or political
systems preserving (or eliminating) such remarkable and
important features.

ATHENIAN: What a stroke of luck! It looks as if we've
somehow got on to a crucial point.

MEGILLUS: No doubt about it.

ATHENIAN: Well now, my fine fellow, what hackneyed
thoughts we've been having, without realizing it! When
people see some tremendous achievement, they always think
to themselves, 'What terrific results it would have led to, if
someone had known how to set about putting it to proper
use!' Here and now, perhaps our ideas on the topic we are
discussing are just as wrong and unrealistic as anybody else's
who looks at anything in that sort of way.

MEGILLUS: Well really, what *do* you mean? What are we supposed to think you're driving at when you say that?

ATHENIAN: I was poking fun at no one but myself, my friend. I was thinking about the army we are discussing and it occurred to me how splendid it was and what a marvellous tool (as I said) had been put into the hands of the Greeks – if only someone had put it to the proper use at the time!

MEGILLUS: And you were quite right and sensible in everything you said, and we heartily agreed with you – equally rightly and sensibly.

ATHENIAN: Maybe so. Still, my view is that everyone who sets eyes on something big and strong and powerful immediately gets the feeling that if the owner knew how to take advantage of its size and scale he would get tremendous results and be a happy man.

MEGILLUS: And this again is surely right and proper. Or 687 do you see it differently?

ATHENIAN: Well now, just consider what criteria a man ought to employ if he is going to be 'right' to give such praise in an individual case. What about the one we are discussing, for a start? Suppose those who undertook the organization of the army in that age had known their job: somehow, they would have succeeded in it – but the question is *how*. They ought, of course, to have consolidated their army and kept it on a permanent footing; this would have ensured them their own freedom while they ruled over anybody else they liked, and in general it would have enabled them to do whatever they or their children wanted all over the world, among Greeks and non-Greeks indifferently. This is what men would praise them for, isn't it?

MEGILLUS: It is indeed.

ATHENIAN: Again, anyone who notices a case of great wealth or exceptional family distinction or something like that takes precisely the same line. He assumes that just because a man enjoys these advantages his every wish will be granted – or at any rate most of them, and the most important ones.

MEGILLUS: Quite likely.

ATHENIAN: Now then, this shows that there is one

specific desire common to all mankind. Isn't this the upshot of our discussion?

MEGILLUS: What desire?

ATHENIAN: That events should obey whatever orders one feels like giving – invariably, if possible, but failing that, at least where human affairs are concerned.

MEGILLUS: Very true.

ATHENIAN: So seeing that this is the constant wish of us all, right from childhood to old age, isn't it inevitably what we are always *praying* for too?

MEGILLUS: Of course.

ATHENIAN: And I suppose our prayers on behalf of those whom we love will be for precisely what they themselves pray for on their own behalf?

MEGILLUS: Certainly.

ATHENIAN: A man who is a father loves the child who is his son?

MEGILLUS: Of course.

ATHENIAN: Yet there is a good deal in the son's prayers that the father will beg the gods never to grant.

MEGILLUS: You mean when the son who prays is still young and irresponsible?

ATHENIAN: Yes, and I'm thinking too of when the father is senile or even unduly impulsive because of second childhood, and has lost all sense of what is right and proper. He gets into the same state as Theseus when he dealt with Hippolytus, who died so wretchedly,[13] and his prayers become very vehement indeed. But if the son understands the situation, do you think he will join in his father's prayers, given those circumstances?

MEGILLUS: I know what you mean. Your point, I take it, is that you should demand your own way in your prayers only if your wishes are supported by your rational judgement –

13. Hippolytus' stepmother Phaedra falsely accused him of sexual misconduct towards herself; Theseus, her husband, prayed for the death of his son. The prayer was granted, but then Theseus discovered Hippolytus' innocence.

and this, a rational outlook, should be the object of the prayers and efforts of us all, states and individuals alike.

ATHENIAN: It should indeed, and in particular – let me 688 remind myself – it should always be the aim of a state's legislator when he frames the provisions of his laws. And I remind *you* again – to recollect the beginning of our discussion – of what you two recommended: you said that the good legislator should construct his entire legal code with a view to war; for my part, I maintained that this was to order him to establish his laws with an eye on only one virtue out of the four. I said he ought to keep virtue as a whole in mind but especially and pre-eminently the virtue that heads the list – judgement and wisdom, and a strength of mind such that desires and appetites are kept under control. Our discussion has come full circle, and being the speaker at the moment I make the same point as before. You can treat it as a joke if you like, but if you prefer, you can take it seriously: I maintain that, if you lack wisdom, praying is a risky business, because you get the opposite of what you want.[14] If you like to suppose that I am in earnest, do so: I'm confident that if you follow the line of argument we opened up a moment ago you'll soon discover that the cause of the ruin of the kings and the whole enterprise was not cowardice nor a lack of military expertise in the commanders or in those whose role it was to obey them. The disaster was caused by every other sort of vice, and in particular ignorance about mankind's most vital concerns. And if that was true then it is even more so today; and precisely the same will be true in the future. If you like, I'll try to press on with the next stages in the argument and develop the point. As you are my friends, I'll do my very best to make it clear.

CLEINIAS: To make a speech in your praise, sir, would be a tasteless thing to do. Our actions rather than our words will show our regard for you: we shall give you our closest attention. This is the best way to tell whether a gentleman approves or not.

14. That is, an unwise man may unwittingly ask for something which will harm him, and see his prayers answered.

MEGILLUS: Well said, Cleinias. Let's do as you say.

CLEINIAS: And so we shall, God willing. Now let's have your explanation.

ATHENIAN: Well then, to get back on to the track of the argument, we maintain that crass ignorance destroyed that great empire, and that it has a natural tendency to produce precisely the same results today. If this is so, it means that the legislator must try to inspire states with as much good sense as possible, and eradicate folly, as far as he can.

CLEINIAS: Obviously.

689 ATHENIAN: So what kind of ignorance would deserve the title 'crass'? See if you agree with my description. I suggest this kind.

CLEINIAS: What?

ATHENIAN: The kind involved when a man thinks something is fine and good, but loathes it instead of liking it, and conversely when he likes and welcomes what he believes is wicked and unjust. I maintain that this disaccord between his feelings of pleasure and pain and his rational judgement constitutes the very lowest depth of ignorance. It is also the most 'crass', in that it affects the most extensive element in the soul (the element that experiences pleasure and pain, which corresponds to the most extensive part of a state, the common people). So when the soul quarrels with knowledge or opinion or reason, its natural ruling principles, you have there what I call 'folly'. This applies both to the state in which people disobey their rulers and laws, and to the individual, when the fine principles in which he really believes prove not only ineffective but actually harmful. It's all these examples of ignorance that I should put down as the worst kind of discord in a state and individual, not the mere professional ignorance of a workman. I hope you see what I mean, gentlemen.

CLEINIAS: We do, my friend, and we agree with what you say.

ATHENIAN: So let's adopt this as an agreed statement of policy: no citizens who suffer from this kind of ignorance should be entrusted with any degree of power. They must be reproved for their ignorance, even if their ability to reason is outstanding and they have worked hard at every nice accomplishment that makes a man quick-witted. It is those whose characters are at the other extreme who must be called 'wise', even if, as the saying is, 'they cannot read, they cannot swim'; and it is these sensible people who must be given the offices of state. You see, my friends, without concord,[15] how could you ever get even a glimmer of sound judgement? It's out of the question. But we should be entirely justified in styling the greatest and most splendid concord of all 'the greatest wisdom'. Anyone who lives a rational life shares in this wisdom, but the man who lacks it will invariably turn out to be a spendthrift and no saviour[16] to the city – quite the reverse, because he suffers from this particular kind of ignorance. So as we said just now, let's adopt this as the statement of our views.

CLEINIAS: Adopted it is.

SEVEN TITLES TO AUTHORITY

ATHENIAN: Now, I take it that states must contain some people who govern and others who are governed?

CLEINIAS: Naturally.

ATHENIAN: Good. Well then, what titles are there to 690 either rank? Can we count them? (I mean both in the state and in the family, in each case irrespective of size.) One claim, surely, could be made by father and mother; and in general the title of parents to exercise control over their children and descendants would be universally acknowledged, wouldn't it?

CLEINIAS: Of course.

ATHENIAN: Close behind comes the title of those of high birth to govern those of low birth. Next in order comes our third demand: that younger people should consent to be governed by their elders.

CLEINIAS: Certainly.

15. That is, the concord between reason and the emotions in the individual, and between rulers and ruled in the state.
16. This word perhaps anticipates p. 140.

ATHENIAN: The fourth is that slaves should be subject to the control of their masters.

CLEINIAS: No doubt about it.

ATHENIAN: And I suppose the fifth is that the stronger should rule and the weaker should obey.

CLEINIAS: A pretty compelling claim to obedience, that!

ATHENIAN: Yes, and one which prevails throughout the animal kingdom – by decree of nature, as Pindar of Thebes once remarked.[17] But it looks as if the most important claim will be the sixth, that the ignorant man should follow the leadership of the wise and obey his orders. In spite of you, my clever Pindar, what I'd call the 'decree of nature' is in fact this spontaneous and willing acceptance of the rule of law; I'm certainly not prepared to say it's *un*natural.

CLEINIAS: Quite right.

ATHENIAN: And we persuade a man to cast lots, by explaining that this, the seventh title to authority, enjoys the favour of the gods and is blessed by fortune. We tell him that the fairest arrangement is for him to exercise authority if he wins, but to be subject to it if he loses.

CLEINIAS: That's very true.

ATHENIAN: 'So you see, O legislator' (as we might jocularly address someone who sets about legislation with undue optimism), 'you see how many titles to authority there are, and how they naturally conflict with each other. Now here's a source of civil strife we've discovered for you, which you must put to rights. First, though, join us in trying to find out how the kings of Argos and Messene went astray and broke these rules, and so destroyed themselves and the power of Greece, for all its splendour at that time. Wasn't it because they didn't appreciate the truth of Hesiod's remark that the half is often greater than the whole.[18] He thought that when

---

17. The Athenian alludes to a few lines of a poem now largely lost: cf. pp. 173 and 417. The text and a translation may be found in J. E. Sandys, *The Odes of Pindar* (2nd edition, London and New York, 1919; Loeb edition, pp. 604–5); for a discussion of Plato's use of the quotation see E. R. Dodds, *Plato, Gorgias* (Oxford, 1959), pp. 270–72.

18. Hesiod, *Works and Days*, 40.

it is harmful to get the whole, and the half is enough, then enough is *better* than a feast, and is the preferable alternative.'

CLEINIAS: True enough.

ATHENIAN: So where do we suppose this destructive process invariably starts? Among kings or people?

CLEINIAS: Most instances suggest that this is probably a 691 disease of kings whose life of luxury has made them arrogant.

ATHENIAN: So it is clear that it was the kings of that era who were first infected by the acquisitive spirit in defiance of the law of the land. The precise point to which they had given their seal of approval by their word and oath became the ground of their disagreement, and this lack of harmony (which is, in our view, the 'crassest' stupidity, though it looks like wisdom) put the whole arrangement jarringly off key and out of tune: hence its destruction.

CLEINIAS: Quite likely.

THE REASONS FOR SPARTA'S SUCCESS

ATHENIAN: Very well. Then what precautions ought a contemporary legislator to have taken in his code to nip this disease in the bud? God knows, the answer's not difficult nowadays, and the point is quite simple to understand – though if anyone had foreseen the problem then, assuming it was possible to do so, he'd have been wiser than we are.

MEGILLUS: What do you mean?

ATHENIAN: Hindsight, Megillus! In the perspective of today it's easy to understand what should have been done then, and once understood it's equally easy to explain.

MEGILLUS: You'd better be even clearer than that.

ATHENIAN: The clearest way of putting it would be this.

MEGILLUS: What?

ATHENIAN: If you neglect the rule of proportion and fit excessively large sails to small ships, or give too much food to a small body, or too high authority to a soul that doesn't measure up to it, the result is always disastrous. Body and soul become puffed up: disease breaks out in the one, and in the other arrogance quickly leads to injustice. Now, what are we getting at? Simply this: the mortal soul simply does not exist, my friends, which by dint of its natural qualities will ever make a success of supreme authority among men while it is still young and responsible to no one. Full of folly, the worst of diseases, it inevitably has its judgement corrupted, and incurs the enmity of its closest friends; and once that happens, its total ruin and the loss of all its power soon follow. A first-class lawgiver's job is to have a sense of proportion and to guard against this danger. Nowadays it is a reasonable guess that this was in fact done at that time. However, it looks as if there was . . .

MEGILLUS: What?

ATHENIAN: . . . some god who was concerned on your behalf and saw what was going to happen. He took your single line of kings and split it into two,[19] so as to restrict its powers to more reasonable proportions. After that, a man[20] who combined human nature with some of the powers of a god observed that your leadership was still in a feverish state, so he blended the obstinacy and vigour of the Spartans with 692 the prudent influence of age by giving the twenty-eight elders the same authority in making important decisions as the kings. Your 'third saviour'[21] saw that your government was still fretting and fuming with restless energy, so he put a kind of bridle on it in the shape of the power of the ephors[22] – a power which came very close to being held by lot. This is the formula that turned your kingship into a mixture of the right elements, so that thanks to its own stability it ensured the stability of the rest of the state. If things had been left to the discretion

19. Procles and Eurysthenes, the first kings of Sparta (see p. 128), were the twin sons of Aristodemus.

20. Lycurgus, who created the Spartan Council of Elders.

21. The expression 'third saviour' is proverbial, and refers to the custom of offering Zeus the Saviour the third libation at banquets. Plato probably means Theopompus, a king of Sparta in the eighth century.

22. Five annually elected officials who in addition to wide executive and judicial powers exercised close control over the conduct of the kings. The origin and development of the ephorate are obscure: for a discussion, see W. G. Forrest, *A History of Sparta, 950–192 B.C.* (London, 1968), especially pp. 76–7, 82–3.

of Temenus and Cresphontes and the legislators of that time, whoever in fact they were, not even Aristodemus' part[23] would have survived. You see, they were tiros in legislation: otherwise it would never have occurred to them to rely on oaths[24] to restrain the soul of a young man who had taken over power from which a tyranny could develop. But the fact is that God has demonstrated the sort of thing a position of authority ought to have been then and should be now, if it is to have any prospects of permanency. As I said before, we don't need any great wisdom to recognize all this now – after all, it's not difficult to see the point if you have a historical example to go by. But if anyone had seen all this then, and had been able to control the various offices and produce a single authority out of the three,[25] he would have saved all the splendid projects of that age from destruction, and neither the Persians nor anyone else would ever have sent a fleet to attack Greece, contemptuously supposing that we were people who counted for very little.

CLEINIAS: That's true.

ATHENIAN: After all, Cleinias, the way the Greeks repulsed them was a disgrace. In saying this, I don't mean that those who won the battles of that war by land and sea did not do so magnificently. By 'disgrace' I mean that, to start with, only one of those three states fought to defend Greece. The other two were rotten to the core. One of them[26] even hindered Sparta's attempts to help the defence, and fought her tooth and nail, while the other, Argos (which used to be paramount when the territory was first divided up), although called upon to repel the barbarian, ignored the request and failed to contribute to the defence. A detailed history of the course of that war would have some pretty ugly charges to make against Greece: indeed, there is no reason why it should report that Greece made any defence at all. If it hadn't been for the joint

23. I.e. Sparta: see page 140, note 19.
24. See p. 129.
25. *Either* kings, elders and ephors, *or* the authorities of the three cities: probably the latter, in view of the context.
26. Messene. Cf. pp. 150–51 and notes.

693 determination of the Athenians and the Spartans to resist the slavery that threatened them, we should have by now virtually a complete mixture of the races – Greek with Greek, Greek with barbarian, and barbarian with Greek. We can see a parallel in the nations whom the Persians lord it over today: they have been split up and then horribly jumbled together again into the scattered communities in which they now live. Well now, Cleinias and Megillus, why are we making these accusations against the so-called 'statesmen' and legislators of that day and this? Because if we find out *why* they went wrong we shall discover what different course of action they ought to have followed. That is what we were doing just now, when we said that legislation providing for powerful or extreme authority is a mistake. One should always remember that a state ought to be free and wise and enjoy internal harmony, and that this is what the lawgiver should concentrate on in his legislation. (It ought not to surprise us if several times before now we have decided on a number of other aims and said *they* were what a lawgiver should concentrate on, so that the aims proposed never seem to be the same from minute to minute. When we say that the legislator should keep self-control or good judgement or friendship in view, we must bear in mind that all these aims are the same, not different. Nor should we be disconcerted if we find a lot of other expressions of which the same is true.)

§5. THE LESSONS OF HISTORY (2): MONARCHY AND DEMOCRACY

The Athenian now suggests that the Persian monarchy, which represents one extreme of government, was destroyed because of the unbridled power and lust for pleasure of the monarch, and his unduly repressive régime; the other extreme, Athenian democracy, was corrupted by the opposite fault, an excess of liberty. If a state is to be happy, the authority of the rulers and the liberty of the subjects must be combined in judicious proportions. The faults of the Persian monarch sprang from a bad education, and those of the Athenian people from a lack of the 'fear' called 'respect': thus two prominent themes of §§1–3 take on a new significance in the context of political organization.

At the very end of the section Cleinias mentions that he has the task of framing laws for a new Cretan colony, and suggests they try to gauge the practical value of these theoretical considerations by applying them to actual legislation. His two companions agree, and the discussion of the new state gets under way.

TWO MOTHER-CONSTITUTIONS

CLEINIAS: Yes, when we think back over the argument we'll certainly try to remember that. But you wanted to explain what the legislator ought to aim at in the matter of friendship and good judgement and liberty. So tell us now what you were going to say.

ATHENIAN: Listen to me then. There are two mother-constitutions, so to speak, which you could fairly say have given birth to all the others. Monarchy is the proper name for the first, and democracy for the second. The former has been taken to extreme lengths by the Persians, the latter by my country; virtually all the others, as I said, are varieties of these two. It is absolutely vital for a political system to combine them, *if* (and this is of course the point of our advice, when we insist that no state formed without these two elements can be constituted properly) – *if* it is to enjoy freedom and friendship allied with good judgement.

CLEINIAS: Of course.

ATHENIAN: One state was over-eager in embracing only the principle of monarchy, the other in embracing only the ideal of liberty; neither has achieved a balance between the two. Your Spartan and Cretan states have done better, and time was when you could say much the same of the Athenians 694 and Persians, but things have changed since then. Let's run through the reasons for this, shall we?

CLEINIAS: Yes, of course – if, that is, we mean to finish what we have set out to do.

THE PERSIAN MONARCHY

ATHENIAN: Then let's listen to the story. Under Cyrus, the life of the Persians was a judicious blend of liberty and subjection, and after gaining their own freedom they became the masters of a great number of other people. As rulers, they granted a degree of liberty to their subjects and put them on the same footing as themselves, with the result that soldiers felt more affection for their commanders and displayed greater zeal in the face of danger. The king felt no jealousy if any of his subjects was intelligent and had some advice to offer; on the contrary, he allowed free speech and valued those who could contribute to the formulation of policy; a sensible man could use his influence to help the common cause. Thanks to freedom, friendship, and the practice of pooling their ideas, during that period the Persians made progress all along the line.

CLEINIAS: It does rather look as if that was the situation in the period you describe.

ATHENIAN: So how are we to explain the disaster under Cambyses, and the virtually complete recovery under Darius?[1] To help our reconstruction of events, shall we have a shot at some inspired guessing?

1. Cambyses, son of Cyrus, was King of Persia from 529 to 521. 'Disaster' refers to the military failures of his reign, his tyrannical madness, and the short-lived seizure of his throne by Gomates (see p. 146, note 3). Cambyses was succeeded by Darius (521–486), who followed the prudent policies described on p. 146. See Herodotus, III, 61 ff.

CLEINIAS: Yes, because this topic we've embarked on will certainly help our inquiry.

ATHENIAN: My guess, then, about Cyrus, is that although he was doubtless a good commander and a loyal patriot, he never considered, even superficially, the problem of correct education; and as for running a household, I'd say he never paid any attention to it at all.

CLEINIAS: And what interpretation are we to put on a remark like that?

ATHENIAN: I mean that he probably spent his entire life after infancy on campaign, and handed over his children to the women to bring up. These women reared them from their earliest years as though they were already Heaven's special favourites and darlings, endowed with all the blessings that implies. They wouldn't allow anyone to thwart 'their Beatitudes' in anything, and they forced everybody to rhapsodize about what the children said or did. You can imagine the sort of person they produced.

CLEINIAS: And a fine old education it must have been, to judge from your account.

ATHENIAN: It was a womanish education, conducted by the royal harem. The teachers of the children had recently come into considerable wealth, but they were left all on their own, without men, because the army was preoccupied by wars and constant dangers.

CLEINIAS: That makes sense.

ATHENIAN: The children's father, for his part, went on accumulating herds and flocks for their benefit – and many a herd of human beings too, quite apart from every other sort of animal; but he didn't know that his intended heirs were ⁶⁹⁵ not being instructed in the traditional Persian discipline. This discipline (the Persians being shepherds, and sons of a stony soil) was a tough one, capable of producing hardy shepherds who could camp out and keep awake on watch and turn soldier if necessary. He just didn't notice that women and eunuchs had given his sons the education of a Mede,[2] and that it had been debased by their so-called 'blessed' status.

2. I.e. an education of extreme luxury.

That is why Cyrus' children turned out as children naturally do when their teachers have never corrected them. So, when they succeeded to their inheritance on the death of Cyrus, they were living in a riot of unrestrained debauchery. First, unwilling to tolerate an equal, one of them killed the other; next, he himself, driven out of his senses by liquor and lack of self-control, was deprived of his dominions by the Medes and 'the Eunuch' (as he was then called), to whom the idiot Cambyses was an object of contempt.[3]

CLEINIAS: So the story goes, and it seems probable enough.

ATHENIAN: And it goes on, I think, to say that the empire was regained for the Persians by Darius and 'the Seven'.

CLEINIAS: Certainly.

ATHENIAN: Now let's carry on with this story of ours and see what happened. Darius was no royal prince, and his upbringing had not encouraged him to self-indulgence. When he came and seized the empire with the aid of the other six, he split it up into seven divisions, of which some faint outlines still survive today. He thought the best policy was to govern it by new laws of his own which introduced a certain degree of equality for all; and he also included in his code regulations about the tribute promised to the people by Cyrus. His generosity in money and gifts rallied all the Persians to his side, and stimulated a feeling of community and friendship among them; consequently his armies regarded him with such affection that they added to the territory Cyrus had bequeathed at least as much again. But Darius was succeeded by Xerxes, whose education had reverted to the royal pampering of old. ('Darius' – as perhaps we'd be entitled to say to him – 'you haven't learnt from Cyrus' mistake, so you've brought up Xerxes in the same habits as Cyrus brought up Cambyses.') So Xerxes, being a product of the same type of education, naturally had a career that closely reproduced the pattern of Cambyses' misfortunes. Ever since then, hardly any king of the Persians has been genuinely 'great', except in style and

3. Gomates impersonated Cambyses' dead brother in order to seize the kingdom.

title. I maintain that the reason for this is not just bad luck, but the shocking life that the children of dictators and 696 fantastically rich parents almost always lead: no man, you see, however old or however young, will ever excel in virtue if he has had this sort of upbringing. We repeat that this is the point the legislator must look out for, and so must we here and now. And in all fairness, my Spartan friends, one must give your state credit for at least this much: rich man, poor man, commoner and king are held in honour to the same degree and are educated in the same way, without privilege, except as determined by the supernatural instructions you received from some god when your state was founded.[4] A man's exceptional wealth is no more reason for a state to confer specially exalted office on him than his ability to run, his good looks, or his physical strength, in the absence of some virtue – or even if he *has* some virtue, if it excludes self-control.

MEGILLUS: What do you mean by that, sir?

ATHENIAN: Courage, I take it, is one part of virtue.

MEGILLUS: Of course.

ATHENIAN: So now that you've heard the story, use your own judgement: would you be glad to have as a resident in your house or as a neighbour a man who in spite of considerable courage was immoderate and licentious?

MEGILLUS: Heaven forbid!

ATHENIAN: Well then, what about a skilled workman, knowledgeable in his own field, but unjust?

MEGILLUS: No, I'd never welcome him.

ATHENIAN: But surely, in the absence of self-control, justice will never spring up.

MEGILLUS: Of course not.

ATHENIAN: Nor indeed will the 'wise' man we put forward just now,[5] who keeps his feelings of pleasure and pain in tune with right reason and obedient to it.

MEGILLUS: No, he certainly won't.

ATHENIAN: Now here's another point for us to consider,

4. Cf. pp. 45 ff and pp. 140 ff.   5 See p. 137.

which will help us to decide whether civic distinctions are, on a given occasion, conferred correctly or incorrectly.

MEGILLUS: And what is that?

ATHENIAN: If we found self-control existing in the soul in isolation from all other virtue, should we be justified in admiring it? Or not?

MEGILLUS: I really couldn't say.

ATHENIAN: A very proper reply. If you had opted for either alternative it would have struck an odd note, I think.

MEGILLUS: So my reply was all right, then.

ATHENIAN: Yes. But if you have something which in itself deserves to be admired or execrated, a mere additional element isn't worth talking about: much better pass it over and say nothing.

MEGILLUS: Self-control is the element you mean, I suppose.

ATHENIAN: It is. And in general, whatever benefits us most, when this element is added, deserves the highest honour, the second most beneficial thing deserves the second highest honour, and so on: as we go down the list, everything will get in due order the honour it deserves.

697 MEGILLUS: True.

ATHENIAN: Well then, shan't we insist again[6] that the distribution of these honours is the business of the legislator?

MEGILLUS: Of course.

ATHENIAN: Would you prefer us to leave the entire distribution to his discretion and let him deal with the details of each individual case? But as we too have something of a taste for legislation, perhaps you'd like us to try our hands at a three-fold division and distinguish the most important class, then the second and the third.

MEGILLUS: Certainly.

ATHENIAN: We maintain that if a state is going to survive to enjoy all the happiness that mankind can achieve, it is vitally necessary for it to distribute honours and marks of disgrace on a proper basis. And the proper basis is to put spiritual goods at the top of the list and hold them – provided

6. Cf. pp. 55–6.

the soul exercises self-control – in the highest esteem; bodily goods and advantages should come second, and third those said to be provided by property and wealth. If a legislator or a state ever ignores these guide-lines by valuing riches above all or by promoting one of the other inferior goods to a more exalted position, it will be an act of political and religious folly. Shall we take this line, or not?

MEGILLUS: Yes, emphatically and unambiguously.

ATHENIAN: It was our scrutiny of the political system of the Persians that made us go into this business at such length. Our verdict was that their corruption increased year by year; and the reason we assign for this is that they were too strict in depriving the people of liberty and too energetic in introducing authoritarian government, so that they destroyed all friendship and community of spirit in the state. And with that gone, the policy of rulers is framed not in the interests of their subjects the people, but to support their own authority: let them only think that a situation offers them the prospect of some profit, even a small one, and they wreck cities and ruin friendly nations by fire and sword; they hate, and are hated in return, with savage and pitiless loathing. When they come to need the common people to fight on their behalf, they discover the army has no loyalty, no eagerness to face danger and fight. They have millions and millions of soldiers – all useless for fighting a war, so that just as if manpower were in short supply, they have to hire it, imagining that mercenaries and foreigners will ensure their safety. Not only this, they inevitably become so stupid that they proclaim by their 698 very actions that as compared with gold and silver everything society regards as good and valuable is in their eyes so much trash.

MEGILLUS: Exactly.

ATHENIAN: So let's have done with the Persians. Our conclusion is that the empire is badly run at the moment because the people are kept in undue subjection and the rulers excessively authoritarian.

MEGILLUS: Precisely.

ATHENS AND THE PERSIAN WARS

ATHENIAN: Next we come to the political system of Attica. We have to demonstrate, on the same lines as before, that complete freedom from all authority is infinitely worse than submitting to a moderate degree of control.

At the time of the Persian attack on the Greeks – on virtually everyone living in Europe, is perhaps a better way of putting it – we Athenians had a constitution, inherited from the distant past, in which a number of public offices were held on the basis of four property-classes. Lady Modesty was the mistress of our hearts, a despot who made us live in willing subjection to the laws then in force. Moreover, the enormous size of the army that was coming at us by land and sea made us desperately afraid, and served to increase our obedience to the authorities and the law. For all these reasons we displayed a tremendous spirit of co-operation. You see, about ten years before the battle of Salamis, Datis had arrived at the head of a Persian army; he had been sent by Darius against the Athenians and the Eretrians with explicit instructions to make slaves of them and bring them home, and he had been warned that failure would mean death.[7] With his vast numbers of soldiers, Datis made short work of the Eretrians, whom he completely overpowered and captured. He then sent to Athens a blood-curdling report that not a single Eretrian had got away – propaganda which asked us to believe that Datis' soldiers, hand in hand in a long line, had combed over every inch of Eretria. Well, whatever the truth or otherwise of this tale, it terrified the Greeks; the Athenians were particularly scared, and they sent off envoys in all directions, but no one was prepared to help them except the Spartans – who were, however, prevented by the Messenian war, which was going on at that time, or perhaps by some other distraction (I'm

7. Athens defeated the Persian fleet near the island of Salamis, off Attica, in September 480; Datis' expedition was in the spring of 490. Eretria was a Euboean city that had assisted the revolt of the Ionians against Persia a few years before. For details, see Herodotus, VI, 94 ff.

not aware of any information being given on the point).
However that may be, the Spartans arrived at Marathon one
day too late for the battle.[8] After this, reports of vast preparations and endless threats on the part of the king came thick
and fast. The years went by, and then we were told that Darius
was dead, but that his son, young and impetuous, had
inherited the kingdom and was determined not to give up the
invasion.[9] The Athenians reckoned that all these preparations 699
were directed against themselves, because of what had happened at Marathon; and when they heard of the canal that
had been dug through Athos, the bridging of the Hellespont
and the huge number of Xerxes' ships, they calculated that
neither land nor sea offered any prospects of safety. No one,
they thought, would come to help them. They remembered
the previous attack and the success of the Persians in Eretria:
no one had assisted the Athenians then, no one had faced the
danger by fighting at their side. On land they expected the
same thing to happen this time; and as for the sea, they
realized that escape by this route was out of the question, in
view of the thousand or more ships coming to the attack.
They could think of only one hope, and a thin, desperate
hope it was; but there was simply no other. Their minds went
back to the previous occasion, and they reflected how the
victory they won in battle had been gained in equally
desperate circumstances. Sustained by this hope, they began
to recognize that no one but they themselves and their gods
could provide a way out of their difficulties. All this inspired
them with a spirit of solidarity. One cause was the actual fear
they felt at the time, but there was another kind too, encouraged by the traditional laws of the state. I mean the 'fear'
they had learned to experience as a result of being subject to

8. The Athenians and Plataeans defeated the Persians on the plain of
Marathon, in north-east Attica, in the summer of 490. Various accounts
are given of the Spartan failure to assist: cf. p. 141 and Herodotus, VI,
106, 108. For discussions, see R. Weil, L' 'Archéologie' de Platon (Paris,
1959), pp. 118–19; G. R. Morrow, Plato's Cretan City (Princeton, 1960),
pp. 71–2.

9. Darius died in 486; his son was Xerxes.

an ancient code of laws. In the course of our earlier discussion[10] we have called this fear 'modesty' often enough, and we said that people who aspire to be good must be its slave. A coward, on the other hand, is free of this particular kind of fear and never experiences it. And if 'ordinary'[11] fear had not overtaken the cowards on that occasion, they would never have combined to defend themselves or protected temples, tombs, fatherland, and friends and relatives as well, in the way they did. We would all have been split up and scattered over the face of the earth.[12]

MEGILLUS: Yes, sir, you are quite right, and your remarks reflect credit both on your country and yourself.

ATHENIAN: No doubt, Megillus; and it is only right and proper to tell you of the history of that period, seeing that you've been blessed with your ancestors' character. Now then, you and Cleinias, consider: have these remarks of ours any relevance at all to legislation? After all, this is the object of the exercise – I'm not going through all this simply for the story. Look: in a way, we Athenians have had the same experience as the Persians. They, of course, reduced the people to a state of complete subjection, and we encouraged the masses to the opposite extreme of unfettered liberty, but the discussion we have had serves well enough as a pointer to the next step in the argument, and shows us the method to follow.

700   MEGILLUS: Splendid! But do try to be even more explicit about what you mean.

THE CORRUPTION OF THE ATHENIAN DEMOCRACY

ATHENIAN: Very well. When the old laws applied, my friends, the people were not in control: on the contrary, they lived in a kind of 'voluntary slavery' to the laws.

10. pp. 78 and 112.

11. The Greek is confusing, and I insert this word to elucidate what I take to be the meaning.

12. Cf. p. 142.

MEGILLUS: Which laws have you in mind?

ATHENIAN: I'm thinking primarily of the regulations about the music[13] of that period (music being the proper place to start a description of how life became progressively freer of controls). In those days Athenian music comprised various categories and forms. One type of song consisted of prayers to the gods, which were termed 'hymns'; and there was another quite different type, which you might well have called 'laments'. 'Paeans'[14] made up a third category, and there was also a fourth, called a 'dithyramb' (whose theme was, I think, the birth of Dionysus). There existed another kind of song too, which they thought of as a separate class, and the name they gave it was this very word that is so often on our lips: 'nomes'[15] ('for the lyre', as they always added). Once these categories and a number of others had been fixed, no one was allowed to pervert them by using one sort of tune in a composition belonging to another category. And what was the authority which had to know these standards and use its knowledge in reaching its verdicts, and crack down on the disobedient? Well, certainly no notice was taken of the catcalls and uncouth yelling of the audience, as it is nowadays, nor yet of the applause that indicates approval. People of taste and education made it a rule to listen to the performance with silent attention right through to the end; children and their attendants and the general public could always be disciplined and controlled by a stick. Such was the rigour with which the mass of the people was prepared to be controlled in the theatre, and to refrain from passing judgement by shouting. Later, as time went on, composers arose who started to set a fashion of breaking the rules and offending good taste. They did have a natural artistic talent, but they were ignorant of the correct and legitimate standards laid down by the Muse. Gripped by a frenzied and excessive lust for pleasure, they jumbled together laments and hymns, mixed paeans and dithyrambs, and even imitated pipe tunes on the lyre. The

13. See §3 *passim*.
14. Hymns in praise of Apollo.
15. The Greek word is *nomoi*, which also means 'laws'. Cf. p. 185.

result was a total confusion of styles. Unintentionally, in their idiotic way, they misrepresented their art, claiming that in music there are no standards of right and wrong at all, but that the most 'correct' criterion is the pleasure of a man who enjoyed the performance, whether he is a good man or not. On these principles they based their compositions, and they accompanied them with propaganda to the same effect. Consequently they gave the ordinary man not only a taste for breaking the laws of music but the arrogance to set himself up 701 as a capable judge. The audiences, once silent, began to use their tongues; they claimed to know what was good and bad in music, and instead of a 'musical meritocracy', a sort of vicious 'theatrocracy' arose.[16] But if this democracy had been limited to gentlemen and had applied only to music, no great harm would have been done; in the event, however, music proved to be the starting-point of everyone's conviction that he was an authority on everything, and of a general disregard for the law. Complete licence was not far behind. The conviction that they *knew* made them unafraid, and assurance engendered effrontery. You see, a reckless lack of respect for one's betters is effrontery of peculiar viciousness, which springs from a freedom from inhibitions that has gone much too far.

MEGILLUS: You're absolutely right.

ATHENIAN: This freedom will then take other forms. First people grow unwilling to submit to the authorities, then they refuse to obey the admonitions of their fathers and mothers and elders. As they hurtle along towards the end of this primrose path, they try to escape the authority of the laws; and the very end of the road comes when they cease to care about oaths and promises and religion in general. They reveal, reincarnated in themselves, the character of the ancient Titans[17] of the story, and thanks to getting into the same position as the Titans did, they live a wretched life of endless misery. Again I ask: what's the purpose of saying all this? My tongue has been galloping on and obviously I ought to curb it con-

16. 'Boxofficeocracy'?

17. Children of Heaven and Earth, and long-standing enemies of the Olympian gods.

stantly; I must keep a bridle in my mouth and not let myself be carried away by the argument so as to 'take a toss from the hoss' as the saying is. Let me repeat the question: what's the point of this speech I've made?

MEGILLUS: Well asked!

RECAPITULATION

ATHENIAN: The point is one we've made before.

MEGILLUS: What?

ATHENIAN: We said[18] that a lawgiver should frame his code with an eye on three things: the freedom, unity and wisdom of the city for which he legislates. That's right, isn't it?

MEGILLUS: Certainly.

ATHENIAN: That was why we selected two political systems, one authoritarian in the highest degree, the other representing an extreme of liberty; and the question is now, which of these two constitutes correct government? We reviewed a moderate authoritarianism and a moderate freedom, and saw the result: tremendous progress in each case. But when either the Persians or the Athenians pushed things to extremes (of subjection in the one case and its opposite in the other), it did neither of them any good at all.

MEGILLUS: You're quite right.

ATHENIAN: [19]We had precisely the same purpose when we looked at the settlement of the Dorian forces, Dardanus' dwellings in the foothills, the foundation by the sea, and the original survivors of the flood; earlier, we discussed music and drink from the same point of view, as well as other topics before that. The object was always to find out what would be the ideal way of administering a state, and the best principles the individual can observe in running his own life. But has it been worth our while? I wonder, Cleinias and Megillus, if there's some test of this that we could set ourselves?

702

18. See p. 142.
19. This paragraph recapitulates in reverse order the themes of §§1-4.

THE PROPOSED NEW CRETAN COLONY

CLEINIAS: I think I can see one, sir. As luck would have it, I find that all the subjects we have discussed in our conversation are relevant to my needs here and now. How fortunate that I've fallen in with you and Megillus! I won't keep you in the dark about my position – indeed, I think that meeting you is a good omen for the future. The greater part of Crete is attempting to found a colony, and has given responsibility for the job to the Cnossians; and the state of Cnossos has delegated it to myself and nine colleagues. Our brief is to compose a legal code on the basis of such local laws as we find satisfactory, and to use foreign laws as well – the fact that they are not Cretan must not count against them, provided their quality seems superior. So what about doing me – and you – a favour? Let's take a selection of the topics we have covered and construct an imaginary community, pretending that we are its original founders. That will allow us to consider the question before us, and it may be that I'll use this framework for the future state.

ATHENIAN: Well, Cleinias, that's certainly welcome news! You may take it that I for my part am entirely at your disposal, unless Megillus has some objection.

CLEINIAS: Splendid!

MEGILLUS: Yes, I too am at your service.

CLEINIAS: I'm delighted you both agree. Now then, let's try – initially only in theory – to found our state.

§6. MAGNESIA AND ITS PEOPLE

*Now that the fundamental ethical questions of §§1–5 have been dealt
with, one might think that the construction of the new state could be
started forthwith, and indeed the Athenian starts off in a business-like
way by asking for some preliminary information about the territory
to be settled and the identity of the new colonists. But it is soon clear
that his major interests are for the moment rather different. For
instance, the possibility of exporting produce leads to a denunciation of
bad habits that can be introduced into the state by foreign merchants,
and the question of whether the land produces timber suitable for
building ships develops into a sermon on the depraved habits of
sailors. (There is an anti-Athenian propaganda here: Athens' navy
and merchant seamen contributed much to her economic and military
ascendency.) Again, the fact that the new colonists will come from
several other states prompts a discussion of the difficulties of reconciling in a new state a number of different social and religious customs.
It is an acutely difficult situation, remarks the Athenian, that may
tempt one to despair; but one should not underrate the professional
skill of a good legislator. He, however, functions most efficiently if he
can enforce his laws with the backing of a dictator in sympathy with
his aims – and such a dictator is a very rare bird. (It is not made
clear how the new colonists are to be brought to submit to the dictator
in the first place; his role seems more appropriate to the reformation
of an already existing state.)*

*The next question is, what constitution should the dictator impose?
No straight answer is given; the Athenian is much more concerned to
make the negative point that the constitution should not favour
particular interests. The government of the state must be conducted
rationally in accordance with the divine will, like the government of
the human race in the age of Cronus. The laws should not serve the
interests of the ruling group; on the contrary, the rulers must themselves obey the laws, and office must be given to those who are most
law-abiding. The section closes with a somewhat high-flown harangue
to the new colonists (whom the three interlocutors pretend are present),*

exhorting them to the punctilious fulfilment of their religious duties. This persuasive address serves as a transition to the subsequent discussion of legal preambles (§7).

Clearly, there is no question – yet, at any rate – of the new colonists framing their own constitution and laws; the initiative comes entirely from above. Human nature is too weak to take complete control of human affairs (p. 171).

NATURAL RESOURCES

BK IV 704 ATHENIAN: Well, now, how should we describe our future state? I don't mean just its name: I'm not asking what it's called now, nor what it ought to be called in the future. (This might well be suggested by some detail of the actual foundation or by some spot nearby: perhaps a river or spring or some local gods will give the new state their own style and title.) This is my real question: is it to be on the coast, or inland?

CLEINIAS: The state I was talking about a moment ago, sir, is approximately eighty stades[1] from the sea.

ATHENIAN: Well, what about harbours? Are there any along the coast on that side of the state, or are they entirely absent?

CLEINIAS: No, sir. The state has harbours in that direction which could hardly be bettered.

ATHENIAN: A pity, that. What about the surrounding countryside? Does it grow everything or are there some deficiencies?

CLEINIAS: No, it grows practically everything.

ATHENIAN: Will it have some nearby state for a neighbour?

CLEINIAS: Absolutely none – that's just why it's being founded. Ages ago, there was a migration from the district, which has left the land deserted for goodness knows how long.

ATHENIAN: What about plains and mountains and forests? How is it off for each of these?

CLEINIAS: Very much like the rest of Crete in general.

ATHENIAN: Rugged rather than flat, you mean?

1. Nine or ten miles.

CLEINIAS: Yes, that's right.

ATHENIAN: Then the state will have tolerably healthy prospects of becoming virtuous. If it were going to be founded near the sea and have good harbours, and were deficient in a great number of crops instead of growing everything itself, then a very great saviour indeed[2] and lawgivers of divine stature would be needed to stop sophisticated and vicious characters developing on a grand scale: such a state would simply invite it. As it is, we can take comfort in those eighty stades. Even so, it lies nearer the sea than it should, and you say that it is rather well off for harbours, which makes matters worse; but let's be thankful for small mercies. For a country 705 to have the sea nearby is pleasant enough for the purpose of everyday life, but in fact it is a 'salty-sharp and bitter neighbour'[3] in more senses than one. It fills the land with wholesaling and retailing, breeds shifty and deceitful habits in a man's soul, and makes the citizens distrustful and hostile, not only among themselves, but also in their dealings with the world outside. Still, the fact that the land produces everything will be some consolation for these disadvantages, and it is obvious in any case that even if it does grow every crop, its ruggedness will stop it doing so in any quantity; if it yielded a surplus that could be exported in bulk, the state would be swamped with the gold and silver money it received in return – and this, if a state means to develop just and noble habits, is pretty nearly the worst thing that could happen to it, all things considered (as we said, if we remember, earlier in our discussion).[4]

CLEINIAS: Of course we remember, and we agree that our argument then was right, and still is now.

ATHENIAN: The next point is this: how well is the surrounding district supplied with timber for building ships?

CLEINIAS: There are no firs or pines worth mentioning,

2. Cf. p. 140.

3. Apparently in part a quotation from Alcman, a Spartan poet of the seventh century. See J. M. Edmonds, *Lyra Graeca* (Loeb edition, 1922), vol. I, pp. 108–9.

4. E.g., p. 122.

and not much by way of cypress, though you'll find a small quantity of plane and Aleppo pine, which is, of course, the standard material shipwrights must have to construct the interior parts of a boat.

ATHENIAN: That too is a feature of the country which will do it no harm.

CLEINIAS: Oh?

ATHENIAN: It's a good thing that a state should find it difficult to lower itself to copy the wicked customs of its enemies.

CLEINIAS: And what on earth has been said to prompt *that* remark?

ATHENIAN: My dear sir, cast your mind back to the beginning of our discussion and watch what I'm up to. Do you remember the point we made about the laws of the Cretans having only one object, and how in particular the two of you asserted that this was warfare? I took you up on the point and argued that in so far as such institutions were established with virtue as their aim, they were to be approved; but I took strong exception to their aiming at only a part of virtue instead of the whole.[5] Now it's your turn: keep a sharp eye on this present legislation, in case I lay down some law which is not conducive to virtue, or which fosters only a part of it. I'm going on the assumption that a law is well enacted only if it 706 constantly aims, like an archer, at that unique target which is the only object of legislation to be invariably and uninterruptedly attended by some good result; the law must ignore everything else (wealth or anything like that), if it happens not to meet the requirements I have stipulated.[6] This 'disgraceful copying of enemies' to which I was referring occurs when people live by the sea and are plagued by such foes as Minos, who once forced the inhabitants of Attica to pay a most onerous tribute (though of course in saying this I've no wish at all to hark back to our old grudges against you).[7]

5. E.g., pp. 54 ff.
6. That is, of having virtue (the 'unique target') as the ultimate aim.
7. The Athenians killed Androgeos, son of Minos, King of Crete, who then exacted a tribute of seven girls and seven boys as victims for the Minotaur, a Cretan monster.

Minos exercised tremendous power at sea, whereas the Athenians had not yet acquired the fighting ships they have today, nor was their country so rich in supplies of suitable timber that they could readily construct a strong fleet; consequently they couldn't turn themselves into sailors at a moment's notice and repel the enemy by copying the Cretan use of the sea. Even if they *had* been able to do that, it would have done them more good to lose seven boys over and over again rather than get into bad habits by forming themselves into a navy. They had previously been infantrymen, and infantrymen can stand their ground; but sailors have the bad habit of dashing forward at frequent intervals and then beating a very rapid retreat indeed back to their ships. They see nothing disgraceful at all in a craven refusal to stand their ground and die as the enemy attacks, nor in the plausible excuses they produce so readily when they drop their weapons and take to their heels – or, as they put it, 'retreat without dishonour'. This is the sort of terminology you must expect if you make your soldiers into sailors; these expressions are not 'beyond praise' (far from it): men ought never to be trained in bad habits, least of all the citizen-*élite*. Even from Homer, I suspect, you can see that this is bad policy. He has Odysseus pitching into Agamemnon for ordering the ships to be put to sea just when the Achaeans were being hard put to it in their fight with the Trojans. In his anger, Odysseus says to him:

'Why bid the well-benched ships be put to sea,
When in our ears the noise of battle rings?
Do you want the Trojans' dearest wish fulfilled,
and utter ruin send us to the grave?
Put the ships to sea, and watch the Achaeans
buckle to the fight! No: they'll scuttle off
and shrink away from battle. The advice you give
will mean the end of us.'[8]

So Homer too realized that it is bad tactics to have triremes lined up at sea in support of infantry in the field. This is the

8. *Iliad* XIV, 96 ff.

sort of habit-training that will soon make even lions run away from deer. And that's not all. When a state which owes its power to its navy wins a victory, the bravest soldiers never get the credit for it, because the battle is won thanks to the skill of steersman, boatswain and rower and the efforts of a motley crowd of ragamuffins, which means that it is impossible to honour each individual in the way he deserves. Rob a state of its power to do that, and you condemn it to failure.

CLEINIAS: I suppose that's more or less inevitable. But in spite of that, sir, it was by fighting at sea at Salamis against the barbarians that the Greeks saved their country – according to us Cretans, anyway.

ATHENIAN: Yes, that's what most people say, Greek and non-Greek alike. Still, my friend, we – Megillus here and myself – are arguing in favour of two battles fought on land: Marathon, which first got the Greeks out of danger, and Plataea, which finally made them really safe. We maintain that these battles *improved* the Greeks, whereas the fighting at sea had the opposite effect. I hope this isn't too strong language to use about battles that at the time certainly helped to ensure our survival (and I'll concede you the battle at Artemisium as well as the one at Salamis).[9] That's all very well, but when we examine the natural features of a country and its legal system, our ultimate object of scrutiny is of course the quality of its social and political arrangements. We do not hold the common view that a man's highest good is to survive and simply continue to exist. His highest good is to become as virtuous as possible and to continue to exist in that state as long as life lasts. But I think we've already taken this line before.

CLEINIAS: Of course.

ATHENIAN: Then we need consider only one thing: is the method we are following the same as before? Can we assume it is the best way to found a state and legislate for it?

CLEINIAS: Yes, it's by far the best.

9. Artemisium was a promontory in north-west Euboea, where the Greek fleet held the Persians at bay in 480. Plataea, a city in southern Boeotia and an ally of Athens, was the scene of a Persian defeat in 479. For Marathon and Salamis, see notes on pp. 150–51.

THE NEW COLONISTS

ATHENIAN: Now for the next point. Tell me, what people will you be settling? Will your policy be to accept all comers from the whole of Crete, on the grounds that the population in the individual cities has exceeded the number that can be supported by the land? I don't suppose you're taking all comers from the Greeks in general – though in fact I notice that some settlers from Argos and Aegina and other parts of Greece have come to settle in your country. But tell me what 708 you intend on this occasion: where do you think your citizen body will come from this time?

CLEINIAS: They will probably come from all over Crete; as for the other Greeks, I imagine settlers from the Peloponnese will be particularly welcome. You are quite right in what you said just now, that there are some here from Argos: they include the Gortynians, the most distinguished of the local people, who hail from the well-known Gortyn in the Peloponnese.

ATHENIAN: So it won't be all that easy for the Cretan states to found their colony. The emigrants, you see, haven't the unity of a swarm of bees: they are not a single people from a single territory settling down to form a colony with mutual goodwill between themselves and those they have left behind. Such migrations occur because of the pressures of land-shortage or some similar misfortune: sometimes a given section of the community may be obliged to go off and settle elsewhere because it is harassed by civil war, and on one occasion a whole state took to its heels after being overcome by an attack it could not resist. In all these cases to found a state and give it laws is, in some ways, comparatively easy, but in others it's rather difficult. When a single people speaks the same language and observes the same laws you get a certain feeling of community, because everyone shares the same religious rites and so forth; but they certainly won't find it easy to accept law or political systems that differ from their own. Sometimes, when it's bad laws that have stimulated the revolt, and the rebels try in their new home to keep to the same familiar habits that ruined them before, their reluctance to toe the line presents the founder and lawgiver with a difficult problem. On the other hand, a miscellaneous combination of all kinds of different people will perhaps be more ready to submit to a new code of laws – but to get them to 'pull and puff as one' (as they say of a team of horses) is very difficult and takes a long time. There's no escaping it: founding a state and legislating for it is a superb test that separates the men from the boys.

CLEINIAS: I dare say; but what do you mean? Please be a little clearer.

THE NEED FOR A BENEVOLENT DICTATOR

ATHENIAN: My dear fellow, now that I'm going back to considering legislators again, I think I'm actually going to insult them: but no matter, so long as the point is relevant. Anyway, why should I have qualms about it? It seems true of pretty nearly all human affairs.

CLEINIAS: What are you getting at?

ATHENIAN: I was going to say that no man ever legislates 709 at all. Accidents and calamities occur in a thousand different ways, and it is they that are the universal legislators of the world. If it isn't pressures of war that overturn a constitution and rewrite the laws, it's the distress of grinding poverty; and disease too forces us to make a great many innovations, when plagues beset us for years on end and bad weather is frequent and prolonged. Realizing all these possibilities, you may jump to conclusions and say what I said just now, that no mortal ever passes any law at all, and that human affairs are almost entirely at the mercy of chance. Now of course this same view could equally plausibly be taken of the profession of the steersman or doctor or general – but at the same time there's another point that could be made about all these examples, and with no less justification.

CLEINIAS: What?

ATHENIAN: That the all-controlling agent in human affairs

is God, assisted by the secondary influences of 'chance' and 'opportunity'. A less uncompromising way of putting it is to acknowledge that there must be a third factor, namely 'skill', to back up the other two. For instance, in a storm the steersman may or may not use his skill to seize any favourable opportunity that may offer. I'd say it would help a great deal if he did, wouldn't you?

CLEINIAS: Yes.

ATHENIAN: So the same will apply in the other cases too, and legislation in particular must be allowed to play the same role. If a state is to live in happiness, certain local conditions must be present, and when all these coincide, what the community needs to find is a legislator who understands the right way to go about things.

CLEINIAS: Very true.

ATHENIAN: So a professional man in each of the fields we've enumerated could hardly go wrong if he prayed for conditions in which the workings of chance needed only to be supplemented by his own skill.

CLEINIAS: Certainly.

ATHENIAN: And all the other people we've instanced would of course be able to tell you what conditions they were praying for, if you asked them.

CLEINIAS: Of course.

ATHENIAN: And I fancy a legislator would do just the same.

CLEINIAS: I agree.

ATHENIAN: 'Well now, legislator,' let's say to him, 'tell us your requirements. What conditions in the state we are going to give you will enable you to run it properly on your own from now on?' What's the right answer to a question like that? (We're giving the legislator's answer for him, I take it.)

CLEINIAS: Yes.

ATHENIAN: Then this is what he'll say: 'Give me a state under the absolute control of a dictator, and let the dictator be young, with a good memory, quick to learn, courageous, and with a character of natural elevation. And if his other abilities

710 are going to be any use, his dictatorial soul should also possess that quality which was earlier agreed to be an essential adjunct to all the parts of virtue.'[10]

CLEINIAS: I think the 'essential adjunct' our companion means, Megillus, is self-control. Right?

ATHENIAN: Yes, Cleinias – but the everyday kind, not the self-control that by an exaggerated and twisted use of language can be identified with good judgement. I mean the spontaneous instinct that flowers early in life in children and animals and in some cases succeeds in imposing a certain restraint in the search for pleasure, but fails in others. We said[11] that if this quality existed in isolation from the many other merits we are discussing, it was not worth consideration. You see my point, I take it.

CLEINIAS: Of course.

ATHENIAN: This is the innate quality our dictator must have, in addition to the others, if the state is going to get, as quickly and efficiently as possible, a political system that will enable it to live a life of supreme happiness. You see, there is no quicker or better method of establishing a political system than this one, nor could there ever be.

CLEINIAS: Well sir, how can a man convince himself that he is talking sense in maintaining all this? What arguments are there for it?

ATHENIAN: It's easy enough, surely, to see that the very facts of the case make the doctrine true.

CLEINIAS: What do you mean? If we were to get a dictator, you say, who is young, restrained, quick to learn, with a retentive memory, courageous and elevated –

ATHENIAN: – and don't forget to add 'lucky' too, in this one point: he should be the contemporary of a distinguished lawgiver, and be fortunate enough to come into contact with him.[12] If that condition is fulfilled, God will have done nearly all that he usually does when he wants to treat a state with particular favour. The next best thing would be a pair of such

---

10. See pp. 147–8.   11. See p. 148.
12. For a discussion of this passage, see Appendix, pp. 545–6.

dictators; the third best would be several of them. The difficulties are in direct proportion to the numbers.

CLEINIAS: It looks as if your position is this: the best state will be the product of a dictatorship, thanks to the efforts of a first-rate legislator and a well-behaved dictator, and this will be the quickest and easiest way to bring about the transformation. The second best will be to start with an oligarchy – is that your point, or what? – and the third to start with a democracy.

ATHENIAN: Certainly not.[13] The ideal starting point is dictatorship, the next best is constitutional kingship, and the third is some sort of democracy. Oligarchy comes fourth, because it has the largest number of powerful people, so that it admits the growth of a new order only with difficulty. And we maintain, of course, that such a growth takes place when circumstances throw up a genuine lawgiver who comes to share a degree of power with the most influential persons in the state. Where the most influential element is both extremely 711 powerful and numerically as small as it could be, as in a dictatorship, you usually get a rapid and trouble-free transition.

CLEINIAS: How? We don't understand.

ATHENIAN: We've made the point more than once, I think. Perhaps you two have not so much as seen a state under the control of a dictator.

CLEINIAS: No, and I don't particularly want to, either.

ATHENIAN: Still, suppose you did: you'd notice something we remarked on just now.

CLEINIAS: What's that?

ATHENIAN: That when a dictator wants to change the morals of a state, he doesn't need to exert himself very much or spend a lot of time on the job. He simply has to be the first to set out on the road along which he wishes to urge the citizens – whether to the practice of virtue or vice – and give them a complete moral blueprint by setting his own personal

13. The upshot of the Athenian's correction, which at first sight seems fussy, is that *formal* power in a state must not be confused with *effective* power. Effective power in a democracy is likely to be in fewer hands than in an oligarchy.

example; he must praise and commend some courses of action and censure others, and in every field of conduct he must see that anyone who disobeys is disgraced.

CLEINIAS: And why should we expect the citizens to obey, with such alacrity, a man who combines persuasion with compulsion like that?

ATHENIAN: My friends, there's no quicker or easier way for a state to change its laws than to follow the leadership of those in positions of power; there is no other way now, nor will there be in the future, and we shouldn't let anyone persuade us to the contrary. Actually, you see, it's not simply this that is impossible or difficult to achieve. What *is* difficult, and a very rare occurrence in the history of the world, is something else; but when it does occur, the state concerned reaps the benefit on a grand scale – indeed, there's no blessing that will pass it by.

CLEINIAS: What occurrence do you mean?

ATHENIAN: A situation in which an inspired passion for the paths of restraint and justice guides those who wield great power. The passion may seize a single supreme ruler, or perhaps men who owe their power to exceptional wealth or high birth; or you may get a reincarnation of Nestor, who, superior as he was to all mankind for the vigour of his speech, is said to have put them in the shade even more by his qualities of restraint. In Trojan times, they say, such a paragon did exist, but he is certainly unheard of today. Still, granted someone like that did in fact exist in the past or is going to in the future, or is alive among us now, blessed is the life of this man of moderation, and blessed they who listen to the words that fall from his lips. And whatever the form of 712 government, the same doctrine holds true: where supreme power in a man joins hands with wise judgement and self-restraint, there you have the birth of the best political system, with laws to match; you'll never achieve it otherwise. So much for my somewhat oracular fiction! Let's take it as established that though in one sense it is difficult for a state to acquire a good set of laws, in another sense nothing could be quicker or easier – granted, of course, the conditions I've laid down.

CLEINIAS: How so?

WHAT CONSTITUTION IS TO BE IMPOSED?

ATHENIAN: What about pretending the fiction[14] is true of your state, Cleinias, and having a shot at making up its laws? Like children, we old men love a bit of make-believe.

CLEINIAS: Yes, what are we waiting for? Let's get down to it.

ATHENIAN: Let us therefore summon God to attend the foundation of the state. May he hear our prayers, and having heard, come graciously and benevolently to help us settle our state and its laws.

CLEINIAS: May he come indeed.

ATHENIAN: Well now, what political system do we intend to impose on the state?

CLEINIAS: Please be a little more explicit about what you really mean by that question. Do you mean we have to choose between a democracy, an oligarchy, and an aristocracy? Presumably you're hardly contemplating a dictatorship – or so we'd think, at any rate.

ATHENIAN: Well then, which of you would be prepared to answer first and tell us which of these terms fits the political system of your homeland?

MEGILLUS: Isn't it right and proper for me to answer first, as the elder?

CLEINIAS: Perhaps so.

MEGILLUS: Very well. When I consider the political system in force at Sparta, sir, I find it impossible to give you a straight answer: I just can't say what one ought to call it. You see, it really does look to me like a dictatorship (it has the ephors, a remarkably dictatorial institution), yet on occasions I think it gets very close to being run democratically. But then again, it would be plain silly to deny that it is an aristocracy; and there is also a kingship (held for life), which both we and

14. That a benevolent dictator is in control.

the rest of the world speak of as the oldest kingship of all. So when I'm asked all of a sudden like this, the fact is, as I said, that I can't distinguish exactly which of these political systems it belongs to.

CLEINIAS: I'm sure I'm in the same predicament as you, Megillus. I find it acutely difficult to say for sure that the constitution we have in Cnossos comes into any of these categories.

ATHENIAN: And the reason, gentlemen, is this: you really do operate constitutions worthy of the name. The ones we called constitutions just now are not really that at all: they are just a number of ways of running a state, all of which involve some citizens living in subjection to others like 713 slaves, and the state is named after the ruling class in each case. But if that's the sort of principle on which your new state is to be named, it should be called after the god who really does rule over men who are rational enough to let him.[15]

CLEINIAS: What god is that?

THE AGE OF CRONUS

ATHENIAN: Well, perhaps we ought to make use of this fiction a little more, if we are going to clear up the question at issue satisfactorily.

CLEINIAS: Yes, that will be the right procedure.

ATHENIAN: It certainly will. Well now, countless ages before the formation of the states we described earlier,[16] they say there existed, in the age of Cronus, a form of government and administration which was a great success, and which served as a blueprint for the best run of our present-day states.

CLEINIAS: Then I think we simply must hear about it.

ATHENIAN: Yes, I agree. That's just why I introduced it into the discussion.

CLEINIAS: You were quite right to do so, and seeing how relevant it is, you'll be entirely justified in giving a systematic account of what happened.

ATHENIAN: I must try to meet your wishes. The traditional

15. In other words the state would be a 'theocracy' (*theos* being the Greek for 'god' – here presumably *Nomos*, 'Law').   16. In §4.

account that has come down to us tells of the wonderfully happy life people lived then, and how they were provided with everything in abundance and without any effort on their part. The reason is alleged to be this: Cronus was of course aware that human nature, as we've explained,[17] is never able to take complete control of all human affairs without being filled with arrogance and injustice. Bearing this in mind, he appointed kings and rulers for our states; they were not men, but beings of a superior and more divine order – spirits. We act on the same principle nowadays in dealing with our flocks of sheep and herds of other domesticated animals: we don't put cattle in charge of cattle or goats in charge of goats, but control them ourselves, because we are a superior species. So Cronus too, who was well-disposed to man, did the same: he placed us in the care of the spirits, a superior order of beings, who were to look after our interests – an easy enough task for them, and a tremendous boon to us, because the result of their attentions was peace, respect for others, good laws, justice in full measure, and a state of happiness and harmony among the races of the world. The story has a moral for us even today, and there is a lot of truth in it: where the ruler of a state is not a god but a mortal, people have no respite from toil and misfortune. The lesson is that we should make every effort to imitate the life men are said to have led under Cronus; we should run our public and our private life, our homes and our cities, in obedience to what little spark of immortality lies in us, and dignify this distribution of reason 714 with the name of 'law'.[18] But take an individual man or an oligarchy, or even a democracy, that lusts in its heart for pleasure and demands to have its fill of everything it wants – the perpetually unsatisfied victim of an evil greed that attacks it like the plague – well, as we said just now, if a power like that controls a state or an individual and rides roughshod over

17. See p. 140.
18. The punning in the Greek defies rendering into English. The 'divine spark' in us is reason (*nous*), which 'dispenses' (*dianomē*) law (*nomos*) in place of the spirits (*daimones*) of Cronus' age. The Greek word 'to name' (*eponomazō*) adds to the jingling effect. Cf. p. 510.

the laws, it's impossible to escape disaster. This is the doctrine we have to examine, Cleinias, and see whether we are prepared to go along with it – or what?

CLEINIAS: Of course we must go along with it.

LAW SHOULD BE SUPREME

ATHENIAN: You realize that some people maintain that there are as many different kinds of laws as there are of political systems? (And of course we've just run through the many types of political systems there are popularly supposed to be.) Don't think the question at issue is a triviality: it's supremely important, because in effect we've got back to arguing about the criteria of justice and injustice. These people take the line that legislation should be directed not to waging war or attaining complete virtue, but to safeguarding the interests of the established political system, whatever that is, so that it is never overthrown and remains permanently in force. They say that the definition of justice that measures up to the facts is best formulated like this.

CLEINIAS: How?

ATHENIAN: It runs: 'Whatever serves the interest of the stronger'.

CLEINIAS: Be a little more explicit, will you?

ATHENIAN: The point is this: according to them, the element in control at any given moment lays down the law of the land. Right?

CLEINIAS: True enough.

ATHENIAN: 'So do you imagine,' they say, 'that when a democracy has won its way to power, or some other constitution has been established (such as dictatorship), it will ever pass any laws, unless under pressure, except those designed to further its own interests and ensure that it remains permanently in power? That'll be its main preoccupation, won't it?'

CLEINIAS: Naturally.

ATHENIAN: So the author of these rules will call them 'just' and claim that anyone who breaks them is acting 'unjustly', and punish him?

CLEINIAS: Quite likely.

ATHENIAN: So this is why such rules will always add up to 'justice'.

CLEINIAS: Certainly, on the present argument.

ATHENIAN: We are, you see, dealing with one of those 'claims to authority'.[19]

CLEINIAS: What claims?

ATHENIAN: The ones we examined before, when we asked who should rule whom. It seemed that parents should rule children, the elder the younger, and the noble those of low birth; and there was a large number of other titles to authority, if you remember, some of which conflicted with others. The claim we're talking about now[20] was certainly one of these: we said, I think, that Pindar turned it into a law of nature – which meant that he 'justified the use of force extreme', to quote his actual words.[21]

CLEINIAS: Yes, those are the points that were made.

ATHENIAN: Now look: to which side in the dispute should we entrust our state? In some cities, you see, this is the sort of thing that has happened thousands of times.

CLEINIAS: What?

ATHENIAN: When offices are filled competitively, the winners take over the affairs of state so completely that they totally deny the losers and the losers' descendants any share of power. Each side passes its time in a narrow scrutiny of the other, apprehensive lest someone with memories of past injustices should gain some office and lead a revolution. Of course, our position is that this kind of arrangement is very far from being a genuine political system; we maintain that laws which are not established for the good of the whole state are bogus laws, and when they favour particular sections of the community, their authors are not citizens but party-men; and people who say those laws have a claim to be obeyed are wasting their breath. We've said all this because in your new state we aren't going to appoint a man to office because of his

715

19. See pp. 137ff.
20. I.e. that the stronger should rule the weaker.
21. See p. 138 and note.

wealth or some other claim like that, say strength or stature or birth. We insist that the highest office in the service of the gods must be allocated to the man who is best at obeying the established laws and wins *that* sort of victory in the state; the man who wins the second prize must be given second rank in that service, and so on, the remaining posts being allocated in order on the same system. Such people are usually referred to as 'rulers', and if I have called them 'servants of the laws' it's not because I want to mint a new expression but because I believe that the success or failure of a state hinges on this point more than on anything else. Where the law is subject to some other authority and has none of its own, the collapse of the state, in my view, is not far off; but if law is the master of the government and the government is its slave, then the situation is full of promise and men enjoy all the blessings that the gods shower on a state. That's the way I see it.

CLEINIAS: By heaven, sir, you're quite right. You've the sharp eye of an old man for these things.

ATHENIAN: Yes, when we're young, we're all pretty blind to them; old age is the best time to see them clearly.

CLEINIAS: Very true.

ADDRESS TO THE NEW COLONISTS

ATHENIAN: Well, what now? I suppose we should assume our colonists have arrived and are standing before us. So we shall have to finish off the topic by addressing them.

CLEINIAS: Of course.

ATHENIAN: Now then, our address should go like this: 'Men, according to the ancient story, there is a god who holds in his hands the beginning and end and middle of all 716 things, and straight he marches in the cycle of nature. Justice, who takes vengeance on those who abandon the divine law, never leaves his side. The man who means to live in happiness latches on to her and follows her with meekness and humility. But he who bursts with pride, elated by wealth or honours or by physical beauty when young and foolish, whose soul is afire with the arrogant belief that so far from needing someone to control and lead him, he can play the leader to others – there's a man whom God has deserted. And in his desolation he collects others like himself, and in his soaring frenzy he causes universal chaos. Many people think he cuts a fine figure, but before very long he pays to Justice no trifling penalty and brings himself, his home and state to rack and ruin. Thus it is ordained. What action, then, should a sensible man take, and what should his outlook be? What must he *avoid* doing or thinking?'

CLEINIAS: This much is obvious: every man must resolve to belong to those who follow in the company of God.

ATHENIAN: 'So what conduct recommends itself to God and reflects his wishes? There is only one sort, epitomized in the old saying "like approves of like" (excess apart, which is both its own enemy and that of due proportion). In our view it is God who is pre-eminently the "measure of all things", much more so than any "man", as they say.[22] So if you want to recommend yourself to someone of this character, you must do your level best to make your own character reflect his, and on this principle the moderate man is God's friend, being like him, whereas the immoderate and unjust man is not like him and is his enemy; and the same reasoning applies to the other vices too.

'Let's be clear that the consequence of all this is the following doctrine (which is, I think, of all doctrines the finest and truest): If a good man sacrifices to the gods and keeps them constant company in his prayers and offerings and every kind of worship he can give them, this will be the best and noblest policy he can follow; it is the conduct that fits his character as nothing else can, and it is his most effective way of achieving a happy life. But if the wicked man does it, the results are bound to be just the opposite. Whereas the good man's soul is clean, the wicked man's soul is polluted, and it is never right for a good man or for God to receive gifts from unclean hands – which means that even if impious people do lavish a lot of 717 attention on the gods, they are wasting their time, whereas

22. Protagoras, a philosopher of the fifth century, maintained that 'man is the measure of all things'.

the trouble taken by the pious is very much in season. So this is the target at which we should aim – but what "missiles" are we to use to hit it, and what "bow" is best carried to shoot them? Can we name these "weapons"? The first weapon in our armoury will be to honour the gods of the underworld next after those of Olympus, the patron-gods of the state; the former should be allotted such secondary honours as the Even and the Left, while the latter should receive superior and contrasting honours like the Odd.[23] That's the best way a man can hit his target, piety. After these gods, a sensible man will worship the spirits, and after them the heroes. Next in priority will be rites celebrated according to law at private shrines dedicated to ancestral gods.[24] Last come honours paid to living parents. It is meet and right that a debtor should discharge his first and greatest obligation and pay the debt which comes before all others; he must consider that all he has and holds belongs to those who bore and bred him, and he is meant to use it in their service to the limit of his powers. He must serve them first with his property, then with hand and brain, and so give to the old people what they desperately need in view of their age: repayment of all that anxious care and attention they lavished on him, the long-standing "loan" they made him as a child. Throughout his life the son must be very careful to watch his tongue in addressing his parents, because there is a very heavy penalty for careless and ill-considered language; Retribution, messenger of Justice, is the appointed overseer of these things. If his parents get angry, he must submit to them, and whether they satisfy their anger in speech or in action, he must forgive them; after all, he must reflect, it's natural enough for a father to get very angry if he thinks he's being harmed by his own son. When the parents die, the most modest burial will be best, and the ceremonies should not be more elaborate than custom demands nor inferior to those with which his

23. A reference to the Pythagorean list of opposites: Odd, Even; Right, Left; Male, Female; Good, Bad; and a number of others. The ritual details glanced at are obscure.

24. Probably deceased ancestors: see p. 209.

forefathers laid their own parents to rest. Year by year he should honour the departed by similar acts of devotion; he will honour them best by never failing to provide a perpetual memorial to them, spending on the dead a proper proportion 718 of the money he happens to have available. If we do that, and live in accordance with these rules, each of us will get the reward we deserve from the gods and such beings as are superior to ourselves, and live in a spirit of cheerful confidence for most of the years of our life.'

§7. THE CORRECT WAY TO LEGISLATE: LAWS AND PREAMBLES

It was noticed (p. 158) that the initiative for framing the constitution and laws of the new state comes entirely from above; the colonists themselves have no say in the matter. But the Athenian is not so authoritarian as to be indifferent to the feelings of the citizens: he insists that they must welcome and accept the laws that will be framed for them. They must not be browbeaten into obedience like a slave-patient being treated by a slave-doctor. Just as a 'free' doctor explains the patient's illness to him, and tries to make him understand the reasons for the measures to be prescribed, in order to gain his co-operation, so the legislator must explain and justify his laws. Hence every law must be headed by a preamble justifying its provisions; further, the preamble must be rhetorical in character: it must not only instruct, but persuade. Only if a man ignores the preambles must the sanction of actual law be applied.

We shall interpret the doctrine of this section in accordance with our overall approach to Plato's political philosophy. We may feel that it shows a praiseworthy awareness of the importance of public opinion and a desire that the government should carry the people with it. On the other hand we may think that an efficient authoritarian regime will naturally prefer, if it can get away with it, to use the carrot rather than the stick.

THE LEGISLATOR MUST JUSTIFY HIS LAWS

ATHENIAN: The laws themselves will explain the duties we owe to children, relatives, friends and fellow-citizens, as well as the service heaven demands we render to foreigners; they will tell us the way we have to behave in the company of each of these categories of people, if we want to lead a full and varied life without breaking the law. The laws' method will be partly persuasion and partly (when they have to deal with characters that defy persuasion) compulsion and chastisement;

178

and with the good wishes of the gods they will make our state happy and prosperous. There are a number of other topics which a legislator who thinks as I do simply must mention, but they are not easily expressed in the form of a law. So he should, I think, put up to himself and those for whom he is going to legislate an example of the way to deal with the remaining subjects, and when he has explained them all as well as he can, he should set about laying down his actual code of laws. So what's the particular form in which such topics are expressed? It's none too easy to confine one's exposition of them to a single example, but let's see if we can crystallize our ideas by looking at the matter rather like this.

CLEINIAS: Tell us what you have in mind.

ATHENIAN: I should like the citizens to be supremely easy to persuade along the paths of virtue; and clearly this is the effect the legislator will try to achieve throughout his legislation.

CLEINIAS: Of course.

ATHENIAN: It occurs to me that the sort of approach I've just explained, provided it is not made to totally uncouth souls, will help to make people more amenable and better disposed to listen to what the lawgiver recommends. So even if the address has no great effect but only makes his listener a trifle easier to handle, and so that much easier to teach, the legislator should be well pleased. People who are anxious to attain moral excellence with all possible speed are pretty thin on the ground and it isn't easy to find them: most only go to prove the wisdom of Hesiod's remark that the road to vice is smooth and can be travelled without sweating, because it is very short; but 'as the price of virtue', he says,

'the gods have imposed the sweat of our brows,
And long and steep is the ascent that you have to make
And rough, at first; but when you get to the top,   719
Then the rugged road is easy to endure.'[1]

CLEINIAS: It sounds as if he hit off the situation very well.

ATHENIAN: He certainly did. But after this discussion I'm

---

1. Hesiod, *Works and Days*, 287–92.

left with certain impressions which I want to put forward for your consideration.

CLEINIAS: Do so, then.

ATHENIAN: Let's have a word with the legislator and address him like this: 'Tell us, legislator, if you were to discover what we ought to do and say, surely you'd tell us?'

CLEINIAS: Of course.

ATHENIAN: 'Now didn't we hear you saying a few minutes ago[2] that a legislator ought not to allow the poets to compose whatever happened to take their fancy? You see, they'd never know when they were saying something in opposition to the law and harming the state.'

CLEINIAS: You're quite right.

ATHENIAN: Well, then, if we took the poets' side and addressed the legislator, would this be a reasonable line to take?

CLEINIAS: What?

ATHENIAN: This: 'There is an old proverb, legislator, which we poets never tire of telling and which all laymen confirm, to the effect that when a poet takes his seat on the tripod of the Muse, he cannot control his thoughts. He's like a fountain where the water is allowed to gush forth unchecked. His art is the art of representation, and when he represents men with contrasting characters he is often obliged to contradict himself, and he doesn't know which of the opposing speeches contains the truth. But for the legislator, this is impossible: he must not let his laws say two different things on the same subject; his rule has to be "one topic, one doctrine". For example, consider what you said just now. A funeral can be extravagant, inadequate or modest, and your choice falls on one of these three – the moderate – which you recommend with unqualified praise. But if I were composing a poem about a woman of great wealth and how she gave instructions for her own funeral, I should recommend the elaborate burial; a poor and frugal character, on the other hand, would be in favour of the cheap funeral, while the moderate man of moderate means would recommend accord-

2. See pp. 91 ff.

ingly. But you ought not to use the term "moderate" in the way you did just now: you must say what "moderate" means and how big or small it may be. If you don't, you must realize that a remark such as you made still has some way to go before it can be a law.'

CLEINIAS: That's quite right.

TWO CATEGORIES OF DOCTORS

ATHENIAN: So should the legislator whom we appoint skip any such announcement at the beginning of his laws? Is he to say without ceremony what one should and should not do, and simply threaten the penalty for disobedience before 720 passing on to the next law, without adding to his statutes a single word of encouragement or persuasion? It's just the same with doctors, you know, when we're ill: one follows one method of treatment, one another. Let's recall the two methods, so that we can make the same request of the legislator that a child might make of its doctor, to treat him as gently as possible. You want an example? Well, we usually speak, I think, of doctors and doctors' assistants, but of course we call the latter 'doctors' too.

CLEINIAS: Certainly.

ATHENIAN: And these 'doctors' (who may be free men or slaves) pick up the skill empirically, by watching and obeying their masters; they've no systematic knowledge such as the free doctors have learned for themselves and pass on to their pupils. You'd agree in putting 'doctors' into these two categories?

CLEINIAS: Of course.

ATHENIAN: Now here's another thing you notice. A state's invalids include not only free men but slaves too, who are almost always treated by other slaves who either rush about on flying visits or wait to be consulted in their surgeries. This kind of doctor never gives any account of the particular illness of the individual slave, or is prepared to listen to one; he simply prescribes what he thinks best in the light of experience, as if he had precise knowledge, and with the self-confidence of a dictator. Then he dashes off on his way to the next slave-patient, and so takes off his master's shoulders some of the work of attending the sick. The visits of the free doctor, by contrast, are mostly concerned with treating the illnesses of free men; *his* method is to construct an empirical case-history by consulting the invalid and his friends; in this way he himself learns something from the sick and at the same time he gives the individual patient all the instruction he can. He gives no prescription until he has somehow gained the invalid's consent; then, coaxing him into continued co-operation, he tries to complete his restoration to health. Which of the two methods do you think makes a doctor a better healer, or a trainer more efficient? Should they use the *double* method to achieve a *single* effect,[3] or should the method too be single – the less satisfactory approach that makes the invalid more recalcitrant?

CLEINIAS: The double, sir, is much better, I think.

TWO CATEGORIES OF LAWS: AN EXAMPLE

ATHENIAN: Would you like us to see how this double method and the single work out when applied to legislation?

CLEINIAS: Yes, I'd like that very much.

ATHENIAN: Well then, in heaven's name, what will be the first law our legislator will establish? Surely the first subject he will turn to in his regulations will be the very first step that 721 leads to the birth of children in the state.

CLEINIAS: Of course.

ATHENIAN: And this first step is, in all states, the union of two people in the partnership of marriage?

CLEINIAS: Naturally.

ATHENIAN: So the correct policy for every state will probably be to pass marriage laws first.

CLEINIAS: No doubt about it.

ATHENIAN: Now then, to start with, let's have the simple form. It might run more or less like this:

A man must marry between the ages of thirty and thirty-five.

3. That is, I take it, the patient's health.

If he does not,
he must be punished by fines and disgrace –

and the fines and disgrace will then be specified. So much for
the simple version of the marriage law; this will be the double
version:

A man must marry between the ages of thirty and thirty-five,[4]

> reflecting that there is a sense in which nature has not only
> somehow endowed the human race with a degree of im-
> mortality, but also planted in us all a longing to achieve it,
> which we express in every way we can. One expression of
> that longing is the desire for fame and the wish not to lie
> nameless in the grave. Thus mankind is by nature a com-
> panion of eternity, and is linked to it, and will be linked to
> it, for ever. Mankind is immortal because it always leaves
> later generations behind to preserve its unity and identity
> for all time: it gets its share of immortality by means of
> procreation. It is never a holy thing voluntarily to deny
> oneself this prize, and he who neglects to take a wife and
> have children does precisely that. So if a man obeys the
> law he will be allowed to go his way without penalty, but

If a man disobeys, and reaches the age of thirty-five without
having married,
he must pay a yearly fine

(of a sum to be specified; that ought to stop him thinking that
life as a bachelor is all cakes and ale),

> *and be* deprived too of all the honours which the younger
> people in the state pay to their elders on the appropriate
> occasions.

When one has heard this law and compared it with the other,
one can judge whether in general laws should run to at least
twice the length by combining persuasion and threats, or
restrict themselves to threats alone and be of 'single' length
only.

MEGILLUS: The Spartan instinct, sir, is always to prefer
brevity. But if I were asked to sit in judgement on these

4. These figures are perhaps only *exempli gratia*: see pp. 251 and 269.

statutes and say which of the two I'd like to see committed to
722 writing in the state, I'd choose the longer one, and my choice
would be precisely the same for every law drafted in the
alternative versions of which you've given us specimens. Still,
I suppose Cleinias here too must approve this present legislation, seeing that it's his state that is contemplating the adoption
of laws modelled on it.

CLEINIAS: You've put it all very well, Megillus.

ATHENIAN: However, it would be pretty fatuous to spend
our time talking about the length or brevity of the text: it's
high quality that we should value, I think, not extreme brevity
or length. One of the kinds of laws we mentioned just now is
twice as valuable for practical purposes as the other, but that's
not all: as we said a little while ago, the two types of doctors
were an extremely apt parallel.[5] A relevant point here is that
no legislator ever seems to have noticed that in spite of its
being open to them to use two methods in their legislation,
compulsion and persuasion (subject to the limitations imposed
by the uneducated masses), in fact they use only one. They
never mix in persuasion with force when they brew their laws,
but administer compulsion neat. As for myself, my dear sirs,
I can see a third condition that should be observed in legislation – not that it ever is.

CLEINIAS: What condition do you mean?

PREAMBLES ESSENTIAL

ATHENIAN: Providentially enough, the point is brought out
by the very conversation we've had today. Since we began to
discuss legislation dawn has become noon and we've reached
this splendid resting-place; we've talked about nothing but
laws – and yet I suspect it was only a moment ago that we
really got round to framing any, and that everything we've
said up till now has been simply legislative preamble. Now

5. The point seems to be that in the case of the doctors, one kind of
treatment was 'much better' (p. 182) than the other (not simply twice as
good). In other words, if you double the length of your laws, you *more*
than double their value.

why have I pointed this out? I want to make the point that the spoken word, and in general all compositions that involve using the voice, employ 'preludes' (a sort of limbering up, so to speak), and that these introductions are artistically designed to aid the coming performance. For instance, the 'nomes' of songs to the harp, and all other kinds of musical composition, are preceded by preludes of fantastic elaboration. But in the case of the real 'nomes',[6] the kind we call 'administrative', nobody has ever so much as breathed the word 'prelude' or composed one and given it to the world; the assumption has been that such a thing would be repugnant to nature. But in my opinion the discussion we've had indicates that it is perfectly natural; and this means that the laws which seemed 'double' when I described them a moment ago are not really 'double' in the straightforward sense the term suggests: it's just that they have *two elements*, 'law' and 'preface to law'. The 'dictatorial prescription', which we compared to the prescriptions of the 'slavish' doctors, is the law pure and simple; and the part that comes before it, which is essentially 'persuasive' (as Megillus put it), has an additional function, analogous to that of a preamble in a speech. It seems obvious to me that the reason why the legislator gave that entire persuasive address was to make the person to whom he promulgated his law accept his orders – the law – in a more co-operative frame of mind and with a correspondingly greater readiness to learn. That's why, as I see it, this element ought properly to be termed not the 'text' of the law, but the 'preamble'. So after all that, what's the next point I'd like made? It's this: the legislator must see that both the permanent body of laws and the individual sub-divisions are always supplied with preambles. The gain will be just as great as it was in the case of the two specimens we gave just now.[7]

CLEINIAS: As far as I'm concerned, I'd certainly instruct our lawgiver, master of his art though he is, to legislate in no way but that.

6. I.e. laws, the Greek word *nomoi* meaning both 'laws' and 'melodies'. Cf. pp. 153 and 255.

7. I.e. the two marriage laws on pp. 182–3.

ATHENIAN: Yes, Cleinias, I think you're right to agree that all laws have their preambles and that the first task must be to preface the text of each part of the legal code with the appropriate introduction, because the announcement it introduces is important, and it matters a great deal whether it is clearly remembered or not. However, we should be wrong to demand that both 'major' laws and minor rules should *invariably* be headed by a preface. Not every song and speech, after all, needs this treatment. (They all have introductions in the nature of the case, but it's not always appropriate to use them.) Still, the decision in all these cases must be left to the discretion of the orator or singer or legislator.

§8. GENERAL PREAMBLE TO THE LEGAL CODE

Cleinias now asks that the earlier remarks (pp. 174–7) about religious duties should be repeated and followed up in specifically preamble form. The Athenian more than obliges, and delivers a long sermon (as we might want to call it) on the whole moral basis of the coming detailed legislation. This preamble serves as the general preface (mentioned on p. 185) to the entire legal code as opposed to the individual prefaces to the various sections of it.

The preface is very earnest, and sounds quite Victorian. It is chiefly concerned to extol the virtues of thrift, piety, honesty, restraint, etc., and to condemn their opposites. The Athenian deals with a man's duties under three main headings: duties to the soul, the body and one's fellow-men. Today we are apt to be somewhat mystified by the first two of these: what does the Athenian mean by 'honouring' the soul and the body? The Greek terms are somewhat emotive and not at all precise; equivalent modern English expressions are hard to come by. 'Giving priority to spiritual values' gets something of the sense of 'honouring the soul', and 'treating the body as it deserves' roughly expresses 'honouring the body'. Even though the literal translation sounds a trifle odd to modern ears, I have thought it best to keep it: even today we have by no means lost the notion that we consist of body and soul and that there is somehow an 'I' who can (say) ruin or do good to either. (Compare 'I owe it to myself'.) A literal translation reflects this popular and non-philosophical point of view. But the central point the Athenian wants to make is that the 'honour' of the soul is paramount, and that of the body secondary, while external goods come last: he insists on a scale of value, and the literal translation has the added advantage of clarifying this, as he speaks of 'honouring' not only the soul and the body but possessions too. The modern reader has simply to make the slight effort required to adapt himself to the Athenian's conceptual framework.

The closing topic ('Virtue and Happiness') is an elaborate and fascinating attempt to show that the virtuous life offers us the maximum pleasure, whereas vice offers the maximum pain, so that what we really want is virtue (assuming, of course, that we all wish to maximize our pleasures); if we do wrong it must be because we cannot control ourselves or act in ignorance of the truth. The thesis the Athenian wishes to refute is the common one that 'Vice may be vice but I enjoy it'. The 'proof' depends on our agreeing (and of course Cleinias and Megillus are never given the chance not to) that vice involves extremes of emotion, and extremes are more painful than pleasurable. Clearly there is much here that one might wish to question.

The whole section is written very discursively: the Athenian has a broad plan of procedure but deals with various side issues as they occur to him. This grand preface to the whole body of legislation depends for its effect not so much on the cogency of its arguments as on its serious and elevated tone; after all, the function of a preface is to persuade rather than to demonstrate. Whatever we may think of its theoretical underpinning (or lack of it), the actual advice given ('be honest', etc.) seems mostly admirable enough (doubtless Samuel Smiles would have thoroughly approved); on occasions it shows considerable wordly-wisdom (e.g. p. 193 on duties to friends).

INTRODUCTION

CLEINIAS: I think all this is very true. But let's not waste any more time delaying, sir. Let's get back to our theme and make a fresh start, if you are agreeable, on the subject you dealt with before, when you were not professing to compose in preamble form; let's go over the topic again ('second time lucky', as they say in games), on the understanding that we are not talking at random, as we did just now, but composing a preface; and we should begin by agreeing that this is what we are doing. We've heard enough said just now about the worship of the gods and the services to be rendered to our ancestors;[1] let's try to deal with the subsequent topics until you think the entire preface has been adequately put together. Then you will go on to work through the actual laws.

724 ATHENIAN: So our feeling at the moment is that we have

1. See pp. 174–7.

already produced an adequate preface about the gods and the powers below them, and about parents living and dead. Your instructions now, I think, are that I should, as it were, take the covers off the remainder of the preface.

CLEINIAS: Certainly.

ATHENIAN: Well now, the next thing is this: how far should a man concentrate or relax the efforts he devotes to looking after his soul, his body, and his property? This is a suitable topic, and it will be to the mutual advantage of both speaker and listeners to ponder it and so perfect their education as far as they can. So beyond a shadow of a doubt here's the next subject for explanation and the next topic to listen to.

CLEINIAS: You're quite right.

ATHENIAN: Everyone who was listening to the address just now about the gods and our dearly beloved ancestors, should now pay attention.

BK
V
726

THE IMPORTANCE OF HONOURING THE SOUL

Of all the things a man can call his own, the holiest (though the gods are holier still) is his soul, his most intimate possession. There are two elements that make up the whole of every man. One is stronger and superior, and acts as master; the other, which is weaker and inferior, is a slave; and so a man must always respect the master in him in preference to the slave. Thus when I say that next after the gods – our masters – and their attendant spirits, a man must honour his soul, my recommendation is correct. But hardly a man among us honours it in the right way: he only thinks he does. You see, nothing that is evil can confer honour, because to honour something is to confer marvellous benefits upon it; and anyone who reckons he is magnifying his soul by flattery or gifts or indulgence, so that he fails to make it better than it was before, may *think* he is honouring it, but in fact that is not what he is doing at all. For instance, a person has only to reach adolescence to imagine he is capable of deciding everything; he thinks he is honouring his soul if he praises it, and he is only too keen to tell it to

727

do what it likes. But our present doctrine is that in doing this he is not honouring but harming it; whereas we are arguing that he should honour it next after the gods. Similarly when a man thinks that the responsibility for his every fault lies not in himself but in others, whom he blames for his most frequent and serious misfortunes, while exonerating himself, he doubtless supposes he is honouring his soul. But far from doing that, he is injuring it. Again, when he indulges his pleasures and disobeys the recommendations and advice of the legislator, he is not honouring his soul at all, but dishonouring it, by filling it with misery and repentance. Or, to take the opposite case, he may not brace himself to endure the recommended toils and fears and troubles and pains, and simply give up; but his surrender confers no honour on his soul, because all such conduct brings disgrace upon it. Nor does he do it any honour if he thinks that life is a good thing no matter what the cost. This too dishonours his soul, because he surrenders to its fancy that everything in the next world is an evil, whereas he should resist the thought and enlighten his soul by demonstrating that he does not really know whether our encounter with the gods in the next world may not be in fact the best thing that ever happens to us. And when a man values beauty above virtue, the disrespect he shows his soul is total and fundamental, because he would argue that the body is more to be honoured than the soul – falsely, because nothing born of earth is to be honoured more than what comes from heaven; and anyone who holds a different view of the soul does not realize how wonderful is this possession which he scorns. Again, a man who is seized by lust to obtain money by improper means and feels no disgust in the acquisition, will find that in the event he does his soul no honour by such gifts – far from it: he sells all that gives the soul its beauty and value for a few paltry pieces of gold; but all the gold upon the earth and all the gold beneath it does not compensate for lack of virtue.

To sum up, the legislator will list and classify certain things as disgraceful and wicked, and others as fine and good; everyone who is not prepared to make all efforts to refrain from the one kind of action and practise the other to the limits of his power must be unaware that in all such conduct he is treating his soul, the most holy possession he has, in the most disrespectful and abominable manner. You see, practically no one takes into account the greatest 'judgement', as it is called, on wrongdoing. This is to grow to resemble men who are evil, and as the resemblance increases to shun good men and their wholesome conversation and to cut oneself off from them, while seeking to attach oneself to the other kind and keep their company. The inevitable result of consorting with such people is that what you do and have done to you is exactly what *they* naturally do and say to each other. Consequently, this condition is not really a 'judgement' at all, because justice and judgement are fine things: it is mere punishment, suffering that follows a wrongdoing. Now whether a man is made to suffer or not, he is equally wretched. In the former case he is not cured, in the latter he will ultimately be killed to ensure the safety of many others.[2]

To put it in a nutshell, 'honour' is to cleave to what is superior, and, where practicable, to make as perfect as possible what is deficient. Nothing that nature gives a man is better adapted than his soul to enable him to avoid evil, keep on the track of the highest good, and when he has captured his quarry to live in intimacy with it for the rest of his life.

PHYSICAL FITNESS

For those reasons the soul has been allotted the second rank of honour;[3] third – as everyone will realize – comes the

2. That is, absence of punishment (suffering) will mean you are not deterred from crime and will go from bad to worse until you have to be executed as incorrigible (cf. p. 358), and as an example to deter others from inviting the same fate. But if you *are* made to suffer, you will become resentful and turn to crime again. 'Judgement' is a scientifically designed measure to *cure* vice; retributive 'punishment' is only the infliction of suffering.

3. The first rank being given to the gods (p. 189).

honour naturally due to the body. Here again it is necessary to examine the various reasons for honouring it, and see which are genuine and which are false; this is the job of a legislator, and I imagine he will list them as follows. The body that deserves to be honoured is not the handsome one or the strong or the swift – nor yet the healthy (though a good many people would think it was); and it is certainly not the one with the opposite qualities to all these. He will say that the body which achieves a mean between all these extreme conditions is by far the soundest and best-balanced, because the one extreme makes the soul bold and boastful, while the other makes it abject and grovelling.

WEALTH

The same is true of the possession of money and goods: its value is measured by the same yardstick. Both, in excess, produce enmity and feuds in private and public life, while a deficiency almost invariably leads to slavery.

THE CORRECT TREATMENT OF CHILDREN

No one should be keen on making money for the sake of leaving his children as rich as possible, because it will not do them any good, or the state either. A child's fortune will be most in harmony with his circumstances, and superior to all other fortunes, if it is modest enough not to attract flatterers, but sufficient to supply all his needs; to our ears such a fortune strikes exactly the right note, and it frees our life from anxiety. Extreme modesty, not gold, is the legacy we should leave our children. We imagine that the way to bequeath them modesty is to rebuke them when they are immodest, but that is not the result produced in the young when people admonish them nowadays and tell them that youth must show respect to everyone. The sensible legislator will prefer to instruct the older men to show respect to their juniors, and to take especial care not to let any young man see or hear them doing or saying anything disgraceful: where the old are shameless the young too will inevitably be disrespectful to a degree. The best way to educate the younger generation (as well as yourself) is not to rebuke them but patently to practise all your life what you preach to others.

DUTIES TO RELATIVES, FRIENDS AND STATE

If a man honours and respects his relatives, who all share the worship of the family gods and have the same blood in their veins, he can reasonably expect to have the gods of birth look with benevolence on the procreation of his own children. And as for friends and companions, you will find them easier to get on with in day-to-day contact if you make more of their services to you and esteem them more highly than they do, and put a smaller value on your own good turns to your friends and companions than they do themselves. In dealings with the state and one's fellow-citizens, the best man by far is the one who, rather than win a prize at Olympia or in any of the other contests in war and peace, would prefer to beat everyone by his reputation for serving the laws of his country – a reputation for having devoted a lifetime of service to them with more distinction than anyone else.

DUTIES TO FOREIGNERS

As to foreigners, one should regard agreements made with them as particularly sacrosanct. Practically all offences committed as between or against foreigners are quicker to attract the vengeance of God than offences as between fellow-citizens. The foreigner is not surrounded by friends and companions, and stirs the compassion of gods and men that much more, so that anyone who has the power to avenge him comes to his aid more readily; and that power is possessed pre-eminently by the guardian spirit or god, companion of Zeus the God of Strangers, who is concerned 730 in each case. Anyone who takes the smallest thought for the future will therefore take great care to reach the end of his days without having committed during his life any crime involving foreigners. The most serious of offences against foreigners or natives is always that affecting suppliants; the god the victim supplicated and invoked when he won his promise becomes a devoted protector of his suppliant, who can consequently rely on the promise he received never to suffer without vengeance being taken for the wrongs done to him.

We've now dealt fairly thoroughly with a man's treatment of his parents, himself and his own possessions, and his contacts with the state, his friends, his relatives, foreigners and countrymen. The next question for consideration is the sort of person he must be himself, if he is to acquit himself with distinction in his journey through life; it's not the influence of law that we're concerned with now, but the educational effect of praise and blame, which makes the individual easier to handle and better disposed towards the laws that are to be established.

PERSONAL MORALITY

Truth heads the list of all things good, for gods and men alike. Let anyone who intends to be happy and blessed be its partner from the start, so that he may live as much of his life as possible a man of truth. You can trust a man like that, but not the man who is fond of telling deliberate lies (and anyone who is happy to go on producing falsehoods in *ignorance* of the truth is an idiot). Neither state is anything to envy: no one has any friends if he is a fool or cannot be trusted. As the years go by he is recognized for what he is, and in the difficulties of old age as life draws to its close he isolates himself completely; he has just about as much contact with his surviving friends and children as with those who are already dead.

A man who commits no crime is to be honoured; yet the man who will not even allow the wicked to do wrong deserves more than twice as much respect. The former has the value of a single individual, but the latter, who reveals the wickedness of another to the authorities, is worth a legion. Anyone who makes every effort to assist the authorities in checking crime should be declared to be the great and perfect citizen of his state, winner of the prize for virtue.

The same praise should also be given to self-control and good judgement, and to all the other virtues which the possessor can communicate to others as well as displaying in his own person. If a man does so communicate them, he should be honoured as in the top rank; if he is prepared to communicate them but lacks the ability, he must be left in second place; but if he is a jealous fellow and churlishly wants to monopolize his virtues, then we should certainly censure him, but without holding the virtue itself in less 731 esteem because of its possessor – on the contrary, we should do our best to acquire it. We want everyone to compete in the struggle for virtue in a generous spirit, because this is the way a man will be a credit to his state – by competing on his own account but refraining from fouling the chances of others by slander. The jealous man, who thinks he has to get the better of others by being rude about them, makes less effort himself to attain true virtue and discourages his competitors by unfair criticism. In this way he hinders the whole state's struggle to achieve virtue and diminishes its reputation, in so far as it depends on him.

HOW TO HANDLE CRIMINALS

Every man should combine in his character high spirit with the utmost gentleness, because there is only one way to get out of the reach of crimes committed by other people and which are dangerous or even impossible to cure: you have to overcome them by fighting in self-defence and rigidly punishing them, and no soul can do this without righteous indignation. On the other hand there are some criminals whose crimes are curable, and the first thing to realize here is that every unjust man is unjust against his will. No man on earth would ever deliberately embrace any of the supreme evils, least of all in the most precious parts of himself – and as we said, the truth is that the most precious part of every man is his soul. So no one will ever voluntarily accept the supreme evil into the most valuable part of himself and live with it throughout his life. No: in general, the unjust man deserves just as much pity as any other sufferer. And you may pity the criminal whose disease is curable, and restrain and abate your anger, instead of persisting in it with the spitefulness of a shrew; but when you have to deal with complete and unmanageably vicious corruption, you must let your anger off its leash. That is why we say that it must be the good man's duty to be high-spirited or gentle as circumstances require.

SELFISHNESS

The most serious vice innate in most men's souls is one for which everybody forgives himself and so never tries to find a way of escaping. You can get some idea of this vice from the saying that a man is in the nature of the case 'his own best friend', and that it is perfectly proper for him to have to play this role. It is truer to say that the cause of each and every crime we commit is precisely this excessive love of ourselves, a love which blinds us to the faults of the beloved and makes us bad judges of goodness and beauty and justice, because we believe we should honour our own ego rather than the truth. Anyone with aspirations to greatness must admire not himself and his own possessions, but acts of justice, not only when they are his own, but especially when they happen to be done by someone else. It's because of this same vice of selfishness that stupid people are always convinced of their own shrewdness, which is why we think we know everything when we are almost totally ignorant, so that thanks to not leaving to others what we don't know how to handle, we inevitably come to grief when we try to tackle it ourselves. For these reasons, then, every man must steer clear of extreme love of himself, and be loyal to his superior instead; and he mustn't be put off by shame at the thought of abandoning that 'best friend'.

EXTREMES OF EMOTION TO BE AVOIDED

There is a certain amount of more detailed but no less useful advice which one hears often enough, and one should go through it to oneself by way of reminder. (Where waters ebb, there is always a corresponding flow, and the act of remembering is the 'flow' of thought that has drained away.[4])

So then: excessive laughter and tears must be avoided, and this is the advice every man must give to every other; one should try to behave decently by suppressing all extremes of joy and grief, both when one's guardian angel brings continued prosperity and when in times of trouble our guardians face difficulties as insurmountable as a high, sheer cliff. We should always have the hope that the blessings God sends will decrease the troubles that assail us, change our present circumstances for the better, and make us lucky enough to see our good fortune always increase. These are the hopes that every man should live by; he must remember all this advice and never spare any effort to recall it vividly to his own mind and that of others, at work and in leisure time alike.

Now then, from the point of view of religion, we've expounded pretty thoroughly what sort of activities we should pursue and what sort of person the individual ought to be; but we have not yet come down to the purely secular level. But we must, because we are addressing men, not gods.

VIRTUE AND HAPPINESS

Human nature involves, above all, pleasures, pains, and desires, and no mortal animal can help being hung up dangling in the air (so to speak) in total dependence on these powerful influences. That is why we should praise the noblest life – not only because it enjoys a fine and glorious reputation, but because (provided one is prepared to try it 733

4. This curious parenthesis may be a note Plato intended to elaborate later.

out instead of recoiling from it as a youth) it excels in providing what we all seek: a predominance of pleasure over pain throughout our lives. That this result is guaranteed, if it is tried out in the correct manner, will be perfectly obvious in an instant. But what is 'correctness' here? One should consider this point in the light of the following thesis. We have to ask if one condition suits our nature while another does not, and weigh the pleasant life against the painful with that question in mind. We want to have pleasure; we neither choose nor want pain; we prefer the neutral state if we are thereby relieved of pain, but not if it involves the loss of pleasure. We want less pain and more pleasure, we do not want less pleasure and more pain; but we should be hard put to it to be clear about our wishes when faced with a choice of two situations bringing pleasure and pain in the same proportions. These considerations of number or size or intensity or equality (or their opposites) which determine our wishes all influence or fail to influence us whenever we make a choice. This being inevitably the way of things, we want a life in which pleasures and pains come frequently and with great intensity, but with pleasure predominating; if pains predominate, we reject that life. Similarly when pleasures and pains are few and small and feeble: if pain outweighs pleasure, we do not want that life, but we do when pleasure outweighs pain. As for the 'average' life, which experiences only moderate pleasures or pains, we should observe the same point as before: we desire it when it offers us a preponderance of pleasure (which we enjoy), but not when it offers us a preponderance of pain (which we abhor). In that sense, then, we should think of all human lives as bound up in these two feelings, and we must think to what kind of life our natural wishes incline. But if we assert that we want anything outside this range, we are talking out of ignorance and inexperience of life as it is really lived.

So when a man has decided his wishes and aversions, what he would willingly do and what not, and adopted that as a working rule to guide him in choosing what he finds congenial and pleasant and supremely excellent, he will select a life that will enable him to live as happily as a man can. So what are these lives, and how many are there, from which he must make this choice? Let us list them: there is the life of self-control for one, the life of wisdom for another, and the life of courage too; and let us treat the healthy life as another. As opposed to these, we have another four lives – the licentious, the foolish, the cowardly and the diseased. Now anyone who knows what the life of self-control is like will describe it as gentle in all respects, with mild pleasures and pains, light appetites, and desires without frenzy; the licentious life he will say is violent through and through, involving extreme pleasures and pains, intense and raging appetites and desires of extreme fury. He will say that in the life of self-control the pleasures outweigh the pains, and in the licentious life the pains exceed the pleasures, in point of size, number and frequency. That is why we inevitably and naturally find the former life more pleasant, the latter more painful, and anyone who means to live a pleasant life no longer has the option of living licentiously. On the contrary, it is already clear (if our present position is correct) that if a man is licentious it must be without intending to be. It is either because of ignorance or lack of self-control, or both, that the world at large lives immoderately. The healthy and unhealthy life should be regarded in the same way: they both offer pleasures and pains, but the pleasures outweigh the pains in the healthy life, vice versa in the unhealthy. But what we want when we choose between lives is not a predominance of pain: we have chosen as the pleasanter life the one where pain is the weaker element. And so we can say that the self-controlled, the wise and the courageous, experience pleasure and pain with less intensity and on a smaller and more restricted scale than the profligate, the fool and the coward. The first category beats the second on the score of pleasure, while the second beats the other when it comes to pain. The courageous man does better than the coward, the wise man than the fool; so that, life for life, the former

734

kind – the restrained, the courageous, the wise and the healthy – is pleasanter than the cowardly, the foolish, the licentious and the unhealthy.

To sum up, the life of physical fitness, and spiritual virtue too, is not only pleasanter than the life of depravity but superior in other ways as well: it makes for beauty, an upright posture, efficiency and a good reputation, so that if a man lives a life like that it will make his whole existence infinitely happier than his opposite number's.

§9. THE FOUNDATION OF THE NEW STATE

The Athenian now passes from preface to law. He deals with the choice of a site for the new state, the selection of the first citizens, the various divisions of land and people, and some of the basic economic rules that will be observed. He takes the opportunity at this early stage in the new state's history to make it quite clear that the legislator will have to modify his plans in the light of prevailing circumstances, and to illustrate the point he takes the institution of property. Complete communism is the ideal, but in the present case limited private property will have to be allowed, and perhaps in other circumstances it might be necessary to go even further. The essential point for us, however, is that this is utopian political philosophy: the legislator is always to keep an ideal pattern in mind, to which men must conform as closely as they can be made to. The section is largely self-explanatory, but the reader should be warned that some of the details of the division of the land and people are rather difficult to understand: the Athenian's exposition is not as clear as we should like.

The word 'colony' occurs frequently: it is of course used not in the modern sense of 'subject territory', but in the sense of 'new state formed by citizens who have left their home land' (though the mother city might still retain some degree of control).

The 'Preliminary Analysis' is something of a false start, because the distinction it makes is not in fact developed and utilized until the beginning of §10.

PRELIMINARY ANALYSIS OF THE STATE

ATHENIAN: At this point we may stop expounding the preface to the laws, it being now complete. After the 'prelude' should come the 'tune',[1] or (more accurately) a sketch of a legal and political framework. Now it is impossible, when

1. A pun: the Greek *nomos* means both 'tune' and 'law'. Cf. p. 185.

dealing with a web or any piece of weaving, to construct the warp and the woof from the same stuff: the warp must be of 735 a superior type of material (strong and firm in character, while the woof is softer and suitably workable). In a rather similar way it will be reasonable to distinguish between the authorities who are going to rule in a city and the citizens whose education has been slighter and less testing. You may assume, you see, that there are two elements in a political system: the installation of individuals in office, and equipping those officials with a code of laws.

THE SELECTION OF THE CITIZENS

But before all that, here are some further points to notice. Anyone who takes charge of a herd of animals – a shepherd or cattle-man or breeder of horses or what have you – will never get down to looking after them without first performing the purge appropriate to his particular animal-community: that is, he will weed out the unhealthy and inferior stock and send it off to other herds, and keep only the thoroughbreds and the healthy animals to look after. He knows that otherwise he would have to waste endless effort on sickly and refractory beasts, degenerate by nature and ruined by incompetent breeding, and that unless he purges the existing stock these faults will spread in any herd to the animals that are still physically and temperamentally healthy and unspoilt. This is not too serious in the case of the lower animals, and we need mention it only by way of illustration, but with human beings it is vitally important for the legislator to ascertain and explain the appropriate measures in each case, not only as regards a purge, but in general. To purge a whole state, for instance, several methods may be employed, some mild, some drastic; and if a legislator were a dictator too he'd be able to purge the state drastically, which is the best way. But if he has to establish a new society and new laws without dictatorial powers, and succeeds in administering no more than the mildest purge, he'll be well content even with this limited achievement. Like drastic medicines, the best purge is a painful business: it involves chastisement by a combination of 'judgement' and 'punishment',[2] and takes the latter, ultimately, to the point of death or exile. That usually gets rid of the major criminals who are incurable and do the state enormous harm. The milder purge we could adopt is this. When there is a shortage of food, and the underprivileged show themselves ready to follow their leaders in an attack on the property of the privileged, they are to be regarded as a disease that has developed in the body politic, and in the friendliest possible way they should be (as it will tactfully be put) 'transferred to a colony'. Somehow or other everyone who legislates must do this in good time; but our position at the moment is even more unusual. There's no need for us here and now to have resort to a colony or arrange to make a selection of people by a purge. No: it's as though we have a number of streams from several sources, some from springs, some from mountain torrents, all flowing down to unite in one lake. We have to apply ourselves to seeing that the water, as it mingles, is as pure as possible, partly by draining some of it off, partly by diverting it into different channels. Even so, however you organize a society, it looks as if there will always be trouble and risk. True enough: but seeing that we are operating at the moment on a theoretical rather than a practical level, let's suppose we've recruited our citizens and their purity meets with our approval. After all, when we have screened the bad candidates over a suitable period and given them every chance to be converted, we can refuse their application to enter and become citizens of the state; but we should greet the good ones with all possible courtesy and kindness.

DISTRIBUTING THE LAND (I)

We should not forget that we are in the same fortunate position as the Heraclids when they founded their colony: we noticed[3] how they avoided vicious and dangerous disputes

---

2. See p. 191 and note there. 'Judgement' can evidently involve the use of mere 'punishment': see p. 368.

3. See p. 130.

about land and cancellations of debts and distribution of property. When an old-established state is forced to resort to legislation to deal with these problems, it finds that both leaving things as they are and reforming them are somehow equally impossible. The only policy left them is to mouth pious hopes and make a little cautious progress over a long period by advancing a step at a time. (This is the way it can be done. From time to time some of the reformers should be themselves great land-owners and have a large number of debtors; and they should be prepared, in a philanthropic spirit, to share their prosperity with those debtors who are in distress, partly by remitting debts and partly by making land available for distribution. Their policy will be a policy of moderation, dictated by the conviction that poverty is a matter of increased greed rather than diminished wealth. This belief is fundamental to the success of a state, and is the firm base on which you can later build whatever political structure is appropriate to such conditions[4] as we have described. But 737 when these first steps towards reform falter,[5] subsequent constitutional action in any state will be hard going.) Now as we say, such difficulties do not affect us. Nevertheless, it's better to have explained how we could have escaped them if they had. Let's take it, then, that the explanation has been given: the way to escape those difficulties is through a sense of justice combined with an indifference to wealth; there is no other route, broad or narrow, by which we can avoid them. So let's adopt this principle as a prop for our state. Somehow or other we must ensure that the citizens' property does not lead to disputes among them – otherwise, if people have long-standing complaints against each other, anyone with any sense at all will not go any further with organizing them, if he can help it. But when, as with us now, God has given a group of people a new state to found, in which so far there is no

4. I.e. sharing of property, etc. The thought is cloudily expressed. I suppose the Athenian means that if you want a political structure that presupposes a sharing of land, this in turn must presuppose citizens who believe that poverty is a state of mind.

5. I.e. they are not sufficiently inspired by this belief about poverty.

mutual malice – well, to stir up ill-will towards each other because of the way they distribute the land and houses would be so criminally stupid that no man could bring himself to do it.

So what's the correct method of distribution? First, one has to determine what the total number of people ought to be, then agree on the question of the distribution of the citizens and decide the number and size of the subsections into which they ought to be divided; and the land and houses must be divided equally (so far as possible) among these subsections. A suitable total for the number of citizens cannot be fixed without considering the land and the neighbouring states. The land must be extensive enough to support a given number of people in modest comfort, and not a foot more is needed. The inhabitants should be numerous enough to be able to defend themselves when the adjacent peoples attack them, and contribute at any rate some assistance to neighbouring societies when they are wronged. When we have inspected the land and its neighbours, we'll determine these points and give reasons for the action we take; but for the moment let's just give an outline sketch and get on with finishing our legislation.

THE SIZE OF THE POPULATION (I)

Let's assume we have the convenient number of five thousand and forty farmers and protectors of their holdings, and let the land with its houses be divided up into the same number of parts, so that a man and his holding always go together. Divide the total first by two, then by three: you'll see it can be divided by four and five and every number right up to ten. Everyone who legislates should have sufficient appreciation of arithmetic to know what number will be most use in every 738 state, and why. So let's fix on the one which has the largest number of consecutive divisors. Of course, an infinite series of numbers would admit all possible divisions for all possible uses, but our 5040 admits no more than 59 (including 1 to 10 without a break), which will have to suffice for purposes of war and every peacetime activity, all contracts and dealings, and for taxes and grants.

RELIGIOUS AND SOCIAL OCCASIONS

Anyone who is legally obliged to understand these mathematical facts should try to deepen his understanding of them even in his spare time. They really are just as I say, and the founder of a state needs to be told of them, for the following reasons. It doesn't matter whether he's founding a new state from scratch or reconstructing an old one that has gone to ruin: in either case, if he has any sense, he will never dream of altering whatever instructions may have been received from Delphi or Dodona or Ammon[6] about the gods and temples that ought to be founded by the various groups in the state, and the gods or spirits after whom the temples should be named. (Alternatively, such details may have been suggested by stories told long ago of visions or divine inspiration, which somehow moved people to institute sacrifices with their rituals – either native or taken from Etruria or Cyprus or some other country – so that on the strength of these reports they consecrated statues, altars, temples and sites of oracles, providing each with its own sacred plot of land.) The legislator must not tamper with any of this in the slightest detail. He must allocate to each division of citizens a god or spirit or perhaps a hero,[7] and when he divides up the territory he must give these priority by setting aside plots of land for them, endowed with all the appropriate resources. Thus when the different divisions gather together at fixed times they will have an opportunity of satisfying their various needs, and the citizens will recognize and greet each other at the sacrifices in mutual friendship – and there can be no greater benefit for a state than that the citizens should be well-known one to another. Where they have no insight into each other's

6. The most celebrated of these oracles was that of Apollo at Delphi, on the southern slopes of Mount Parnassus, north of the gulf of Corinth. Dodona was an oracle of Zeus in Epirus (north-west Greece); Ammon was a deity whose oracle was established at the oasis of Siwa in the Libyan desert.

7. Illustrious men who have become minor deities after death.

characters and are kept in the dark about them, no one will ever enjoy the respect he merits or fill the office he deserves or obtain the legal verdict to which he is entitled. So every citizen of every state should make a particular effort to show that he is straightforward and genuine, not shifty, and try to avoid being hoodwinked by anyone who is.

STATES IDEAL AND REAL: COMMUNITY OF PROPERTY

The next gambit in this game of legislation is as unusual as 739 going 'across the line' in draughts, and may well cause surprise at first hearing.[8] But reflection and experience will soon show that the organization of a state is almost bound to fall short of the ideal. You may, perhaps – if you don't know what it means to be a legislator without dictatorial powers – refuse to countenance such a state; nevertheless the right procedure is to describe not only the ideal society but the second and third best too, and then leave it to anyone in charge of founding a community to make a choice between them. So let's follow this procedure now: let's describe the absolutely ideal society, then the second-best, then the third. On this occasion we ought to leave the choice to Cleinias, but we should not forget anyone else who may at some time be faced with such a choice and wish to adopt for his own purposes customs of his native country which he finds valuable.

You'll find the ideal society and state, and the best code of laws, where the old saying 'friends' property is genuinely shared'[9] is put into practice as widely as possible throughout the entire state. Now I don't know whether in fact this situation – a community of wives, children and all property – exists anywhere today, or will ever exist, but at any rate in such a state the notion of 'private property' will have been

8. The (risky) 'gambit' of the legislator is to recognize that the ideal state is impracticable, given the weakness of human nature.

9. The Athenian slips in the word 'genuinely', thus suggesting that he will apply the proverb in a special way.

by hook or by crook completely eliminated from life. Everything possible will have been done to throw into a sort of common pool even what is by nature 'my own', like eyes and ears and hands, in the sense that to judge by appearances they all see and hear and act in concert. Everybody feels pleasure and pain at the same things, so that they all praise and blame with complete unanimity. To sum up, the laws in force impose the greatest possible unity on the state – and you'll never produce a better or truer criterion of an absolutely perfect law than that. It may be that gods or a number of the children of gods inhabit this kind of state: if so, the life they live there, observing these rules, is a happy one indeed. And so men need look no further for their ideal: they should keep this state in view and try to find the one that most nearly resembles it. This is what we've put our hand to, and if in some way it could be realized, it would come very near immortality and be second only to the ideal. Later, God willing, we'll describe a third best. But for the moment, what description should we give of this second-best state? What's the method by which a state like that is produced?

DISTRIBUTING THE LAND (2)

First of all, the citizens must make a distribution of land and houses; they must not farm in common, which is a practice too demanding for those born and bred and educated as ours are. But the distribution should be made with some such intention as this: each man who receives a portion of land should regard it as the common possession of the entire state. The land is his ancestral home and he must cherish it even more than children cherish their mother; furthermore, Earth is a goddess, and mistress of mortal men. (And the gods and spirits already established in the locality must be treated with the same respect.)

THE SIZE OF THE POPULATION (2)

Additional measures must be taken to make sure that these arrangements are permanent: the number of hearths established by the initial distribution must always remain the same; it must neither increase nor decrease. The best way for every state to ensure this will be as follows: the recipient of a holding should always leave from among his children only *one* heir to inherit his establishment. This will be his favourite son, who will succeed him and give due worship to the ancestors (who rank as gods) of the family and state; these must be taken to include not only those who have already passed on, but also those who are still alive. As for the other children, in cases where there are more than one, the head of the family should marry off the females in accordance with the law we shall establish later; the males he must present for adoption to those citizens who have no children of their own — priority to be given to personal preferences as far as possible. But some people may have no preferences, or other families too may have surplus offspring, male or female; or, to take the opposite problem, they may have too few, because of the onset of sterility. All these cases will be investigated by the highest and most distinguished official we shall appoint. He will decide what is to be done with the surpluses or deficiencies, and will do his best to discover a device to keep the number of households down to 5040. There are many devices available: if too many children are being born, there are measures to check propagation; on the other hand, a high birth-rate can be encouraged and stimulated by conferring marks of distinction or disgrace, and the young can be admonished by words of warning from their elders. This approach should do the trick, and if in the last resort we are in complete despair about variations from our number of 5040 households, and the mutal love of wives and husbands produces an excessive flow of citizens that drives us to distraction, we have that old expedient at hand, which we have often mentioned before. We can send out colonies of people that seem suitable, with mutual goodwill between the emigrants and their mother-city. By contrast, we may be flooded with a wave of diseases or by the ravages of wars, so that bereave- 741 ments depress the citizens far below the appointed number. In this event we ought not to import citizens who have been brought up by a bastard education, if we can help it; but not even God, they say, can grapple with necessity.

HOLDINGS ARE INALIENABLE

So let's pretend our thesis can talk and gives us this advice: 'My dear sirs, don't ignore the facts and be careless enough to undervalue the concepts of likeness, equality, identity and agreement, either in mathematics or in any other useful and productive science. In particular, your first task now is to keep to the said number as long as you live; you must respect the upper limits of the total property which you originally distributed as being reasonable, and not buy and sell your holdings among yourselves. The lot by which they were distributed is a god, so there will be no support for you there, or from the legislator either. And there are two warnings the law has for the disobedient: (A) You may choose or decline to take part in the distribution, but if you do take part you must observe the following conditions: (i) you must acknowledge that the land is sacred to all the gods; (ii) after priests and priestesses have offered prayers for that intention at the first, second and third sacrifices,

1. anyone buying or selling his allotted land or house *must suffer* the penalty appropriate to the crime.

You are to inscribe the details on pieces of cypress-wood and put these written records on permanent deposit in the temples. (B) You must appoint the official who seems to have the sharpest eyes to superintend the observance of the rule, so that the various contraventions may be brought to your notice and the disobedient punished by the law and the god[10] alike. What a boon this rule is to all the states that observe it, given the appropriate arrangements, no wicked men – as the saying goes – will ever understand; such knowledge is the fruit of experience and virtuous habits.[11] Such arrangements, you see, involve very little by way of profit-making, and there is

10. Presumably the one mentioned above on this page.
11. Cf. pp. 197-8.

no need or opportunity for anyone to engage in any of the vulgar branches of commerce (you know how a gentleman's character is coarsened by manual labour, which is generally admitted to be degrading), and no one will presume to rake in money from occupations such as that.'

THE POSSESSION OF MONEY

All these considerations suggest a further law that runs like this: no private person shall be allowed to possess any gold or silver, but only coinage for day-to-day dealings which one 742 can hardly avoid having with workmen and all other indispensable people of that kind (we have to pay wages to slaves and foreigners who work for money). For these purposes, we agree, they must possess coinage, legal tender among themselves, but valueless to the rest of mankind. The common Greek coinage is to be used for expeditions and visits to the outside world, such as when a man has to be sent abroad as an ambassador or to convey some official message; to meet these occasions the state must always have a supply of Greek coinage. If a private individual should ever need to go abroad, he should first obtain leave of the authorities, and if he returns home with some surplus foreign money in his pocket he must deposit it with the state and take local money to the same value in exchange.

2. If he is found keeping it for himself,
it must be confiscated by the state.

3. If anyone who knows of its concealment fails to report it, *he must* be liable to a curse and a reproach (and so must the importer), and in addition be fined in a sum not less than that of the foreign currency brought in.

When a man marries or gives in marriage, no dowry whatsoever must be given or received. Money must not be deposited with anybody whom one does not trust. There must be no lending at interest, because it will be quite in order for the borrower to refuse absolutely to return both interest and principal.

The best way to appreciate that these are the best policies for a state to follow is to examine them in the light of the fundamental aim. Now we maintain that the aim of a statesman who knows what he's about is not in fact the one which most people say the good legislator should have. They'd say that if he knows what he's doing his laws should make the state as huge and as rich as possible; he should give the citizens gold mines and silver mines, and enable them to control as many people as possible by land and sea. And they'd add, too, that to be a satisfactory legislator he must want to see the state as good and as happy as possible. But some of these demands are practical politics, and some are not, and the legislator will confine himself to what can be done, without bothering his head with wishful thinking about impossibilities. I mean, it's pretty well inevitable that happiness and virtue should come hand in hand (and this is the situation the legislator will want to see), but virtue and great wealth are quite incompatible, at any rate great wealth as generally understood (most people would think of the extreme case of a millionaire, who will of course be a rogue into the bargain). 743 In view of all this, I'll never concede to them that the rich man can become really happy without being virtuous as well: to be extremely virtuous and exceptionally rich at the same time is absolutely out of the question. 'Why?' it may be asked.[12] 'Because,' we shall reply, 'the profit from using just *and* unjust methods is more than twice as much as that from just methods alone, and a man who refuses to spend his money either honestly or dishonestly spends only half the sum laid out by honest people who are prepared to spend on honest purposes too.[13] So anyone who follows the opposite policy[14]

12. The answer to this question is confusing and extraordinarily elaborate, but in essence it seems to be only an appeal to the 'facts'. Great wealth is the result either of unjust gains or at best parsimony; honesty leads to modest wealth or a competence; and poverty is likely to be the result of extravagance. Thus anything but the mean seems incompatible with virtue.

13. I.e. as well as on 'neutral' objects.

14. I.e. of spending on good objects and confining his receipts to those obtainable by honest methods.

will never become richer than the man who gets twice as much profit from half the expenditure. The former is a good man; the latter is not actually a rogue so long as he uses his money sparingly, but on some occasions[15] he is an absolute villain; thus, as we have said, he is *never* good. Ill-gotten and well-gotten gains plus expenditure that is neither just nor unjust, when a man is also sparing with his money, add up to wealth; the absolute rogue, who is generally a spendthrift, is quite impoverished. The man who spends his money for honest ends and uses only just methods to come by it, will not easily become particularly rich or particularly poor. Our thesis is therefore correct: the very rich are not good; and if they are not good, they are not happy either.'

The whole point of our legislation was to allow the citizens to live supremely happy lives in the greatest possible mutual friendship. However, they will never be friends if injuries and lawsuits arise among them on a grand scale, but only if they are trivial and rare. That is why we maintain that neither gold nor silver should exist in the state, and there should not be much money made out of menial trades and charging interest, nor from prostitutes;[16] the citizens' wealth should be limited to the products of farming, and even here a man should not be able to make so much that he can't help forgetting the real reason why money was invented (I mean for the care of the soul and body, which without physical and cultural education respectively will never develop into anything worth mentioning). That's what has made us say more than once[17] that the pursuit of money should come last in the scale of value. Every man directs his efforts to three things in all, and if his efforts are directed with a correct sense of priorities he will give money the third and lowest place, and his soul the highest, with his body coming somewhere between the two. In particular, if this scale of values prevails in the society we're now describing, then it has been equipped with a good code of laws. But if any of the laws subsequently passed is found

15. I.e. when he *makes* money (by dishonest means).
16. Literally, 'shocking fatted beasts', presumably a euphemism.
17. E.g. pp. 55 and 149.

744 giving pride of place to health in the state rather than the virtue of self-control, or to wealth rather than health and habits of restraint, then quite obviously its priorities will be wrong. So the legislator must repeatedly try to get this sort of thing straight in his own mind by asking 'What do I want to achieve?' and 'Am I achieving it, or am I off target?' If he does that, perhaps he'll complete his legislation by his own efforts and leave nothing to be done by others. There's no other way he could possibly succeed.

THE FOUR PROPERTY-CLASSES

So when a man has drawn his lot, he must take over his holding on the terms stated.[18] It would have been an advantage if no one entering the colony had had any more property than anyone else; but that's out of the question, and some people will arrive with relatively large fortunes, others with relatively little. So for a number of reasons, and especially because the state offers equality[19] of opportunity, there must be graded property-classes, to ensure that offices and taxes and grants may be arranged on the basis of what a man is worth. It's not only his personal virtues or his ancestors' that should be considered, or his physical strength or good looks: what he's made of his wealth or poverty should also be taken into account. In short, the citizens must be esteemed and given office, so far as possible, on exactly equal terms of 'proportional inequality',[19] so as to avoid ill-feeling. For these reasons four permanent property-classes must be established, graded according to wealth: the 'first', 'second', 'third', and 'fourth' classes, or whatever other names are employed. A man will either keep his original classification, or, when he has grown richer or poorer than he was before, transfer to the appropriate class.

In view of all this, the next law I'd pass would be along the following lines. (We maintain that if a state is to avoid the greatest plague of all – I mean civil war, though civil disintegration would be a better term – extreme poverty and

18. See p. 210.   19. These words are elucidated on pp. 229–30.

wealth must not be allowed to arise in any section of the citizen-body, because both lead to both these disasters. That is why the legislator must now announce the acceptable limits of wealth and poverty.) The lower limit of poverty must be the value of the holding (which is to be permanent: no official nor anyone else who has ambitions to be thought virtuous will ever overlook the diminution of any man's holding). The legislator will use the holding as his unit of measure and allow a man to possess twice, thrice, and up to four times its value. If anyone acquires more than this, by finding treasure-trove or by gift or by a good stroke of business or some other similar lucky chance which presents 745 him with more than he's allowed, he should hand over the surplus to the state and its patron deities, thereby escaping punishment and getting a good name for himself.

4. If a man breaks this law,
anyone who wishes may lay information and be rewarded with half the amount involved, the other half being given to the gods; and besides this the guilty person must pay a fine equivalent to the surplus out of his own pocket.

The total property of each citizen over and above his holding of land should be recorded in a public register kept in the custody of officials legally appointed for that duty, so that lawsuits on all subjects – in so far as they affect property – may go smoothly because the facts are clear.

ADMINISTRATIVE UNITS OF THE STATE

After this, the legislator's first job is to locate the city as precisely as possible in the centre of the country, provided that the site he chooses is a convenient one for a city in all other respects too (these are details which can be understood and specified easily enough). Next he must divide the country into twelve sections. But first he ought to reserve a sacred area for Hestia, Zeus and Athena[20] (calling it the 'acropolis'),

20. Hestia was the goddess of the hearth. Zeus and Athena have various functions (see the index): here they appear in their role as chief deities and patrons of the state: cf. p. 461.

and enclose its boundaries; he will then divide the city itself and the whole country into twelve sections by lines radiating from this central point.[21] The twelve sections should be made equal in the sense that a section should be smaller if the soil is good, bigger if it is poor. The legislator must then mark out five thousand and forty holdings, and further divide each into two parts; he should then make an individual holding consist of two such parts coupled so that each has a partner near the centre or the boundary of the state as the case may be. (A part near the city and a part next to the boundary should form one holding, the second nearest the city with the second from the boundary should form another, and so on.) He must apply to the two parts the rule I've just mentioned about the relative quality of the soil, making them equal by varying their size. He should also divide the population into twelve sections, and arrange to distribute among them as equally as possible all wealth over and above the actual holdings[22] (a comprehensive list will be compiled). Finally, they must allocate the sections as twelve 'holdings' for the twelve gods, consecrate each section to the particular god which it has drawn by lot, name it after him, and call it a 'tribe'. Again, they must divide the city into twelve sections in the same way as they divided the rest of the country; and each man should be allotted two houses, one near the centre of the state, one near the boundary.[23] That will finish off the job of getting the state founded.

THEORY TO BE MODIFIED BY FACTS

But there's a lesson here that we must take to heart. This blueprint as a whole is never likely to find such favourable circumstances that every single detail will turn out precisely

21. The sacred area is at the centre of the city, which is itself at the centre of the state. I slightly expand this and a few other sentences in this paragraph in the interests of clarity.

22. I.e. so that each section has about the same number of rich and poor men.

23. Cf. p. 256.

according to plan. It presupposes men who won't turn up [746] their noses at living in such a community, and who will tolerate a moderate and fixed level of wealth throughout their lives, and the supervision of the size of each individual's family as we've suggested.[24] Will people really put up with being deprived of gold and other things which, for reasons we went into just now, the legislator is obviously going to add to his list of forbidden articles? What about this description of a city and countryside with houses at the centre and in all directions round about? He might have been relating a dream, or modelling a state and its citizens out of wax. The ideal impresses well enough, but the legislator must reconsider it as follows (this being, then, a *reprise* of his address to us):[25] 'My friends, in these talks we're having, don't think it has escaped me either that the point of view you are urging has some truth in it. But I believe that in every project for future action, when you are displaying the ideal plan that ought to be put into effect, the most satisfactory procedure is to spare no detail of absolute truth and beauty. But if you find that one of these details is impossible in practice, you ought to put it on one side and not attempt it: you should see which of the remaining alternatives comes closest to it and is most nearly akin to your policy, and arrange to have that done instead. But you must let the legislator finish describing what he really wants to do, and only then join him in considering which of his proposals for legislation are feasible, and which are too difficult. You see, even the maker of the most trivial object must make it internally consistent if he is going to get any sort of reputation.'[26]

THE PRE-EMINENCE OF MATHEMATICS

Now that we've decided to divide the citizens into twelve sections, we should try to realize (after all, it's clear enough) the enormous number of divisors the subdivisions of each

24. See p. 209.   25. See pp. 207–8.

26. That is, the legislator must not mix ideal and second-best in the same programme.

section have, and reflect how these in turn can be further
subdivided and subdivided again until you get to 5040.[27] This
is the mathematical framework which will yield you your
brotherhoods, local administrative units,[28] villages, your military companies and marching-columns, as well as units of
coinage, liquid and dry measures, and weights. The law must
regulate all these details so that the proper proportions and
correspondences are observed. And not only that: the legislator should not be afraid of appearing to give undue attention to detail. He must be bold enough to give instructions
that the citizens are not to be allowed to possess any equipment that is not of standard size. He'll assume it's a general
747 rule that numerical division in all its variety can be usefully
applied to every field of conduct. It may be limited to the
complexities of arithmetic itself, or extended to the subtleties
of plane and solid geometry; it's also relevant to sound, and
to motion (straight up or down or revolution in a circle).
The legislator should take all this into account and instruct
all his citizens to do their best never to operate outside that
framework. For domestic and public purposes, and all professional skills, no single branch of a child's education has
such an enormous range of applications as mathematics; but
its greatest advantage is that it wakes up the sleepy ignoramus
and makes him quick to understand, retentive and sharp-
witted; and thanks to this miraculous science he does better
than his natural abilities would have allowed. These subjects
will form a splendidly appropriate curriculum, *if* by further
laws and customs you can expel the spirit of pettiness and
greed from the souls of those who are to master them and
profit from them. But if you fail, you'll find that without
noticing it you've produced a 'twister' instead of a man of
learning – just what can be seen to have happened in the case

27. $5040 = 12 \times 420$. 420 (a 'section') has many divisors (including
all numbers from 1 to 8), and several (e.g. 12, 15, 20) can be conveniently
subdivided. Division of all the 12 sections, if carried far enough, will
ultimately give you 5040.
28. The brotherhoods and units ('phratries' and 'demes') would be
subdivisions of the tribes (a tribe = 420 citizens).

of the Egyptians and Phoenicians, and many other races whose approach to wealth and life in general shows a narrow-minded outlook. (It may have been an incompetent legislator who was to blame for this state of affairs, or some stroke of bad luck, or even some natural influence that had the same effect.)

INFLUENCES OF CLIMATE

And that's another point about the choice of sites, Cleinias and Megillus, that we mustn't forget. Some localities are more likely than others to produce comparatively good (or bad) characters, and we must take care to lay down laws that do not fly in the face of such influences. Some sites are suitable or unsuitable because of varying winds or periods of heat, others because of the quality of the water; in some cases the very food grown in the soil can nourish or poison not only the body but the soul as well. But best of all will be the places where the breeze of heaven blows, where spirits hold possession of the land and greet with favour (or disfavour) the various people who come and settle there. The sensible legislator will ponder these influences as carefully as a man can, and then try to lay down laws that will take account of them. This is what you must do too, Cleinias. You're going to settle a territory, so here's the first thing you have to attend to.

CLEINIAS: Well said, sir. I must follow your advice.

§10. CIVIL AND LEGAL
ADMINISTRATION

*Now that the site has been chosen, the Athenian goes on to describe
the various officials that will run the new state. The first problem is
that of the transfer of power between the Cnossians who are in charge
of the foundation and the first officials of the colonists themselves.
Thereafter the regulations apply to the period when the state has
been properly founded and can manage its own affairs.*

*The details of the elections are sometimes very brief and confusing.
I have tried to remove some of the worst obscurities by the use of
footnotes, but it will also help the reader to know that elections
typically comprise the following stages:*

*(a) Nomination of a preliminary 'slate' of candidates: the
elector puts a man forward as suitable to be a candidate in stage (b).*

*(b) Voting for your choice from among the specified number of the
names most frequently put forward in (a), e.g. the top 10 or 20.
(a) differs from (b) in that you may nominate anybody, but vote
only for a pre-determined list. (b) may be repeated several times, the
leading names being reduced to a smaller number on each occasion.*

*(c) Casting lots to make the final selection from among the
leading names arrived at in (b).*

*(d) Scrutiny of those chosen by lot. If the scrutiny is satisfactory,
those candidates are then installed in office.*

*The reader should also note the distinction between the assembly
(the full meeting of all adult male citizens), the council (a select
body of 360 members, 90 from each tribe), and the executive
(one-twelfth of the council, 'on duty' for a month to deal with
emergencies and generally take the initiative in running the state).*

*Apart from that, this whole section speaks largely for itself.
Several interesting points of political theory are involved:*

*(a) The very extensive part played by each citizen in selecting the
officials.*

(b) The 'edge' sometimes given to the wealthier classes in electing

and being elected because they will have (possibly) a more informed judgement and the time to devote to affairs of state.

(c) The notion of 'equality'. The section is jerkily and paradoxically written, but its main point is that the lot must be used in elections in order to placate democratic sentiment, which holds that one man is as good as another and all citizens should have an equal chance to play a part in running the state. Ideally, the Athenian argues, the 'best' should always be elected. (Today, we should think of the lot as an irrational and slightly anti-democratic device.)

(d) The elaborate system of courts, uncertain in some of the details but clear in the main outline. The court of first instance is the 'neighbours' court', consisting of arbitrators rather than judges; the second is the 'tribal' court, with a jury chosen by lot; the third is the supreme court, which hears appeals from litigants satisfied with the verdict neither of the first nor of the second court.

(e) The very close connexion between the administration, legislature and judiciary.

There is much else of interest in this part; here, I can mention only some leading features. For further details, see G. R. Morrow, Plato's Cretan City *(Princeton, 1960).*

PROBLEMS OF APPOINTING THE FIRST OFFICIALS

ATHENIAN: Well then, now that I've got all that off my chest, your next job will be to appoint officials for the state.

CLEINIAS: It certainly will.

ATHENIAN: There are two stages involved in organizing a society.[1] First you establish official positions and appoint people to hold them: you decide how many posts there should be and how they ought to be filled. Then each office has to be given its particular laws: you have to decide which laws will be appropriate in each case, and the number and type required. But before we make our choice, let's pause a moment and explain a point that will affect it.

CLEINIAS: And what's that?

ATHENIAN: This. It's obvious to anyone that legislation

1. This passage picks up from p. 202.

is a tremendous task, and that when you have a well constructed state with a well-framed legal code, to put incompetent officials in charge of administering the code is a waste of good laws, and the whole business degenerates into farce. And not only that: the state will find that its laws are doing it damage and injury on a gigantic scale.

CLEINIAS: Naturally.

ATHENIAN: Now let's notice the relevance of this to your present society and state. You appreciate that if your candidates are to deserve promotion to positions of power, their characters and family background must have been adequately tested, right from their childhood until the moment of their election. Furthermore, the intending electors ought to have been well brought up in law-abiding habits, so as to be able to approve or disapprove of the candidates for the right reasons and elect or reject them according to their deserts. But in the present case we are dealing with people who have only just come together and don't know each other – and they're uneducated too. So how could they ever elect their officials without going wrong?

CLEINIAS: It's pretty well impossible.

ATHENIAN: But look here, 'once in the race, you've no excuses', as the saying is. That's just our predicament now: you and your nine colleagues, you tell us, have given an undertaking to the people of Crete to turn your energies to 752 founding this state; I, for my part, have promised to join in with this piece of fiction I'm now relating. Seeing that I've got on to telling a story, I'd be most reluctant to leave it without a head: it would look a grim sight wandering about like that!

CLEINIAS: And a fine story it's been, sir.

ATHENIAN: Surely, but I also intend to give you actual help along those lines, so far as I can.

CLEINIAS: Then let's carry out our programme, certainly.

ATHENIAN: Yes, we shall, God willing, if we can keep old age at bay for long enough.

CLEINIAS: 'God willing' can probably be taken for granted.

ATHENIAN: Of course. So let's be guided by him and notice something else.

CLEINIAS: What?

ATHENIAN: That we'll find we've been pretty bold and foolhardy in launching this state of ours.

CLEINIAS: What's made you say that? What have you in mind?

ATHENIAN: I'm thinking of the cheerful way we're legislating for people who'll be new to the laws we've passed, without bothering how they'll ever be brought to accept them. It's obvious to us all, Cleinias, even if we're not very clever, that at the start they won't readily accept any at all. Ideally, we'd remain on the spot long enough to see people getting a taste of the laws while they're still children; then when they've grown up and have become thoroughly accustomed to them, they can take part in the elections to all the offices of the state. If we can manage that (assuming acceptable ways and means are available), then I reckon that the state would have a firm guarantee of survival when its 'schooldays' are over.

CLEINIAS: That's reasonable enough.

THE ELECTION OF THE GUARDIANS OF THE LAWS

ATHENIAN: So let's see if we can find ways and means. Will this do? I maintain, Cleinias, that of all the Cretans, the citizens of Cnossos have a special duty. They must not be content with simply doing all that religion demands for the mere soil of your settlement: they must also take scrupulous care to see that the first officials are appointed by the best and safest methods. And it's absolutely vital to give your best attention to choosing, first of all, Guardians of the Laws. (Less trouble need be taken over the other officials.)

CLEINIAS: So can we find a reasonable way of going about it?

ATHENIAN: Yes. 'Sons of Crete' (I say), 'as the Cnossians take precedence over your many cities, they should collaborate with the newly arrived settlers in choosing a total of thirty-

seven men from the two sides, nineteen from the settlers, the
753 rest from Cnossos itself' – the gift of the Cnossians to this
state of yours, Cleinias. They should include you in the
eighteen, and make you yourself a citizen of the colony, with
your consent (failing which, you'll be gently compelled).

CLEINIAS: But why on earth, sir, haven't you, and Megillus
too, enrolled as joint administrators?

ATHENIAN: Ah, Cleinias, Athens is a high and mighty
state, and so is Sparta; besides, they're both a long way off.
But it's just the right thing for you and the other founders, and
what I said a moment ago of you applies equally to them. So
let's take it we've explained how to deal with the present
situation. But as time goes on and the constitution has become
established, the election of these officials should be held more
or less as follows. Everyone who serves in the cavalry or
infantry, and has fought in the field while young and strong
enough to do so, should participate. They must proceed to
election in the temple which the state considers to be the most
venerable; each elector should place on the altar of the god a
small tablet on which he has written the name of the person he
wishes to vote for, adding the candidate's father, tribe, and
deme;[2] and he should append his own name with the same
details. For at least thirty days anyone who wishes should be
allowed to remove any tablet bearing a name he finds objectionable and put it on display in the market-place. Then the
officials must exhibit to the state at large the 300 tablets[3] that
head the list; on the basis of this list the voters must then again
record their nominations, and the 100 names that lead this
second time must be publicly displayed as before. On the
third occasion anyone who wishes should walk between the
victims of a sacrifice[4] and record which of these 300 he
chooses. The thirty-seven who receive most votes must then
submit to scrutiny and be declared elected.

Well then, Cleinias and Megillus, who will make all these
arrangements about these officials in our state, and their
scrutiny? We can surely appreciate that as the state apparatus

2. See p. 218, note 28, on demes.   3. I.e. names, in effect.
4. A procedure that would lend particular solemnity to his vote.

is as yet only rudimentary such people have to be on hand; but they could hardly be available before any officials at all have been appointed. Even so, we must have them, and these 200 persons mustn't be feeble specimens, either, but men of the highest calibre. As the proverb says, 'getting started is half the battle', and a *good* beginning we all applaud. But in my view a good start is more than 'half', and no one has yet given 754 it the praise it deserves.

CLEINIAS: That's quite true.

ATHENIAN: So as we acknowledge the value of a good beginning, let's not skip discussion of it in this case. Let's get it quite clear in our own minds how we can tackle it. I've no particular points to make, except one, which is vitally relevant to the situation.

CLEINIAS: And what's that?

ATHENIAN: Apart from the city which is founding it, this state we are about to settle has, so to speak, no father or mother. I'm quite aware, of course, that many a foundation has quarrelled repeatedly with its founder-state, and will again, but in the present circumstances we have, as it were, the merest infant on our hands. I mean, any child is going to fall out with his parents sooner or later, but while he's young and can't help himself, he loves them and they love him; he's for ever scampering back to his family and finding his only allies are his relatives. That's exactly the way I maintain our young state regards the citizens of Cnossos and how they regard it, in virtue of their role as its guardians. I therefore repeat what I said just now – there's no harm in saying a good thing twice – that the citizens of Cnossos should choose colleagues from among the newly arrived colonists and take charge of all these arrangements; they should choose at least 100 of them, the oldest and most virtuous they can find; and they themselves should contribute another 100. They should enter the new state and collaborate in seeing that the officials are designated according to law, and after designation, scrutinized. When they've done all that, the citizens of Cnossos should resume living in Cnossos and leave the infant state to work out its own salvation and flourish unaided.

DUTIES AND TENURE OF THE GUARDIANS; REGISTRATION OF PROPERTY

The duties for which the members of the body of thirty-seven should be appointed are as follows (not only here and now, but permanently): first, they are to act as Guardians of the Laws; second, they are to take charge of the documents in which each person has made his return to the officials of his total property. (A man may leave 400 drachmas undeclared if he belongs to the highest property-class, 300 if to the second, 200 if to the third, and 100 if he belongs to the fourth.)[5]

5. If anyone is found to possess anything in addition to the registered sum,
   the entire surplus should be confiscated by the state,

and on top of that anyone who wants to should bring a charge against him – and an ugly, discreditable and disgraceful charge it will be, if the man is convicted of being enticed by the prospect of gain to hold the laws in contempt. The accuser, who may be anyone, should accordingly enter a charge of 'money-grubbing' against him, and prosecute in the court of the Law-Guardians themselves.

6. If the defendant is found guilty,
755 *he must* be excluded from the common resources of the state, and when a grant of some kind is made, he must go without and be limited to his holding; and for as long as he lives his conviction should be recorded for public inspection by all and sundry.

A Law-Guardian must not hold office for longer than twenty years; he should be not less than fifty years old on appointment, and if he is appointed at sixty, his maximum tenure must be ten years, and so on. And if a man survives beyond seventy, he should no longer expect to hold such an important post as membership of this board.

5. I take it this means one is allowed a certain margin for small inadvertent underestimates.

That gives us three duties[6] to assign to the Guardians of the Laws. As the legal code is extended, every new law will give this body of men additional duties to perform, over and above the ones we've mentioned.

Now for the election of the other officials, one by one.

MILITARY OFFICIALS

Next, then, we have to elect Generals and their *aides-de-camp*, so to speak: Cavalry-Commanders, Tribe-Leaders, and controllers of the tribal companies of infantry ('Company-Commanders' will be a good name for these officers, which is in fact what most people do call them).

Generals. The Guardians of the Laws must compile a preliminary list of candidates, restricted to citizens, and the Generals should then be elected from this list by all those who have served in the armed forces at the proper age, or are serving at the time. If anybody thinks that someone not on the preliminary list is better qualified than someone who is, he must name his proposed substitute, and say whom he should replace; then, having sworn his oath, he must propose the alternative candidate. Whichever of the two the voting favours should be a candidate in the election. The three candidates who receive most votes should become Generals and take over the organization of military affairs, after being scrutinized in the same way as the Guardians of the Laws.

Company-Commanders. The elected Generals should make their own preliminary list of twelve Company-Commanders, one for each tribe; the counter-nominations, the election and the scrutiny must be conducted as they were for the Generals themselves.

The Elections. For the moment, before a council and executive committees[7] have been chosen, your assembly must be

6. Presumably (a) supervision of the laws, (b) custody of the registers of property, (c) trying those accused of 'money-grubbing'.

7. See pp. 230–31.

convened by the Guardians of the Laws in the holiest and most capacious place they can find; and they must seat the heavy-armed soldiers, the cavalry, and finally all other ranks, in separate blocks. The Generals and Cavalry-Commanders should be elected by the whole assembly, the Company-756 Commanders by the shield-bearers, and their[8] Tribe-Leaders by the entire cavalry; as for light-armed troops, archers, or whatever other ranks there may be, the appointment of their leaders should be left to the Generals' discretion.

Cavalry-Commanders. That will leave us with the appointment of the Cavalry-Commanders. The preliminary list must be drawn up by the same persons as drew up the list of Generals, and the election and counter-proposals should be conducted in the same way; the cavalry must hold the election watched by the infantry, and the two candidates with the most votes must become leaders of the entire mounted force.

Disputed Votes. Votes may be disputed no more than twice. If anyone contests the vote on the third occasion, the tellers must decide the issue by voting among themselves.

THE ELECTION OF THE COUNCIL[9]

The council should have thirty dozen members, as 360 will be a convenient number for subdivision. The total will be divided into four sections of ninety, this being the number of members to be elected from each property-class. The first step in the election is to be compulsory for all: everyone must take part in the nomination of members of the highest class, and anybody who neglects his duty must pay the approved fine. When the nominations are completed, the names must be noted down.

On the next day, using the same procedure as before, they will nominate members of the second class.

---

8. It is not clear to whom this word is supposed to refer.

9. For an elucidation of the procedure described here, see G. R. Morrow, *Plato's Cretan City*, p. 166 ff.

On the third day, nominating for Councillors from the third class will be optional, except for voters of the first three classes: voters of the fourth and lowest class will be exempted from the fine if they do not care to make a nomination.

The fourth day will see the nomination for representatives of the fourth and lowest class; everyone must take part, but voters of the third and fourth class who do not wish to nominate should not be fined – unlike voters of the second and first classes, who must be fined treble and quadruple the standard fine respectively if they do not make a nomination.

On the fifth day the officials must display to the entire citizen body the names duly noted down, and on the basis of these lists every man must cast his vote or pay the standard fine. 180 must be selected from each property-class, and half of them finally chosen by lot. These, after scrutiny, are to be Councillors for the year.

THE NOTION OF EQUALITY

A system of selection like that will effect a compromise between a monarchical and a democratic constitution, which is precisely the sort of compromise a constitution should always be. You see, even if you proclaim that a master and his slave shall have equal status, friendship between them is inherently 757 impossible. The same applies to the relations between an honest man and a scoundrel. Indiscriminate equality for all amounts to *in*equality, and both fill a state with quarrels between its citizens. How correct the old saying is, that 'equality leads to friendship'! It's right enough and it rings true, but what *kind* of equality has this potential is a problem which produces ripe confusion. This is because we use the same term for two concepts of 'equality', which in most respects are virtual opposites. The first sort of equality (of measures, weights and numbers) is within the competence of any state and any legislator: that is, one can simply distribute equal awards by lot. But the most genuine equality, and the best, is not so obvious. It needs the wisdom and judgement of Zeus, and only in a limited number of ways does it help the human race; but when states or even individuals do find it profitable, they find it very profitable indeed. The general method I mean is to grant much to the great and less to the less great, adjusting what you give to take account of the real nature of each – specifically, to confer high recognition on great virtue, but when you come to the poorly educated in this respect, to treat them as they deserve. We maintain, in fact, that statesmanship consists of essentially this – strict justice. This is what we should be aiming at now, Cleinias: this is the kind of 'equality' we should concentrate on as we bring our state into the world. The founder of any other state should also concentrate on this same goal when he frames his laws, and take no notice of a bunch of dictators, or a single one, or even the power of the people. He must always make *justice* his aim, and this is precisely as we've described it: it consists of granting the 'equality' that unequals deserve to get. Yet on occasion a state as a whole (unless it is prepared to put up with a degree of friction in one part or another) will be obliged to apply these concepts in a rather rough and ready way, because complaisance and toleration, which always wreck complete precision, are the enemies of strict justice. You can now see why it was necessary to avoid the anger of the man in the street by giving him an equal chance in the lot (though even then we prayed to the gods of good luck to make the lot give the right decisions). So though force of circumstances compels us to employ both sorts of equality, we should employ 758 the second, which demands good luck to prove successful, as little as possible.

THE EXECUTIVE COMMITTEE OF THE COUNCIL

So much, my friends, for the justification of our policy, which is the policy a state must follow if it means to survive. The state is just like a ship at sea, which always needs someone to keep watch night and day: as it is steered through the waves of international affairs, it lives in constant peril of being captured by all sorts of conspiracies. Hence the need of an unbroken chain of authority right through the day and into the night and then on into the next day, guard relieving guard in endless succession. But a large body will never be able to act quickly enough, and most of the time we have to leave the majority of council members free to live their private lives and administer their own establishments. We must therefore divide the members of the council into twelve groups, one for each month, and have them go on guard by turns. They must be available promptly, whenever anyone from abroad or from within the state itself approaches them wishing to give information or inquire about those topics on which a state must arrange to answer the questions of other states and receive replies to its own. They must be particularly concerned with the constant revolutions of all kinds that are apt to occur in a state; if possible, they must prevent them, but failing that they must see that the state gets to know as soon as possible, so that the outbreak can be cured. That is why this executive committee has to be in charge of convening and dissolving not only statutory meetings but also those held in some national emergency. The authority that should see to all this – a twelfth of the council – will of course be *off* duty for eleven-twelfths of the year: it's the section of the council *on* duty that must co-operate with other officials and keep a watchful eye on the state.

OTHER OFFICIALS; PRIESTS

That will be a reasonable arrangement for the city, but what about the rest of the country? How should it be superintended and organized? Well now, the entire city and the entire country have been divided into twelve sections; there are the roads of the central city; there are houses, public buildings, harbours, the market, and fountains; there are, above all, sacred enclosures and similar places. Shouldn't all these things have officials appointed to look after them?

CLEINIAS: Naturally.

ATHENIAN: We can say, then, that the temples should have [759] Attendants and Priests and Priestesses. Next, there are the duties of looking after streets and public buildings, ensuring that they reach the proper standards, stopping men and animals doing them damage, and seeing that conditions both in the suburbs and the city itself are in keeping with a civilized life. All these duties require three[10] types of officials to be chosen: the 'City-Wardens' (as they will be called) will be responsible for the points we've just mentioned, and the 'Market-Wardens' for the correct conduct of the market.

Priests or Priestesses of temples who have hereditary priesthoods should not be turned out of office. But if (as is quite likely in a new foundation) few or no temples are thus provided for, the deficiencies must be made good by appointing Priests and Priestesses to be Attendants in the temples of the gods. In all these cases the appointments should be made partly by election and partly by lot, so that a mixture of democratic and non-democratic methods in every rural and urban division may lead to the greatest possible feeling of solidarity. In electing Priests, one should leave it to the god himself to express his wishes, and allow him to guide the luck of the draw. But the man whom the lot favours must be screened to see that he is healthy and legitimate, reared in a family whose moral standards could hardly be higher, and that he himself and his father and mother have lived unpolluted by homicide and all such offences against heaven.

They must get laws on all religious matters from Delphi, and appoint Expounders of them; that will provide them with a code to be obeyed. Each priesthood must be held for a year and no longer, and anyone who intends to celebrate our rites in due conformity with religious law should not be less than sixty years old. The same rules should apply to Priestesses too.

THE ELECTION OF THE EXPOUNDERS[11]

There should be three Expounders. The tribes will be arranged in three sets of four, and every man should nominate four

10. The first category being, presumably, the Priests, etc.
11. Officials charged with the duty of interpreting religious law and advising on the celebration of rites. I adopt Hammond's interpretation

persons, each from the same set as himself; the three candidates who receive most votes should be scrutinized, and nine names should then be sent to Delphi for the oracle to select one from each group of three. Their scrutiny, and the requirement as to age, should be the same as in the case of the Priests; these three must hold office for life, and when one dies the group of four tribes in which the vacancy occurs should make nominations for a replacement.

TREASURERS

The highest property-class must elect Treasurers to control the sacred funds of each temple, and to look after the temple-enclosures and their produce and revenues; three should be 760 chosen to take charge of the largest temples, two for the less large, and one for the very small. The election and scrutiny of these officials should be conducted as it was for the Generals.

So much by way of provision for the holy places.

THE PROTECTION OF THE TERRITORY

As far as practicable, nothing should be left unguarded. The protection of the city is to be the business of the Generals, Company-Commanders, Cavalry-Commanders, Tribe-Leaders and members of the Executive – and the City-Wardens and Market-Wardens too, once we have them elected and satisfactorily installed in office. The whole of the rest of the country should be protected as follows. Our entire territory has been divided as exactly as possible into twelve equal sections, and every year one tribe must be allocated by lot to each of them. Every tribe must provide five 'Country-Wardens' or 'Guards-in-Chief', each of whom[12] will be allowed to choose from

---

of this horrid passage, and have expanded the translation considerably in the interests of intelligibility. See N. G. L. Hammond, 'The Exegetai in Plato's *Laws*', *Classical Quarterly*, II (1952), 4 ff.; G. R. Morrow, *Plato's Cretan City*, 419 ff., 496 ff.

12. Plato does not make clear whether the five chiefs are to choose twelve assistants or sixty (i.e. twelve *each*). I have adopted the latter interpretation: see Morris Davis, 'How many *Agronomoi* in Plato's *Laws*?', *Classical Philology*, LX (1965), 28–9.

his own tribe twelve young men who must be not younger than twenty-five nor older than thirty. The effect of the lot will be that each group will take a different section every month, so that they all get experience and knowledge of the entire country. The guards and their officers in charge are to hold their respective commissions for two years. Starting from the original sections (i.e. districts of the country) assigned by lot, the Guards-in-Chief are to take their groups round in a circle, transferring them each month to the next district on the right ('on the right' should be understood to mean 'to the East'). But it's not enough that as many of the guards as possible should get experience of the country at only one season of the year: we want them to add to their knowledge of the actual territory by discovering what goes on in every district at every season. So their leaders for the time being should follow up the first year by spending a second leading them back through the various districts, moving this time to the left. For the third year, a tribe must choose other Country-Wardens, and five new Guards-in-Chief, each in charge of twelve assistants.

While stationed in the various districts, their duties should be as follows. To start with, they must see that the territory is protected against enemies as thoroughly as possible. They must dig ditches wherever necessary, and excavate trenches and erect fortifications to check any attempt to harm the land and the livestock. They will requisition the beasts of burden 761 and slaves of the local residents for these purposes, and employ them at their discretion, picking as far as possible times when they are not required for their normal duties. The wardens must arrange that the enemy would be impeded at every turn, whereas movement by our own side (by men or beasts of burden or cattle) would be facilitated; and they must see that every road is as easy for the traveller as can be managed.

The rain God sends must do the countryside good, not harm, so the wardens must see that the water flowing off the high ground down into any sufficiently deep ravines between the hills is collected by dikes and ditches, so that the ravines can retain and absorb it, and supply streams and springs for all the districts in the countryside below, and give even the driest of spots a copious supply of pure water. As for water that springs from the ground, the wardens must beautify the fountains and rivers that form by adorning them with trees and buildings; they must use drains to tap the individual streams and collect an abundant supply, and any grove or sacred enclosure which has been dedicated nearby must be embellished by having a perennial flow of water directed by irrigation into the very temples of the gods. The young men should erect in every quarter gymnasia for themselves and senior citizens, construct warm baths for the old folk, and lay up a large stock of thoroughly dry wood. All this will help to relieve invalids, and farmers wearied by the labour of the fields – and it will be a much kinder treatment than the tender mercies of some fool of a doctor.

THE RURAL COURTS

All these and similar projects will beautify and improve a district, and permit some welcome recreation into the bargain. The Wardens' really serious duties should be as follows. Each squad of sixty must protect its own district not only from enemies, but from those who profess to be friends. If a slave or a free man injures a neighbour or any other citizen, the Wardens must try the case brought by the plaintiff. The five leaders should deal with the trivial cases on their own authority, but in the more important cases (when one man sues another for any sum up to three minas) they should sit in judgement with one group of twelve assistants as a bench of 17. Apart from the officials whose decisions (like those of kings) are final, no judge shall hold court, and no official shall fill his position, without being liable to be called to account for his actions. The Country-Wardens are to be no exception, if they treat the people in their care at all high-handedly by giving them unfair orders or by trying to grab 762 and remove any agricultural equipment without permission, or allow their palms to be greased, or go so far as to deliver unjust verdicts. For giving way to boot-lickers they must be publicly disgraced. When the actual injury they have done to an inhabitant of their district does not exceed one mina in value, they should voluntarily submit to a trial before the villagers and neighbours. Whenever larger sums are involved (or even smaller sums, if the accused is not prepared to submit to trial because he's confident that by moving to a fresh district every month he will get away and 'get off' too), the injured party should file suit against him in the common courts.

7. If the plaintiff wins the day,
then this elusive fellow who was not prepared to pay a penalty with a good grace must pay him double the amount at issue.

HOW THE COUNTRY-WARDENS ARE TO LIVE

The way of life of the Country-Wardens and their officers during their two years on duty will be something like this. First, in every district of the country there should be communal restaurants, at which everyone will have to eat together.

8. If a Warden fails to turn up at these meals even for one day, or sleeps away from his quarters at night, except on the express orders of his superiors or because of some unavoidable necessity,
the five leaders may post his name in the market-place as a deserter from his post; if they do, he will have to bear the disgrace of having turned traitor to the state, and anyone who happens to meet him will be entitled to give him a beating if he wants to, without being punished for it.

If one of the actual officers goes so far as to commit this sort of offence, all his fifty-nine colleagues must look into the business.

9. If one of them notices (or is told) what is going on and fails to bring a case,
the same laws should be invoked against him, and he must be punished with greater severity than his juniors: that is, he is to be stripped of his right to exercise any authority over the young.

The Guardians of the Laws should keep a sharp eye on these offences and try to stop them being committed at all; failing that, they must see that the proper penalties are inflicted.

No one will ever make a commendable master without having been a servant first; one should be proud not so much of ruling well but of serving well – and serving the laws above all (because this is the way we serve the gods), and secondly, if we are young, those who are full of years and honour. It is vital that everyone should be convinced that this rule applies to us all. The next point, then, is that when someone who has joined the Country-Wardens gets to the end of his two years, he ought to be no stranger to a meagre daily ration of uncooked food. In fact, after being selected, the groups of twelve assistant Wardens must assemble with the five officers and resolve that, being servants, they will not possess other 763 servants and slaves for themselves, nor employ the attendants of other people (the farmers and villagers) for their own private needs, but only for public tasks. With that exception, they must expect to double as their own servants and fend for themselves; and on top of all that they must reckon to investigate the entire country, summer and winter, in arms, to protect and get to know every district in succession. Everyone should be closely familiar with his own country: probably no study is more valuable. This is the real reason why the youths must go in for hunting with dogs, and other types of chase – quite apart from the pleasure and profit that everyone gets out of such activities.

So much for these 'secret-service men'[13] or 'Country-Wardens' (call them what you will), and their regimen – a regimen into which everyone who means to play his part in keeping his country safe must throw himself heart and soul.

THE CITY-WARDENS

The next election on our list was that of the Market-Wardens and City-Wardens.[14] There are to be three of the latter, who

13. See p. 57 and G. R. Morrow, *Plato's Cretan City*, 189–90. The expression is probably not as sinister as it sounds.
14. See p. 233.

will divide the twelve sections of the city into three groups, and like their counterparts (the 60 Country-Wardens), will look after the roads, both the streets within the city boundaries and the various routes that extend into the capital from the country; and they must also supervise the buildings, to see that they are constructed to the statutory standards. In particular, they must ensure that the water which the Guards-in-Chief have transmitted and sent on to them in good condition reaches the fountains pure and in sufficient quantities, so that it enhances the beauty and amenities of the city. So these officials too must be men of some calibre, with time to go in for public affairs, which means that every citizen nominating City-Wardens must confine his choice to members of the highest property-class. When they have held the election and produced a short list of six candidates with the most votes, the officials responsible are to select three of them by lot; and these, after scrutiny, should hold office in accordance with the laws provided for them.

THE MARKET-WARDENS

Next, five Market-Wardens must be elected from the first and second property-classes. In general, their election should be conducted as for the City-Wardens: ten should be selected from the list of candidates by voting, and then five selected by lot, who after due scrutiny should be appointed to office. (Voting is compulsory for all in every election, and anyone 764 who fails in his duty and is denounced to the authorities should be fined fifty drachmas and get the reputation of being a scoundrel. Attendance at the assembly (the general meeting of the state) is to be optional, except for members of the first and second property-classes, who will be fined ten drachmas if their absence from such a meeting is proved. But the third and fourth classes will not be forced to attend and should not be subject to any penalty unless the authorities, for some pressing reason, instruct everyone to come.) To get back to the Market-Wardens: they are to maintain due order in the market, and look after the temples and fountains, to see that no one damages them. They must punish anyone who commits an offence, a slave or foreigner by whipping him and putting him in chains; but if a native citizen misbehaves himself in this way, the Market-Wardens should be authorized to decide the case on their own and fine the culprit up to 100 drachmas, the limit being increased to 200 if they sit in association with the City-Wardens. In their own sphere, the City-Wardens too should have the same power of fining and punishing, and inflict fines up to one mina on their own, and up to two minas in association with the Market-Wardens.

EDUCATION OFFICIALS[15]

The right thing to do next will be to appoint officials in charge of (A) culture and (B) physical training – two categories of them in each case, one (1) to handle the educational side and the other (2) to organize competitions. By (1)'education officials' the law means superintendents of gymnasia and schools, who see that they are decently run, supervise the curriculum and organize such related matters as the attendance and accommodation of the boys and girls. (2) 'Officials in charge of competitions' means judges of competitors in athletics and contests of the arts (there being here again two categories (AB) of officials, one for the arts, one for athletics). (B2) Men and horses in athletic contests can have the same judges, but (A2) in the arts, choruses[16] should properly have (A2a) one set of judges, while solo dramatic performances (given by reciters of poetry, lyre-players, pipe-players and such people) ought to have another (A2b). So I suppose a good start will be to select (A2a) the authority to supervise children, men and girls as they enjoy themselves in choruses by dancing and every other type of cultural activity. One official, who is to be not less than forty years old, will suffice, and one of not less than thirty (A2b) will also be enough to present the solo performances and give an adequate decision between the contestants. The Chief Organizer of the Choruses

15. I have attempted to articulate the passage by the use of A, B, etc.
16. See pp. 84–5 for an explanation of this term.

(A2a) must be chosen in some such way as this. All those who are keen on such things should attend the election meeting and be liable to a fine if they don't (this is a point for the Guardians of the Laws to decide), whereas others who do not wish to attend should not be compelled. In proposing their choice the electors should confine themselves to the experts, and in the scrutiny there must be only one reason for accepting or rejecting the candidate the lot has favoured: that he is experienced or inexperienced as the case may be. One of the ten nominees with the most votes must be selected by lot, scrutinized, and be in charge of the choruses for the year according to law. Similarly with the year's entrants for solo performances and combined pieces on the pipes: only after the application of the same criterion should the candidate (A2b) favoured by the lot take charge of them and decide between them, having referred the decision in his own case to his judges.[17] Next, (B2) Umpires for athletic contests and exercises of horses and men must be chosen from the second and also the third property-class; it will be compulsory for members of the first three classes to take part in the election, but the lowest class may be let off without a fine. The Umpires should number three, chosen by lot from the twenty candidates who head the poll, and duly sanctioned by the scrutineers.

If anyone is judged and found wanting in the scrutiny after being drawn by lot for any office, another person must be chosen in his place by the same methods, and his scrutiny conducted in the same way.

THE MINISTER OF EDUCATION

The remaining official in this field is the director of the entire education of the boys and girls. Here too there should be one official in charge under the law. He must be not younger than fifty years old, and the father of legitimate children – prefer-

---

17. In this mysterious and confusing sentence, which I have slightly expanded, Plato seems to me to be drawing a frigid parallel between the official's own examination at the scrutiny and his judgement between the competitors in his charge.

ably both sons and daughters, though either alone will do.
The chosen candidate himself and those who choose him
should appreciate that this is by far the most important of all
the supreme offices in the state. Any living creature that
flourishes in its first stages of growth gets a tremendous
impetus towards its natural perfection and the final development appropriate to it, and this is true of both plants and
animals (tame and wild), and men too. Man is a 'tame'
animal, as we put it, and of course if he enjoys a good educa- 766
tion and happens to have the right natural disposition, he's
apt to be a most heavenly and gentle creature; but his upbringing has only to be inadequate or misguided and he'll
become the wildest animal on the face of the earth. That's
why the legislator should not treat the education of children
cursorily or as a secondary matter; he should regard the
right choice of the man who is going to be in charge of the
children as something of crucial importance, and appoint as
their Minister the best all-round citizen in the state. So all the
officials except the council and members of the Executive[18]
should meet at the temple of Apollo and hold a secret ballot,
each man voting for whichever Guardian of the Laws he
thinks would make the best Minister of Education. The one
who attracts the largest number of votes should be scrutinized
by the officials who have elected him, the Guardians of the
Laws standing aside. The Minister should hold office for five
years, and in the sixth he should be replaced by his successor
after an election held under the same rules.

DEATH IN OFFICE

If any public official dies in office and there are more than
thirty days of his tenure left to run, the officials concerned
must follow the same procedure as before and appoint a
replacement. If a guardian of orphans dies, the relatives on
both the mother's and the father's side (as far as the children
of first cousins), provided they are living in the state, should
appoint a successor within ten days, or be fined a drachma for

18. See pp. 230–31.

every day they let pass without appointing the children's new guardian.

THREE GRADES OF COURT

Of course, any state without duly established courts simply ceases to *be* a state. If a judge is silent, and (as in arbitration) has no more to say than the litigants in a preliminary hearing, he'll never be able to come to a satisfactory decision on the cases before him. That's why a large bench finds it difficult to return good verdicts – and so does a small one, if its members are of poor calibre. The point in dispute between the parties must always be made crystal clear, and leisurely and repeated interrogation over a period of time helps a lot to clarify the issues. That is the justification for making litigants bring their charges initially before a court of neighbours, who will be their friends and understand best the actions which 767 provoke the dispute. If a litigant is dissatisfied with the judgement of this court, he may apply to a second, but if the first two courts are both unable to settle the argument, the verdict of the third must close the case.

In a sense, to establish a court is to elect officials. Every official, you see, sometimes has to set up as a judge as well; and a judge, although strictly he has no official position, becomes in a way an official of considerable importance during the day on which he sits in judgement and gives his verdict. So on the assumption that judges too are officials, let's specify what judges will be appropriate, the disputes they will decide, and how many should sit on each case. The court appointed by the common choice of the litigants themselves for their own private cases should have absolute authority.[19] Cases may be brought before the other courts[20] for two reasons: one private person may charge another with having done him wrong, and bring him to court so that the issue can be decided; or someone may believe that one of the citizens is acting against the public

19. I.e. *if* the contestants accept the verdict. The 'neighbours' court' above is meant.

20. I.e. the second ('tribal') court and third ('appeal') court.

interests, and wish to come to the community's assistance. Now we must specify the character and identity of the judges.

ELECTION OF THE SUPREME COURT

First, let's set up a common court for all private persons who are contesting an issue with each other for the third time.[21] It is to be formed in some such way as this. All officials whose tenure lasts for a year or longer should assemble in a single temple on the day just before the new year opens in the month after the summer solstice; then, after swearing to the god, they must offer him their choicest fruit, so to speak: each board of officials should contribute one judge, the man who appears to be the outstanding member of his board and seems likely to judge the cases of his fellow-citizens during the coming year in the best and most god-fearing manner. When the judges have been chosen, their scrutiny should be conducted before their very electors, and if any one of them is rejected, a replacement should be chosen under the same rules. Those who pass the scrutiny are to sit in judgement on the cases of the litigants who refuse to accept the decision of the other courts. They are to vote openly, and it will be compulsory for the Councillors and the other officials who elected the judges to watch and listen to the trials; others may attend if they wish.

CORRUPT VERDICTS

If anyone accuses a man of having knowingly returned a false verdict, he must go to the Guardians of the Laws to prefer the charge.

10. If the accused is found guilty as charged,
he will have to pay to the injured party half the damages awarded; if he is thought to deserve a stiffer punishment, his judges must calculate the additional penalty he should

21. I.e. *appealing* for the *second* time.

suffer or additional fine he ought to pay to the state and his prosecutor.

THE COURT OF THE PEOPLE[22]

As for charges of crimes against the state, the first need is to
768 let the man in the street play his part in judging them. A wrong done to the state is a wrong done to all its citizens, who would be justifiably annoyed if they were excluded from deciding such cases. But although we should allow the opening and closing stages of this kind of trial to be in the hands of the people, the detailed examination should be conducted by three of the highest officials, chosen by agreement between prosecutor and defendant. If they are unable to reach agreement themselves, the council should decide between their respective choices.

THE TRIBAL COURTS

Everyone should have a part to play in private suits too, because anyone excluded from the right to participate in trying cases feels he has no stake in the community whatever. Hence we must also have courts organized on a tribal basis, where the judges, being chosen by lot as occasion arises, will give their verdicts uncorrupted by external pressures. But the final decision in all these cases is to be given by that other court[23] which deals with litigants who cannot settle their case either before their neighbours or in the tribal courts, and which for their benefit has been made (we claim) as incorruptible a court as can be assembled by human power.

OUR SCHEME IS ONLY A SKETCH[24]

So much for our courts (and we admit that to call their members either 'officials' or 'non-officials' without qualification

22. Such a court may or may not be implied by the next few sentences.
23. The Supreme Court.
24. The main point of this foggy paragraph seems to be that after a certain stage the details of one topic cannot be described without reference to some other topic. The Athenian Stranger now passes from organization and administration to legislation.

raises difficulties of terminology). We've given a sort of superficial sketch, which in spite of including a number of details,
nevertheless omitted a good many, because a better place for
presenting an exact legal procedure and classification of suits
will be towards the end of our legislation. So this theme may
be dismissed till we are finishing off. We have already explained most of the rules for establishing official posts, but
we still can't get a completely clear and exact picture of every
individual detail of the entire constitutional organization of
the state: for that, we need to take every single topic in
proper sequence and go through the whole subject from
beginning to end. So far, then, we've described the election of
officials, and that brings us to the end of our introduction.
Now to start the actual legislation: there's no need to postpone or delay it any longer.

§11. MARRIAGE AND RELATED TOPICS

The Athenian now abandons organization in favour of legislation, and starts, reasonably enough, with marriage and the birth of children. Some of the topics handled in this section are linked to the theme of marriage rather tenuously (e.g. slavery): the Athenian's exposition moves by association of ideas from one subject to another (for instance, mention of the familiarity to be encouraged by religious festivals leads him on to discuss marriage, because it is by getting to know one another at the festivals that the young people will form suitable matches). Towards the end of the section there is considerable evidence of a lack of revision, and the train of thought becomes a little difficult to grasp. The section 'Three Instinctive Drives' seems particularly loosely included, but I take it that it is put in this particular position to show why the preceding law about communal meals and the succeeding one about procreation are justified: they are intended to regulate properly the basic drives of mankind for food and sexual intercourse.

THE YOUNGER LEGISLATORS

CLEINIAS: I very much approve of your introduction, sir, and I'm even more impressed by the way you've rounded it off so that it leads into the opening of the next theme.

769 ATHENIAN: So far, then, these ideas we old men have been tossing about have given us splendid sport.[1]

CLEINIAS: Splendid indeed, but I fancy you really meant they were 'a splendid challenge for men in their prime of life'.

ATHENIAN: I dare say. But here's another point. I wonder if you agree with me?

CLEINIAS: What about? What point?

ATHENIAN: You know how painting a picture of anything seems to be a never-ending business. It always looks as if the process of touching up by adding colour or relief (or whatever

1. See p. 131.

it's called in the trade) will never finally get to the point where the clarity and beauty of the picture are beyond improvement.

CLEINIAS: Yes, I too get much the same sort of impression, though only from hearsay – I've never gone in for that sort of skill.

ATHENIAN: Well, you haven't missed anything. But we can still use this passing mention of it to illustrate the next point. Suppose that one day somebody were to take it into his head to paint the most beautiful picture in the world, which would never deteriorate but always improve at his hands as the years went by. You realize that as the painter is not immortal, he won't achieve anything very permanent by lavishing such care and attention on his picture unless he leaves some successor to repair the ravages of time? Won't his successor also have to be able to supplement deficiencies in his master's skill and improve the picture by touching it up?

CLEINIAS: True.

ATHENIAN: Well then, don't you think the legislator will want to do something similar? First of all he'll want to write his laws and make them as accurate as he can; then as time goes on and he tries to put his pet theories into practice – well, do you think there's any legislator so stupid as not to realize that his code has many inevitable deficiencies which must be put right by a successor, if the state he's founded is to enjoy a continuous improvement in its administrative arrangements, rather than suffer a decline?

CLEINIAS: Yes, I think – indeed I'm sure – that this is the sort of thing any legislator will want to do.

ATHENIAN: So if a legislator were able to discover a way of doing this – that is, if by instruction or pointing to concrete examples he could make someone else understand (perfectly or imperfectly) how to keep laws in good repair by amending them – I suppose he'd never give up explaining his method until he'd got it across?

CLEINIAS: Of course.

ATHENIAN: So isn't this what you two and I ought to be doing now?

247

CLEINIAS: What do you mean?

ATHENIAN: Now that we (in the evening of life) are on the point of framing laws, for which we have guardians already chosen (our juniors), oughtn't we to combine our law-giving with an attempt to turn *them* into law-'givers' as well as law-'guardians', as far as we can?

CLEINIAS: Of course we ought, assuming we're up to it.

ATHENIAN: Anyhow, we ought to try, and do our level best.

CLEINIAS: Certainly.

ATHENIAN: Let's address them as follows: 'Colleagues and protectors of our laws, we shall – inevitably – leave a great many gaps in every section of our code. However, we shall certainly take care to outline a sort of sketch of the complete system with its main points, and it will be your job to take this sketch and fill in the details. You ought to hear what your aims should be when you do this. Megillus and Cleinias and I have mentioned it to each other more than once, and we are agreed that our formula is a good one. We want you to be sympathetic to our way of thinking and become our pupils, keeping in view this aim which the three of us are unanimous a giver and guardian of laws should have. The central point on which we agree amounted to this. "Our aim in life should be goodness and the spiritual virtue appropriate to mankind. There are various things that can assist us: it may be some pursuit we follow, a particular habit, or something we possess; we may get help from some desire we have or some opinion we hold or some course of study; and all this is true of both male and female members of the community, young or old. Whatever the means, it's this aim we've described that we must all strain every muscle to achieve throughout our lives. No man, whoever he is, should ever be found valuing anything else, if it impedes his progress – not even, in the last resort, the state. Rather than have the state tolerate the yoke of slavery and be ruled by unworthy hands, it may be absolutely necessary to allow it to be destroyed, or abandon it by going into exile. All that sort of hardship we simply have to endure, rather than permit a change to the sort of political system which will make men worse." This, then, is the agreed statement; now it's up to you to consider this double[2] aim of ours and censure the laws that can do nothing to help us; but you must commend and welcome the effective ones with enthusiasm, and cheerfully live as they dictate. You must have no truck with other pursuits which aim at different "goods"[3] (as people call them).'

THE ORGANIZATION OF RELIGIOUS FESTIVALS

The best way to start the next section of our code will be to deal with matters of religion. First, we should go back to the figure of 5040 and reflect again how many convenient divisors we found both in this total and its subdivision the tribe (which is one-twelfth of the total, as we specified, i.e. exactly the product of twenty-one multiplied by twenty). Our grand total is divisible by twelve, and so is the number of persons in a tribe,[4] and in each case this subdivision must be regarded as holy, a gift of God, corresponding to the months of the year and the revolution of the universe. This is exactly why every state is guided by innate intuition to give these fractions the sanction of religion, though in some cases the divisions have been made more correctly than in others and the religious backing has proved more successful. So for our part we claim that we had every justification for preferring 5040, which can be divided by every number from one to twelve, except eleven (a drawback that's very easily cured: one way to remedy it is simply to omit two hearths).[5] The truth of this could be demonstrated very briefly in any idle moment. So let's trust to the rule we've just explained, and divide our number along those lines. We must allocate a god, or child of a god, to each division and subdivision of the state[6] and provide altars and the associated equipment; we must establish two meetings per month for the purposes of sacrifice, one

2. Presumably virtue itself and conditions conducive to it.
3. Health, wealth, etc.   4. 420.
5. 5038 is divisible by 11.   6. Cf. pp. 206 and 216.

in each of the twelve tribes into which the state is divided, and another in each of the twelve local communities that form the divisions of each tribe.[7] This arrangement is intended to ensure, first, that we enjoy the favour of the gods and heaven in general, and secondly (as we'd be inclined to stress[8]) that we should grow familiar and intimate with each other in every kind of social contact.

MARRIAGE: CHOOSING A PARTNER (1)

You see, when people are going to live together as partners in marriage, it is vital that the fullest possible information should be available about the bride and her background and the family she'll marry into. One should regard the prevention of mistakes here as a matter of supreme importance – so important and serious, in fact, that even the young people's recreation must be arranged with this in mind. Boys and girls must 772 dance together at an age when plausible occasions can be found for their doing so, in order that they may have a reasonable look at each other; and they should dance naked, provided sufficient modesty and restraint are displayed by all concerned.

CHANGING THE LAWS

The controllers and organizers of the choruses should be in charge of all these arrangements and maintain due order; and in conjunction with the Guardians of the Laws they will settle anything we leave out. As we said, it's inevitable that a legislator will omit the numerous details of such a topic; those who administer his laws from year to year will have to learn from experience and settle the details by annual refinements and amendments, until they think they've made the rules and procedures sufficiently precise. In the case of

7. The Greek of this sentence is allusive and I expand it somewhat. The point is that each month each person will attend the festival both of his tribe and of his local community (deme). See W. E. Thompson, 'The Demes in Plato's *Laws*', *Eranos*, LXIII (1965), 134–6.

8. See pp. 206–7.

sacrifices and dances, a reasonable and adequate period to allow for experiment, in general and in detail, will be ten years. So long as the original legislator is alive, the various officials should bring him into the consultations, but when he is dead they must use their own initiative in putting up to the Guardians of the Laws proposals for remedying the deficiencies in their respective spheres. This process should continue until every detail is thought to have received its final polish. After that, they must assume that the rules are immutable, and observe them along with the rest of the code which the legislator laid down and imposed on them originally. Not a single detail should be altered, if they can help it; but if they ever believe that the force of circumstances has become irresistible, they must consult all the officials, the entire citizen body and all the oracles of the gods. If the verdict is unanimously in favour, then they may amend, but never in any other conditions whatever; the law will be that the opposition must always win the day.

THE LAW OF MARRIAGE

To resume, then: when a man of twenty-five has observed others and been observed by them and is confident that he has found a family offering someone to his taste who would make a suitable partner for the procreation of children, he should get married, and in any case before he reaches thirty. First, however, he ought to hear the correct method of trying to find a suitable and congenial partner. As Cleinias says[9], the appropriate preface should stand at the head of every law.

CLEINIAS: Well reminded, sir – and at just the right moment in our conversation, I fancy.

PREAMBLE TO THE LAW OF MARRIAGE:
CHOOSING A PARTNER (2)

ATHENIAN: Quite so. 'My boy,' let's say to this son of a good family,

9. See p. 186.

773 'you must make a marriage that will be approved by sensible
folk. They will advise you not to be over keen to avoid
marrying into a poor family or to seek to marry into a rich
one; other things being equal, you should always prefer
to marry somewhat beneath you. That will be best both for
the state and the union of your two hearths and homes,
because it is infinitely better for the virtue of a man and
wife if they balance and complement each other than if they
are both at the same extreme. If a man knows he's rather
headstrong and apt to be too quick off the mark in everything he does, he ought to be anxious to ally himself to a
family of quiet habits, and if he has the opposite kind of
temperament he should marry into the opposite kind of
family. One general rule should apply to marriage: we
should seek to contract the alliance that will benefit the
state, not the one that we personally find most alluring.
Everyone is naturally drawn to the person most like himself, and that puts the whole state off balance, because of
discrepancies in wealth and character;[10] and these in turn
generally lead, in most states, to results we certainly don't
want to see in ours.'

If we give explicit instructions in the form of a law – 'no
rich man to marry into a rich family, no powerful person to
marry into a powerful house, the headstrong must be forced
to join in marriage with the phlegmatic and the phlegmatic
with the headstrong' – well, it's ludicrous, of course, but it
will also annoy a great many people who find it hard to
understand why the state should be like the mixture in a
mixing-bowl. When you pour in the wine it seethes furiously,
but once dilute it with the god of the teetotallers, and you
have a splendid combination which will make you a good and
reasonable drink. Very few people have it in them to see that
the same principle applies to the alliance that produces children. For these reasons we are forced to omit such topics from
our actual laws. However, we must resort to our 'charms'[11]

10. I.e. if the rich marry the rich, they will get richer and the poor
poorer, and this will lead to tension. See pp. 214–15.
11. See pp. 95–6.

and try to persuade everybody to think it more important to produce well-balanced children than to marry his equal and never stop lusting for wealth. Anyone who is set on enriching himself by his marriage should be headed off by reproaches rather than compelled by a written law.

FAILURE TO MARRY

So much for marriage: these exhortations should be added to our previous account of how we should become partners in eternity by leaving a line of descendants to serve God for ever in our stead.[12] A correctly composed preface would have all 774 that and more to say about the obligation to marry.

11. If anyone disobeys (except involuntarily), and unsociably keeps himself to himself so that he is still unmarried at the age of thirty-five,

he must pay an annual fine: 100 drachmas if he belongs to the highest property-class, seventy if to the second, sixty if to the third, and thirty if to the fourth; the sum to be consecrated to Hera.

12. If he refuses to pay his annual fine,
his debt must be increased ten times.

(The fine is to be collected by the treasurer of the goddess.

13. If he fails to collect it,
he will have to owe the sum himself.

Every treasurer must give an account of himself in this respect at the scrutiny.) So much for the financial penalty to be paid by anyone refusing to marry, but

12. (cont.)
he should also be barred from receiving the respect due to him from his juniors, none of whom should ever readily take the slightest notice of him. If the bachelor tries to chastise a man, everyone should take the victim's side and protect him.

12. See p. 183.

14. If a bystander fails to give the victim help,
the law should see that he gets the reputation of being a rotten, lily-livered citizen.

DOWRIES

We've already discussed dowries,[13] but we ought to repeat that even if the poor do have to marry and give in marriage on limited resources, it will not affect their prospects of a long life one way or the other, because in this state no one will go without the necessities of life. Nor will wives be so inclined to give themselves airs, and their husbands will be less humiliated by kowtowing to them for financial reasons.[14] If a man obeys this law, so much to his credit.

15. If he does not, and gives or receives more than fifty drachmas for the trousseau in the case of the lowest property-class (or more than a hundred or a hundred and fifty or two hundred according to class),
he must owe as much again to the treasury, and the amount given or received must be dedicated to Hera and Zeus.

16. The treasurers of these gods are to exact these sums in the same way as we said the treasurers of Hera had to collect the fines in every case of refusal to marry,
or pay out of their own pockets.

The right to make a valid betrothal should rest initially with the bride's father, secondly with her grandfather, thirdly with her brothers by the same father. If none of these is available, the right should belong to the relatives on the mother's side in the same order. If any exceptional misfortune occurs, the nearest relatives shall be authorized to act in conjunction with the girl's guardians.

That leaves us with the pre-marriage sacrifices and any 775 other relevant rites that should be performed before, during or after the wedding. A citizen should ask the Expounders

13. See p. 211.
14. A wife with a large dowry enjoyed a certain edge in domestic arguments.

about these matters, and be confident that if he does as they tell him, everything will be in order.

THE WEDDING-FEAST

As for the wedding-feast, neither family should invite more than five friends of both sexes, and the number of relatives and kinsmen from either side should be limited similarly. No one should incur expense beyond his means: that is, no more than a mina in the case of the wealthiest class, half a mina for the next and so on down the scale according to class. Everyone should commend the man who obeys the regulation, but

17. the Guardians of the Laws must chastise the disobedient as a philistine who has never been trained to appreciate the melodies[15] of the Muses of marriage.

CORRECT PROCREATION (1)

To drink to the point of inebriation is improper whatever the place (except at the feasts of the god who made us the gift of wine), and it's dangerous too, especially if you want to make your marriage a success. On the day of their wedding particularly, when they are at a turning-point in their lives, bride and groom ought to show restraint, so as to make as sure as they can (it being practically impossible to tell the day or night in which by the favour of God conception will take place) that any child they may have should have parents who were sober when they conceived him. Apart from that, children should not be conceived when the parents' bodies are in a state of drunken relaxation; the foetus should be compactly formed and firmly planted, and its growth should be orderly and undisturbed. But when he's drunk a man reels about all over the place and bumps into things, and a raging passion invades his body and soul; this means that as a sower of his seed a drunkard will be clumsy and inefficient, and he'll produce unbalanced children who are not to be trusted, with devious characters, and in all probability with misshapen

15. 'Nomes': the same pun as on p. 185.

bodies too. That's why all the year round, throughout his life (but particularly during the age of procreation), a man must take great care to do nothing to injure his health, if he can help it, and nothing with any hint of insolence or injustice, which will inevitably rub off on to the souls and bodies of his children, and produce absolutely degenerate creatures who have been stamped with the likeness of their father. At the very least, he must shun such vices on the day of his wedding and the following night, because if a human institution gets off to a good and careful start, there is a sort of divine guarantee that it will prosper.

THE LIFE OF THE NEWLY-WEDS

The bridegroom must regard one of the two homes included 776 in the lot as the nest in which he will bring up his brood of young; here he must be married, after leaving his father and mother, and here he must make his home and become the breadwinner for himself and his children. You see, when people feel the need of absent friends, the ties that bind them are strengthened, but when they overdo it and are too much together so that they're not apart long enough to miss each other, they drift apart. That's why the newly-weds must leave their father and mother and the wife's relatives in the old home and live somewhere else, rather as if they had gone off to a colony; and each side should visit, and be visited by, the other. The young couple should produce children and bring them up, handing on the torch of life from generation to generation, and always worshipping the gods in the manner prescribed by law.

THE PROBLEM OF SLAVERY

Now for the question of property: what will it be reasonable for a man to possess? Mostly, it's not difficult to see what it would be, and acquire it; but slaves offer difficulties at every turn. The reason is this. The terms we employ are partly correct and partly not, in that the actual language we use about slaves is partly a reflection and partly a contradiction of our practical experience of them.

MEGILLUS: Oh? What do you mean? We don't yet see your point, sir.

ATHENIAN: No wonder, Megillus. The Spartan helot-system is probably just about the most difficult and contentious institution in the entire Greek world; some people think it's a good idea, others are against it (though less feeling is aroused by the slavery to which the Mariandynoi have been reduced at Heraclea, and by the race of serfs to be found in Thessaly).[16] Faced with these and similar cases, what should our policy be on the ownership of slaves? The point I happened to bring up in my discussion of the subject, and which naturally made you ask what I meant, was this: we know we'd all agree that a man should own the best and most docile slaves he can get – after all, many a paragon of a slave has done much more for a man than his own brother or son, and they have often been the salvation of their masters' persons and property and entire homes. We know quite well, don't we, that some people do tell such stories about slaves?

MEGILLUS: Certainly.

ATHENIAN: And don't others take the opposite line, and say that a slave's soul is rotten through and through, and that if we have any sense we won't trust such a pack at all? The most profound of our poets actually says (speaking of Zeus) that   777

If you make a man a slave, that very day
Far-sounding Zeus takes half his wits away.[17]

Everyone sees the problem differently, and takes one side or

16. The Spartan helots were a numerous class of state serfs, in part the descendants of the original non-Doric population conquered by the Dorian invaders (c. 1000 B.C.); they differed in status from ordinary slaves in various respects, and were kept under control by a 'secret police' of young Spartans. For further details, see W. G. Forrest, A History of Sparta, 950–192 B.C. (London, 1968), especially pp. 30 ff., 101 ff., 113 ff. The helots' counterparts in Heraclea were the Mariandynoi and in Thessaly the Penestai. These and other Greek serf systems are similar in kind rather than identical in all details.

17. Homer, Odyssey XVII, 322–3.

the other. Some people don't trust slaves as a class in anything: they treat them like animals, and whip and goad them so that they make the souls of their slaves three times – no, a thousand times – more slavish than they were. Others follow precisely the opposite policy.

MEGILLUS: True.

CLEINIAS: Well then, sir, in view of this conflict of opinion, what should we do about our own country? What's our line on the possession of slaves, and the way to punish them?

ATHENIAN: Look here, Cleinias: the animal 'man' quite obviously has a touchy temper, and it looks as if it won't be easy, now or in the future, to persuade him to fall neatly into the two categories (slave and freeman master) which are necessary for practical purposes. Your slave, therefore, will be a difficult beast to handle. The frequent and repeated revolts in Messenia, and in the states where people possess a lot of slaves who all speak the same language, have shown the evils of the system often enough; and we can also point to the various crimes and adventures of the robbers who plague Italy, the 'Rangers', as they're called. In view of all this you may well be puzzled to know what your general policy ought to be. In fact, there are just two ways of dealing with the problem open to us: first, if the slaves are to submit to their condition without giving trouble, they should not all come from the same country or speak the same tongue, as far as it can be arranged; secondly, we ought to train them properly, not only for their sakes but above all for our own. The best way to train slaves is to refrain from arrogantly ill-treating them, and to harm them even less (assuming that's possible)[18] than you would your equals. You see, when a man can hurt someone as often as he likes, he'll soon show whether or not his respect for justice is natural and unfeigned and springs from a genuine hatred of injustice. If his attitude to his slaves and his conduct towards them are free of any taint of impiety and injustice, he'll be splendidly effective at sowing the seeds of virtue. Just the same can be said of the

18. I.e. if 'less' than 'not at all' is possible.

way in which any master or dictator or person in any position of authority deals with someone weaker than himself. Even so, we should certainly punish slaves if they deserve it, and not spoil them by simply giving them a warning, as we would free men. Virtually everything you say to a slave should be an order, and you should never become at all familiar with them – neither the women nor the men. 778 (Though this is how a lot of silly folk do treat their slaves, and usually only succeed in spoiling them and in making life more difficult – more difficult, I mean, for the slaves to take orders and for themselves to maintain their authority.)

CLEINIAS: You're quite right.

THE BUILDINGS OF THE STATE

ATHENIAN: So now that the citizen has been supplied with a sufficient number of suitable slaves to help him in his various tasks, the next thing will be to outline a housing-plan, won't it?

CLEINIAS: Certainly.

ATHENIAN: Our state is new, and has no buildings already existing, so it rather looks as if it will have to work out the details of its entire architectural scheme for itself, particularly those of the temples and city walls. Ideally, Cleinias, this subject would have been dealt with before we discussed marriage, but as the whole picture is theoretical anyway, it's perfectly possible to turn to it now, as we are doing. Still, when we put the scheme into practice, we'll see to the buildings, God willing, *before* we regulate marriage, and marriage will then crown our labours in this field. But here and now, let's just give a swift sketch of the building programme.

CLEINIAS: By all means.

ATHENIAN: Temples should be built all round the market-place and on high ground round the perimeter of the city, for purposes of protection and sanitation. Next to them should be administrative offices and courts of law. This is holy ground, and here – partly because the legal cases involve solemn religious issues, partly because of the august divinities whose temples are nearby – judgement will be given and sentence received. Among these buildings will be the courts in which cases of murder, and all other crimes which deserve the death penalty, may properly be heard.

As for city walls, Megillus, I'd agree with the Spartan view that they should be left lying asleep and undisturbed in the ground. My reasons? As the poet neatly puts it, in those words so often cited, 'a city's walls should be made of bronze and iron, not stone'.[19] Besides, what fools people would take us for, and rightly, if we sent our young men out into the countryside every year to excavate trenches and ditches and various structures to ward off the enemy and stop them coming over the boundaries at all[20] – and then were to build a wall round the city! A wall never contributes anything to a town's health, and in any case is apt to encourage a certain softness in the souls of the inhabitants. It invites them to take refuge behind it instead of tackling the enemy and ensuring their own safety by mounting guard night and day; it tempts them to suppose that a foolproof way of protecting themselves is to barricade themselves in behind their walls and gates, and then drop off to sleep, as if they were brought into this world for a life of luxury. It never occurs to them that comfort is really to be won by the sweat of the brow, whereas the only result of such disgusting luxury and idleness is a fresh round of troubles, in my view. However, if men are to have a city wall at all, the private houses should be constructed right from the foundations so that the whole city forms in effect a single wall: that is, all the houses should be easy to defend because they present to the street a regular and unbroken front. A whole city looking like a single house will be quite a pretty sight, and being easy to guard it will be superior to any other for safety. The job of seeing that the buildings always keep to the original scheme should properly belong to their occupants, but the City-Wardens should keep an eye on them and even impose fines to force any negligent

19. We do not know the poet referred to, but the sentiment is fairly common: see e.g. Aeschylus, *Persians*, 349.
20. See p. 234.

person to do his duty. They should also supervise all the
sanitary arrangements of the town and stop any private person
encroaching on public land by buildings or excavations. The
same officials must take particular care to see that rainwater
flows away properly, and in general they must make all the
appropriate arrangements inside and outside the city. To deal
with all these points, and to supplement any other deficiency
in the law (which cannot be exhaustive), the Guardians of the
Laws are to make additional rules in the light of experience.

WOMEN MUST JOIN THE COMMUNAL MEALS

So much for these buildings, together with those round the
market-place, and gymnasia and all the schools: they are now
ready and waiting to be entered, and the theatres are prepared
for the arrival of their audiences. Now let's pass on to the
next item in our legislation, the time after the wedding.

CLEINIAS: By all means.

ATHENIAN: Let's suppose the ceremony is over, Cleinias;
between then and the birth of a child there may well be a
complete year. Now, in a state which sets its sights higher
than others, how this year is to be spent by a bride and groom
(you remember we broke off when we got to this point)[21]
is not the easiest thing in the world to specify. We've had
knotty problems like this before, but the common man will
find our policy this time more difficult to swallow than ever.
However, we should never shrink from speaking the truth as
we see it, Cleinias.

CLEINIAS: Of course.

ATHENIAN: Take someone who proposes to promulgate 780
laws to a state about the correct conduct of the public life of
the community. What if he reckons that *in principle* one ought
not to use compulsion – even in so far as one *can* use it in
private affairs? Suppose he thinks that a man ought to be
allowed to do what he likes with the day, instead of being
regulated at every turn. Well, if he excludes private life from
his legislation, and expects that the citizens will be prepared

21. See p. 256.

to be law-abiding in their public life as a community, he's making a big mistake. Now, what's made me say this? It's because we are going to assert that our newly-marrieds ought to attend communal meals no more and no less than they did before their wedding. I know that this custom of eating together caused eyebrows to be raised when it was introduced in your parts of the world, but I suppose it was dictated by war or some other equally serious emergency that pressed hard on a small people in a critical situation. But once you had had this enforced experience of communal meals, you realized just how much the custom contributed to your security. It must have been in some such way that the practice of communal feeding established itself among you.

CLEINIAS: That sounds plausible enough.

ATHENIAN: As I was saying, it was once an astonishing custom and some people were apprehensive about imposing it. But if a legislator wanted to impose it today, he wouldn't have half so much trouble. But the custom points to another measure, which would probably prove equally successful, if tried. Today, it's absolutely unheard-of, and that's what makes the legislator 'card his wool into the fire', as the saying is, and make so many efforts fruitlessly. This measure is neither easy to describe nor simple in execution.

CLEINIAS: Well then, sir, what's the point you're trying to make? You seem to be awfully reluctant to tell us.

ATHENIAN: Listen to me, then: let's not waste time lingering over this business. The blessings that a state enjoys are in direct proportion to the degree of law and order to be found in it, and the effects of good regulations in some fields are usually vitiated to the extent that things are controlled either incompetently or not at all in others. The point is relevant to the subject in hand. Thanks to some providential necessity, Cleinias and Megillus, you have a splendid and – as I was saying – astonishing institution: communal meals
781 for men. But it is entirely wrong of you to have omitted from your legal code any provision for your women, so that the practice of communal meals for them has never got under way. On the contrary, half the human race – the female sex,

the half which in any case is inclined to be secretive and crafty, because of its weakness – has been left to its own devices because of the misguided indulgence of the legislator. Because you neglected this sex, you gradually lost control of a great many things which would be in a far better state today if they had been regulated by law. You see, leaving women to do what they like is not just to lose *half* the battle (as it may seem): a woman's natural potential for virtue is inferior to a man's, so she's proportionately a greater danger, perhaps even twice as great. So the happiness of the state will be better served if we reconsider the point and put things right, by providing that all our arrangements apply to men and women alike. But at present, unhappily, the human race has not progressed as far as that, and if you're wise you won't breathe a word about such a practice in other parts of the world where states do not recognize communal meals as a public institution at all. So when it comes to the point, how on earth are you going to avoid being laughed to scorn when you try to force women to take their food and drink in public? There's nothing the sex is likely to put up with more reluctantly: women have got used to a life of obscurity and retirement, and any attempt to force them into the open will provoke tremendous resistance from them, and they'll be more than a match for the legislator. Elsewhere, as I said, the very mention of the correct policy will be met with howls of protest. But perhaps this state will be different. So if you want our discussion about political systems to be as complete as theory can ever be, I'd like to explain the merits and advantages of this institution – that is, if you are equally keen to listen to me. If not, then let's skip it.

CLEINIAS: No, no, sir: we're very anxious to hear the explanation.

THREE INSTINCTIVE DRIVES: FOOD, DRINK, SEX

ATHENIAN: Let's listen, then. But don't be disconcerted if I appear to be starting a long way back. We've time to spare, and there's no compelling reason why we shouldn't look into the business of legislation from all possible angles.

CLEINIAS: You're quite right.

ATHENIAN: Let's go back to what we said at the beginning.[22] Here's something that everyone must be perfectly clear about: *either* mankind had absolutely no beginning in time and will have no end, but always existed and always will, *or* it has existed for an incalculably long time from its origin.

CLEINIAS: Naturally.

ATHENIAN: Well, now we may surely assume that in every part of the world cities have been formed and destroyed, and all sorts of customs have been adopted, some orderly, some not, along with the growth of every sort of taste in food, solid and liquid. And the various changes in the seasons have developed, which have probably stimulated a vast number of natural changes in living beings.

CLEINIAS: Of course.

ATHENIAN: Well, we believe, don't we, that at a certain point vines made their appearance, not having existed before, and olives likewise, and the gifts[23] of Demeter and Kore, which Triptolemus, or whoever it was, handed on to us? So long as these things did not exist, we can take it that animals resorted to feeding on each other, as they do now?

CLEINIAS: Certainly.

ATHENIAN: We observe, of course, the survival of human sacrifice among many people today. Elsewhere, we gather, the opposite practice prevailed, and there was a time when we didn't even dare to eat beef, and the sacrifices offered to the gods were not animals, but cakes and meal soaked in honey and other 'pure' offerings like that. People kept off meat on the grounds that it was an act of impiety to eat it, or to pollute the altars of the gods with blood. So at that time men lived a sort of 'Orphic'[24] life, keeping exclusively to in-

22. See pp. 118 ff.

23. Cereals. Demeter was the goddess in control of the fruits of the earth, especially corn, and was commonly worshipped in association with Kore ('the Virgin'). Triptolemus was sent by Demeter to spread the knowledge of agricultural techniques among mankind.

24. The Orphics held that the soul of a man could be reborn in the body of another man or of an animal, and the soul of an animal in the

animate food and entirely abstaining from eating the flesh of animals.

CLEINIAS: So it's commonly said, and it's easy enough to believe.

ATHENIAN: Then the question naturally arises, why have I related all this to you now?

CLEINIAS: A perfectly correct assumption, sir.

ATHENIAN: Now then, Cleinias, I'll try to explain the next point, if I can.

CLEINIAS: Carry on, then.

ATHENIAN: Observation tells me that all human actions are motivated by a set of three needs and desires. Give a man a correct education, and these instincts will lead him to virtue, but educate him badly and he'll end up at the other extreme. From the moment of their birth men have a desire for food and drink. Every living creature has an instinctive love of satisfying this desire whenever it occurs, and the craving to do so can fill a man's whole being, so that he remains quite unmoved by the plea that he should do anything except satisfy his lust for the pleasures of the body, so as to make himself immune to all discomfort. Our third and greatest 783 need, the longing we feel most keenly, is the last to come upon us: it is the flame of the imperious lust to procreate, which kindles the fires of passion in mankind. These three unhealthy instincts must be directed beyond what men call supreme pleasure, towards the *best* supreme pleasure. We must try to keep them in check by the three powerful influences of fear, law, and correct argument; but in addition, we should invoke the help of the Muses and the gods who preside over competitions, to smother their growth and dam their tide.[25]

---

body of another animal or of a man. This belief in the kinship of life was the reason for the Orphics' strict prohibition of killing and meat-eating.

25. The appetites are presumably unhealthy not in themselves, but only when excessive or misdirected. In modern terms, I suppose, the Athenian advocates 'sublimating' our desires.

CORRECT PROCREATION (2)

The topic which should come after marriage, and before training and education, is the birth of children. Perhaps, as we take these topics in order, we shall be able to complete each individual law as we did before, when we approached the question of communal meals – I mean that when we've become intimate with our citizens, perhaps we shall be able to see more clearly whether such gatherings should consist of men only or whether, after all, they should include women. Similarly, when we've won control of certain institutions that have never yet been controlled by law, we'll use them as 'cover', just as other people do, with the result I indicated just now: thanks to a more detailed inspection of these institutions, we may be able to lay down laws that take account of them better.[26]

CLEINIAS: Quite right.

ATHENIAN: So let's bear in mind the points we've just made, in case we find we need to refer to them later on.

CLEINIAS: What points in particular are you telling us to remember?

ATHENIAN: The three impulses we distinguished by our three terms: the desire for 'food' (I think we said) and 'drink', and thirdly 'sexual stimulation'.

CLEINIAS: Yes, sir, we'll certainly remember, just as you tell us.

ATHENIAN: Splendid. Let's turn our attention to the bridal pair, and instruct them in the manner and method by which they should produce children. (And if we fail to persuade them, we'll threaten them with a law or two.)

26. If the English is obscure, the Greek is even worse. I understand Plato to say that family life must not afford 'cover' to undesirable habits, but be subject to control by legislation (cf. p. 270 ff.); but just as legislation on common meals had to wait on a fuller knowledge of the future citizens, so legislation about education etc. must wait until such officials as the 'marriage inspectors' of pp. 267-8 have penetrated family life 'under cover' of assisting it, and reported on the habits and customs that need legislation. I have built this interpretation into the translation.

CLEINIAS: How do you mean?

ATHENIAN: The bride and groom should resolve to present the state with the best and finest children they can produce. Now, when human beings co-operate in any project, and give due attention to its planning and execution, the results they achieve are always of the best and finest quality; but if they act carelessly, or are incapable of intelligent action in the first place, the results are deplorable. So the bridegroom had better deal with his wife and approach the task of begetting children with a sense of responsibility, and the bride should do the same, especially during the period when no children have yet been born to them. They should be supervised by women whom we have chosen[27] (several or only a few – the officials should appoint the number they think right, at times within their discretion). These women must assemble daily at the temple of Eileithuia[28] for not more than a third of the day, and when they have convened each must report to her colleagues any wife or husband of childbearing age she has seen who is concerned with anything but the duties imposed on him or her at the time of the sacrifices and rites of their marriage. If children come in suitable numbers, the period of supervised procreation should be ten years and no longer. But if a couple remain childless throughout this period, they should part, and call in their relatives and the female officials to help them decide terms of divorce that will safeguard the interests of them both. If some dispute arises about the duties and interests of the parties, they must choose ten of the Guardians of the Laws as arbitrators, and abide by their decisions on the points referred to them. The female officials must enter the homes of the young people and by a combination of admonition and threats try to make them give up their ignorant and sinful ways. If this has no effect, they must go and report the case to the Guardians of the Laws, who must resort to sterner methods. If even the Guardians prove ineffective, they should make the case public and post

784

27. No such women have been mentioned. (In other ways too the state of the text hereabouts suggests a lack of revision.)

28. Goddess of childbirth.

up the relevant name, swearing on their oath that they are unable to reform so-and-so.

18. (a) Unless the person whose name is posted up succeeds in convicting in court those who published the notice,

he must be deprived of the privilege of attending weddings and parties celebrating the birth of children.

19. If he persists in attending,

anyone who wishes should chastise him by beating him, and not be punished for it.

18. (b) If a woman misbehaves and her name is posted up, and she fails to win the day in court,

the same regulations are to apply to her too: she must be excluded from female processions and distinctions, and be forbidden to attend weddings and parties celebrating the birth of children.

ADULTERY

20. When children have been produced as demanded by law, if a man has intercourse with another woman, or a woman with another man, and the other party is still of an age to bear children,

they must suffer the same penalty as was specified for those who are still having children.

21. After the period of child-bearing, the chaste man or woman should be highly respected;

the promiscuous should be held in the opposite kind of 'repute' (though *dis*repute would be a better word).

When the majority of people conduct themselves with 785 moderation in sexual matters, no such regulations should be mentioned or enacted; but if there is misbehaviour, regulations should be made and enforced after the pattern of the laws we've just laid down.

REGISTRATION OF BIRTHS AND DEATHS

Our first year is the beginning of our whole life, and every boy's and girl's year of birth should be recorded in their family shrines under the heading 'born'. Alongside, on a whitened wall, should be written up in every brotherhood the sequence-numbers of the officials who facilitate the numbering of the years. The names of the living members of the brotherhood should be inscribed nearby, and those of the deceased expunged.

AGE LIMITS

The age limits for marriage shall be: for a girl, from sixteen to twenty (these will be the extreme limits specified), and for a man, from thirty to thirty-five. A woman may hold office from the age of forty, a man from thirty. Service in the armed forces shall be required of a man from twenty to sixty. As for women, whatever military service it may be thought necessary to impose (after they have finished bearing children) should be performed up to the age of fifty; practicable and appropriate duties should be specified for each individual.

A glance at the subheadings of this section will show that by the term 'education' Plato understands much more than we commonly do today. 'Entertainment', 'good manners', and 'use of leisure time' are only some of the many apparently trivial and irrelevant topics that he discusses. Education, he believes, is not simply narrow vocational training, but the moral formation of the 'whole man'. We are always learning something, and always being affected, for better or worse, at all stages of our existence, even in the womb; education must accordingly penetrate to the smallest detail of our private lives.

Plato's approach is, in general, conservative: he deplores, for instance, contemporary developments in music and literature as pernicious moral influences stimulating our desire for pleasure at the expense of virtue. On the other hand he can be surprisingly radical, as in his proposals for the emancipation of women from the somewhat cloistered and restricted life they led in his day. But the most important point is not the merits or demerits of his total programme or any part of it. What is crucial is his whole 'philosophy' of education, which is so hostile to the freedom of inquiry and expression that we take for granted today. Plato fervently believes that certain eternally valid norms exist, laid down for man by divine fiat; that these norms are ascertainable and leave no room for others; that real 'freedom' is to obey this divine law, and to do otherwise is to be a slave to one's passions; and that a man's education must therefore train him in this obedience. It is an uncompromising and unfashionable point of view.

WRITTEN AND UNWRITTEN RULES

BK VII 788 ATHENIAN: Now that the boys and girls have been born, I suppose their education and training will be the most suitable topic to deal with next. This is not something we can leave on one side: that would be out of the question. However, we shall clearly do better to confine our remarks to advice and instruction, and not venture on precise regulations. In the privacy of family life, you see, a great many trivial activities never get publicity, and under the stimulus of feelings of pleasure or pain or desire they can all too easily fly in the face of the lawgiver's recommendations and produce citizens whose characters are varied and conflicting, which is a social evil. Now although these activities are so trivial and so common that one cannot decently arrange to punish them by law, they do tend to undermine the written statutes, because men get into the habit of repeatedly breaking rules in small matters. That's why in spite of all the difficulties of legislating on such points, we can't simply say nothing about them. But I must try to clarify my point by showing you some samples, as it were. At the moment, I expect it looks as if I'm rather concealing my meaning.

CLEINIAS: You're quite right, it does.

EDUCATION IN THE WOMB

ATHENIAN: I take it we were justified in asserting that if an education is to qualify as 'correct', it simply must show that it is capable of making our souls and bodies as fine and as handsome as they can be?

CLEINIAS: Of course.

ATHENIAN: And I suppose (to take the most elementary requirement), that if a person is going to be supremely good-looking, his posture must be as erect as possible, right from his earliest years?

CLEINIAS: Certainly.

ATHENIAN: Well now, we observe, don't we, that the earliest stages of growth of every animal are by far the most vigorous and rapid? That's why a lot of people actually maintain that in the case of man, the first five years of life see more growth than the next twenty.

CLEINIAS: That's true.

ATHENIAN: But we're aware that rapid growth without 789 frequent and appropriately graded exercises leads to a lot of trouble for the body?

CLEINIAS: Yes, indeed.

ATHENIAN: And isn't it precisely when a body is getting most nourishment that it needs most exercise?

CLEINIAS: Good Heavens, sir, are we going to demand such a thing of new-born babies and little children?

ATHENIAN: No – I mean even earlier, when they're getting nourishment in their mother's body.

CLEINIAS: What's that you say? My dear sir! Do you really mean in the womb?

ATHENIAN: Yes, I do. But it's hardly surprising you haven't heard of these athletics of the embryo. It's a curious subject, but I'd like to tell you about it.

CLEINIAS: Do so, of course.

ATHENIAN: It's something it would be easier to understand in Athens, where some people go in for sport more than they should. Not only boys, but some elderly men as well, rear young birds and set them to fight one another. But they certainly don't think just pitting them one against another will give such creatures adequate exercise. To supplement this, each man keeps birds somewhere about his person – a small one in the cup of his hand, a larger one under his arm – and covers countless stades in walking about, not for the sake of his own health, but to keep these animals in good shape. To the intelligent person, the lesson is obvious: all bodies find it helpful and invigorating to be shaken by movements and joltings of all kinds, whether the motion is due to their own efforts or they are carried on a vehicle or boat or horse or any other mode of conveyance. All this enables the body to assimilate its solid and liquid food, so that we grow healthy and handsome and strong into the bargain. In view of all this, can we say what our future policy should be? If you like, we could lay down precise rules (and how people would laugh at us!): (1) A pregnant woman should go for walks, and when her child is born she should mould it like wax while it is still supple, and keep it well wrapped up for the first two years of its life. (2) The nurses must be compelled under legal penalty to contrive that the children are always being carried to the country or temples or relatives, until they are sturdy enough to stand on their own feet. (3) Even then, the nurses should persist in carrying the child around until it's three, to keep it from distorting its young limbs by subjecting them to too much pressure. (4) The nurses should be as strong as possible, and there must be plenty of them – and we could provide written penalties for each infringement of 790 the rules. But no! That would lead to far too much of what I mentioned just now.

CLEINIAS: You mean . . .

ATHENIAN: . . . the tremendous ridicule we'd provoke. And the nurses (women and slaves, with characters to match) would refuse to obey us anyway.

CLEINIAS: Then why did we insist that the rules should be specified?

ATHENIAN: For this reason. A state's free men and masters have quite different characters to the nurses', and there's a chance that if they hear these regulations they may be led to the correct conclusion: the state's general code of laws will never rest on a firm foundation as long as private life is badly regulated, and it's silly to expect otherwise. Realizing the truth of this, they may themselves spontaneously adopt our recent suggestions as rules, and thereby achieve the happiness that results from running their households and their state on proper lines.

CLEINIAS: Yes, that's all very reasonable.

ATHENIAN: Still, let's not abandon this style of legislation yet. We started to talk about young children's bodies: let's use the same sort of approach to explain how to shape their personalities.

CLEINIAS: Good idea.

THE IMPORTANCE OF MOVEMENT:
THE EVIDENCE OF CORYBANTIC RITUAL

ATHENIAN: So let's take this as our basic principle in both cases: all young children, and especially very tiny infants, benefit both physically and mentally from being nursed and kept in motion, as far as practicable, throughout the day and night; indeed, if only it could be managed, they ought to live

273

as though they were permanently on board ship. But as that's impossible, we must aim to provide our new-born infants with the closest possible approximation to this ideal.

Here's some further evidence, from which the same conclusions should be drawn: the fact that young children's nurses, and the women who cure Corybantic conditions,[1] have learnt this treatment from experience and have come to recognize its value. And I suppose you know what a mother does when she wants to get a wakeful child to sleep. Far from keeping him still, she takes care to move him about, rocking him constantly in her arms, not silently, but humming a kind of tune. The cure consists of *movement*, to the rhythms of dance and song; the mother makes her child '*pipe down*' just as surely as the music of the *pipes* bewitches the frenzied Bacchic[2] reveller.

CLEINIAS: Well then, sir, have we any particular explanation for all this?

ATHENIAN: The reason's not very hard to find.

CLEINIAS: What is it?

ATHENIAN: Both these conditions are a species of fear, and fear is the result of some inadequacy in the personality. When one treats such conditions by vigorous movement, this external motion, by cancelling out the internal agitation that gives rise to the fear and frenzy, induces a feeling of calm and peace in the soul, in spite of the painful thumping of the heart experienced by each patient. The result is very gratifying. Whereas the wakeful children are sent to sleep, the revellers (far from asleep!), by being set to dance to the music of the pipes, are restored to mental health after their derangement,

791

1. Frenzied pathological states accompanied by a strong desire to dance, popularly supposed to be caused by the Corybantes, spirits in attendance on the goddess Cybele. The condition was cured homoeopathically by the *disciplined* music and dancing of Corybantic ritual. For a different view, see I. M. Linforth, 'The Corybantic Rites in Plato', *University of California Publications in Classical Philology*, XIII (1946), 121–62.

2. For the purpose of his illustration, Plato seems to treat 'Corybantic' and 'Bacchic' ritual (ecstatic dancing to music, in honour of Dionysus) as essentially similar.

with the assistance of the gods to whom they sacrifice so propitiously. This explanation, brief as it is, is convincing enough.

CLEINIAS: Yes, indeed.

ATHENIAN: Well then, seeing how effective these measures are, here's another point to notice about the patient. Any man who has experienced terrors from his earliest years will be that much more likely to grow up timid. But no one will deny that this is to train him to be a coward, not a hero.

CLEINIAS: Of course.

ATHENIAN: Contrariwise, we'd agree that a training in courage right from infancy demands that we overcome the terrors and fears that assail us?

CLEINIAS: Exactly.

ATHENIAN: So we can say that exercising very young children by keeping them in motion contributes a great deal towards the perfection of one aspect of the soul's virtue.

CLEINIAS: Certainly.

HOW FAR SHOULD A CHILD BE HUMOURED?

ATHENIAN: Further, good humour and bad humour will be a conspicuous element in a good or bad moral character respectively.

CLEINIAS: Of course.

ATHENIAN: So how can we instil into the new-born child, right from the start, whichever of these two characteristics we want? We must try to indicate how far they are within our control, and the methods we have to use.

CLEINIAS: Quite so.

ATHENIAN: I belong to the school of thought which maintains that luxury makes a child bad-tempered, irritable, and apt to react violently to trivial things. At the other extreme, unduly savage repression turns children into cringing slaves and puts them so much at odds with the world that they become unfit to be members of a community.

CLEINIAS: So how should the state as a whole set about bringing up children who are as yet unable to understand what is said to them or respond to any attempt to educate them?

ATHENIAN: More or less like this. Every new-born animal is apt to give a sort of loud yell – especially the human child, who in addition to yelling is also exceptionally prone to tears.

CLEINIAS: He certainly is.

ATHENIAN: So if a nurse is trying to discover what a child
792 wants, she judges from these reactions to what it is offered. Silence, she thinks, means she is giving it the right thing, whereas crying and bawling indicate the wrong one. Clearly these tears and yells are the child's way of signalling his likes and dislikes – and ominous signs they are, too, because this stage lasts at least three years, and that's quite a large part of one's life to spend badly (or well).

CLEINIAS: You're right.

ATHENIAN: Now don't you two think that a morose and ungenial fellow will on the whole be more of a moaner and a grumbler than a good man has any right to be?

CLEINIAS: Yes, *I* think so, at any rate.

ATHENIAN: Well then, suppose you do your level best during these years to shelter him from distress and fright and any kind of pain at all. Shouldn't we expect that child to be educated into a more cheerful and genial disposition?

CLEINIAS: Certainly, and especially, sir, if one surrounded him with lots of pleasures.

ATHENIAN: Now here, my dear sir, is just where Cleinias no longer carries me with him. That's the best way to ruin a child, because the corruption invariably sets in at the very earliest stages of his education. But perhaps I'm wrong about this: let's see.

CLEINIAS: Tell us what you mean.

ATHENIAN: I mean that we're now discussing a topic of great importance. So you too, Megillus, see what your views are, and help us to make up our minds. My position is this: the right way of life is neither a single-minded pursuit of pleasure nor an absolute avoidance of pain, but a genial (the word I used just now) contentment with the state between those extremes – precisely the state, in fact, which we always say is that of God himself (a conjecture that's reasonable enough, supported as it is by the statements of the oracles). Similarly if one of *us* aspires to live like a god, this is the state he must try to attain. He must refuse to go looking for pleasure on his own account, aware that this is not a way of avoiding pain; nor must he allow anyone else to behave like that, young or old, male or female – least of all newly-born children, if he can help it, because that's the age when habits, the seeds of the entire character, are most effectively implanted. I'd even say, at the risk of appearing flippant, that all expectant mothers, during the year of their pregnancy, should be supervised more closely than other women, to ensure that they don't experience frequent and excessive pleasures, or pains either. An expectant mother should think it important to keep calm and cheerful and sweet-tempered throughout her pregnancy.

CLEINIAS: There's no need to ask Megillus which of us 793 two has made the better case, sir. I agree with you that everyone should avoid a life of extreme pleasure and pain, and always take the middle course between them. Your point has been well and truly put, and you've heard it well and truly endorsed.

ATHENIAN: Admirable, Cleinias! Well then, here's a related point that the three of us should consider.

CLEINIAS: What's that?

UNWRITTEN RULES: A REMINDER

ATHENIAN: That all the rules we are now working through are what people generally call 'unwritten customs', and all this sort of thing is precisely what they mean when they speak of 'ancestral law'. Not only that, but the conclusion to which we were driven a moment ago was the right one: that although 'laws' is the wrong term for these things, we can't afford to say *nothing* about them, because they are the bonds of the entire social framework, linking all written and established laws with those yet to be passed. They act in the same way as ancestral customs dating from time immemorial, which by virtue of being soundly established and instinctively observed, shield and protect existing written law. But if they go wrong and get 'out of true' – well, you know what happens when carpenters' props buckle in a house: they bring the whole building crashing down, one thing on top of another, stays and superstructure (however well built) alike – all because the original timberwork has given way. So you see, Cleinias, this is what we have to bear in mind in thoroughly binding your state together while it is still a new foundation; we must do our best not to omit anything, great or small, whether 'laws', 'habits' or 'institutions', because they are all needed to bind a state together, and the permanence of the one kind of norm depends on that of the other. So we ought not to be surprised to see a flood of apparently unimportant customs or usages making our legal code a bit on the long side.

CLEINIAS: You're quite right, and we'll keep the point in mind.

EARLY EDUCATION

ATHENIAN: Up to the age of three the early training of a boy or girl will be helped enormously by this regimen, provided it is observed punctiliously and systematically. In the fourth, fifth, sixth and even seventh year of life, a child's character will need to be formed while he plays; we should now stop spoiling him, and resort to discipline, but not such as to humiliate him. We said, in the case of slaves,[3] that discipline should not be enforced so high-handedly that they become resentful, though on the other hand we mustn't spoil them by letting them go uncorrected; the same rule should apply to free persons too. When children are brought together, they discover more or less spontaneously the games which come naturally to them at that age. As soon as they are three, and until they reach the age of six, all children must congregate at the village temples – the children of each village to assemble at the same place. They should be kept in order and restrained from bad behaviour by their nurses, who should

3. See p. 258.

themselves be supervised, along with their groups as a whole, by the twelve women elected for the purpose, one to be in charge of one group for a year at a time, the allocations to be made by the Guardians of the Law. The twelve must be elected by the women in charge of supervising marriage;[4] one must be chosen from each tribe, and they must be of the same age as their electors. The woman allotted to a given tribe will discharge her duties by visiting the temple daily and punishing any cases of wrong-doing. She may use a number of state slaves to deal with male and female slaves and aliens on her own authority; however, if a citizen disputes his punishment, she must take the case to the City-Wardens, but if he does not dispute it, she may punish him too on her own authority. When the boys and girls have reached the age of six, the sexes should be separated; boys should spend their days with boys, and girls with girls. Each should attend lessons. The males should go to teachers of riding, archery, javelin-throwing and slinging – and the females too, if they are agreeable, may attend at any rate the lessons,[5] especially those in the use of weapons. In this business, you see, pretty nearly everyone misunderstands the current practice.

CLEINIAS: How so?

AMBIDEXTERITY

ATHENIAN: People think that where the hands are concerned right and left are *by nature* suited for different specialized tasks – whereas of course in the case of the feet and the lower limbs there is obviously no difference in efficiency at all. Thanks to the silly ideas of nurses and mothers we've all been made lame-handed, so to speak. The natural potential of each arm is just about the same, and the difference between them is our own fault, because we've habitually misused them. Of course, in activities of no consequence – using the left hand for the lyre and the right for the *plectrum*[6] and so on – it

4. Presumably a reference to p. 267.
5. As distinct from mock battles. See p. 322 and cf. p. 330.
6. The instrument used for striking the lyre.

doesn't matter in the slightest. But to take these examples as a model for other activities too, when there's no need, is 795 pretty stupid. The Scythian practice is an illustration of this: a Scythian doesn't use his left hand exclusively to draw his bow and his right hand exclusively to fit in the arrow, but uses both hands for both jobs indifferently. There are a lot of other similar examples to be found – in driving chariots, for instance, and other activities – from which we can see that when people train the left hand to be weaker than the right they are going *against* nature. As we said, that doesn't matter when it's a case of *plectra* of horn and similar instruments. But it matters enormously when one has to use iron weapons of war (javelins, arrows or whatever), and it matters most of all when you have to use your weapons in fighting hand to hand. And what a difference there is between a man who has learnt this lesson and one who has not, between the trained and the untrained fighter! You know how a trained pancratiast[7] or boxer or wrestler can fight on his left, so that when his opponent makes him change over and fight on that side, he doesn't stagger round as though he were lame, but keeps his poise. And I reckon we have to suppose that precisely the same rule applies to the use of weapons and to all other activities: when a man has two sets of limbs for attack and defence, he ought to leave neither of them idle and untrained if he can help it. In fact, if you were born with the body of a Geryon or a Briareus,[8] you ought to be able to throw a hundred shafts with your hundred hands. All these points should come under the supervision of the male and female officials, the latter keeping an eye on the training the children get at play, the former superintending their lessons. They must see that every boy and girl grows up versatile in the use of both hands and both feet, so that they don't ruin their natural abilities by their acquired habits, so far as they can be prevented.

7. See note on p. 323.
8. Monsters: Geryon had a triple body, Briareus a hundred hands.

PHYSICAL TRAINING (I)

In practice, formal lessons will fall into two categories, physical training for the body, and cultural education to perfect the personality. Physical training can be further subdivided into two branches: dancing and wrestling. Now when people dance, they are either acting the words of the composer,[9] and a dignified and civilized style is their prime concern, or they are aiming at physical fitness, agility and beauty. In this case they are preoccupied with bending and stretching in the approved fashion, so that each limb and other part of the body can move with its own peculiar grace – a grace which is then carried over and infused into dancing in general.[10] As for wrestling, the kind of trick introduced as part of their technique by Antaeus and Cercyon because of their wretched obsession with winning, and the boxing devices invented by Epeius and Amycus, are absolutely useless in a military encounter and don't merit the honour of being described.[11] But if the legitimate manoeuvres of *regular* wrestling – extricating the neck and hands and sides from entanglement – are practised for the sake of strength and health with a vigorous desire to win and without resort to undignified postures, then they are extremely useful, and we mustn't neglect them. So when we reach the proper place in our legal code we must tell the future teachers to present all this kind of instruction in an attractive way, and the pupils to receive it with gratitude. Nor should we omit to mention the chorus-performances that may appropriately be imitated: for instance, here in Crete the 'games in armour' of the Curetes,[12] and those of the Dioscuri[13] in Sparta. And at Athens our Virgin Lady,[14] I believe, charmed by the pleasure of

796

9. See note on Greek 'music' on p. 85. Dancing can be *either* by way of dramatic performance *or* merely callisthenic.

10. I.e. callisthenics are an aid to dancing in the drama, etc.

11. E.g. dropping on to the ground in wrestling (Antaeus), and the use of gloves in boxing (Amycus).

12. Cretan spirits who protected the infant Zeus.

13. Castor and Pollux.   14. Athena.

performing in a chorus,[15] and disapproving of empty hands in recreation, thought she should perform the dance only when arrayed in full armour. Our boys and girls should imitate her example wholeheartedly, and prize the gift[16] which the goddess has made them, because it increases their fighting skill and embellishes their festivals. Young boys, right from the early stages up to the age of military service, should be equipped with weapons and horses whenever they parade and process in honour of any god; and when they supplicate the gods and sons of gods they must dance and march in step, sometimes briskly, sometimes slowly. Even contests and preliminary heats, if they are to prove their worth in war and peace to the state and private households, must be conducted with these purposes[17] in view and no other. Other kinds of physical exercise, Megillus and Cleinias, whether serious or by way of recreation, are beneath the dignity of a gentleman.

I've now pretty well described the sort of physical education which needed to be described, as I said early on.[18] So there it is, in all its detail. If you know of a better system than that, let's have it.

CLEINIAS: No sir, if we cry off these ideas of yours, a better programme of competitions and physical training won't be easy to describe.

THE DANGERS OF INNOVATION IN
EDUCATION

ATHENIAN: The next subject is the gifts of Apollo and the Muses. When we discussed this before,[19] we thought we'd exhausted the topic, and that physical training alone remained for discussion. But it's clear now that a number of points were omitted – points which everyone ought in fact to hear first. So let's go through them in order.

CLEINIAS: Yes, they should certainly be mentioned.

15. See note on pp. 84–5.
16. I.e. armed dancing.
17. I.e. efficiency in war and good performance in festivals.
18. See p. 115. 19. In §§1–3.

ATHENIAN: Listen to me then. You've done that before, 797
of course, but such a curious eccentricity calls for extreme
caution in the speaker and his audience. You see, I'm going
to spin a line that almost makes me afraid to open my mouth;
still, I'll pluck up my courage and go ahead.

CLEINIAS: What is this thesis of yours, sir?

ATHENIAN: I maintain that no one in any state has really
grasped that children's games affect legislation so crucially as
to determine whether the laws that are passed will survive or
not. If you control the way children play, and the same
children always play the same games under the same rules and
in the same conditions, and get pleasure from the same toys,
you'll find that the conventions of adult life too are left in
peace without alteration. But in fact games are always being
changed and constantly modified and new ones invented, and
the younger generation never enthuses over the same thing
for two days running. They have no permanent agreed
standard of what is becoming or unbecoming either in
deportment or their possessions in general; they worship
anyone who is always introducing some novelty or doing
something unconventional to shapes and colours and all that
sort of thing. In fact, it's no exaggeration to say that this fellow
is the biggest menace that can ever afflict a state, because he
quietly changes the character of the young by making them
despise old things and value novelty. That kind of language
and that kind of outlook is – again I say it – the biggest
disaster any state can suffer. Listen: I'll tell you just how big
an evil I maintain it is.

CLEINIAS: You mean the way the public grumbles at old-
fashioned ways of doing things?

ATHENIAN: Exactly.

CLEINIAS: Well, you won't find us shutting our ears to
that kind of argument – you couldn't have a more sympathetic audience.

ATHENIAN: So I should imagine.

CLEINIAS: Go on then.

ATHENIAN: Well now, let's listen to the argument with
even greater attention than usual, and expound it to each

other with equal care. Change, we shall find, except in something evil,[20] is extremely dangerous. This is true of seasons and winds, the regimen of the body and the character of the soul – in short, of everything without exception (unless, as I said just now, the change affects something evil). Take as an example the way the body gets used to all sorts of food and drink and exercise. At first they upset it, but then in the course of time it's this very regimen that is responsible for its putting on flesh. Then the regimen and the flesh form a kind of partnership, so that the body grows used to this congenial and familiar system, and lives a life of perfect happiness and health. But imagine someone forced to change again to one of the other recommended systems: initially, he's troubled by illnesses, and only slowly, by getting used to his new way of life, does he get back to normal. Well, we must suppose that precisely the same thing happens to a man's outlook and personality. When the laws under which people are brought up have by some heaven-sent good fortune remained unchanged over a very long period, so that no one remembers or has heard of things ever being any different, the soul is filled with such respect for tradition that it shrinks from meddling with it in any way. Somehow or other the legislator must find a method of bringing about this situation in the state. Now here's my own solution of the problem. All legislators suppose that an alteration to children's games really is just a 'game', as I said before, which leads to no serious or genuine damage. Consequently, so far from preventing change, they feebly give it their blessing. They don't appreciate that if children introduce novelties into their games, they'll inevitably turn out to be quite different people from the previous generation; being different, they'll demand a different kind of life, and that will then make them want new institutions and laws. The next stage is what we described just now as the biggest evil that can affect a state – but not a single legislator takes fright at the prospect. Other changes, that affect only deportment, will do less harm, but it is a very serious matter indeed to keep changing the criteria for praising or censuring a man's moral character, and we must take great care to avoid doing so.

CLEINIAS: Of course.

ATHENIAN: Well then, are we still happy about the line we took earlier,[21] when we said that rhythms and music in general were means of representing the characters of good men and bad? Or what?

CLEINIAS: Yes, our view remains exactly the same.

ATHENIAN: So our position is this: we must do everything we possibly can to distract the younger generation from wanting to try their hand at presenting new subjects, either in dance or song; and we must also stop pleasure-mongers seducing them into the attempt.

CLEINIAS: You're absolutely right.

ATHENIAN: Now, does any of us know of a better method 799 of achieving such an object than that of the Egyptians?[22]

CLEINIAS: What method is that?

ATHENIAN: To *sanctify* all our dances and music. The first job will be to settle the festivals by drawing up the year's programme, which should show the dates of the various holidays and the individual gods, children of gods, or spirits in whose honour they should be taken. Second, it has to be decided what hymn should be sung at the various sacrifices to the gods and the type of dancing that should dignify the ritual in question. These decisions should be taken by some authority or other, and then the whole body of the citizens together should ratify them by sacrificing to the Fates and all the other gods, and by pouring a libation to consecrate the various songs to their respective divinities and other powers.

22. If anybody disobeys and introduces any different hymns or dances in honour of any god,

the *priests* and priestesses, in association with the Guardians of the Laws, will have the backing of sacred and secular law in expelling him.

23. If he resists expulsion,

he *must* be liable to a charge of impiety for the rest of his life at the hands of anyone who wishes to bring it.

21. See pp. 87–9.   22. Cf. pp. 91–2.

CLEINIAS: And serve him right.

ATHENIAN: Now seeing that we've got on to this topic, we must watch our step and behave ourselves.[23]

CLEINIAS: How do you mean?

ATHENIAN: No young man, much less an old one, on seeing or hearing anything paradoxical or unfamiliar, is ever going to brush aside his doubts all in a hurry and reach a snap decision about it. More probably, like a traveller who has come to a cross-roads, alone or with others, and is rather uncertain about the right road, he'll pause, and put the problem to himself or his companions; and he won't continue his journey until he's pretty sure of his direction and bearings. That's precisely what we must do now. Our discussion has led us to a legal paradox, and naturally we must go into it in details and not – at our age – rashly claim to pontificate in such an important field off the cuff.

CLEINIAS: You're absolutely right.

ATHENIAN: So we won't hurry over the problem, and only when we've looked into it properly shall we draw any firm conclusions. Still, there's no point in being deterred from completing the formal presentation of these 'laws' we're dealing with now, so let's press on till we get to the end of them. God willing, the completion of the whole exposition may perhaps point to an adequate solution of our present problem.

CLEINIAS: You've put it very well, sir; let's do as you say.

ATHENIAN: So let's assume we've agreed on the paradox: our songs have turned into 'nomes'[24] (apparently the ancients gave some such name to tunes on the lyre – perhaps 800 they had some inkling of what we're saying, thanks to the intuition of someone who saw a vision either in his sleep or while awake). However that may be, let's adopt this as our agreed policy: no one shall sing a note, or perform any dance-movement, other than those in the canon of public songs, sacred music, and the general body of chorus performances of the young – any more than he would violate any

23. I.e. act with the caution demanded of the old (cf. p. 59).
24. An untranslatable pun: 'nome' = 'law' and 'tune'. Cf. p. 185.

other 'nome' or law. If a man obeys, he shall go unmolested by the law; but if he disobeys, the Guardians of the Laws and the priests and priestesses must punish him, as we said just now. Can we accept this as a statement of policy?

CLEINIAS: We can.

SOME MODEL RULES

ATHENIAN: Then how could one put these rules in proper legal form, without being laughed to scorn? Well now, there's a new point we ought to notice: in this business, the safest method is to sketch a few model rules. Here's one for you: imagine a sacrifice has been performed and the offerings burnt as demanded by law and someone standing in a private capacity near the altar and offerings – a son or brother, say – breaks out into the most extreme blasphemy: wouldn't his words fill his father and his other relations with alarm and despondency and forebodings of despair? Isn't that what we'd expect?

CLEINIAS: Of course.

ATHENIAN: But it is hardly an exaggeration to say that in our corner of the world this is exactly what happens in pretty nearly every state. When an official has performed a public sacrifice, a chorus – or rather a mob of choruses – arrives and takes up position not far from the altar and sometimes right next to it. Then they swamp the holy offerings with a flood of absolute blasphemy. With words and rhythms and music of the most morbid kind they work up the emotions of their audience to a tremendous pitch, and the prize is awarded to the chorus which succeeds best in making the community burst into tears – the very community which has just offered sacrifice. Well, that's certainly a 'nome'[25] on which we must pass an unfavourable verdict, isn't it? If there is ever any real need for the public to listen to such lugubrious noises, on days that are unclean and unlucky, it will be much better, and entirely appropriate, to hire some foreign choruses to sing such songs (just as one hires mourners to accompany funerals

25. Another play on *nomos* as 'tune' and 'custom' or 'law'. See p. 185.

with Carian dirges). In particular, the costume appropriate for such funereal dirges will not be garlands or trappings of gilt, but – to polish off the topic as quickly as possible – quite the opposite kind of thing. I merely repeat the question we're always asking ourselves: are we happy to adopt this, for a start, as one of our model rules of singing?

CLEINIAS: What?

ATHENIAN: The rule of auspicious language. This is the characteristic that is absolutely vital for our kind of song. Or shall I simply lay down the rule without repeating the question?

CLEINIAS: Lay it down by all means: your law's been approved without a single vote against it.

ATHENIAN: After auspicious language, then, what will be the second law of music?[26] Surely this: that the gods to whom we sacrifice should always be offered our prayers.

CLEINIAS: Of course.

ATHENIAN: And the third law, I suppose, will be this: poets should appreciate that prayers are requests for something from the gods, so they must take great care that they never inadvertently request an evil under the impression that it is a benefit. What a ludicrous calamity it would be to offer that kind of prayer!

CLEINIAS: It certainly would.

ATHENIAN: Now didn't our remarks a short time ago[27] persuade us that 'Gold and Silver, the gods of Wealth, ought to have neither temple nor home in our state'?[28]

CLEINIAS: Absolutely.

ATHENIAN: So what lesson can we say this doctrine holds for us? Surely this: that authors in general are quite unable to tell good from bad. We conclude that a composer who embodies this error in his words or even in his music,[29] and

26. On Greek 'music', see pp. 84–5.

27. See pp. 190 and 211.

28. Possibly a free quotation from a poet not now identifiable. Cf. p. 260.

29. The error could presumably be embodied 'in the music' by accompanying the portrayal of a rich man with attractive melodies.

who produces mistaken prayers, will make our citizens pray improperly when it comes to matters of importance – and, as we were saying, we shan't find many more glaring mistakes than that. So can we establish this as one of our model laws of music?

CLEINIAS: What?

ATHENIAN: That a poet should compose nothing that conflicts with society's conventional notions of justice, goodness and beauty. No one should be allowed to show his work to any private person without first submitting it to the appointed assessors and to the Guardians of the Laws, and getting their approval. (In effect, we've got our assessors already appointed – I mean the legislators we chose to regulate the arts, and the person we elected as Minister of Education.) Well then, here's the same question yet again: are we satisfied to adopt this as our third principle and our third model law? Or what do you think?

CLEINIAS: Of course we'll adopt it.

ATHENIAN: The next point is that it will be proper to sing hymns and panegyrics, combined with prayers, in honour of the gods. After the gods, we may similarly give the spirits and heroes their meed of praise, and pray to each of them as appropriate.

CLEINIAS: Certainly.

ATHENIAN: And the next law, which should be adopted quite ungrudgingly, will run as follows: deceased citizens who by their physical efforts or force of personality have conspicuous and strenuous achievements to their credit, and who have lived a life of obedience to the laws, should be regarded as proper subjects for our panegyrics.

CLEINIAS: Of course.

ATHENIAN: But to honour a man with hymns and pane- 802 gyrics during his lifetime is to invite trouble: we must wait until he has come to the end of the course after running the race of life successfully. (Men and women who have shown conspicuous merit should qualify for all these honours without distinction of sex.)

THE REGULATION OF MUSIC

The following arrangements should be made with regard to singing and dancing. Among the works we've inherited from the past there are a great many grand old pieces of music – and dances too, for occasions when we want to exercise our bodies – from which we should not hesitate to choose those suitable and appropriate for the society we are organizing. Censors of at least fifty years of age should be appointed to make the selection, and any ancient composition that seems to come up to standard should be approved; absolutely unsuitable material must be totally rejected, and substandard pieces revised and re-arranged, on the advice of poets and musicians. (Although we shall exploit the creative talents of these people, we shan't – with rare exceptions – put our trust in their tastes and inclinations. Instead, we shall interpret the wishes of the lawgiver and arrange to *his* liking our dancing and singing and chorus performances in general.) Music composed in an undisciplined style is always infinitely improved by the imposition of form, even if that makes it less immediately attractive. But music doesn't *have* to be disciplined to be pleasant. Take someone who has right from childhood till the age of maturity and discretion grown familiar with a controlled and restrained style of music. Play him some of the other sort, and how he'll loathe it! 'What vulgar stuff!' he'll say. Yet, if he's been brought up to enjoy the strong appeal of popular music, it's the disciplined kind he'll call frigid and repellent. So as I said just now, on the score of pleasure or the lack of it, neither type is superior nor inferior to the other. The difference is simply this: the one musical environment is invariably a good influence, the other a bad.

CLEINIAS: Well said!

ATHENIAN: In addition, we shall have to distinguish, in a rough and ready way, the songs suitable for men and those suitable for women, and give each its proper mode and rhythm. It would be terrible if the words failed to fit the mode, or if their metre were at odds with the beat of the music, which is what will happen if we don't match properly the songs to each of the other elements in the performance – elements which must therefore be dealt with, at any rate in outline, in our legal code. One possibility is simply to ensure that the songs men and women sing are accompanied by the rhythms and modes imposed by the words in either case; but our regulations about female performances must be more precise than this and be based on the natural difference between the sexes. So an elevated manner and courageous instincts must be regarded as characteristic of the male, while a tendency to modesty and restraint must be presented – in theory and law alike – as a peculiarly feminine trait.

THE RIGHT USE OF LEISURE

Now to deal with how this doctrine should be taught and 80s handed on. What method of instruction should we use? Who should be taught, and when should the lessons take place? Well, you know that when a shipwright is starting to build a boat, the first thing he does is to lay down the keel as a foundation and as a general indication of the shape. I have a feeling my own procedure now is exactly analogous. I'm trying to distinguish for you the various ways in which our character shapes the kind of life we live; I really am trying to 'lay down the keel', because I'm giving proper consideration to the way we should try to live – to the 'character-keel' we need to lay if we are going to sail through this voyage of life successfully.[30] Not that human affairs are worth taking very seriously – but take them seriously is just what we are forced to do, alas. Still, perhaps it will be realistic to recognize the position we're in and direct our serious efforts to some suitable purpose. My meaning? – yes, you'd certainly be right to take me up on that.

CLEINIAS: Exactly.

ATHENIAN: I maintain that serious matters deserve our serious attention, but trivialities do not; that all men of good

30. The play on *tropideia* (keel) and *tropoi* (habits or character) defies rendering into English.

will should put God at the centre of their thoughts; that man, as we said before,[31] has been created as a toy for God; and that this is the great point in his favour. So every man and every woman should play this part and order their whole life accordingly, engaging in the best possible pastimes – in a quite different frame of mind to their present one.

CLEINIAS: How do you mean?

ATHENIAN: The usual view nowadays, I fancy, is that the purpose of serious activity is leisure – that war, for instance, is an important business, and needs to be waged efficiently for the sake of peace. But in cold fact neither the immediate result nor the eventual consequences of warfare ever turn out to be *real* leisure or an education that really deserves the name – and education is in our view just about the most important activity of all. So each of us should spend the greater part of his life at peace, and that will be the best use of his time. What, then, will be the right way to live? A man should spend his whole life at 'play' – sacrificing, singing, dancing – so that he can win the favour of the gods and protect himself from his enemies and conquer them in battle. He'll achieve both these aims if he sings and dances in the way we've outlined; his path, so to speak, has been marked out for him and he must go on his way confident that the poet's words are true:[32]

804
'Some things, Telemachus, your native wit will tell you,
And Heaven will prompt the rest. The very gods, I'm
sure,
Have smiled upon your birth and helped to bring you
up.'

And those *we* bring up, too, must proceed in the same spirit. They must expect that although our advice is sound as far as it goes, their guardian deity will make them further suggestions about sacrifices and dancing – telling them the various divinities in whose honour they should hold their various games, and on what occasions, so as to win the gods' good will and live the life that their own nature demands, puppets that they are, mostly, and hardly real at all.

31. See p. 74.   32. Homer, *Odyssey* III, 26–8.

MEGILLUS: That, sir, is to give the human race a very low rating indeed.

ATHENIAN: Don't be taken aback, Megillus. You must make allowances for me. I said that with my thoughts on God, and was quite carried away. So, if you like, let's take it that our species is *not* worthless, but something rather important.

ATTENDANCE AT SCHOOL

To resume, then. So far, we have provided for the public gymnasia and the state schools to be housed in three groups of buildings at the centre of the city; similarly, on three sites in the suburbs, there should be training grounds for horses, and open spaces adapted for archery and the discharge of other long-range missiles, where the young may practise and learn these skills. Anyway, if we haven't explained all this adequately before, let's do so now, and put our requirements into legal form.

Foreign teachers should be hired to live in these establishments and provide the pupils with complete courses of instruction in both military and cultural subjects. Children must not be allowed to attend or not attend school at the whim of their father; as far as possible, education must be compulsory for 'one and all' (as the saying is), because they belong to the state first and their parents second.

THE EDUCATION OF FEMALES

Let me stress that this law of mine will apply just as much to girls as to boys. The girls must be trained in precisely the same way, and I'd like to make this proposal without any reservations whatever about horse-riding or athletics being suitable activities for males but not for females.[33] You see, although I was already convinced by some ancient stories I have heard, I now know for sure that there are pretty well countless numbers of women, generally called Sarmatians, round the Black Sea, who not only ride horses but use the bow and

33. Cf. pp. 279 and 330.

other weapons. There, men and women have an equal duty to cultivate these skills, so cultivate them equally they do. And while we're on the subject, here's another thought for you. I maintain that if these results can be achieved, the state of affairs in our corner of Greece, where men and women do *not* have a common purpose and do *not* throw all their energies into the same activities, is absolutely stupid. Almost every state, under present conditions, is only half a state, and develops only half its potentialities, whereas with the same cost and effort, it could double its achievement. Yet what a staggering blunder for a legislator to make!

CLEINIAS: I dare say. But a lot of these proposals, sir, are incompatible with the average state's social structure. However, you were quite right when you said we should give the argument its head, and only make up our minds when it had run its course. You've made me reproach myself for having spoken. So carry on, and say what you like.

ATHENIAN: The point I'd like to make, Cleinias, is the same one as I made a moment ago,[34] that there might have been something to be said against our proposal, if it had not been proved by the facts to be workable. But as things are, an opponent of this law must try other tactics. We are not going to withdraw our recommendation that so far as possible, in education and everything else, the female sex should be on the same footing as the male. Consequently, we should approach the problem rather like this. Look: if women are *not* to follow absolutely the same way of life as men, then surely we shall have to work out some other programme for them?

CLEINIAS: Inevitably.

ATHENIAN: Well then, if we deny women this position of equality we're now demanding for them, which of the systems actually in force today shall we adopt instead? What about the practice of the Thracians and many other peoples, who make their women work on the land and mind sheep and cattle, so that they turn into skivvies indistinguishable from slaves? Or what about the Athenians and all the other states in that part of the world? Well, here's how we Athenians deal with the

34. See p. 262.

problem: we 'concentrate our resources', as the expression is, under one roof, and let our women take charge of our stores and the spinning and wool-working in general. Or we could adopt the Spartan system, Megillus, which is a compromise. You make your girls take part in athletics and you give them a compulsory education in the arts; when they grow up, though dispensed from working wool, they have to 'weave' themselves a pretty hard-working sort of life which is by no means despicable or useless: they have to be tolerably efficient at running the home and managing the house and bringing up children – but they *don't* undertake military service. This means that even if some extreme emergency ever led to a battle for their state and the lives of their children, they wouldn't have the expertise to use bows and arrows, like so many Amazons, nor could they join the men in deploying any other missile. They wouldn't be able to take up shield and spear and copy Athena,[35] so as to terrify the enemy (if nothing more) by being seen in some kind of battle-array gallantly resisting the destruction threatening their native land. Living as they do, they'd never be anything like tough enough to imitate the Sarmatian women, who by comparison with such femininity would look like men. Anyone who wants to commend your Spartan legislators for this state of affairs, had better get on with it: I'm not going to change *my* mind. A legislator should go the whole way and not stick at half-measures; he mustn't just regulate the men and allow the women to live as they like and wallow in expensive luxury. That would be to give the state only half the loaf of prosperity instead of the whole of it.

MEGILLUS: What on earth are we to do, Cleinias? Are we going to let our visitor run down Sparta for us like this?

CLEINIAS: Yes, we are. We told him he could be frank, and we must give him his head until we've properly worked through every section of our legal code.

MEGILLUS: Very well.

ATHENIAN: So I suppose I should try to press straight on with the next topic?

CLEINIAS: Naturally.

35. A reference to pp. 281–2.

HOW TO LIVE A LIFE OF LEISURE

ATHENIAN: Now that our citizens are assured of a moderate supply of necessities, and other people have taken over the skilled work, what will be their way of life? Suppose that their farms have been entrusted to slaves, who provide them with sufficient produce of the land to keep them in modest comfort; suppose they take their meals in separate messes, one for themselves, another nearby for their families, including their daughters and their daughters' mothers; assume the messes, are presided over by officials, male and female as the case may be, who have the duty of dismissing their respective assemblies after the day's review and scrutiny of the diners' habits; and 807 that when the official and his company have poured libations to whatever gods that day and night happen to be dedicated, they all duly go home. Now, do such leisured circumstances leave them no pressing work to do, no genuinely appropriate occupation? Must each of them get plumper and plumper every day of his life, like a fatted beast? No: we maintain that's *not* the right and proper thing to do. A man who lives like that won't be able to escape the fate he deserves; and the fate of an idle fattened beast that takes life easy is usually to be torn to pieces by some other animal – one of the skinny kind, who've been emaciated by a life of daring and endurance. (Our ideal, of course, is unlikely to be realized *fully* so long as we persist in our policy of allowing individuals to have their own private establishments, consisting of house, wife, children and so on. But if we could ever put into practice the second-best scheme we're now describing,[36] we'd have every reason to be satisfied.) So we must insist that there is something left to do in a life of leisure, and it's only fair that the task imposed, far from being a light or trivial one, should be the most demanding of all. As it is, to dedicate your life to winning a victory at Delphi or Olympia keeps you far too busy to attend to other tasks; but a life devoted to the cultivation of every physical

36. That is, where a man's household, though his 'own', shares the common meals (cf. pp. 262–3.)

perfection *and* every moral virtue (the only life worth the name) will keep you at least twice as busy. Inessential business must never stop you taking proper food and exercise, or hinder your mental and moral training. To follow this regimen and to get the maximum benefit from it, the whole day and the whole night is scarcely time enough.

In view of this, every gentleman must have a timetable prescribing what he is to do every minute of his life, which he should follow at all times from the dawn of one day until the sun comes up at the dawn of the next. However, a lawgiver would lack dignity if he produced a mass of details about running a house, especially when he came to the regulations for curtailing sleep at night, which will be necessary if the citizens are going to protect the entire state systematically and uninterruptedly. Everyone should think it a disgrace and unworthy of a gentleman, if any citizen devotes the whole of any night to sleep; no, he should always be the first to wake and get up, and let himself be seen by all the servants. (It 808 doesn't matter what we ought to call this kind of thing – either 'law' or 'custom' will do.) In particular, the mistress of the house should be the first to wake up the other women; if she herself is woken by some of the maids, then all the slaves – men, women and children – should say 'How shocking!' to one another, and so too, supposing they could, should the very walls of the house. While awake at night, all citizens should transact a good proportion of their political and domestic business, the officials up and down the town, masters and mistresses in their private households. By nature, prolonged sleep does not suit either body or soul, nor does it help us to be active in all this kind of work. Asleep, a man is useless; he may as well be dead. But a man who is particularly keen to be physically active and mentally alert stays awake as long as possible, and sets aside for sleep only as much time as is necessary for his health – and that is only a little, once that little has become a regular habit. Officials who are wide awake at night in cities inspire fear in the wicked, whether citizens or enemies, but by the just and the virtuous they are honoured and admired; they benefit themselves and are a blessing to the entire state. And an additional advantage of spending the night in this way will be the courage thus inspired in individual members of the state.

FURTHER DUTIES OF THE MINISTER
OF EDUCATION

When dawn comes up and brings another day, the children must be sent off to their teachers. Children must not be left without teachers, nor slaves without masters, any more than flocks and herds must be allowed to live without attendants. Of all wild things, the child is the most unmanageable: an unusually powerful spring of reason, whose waters are not yet canalized in the right direction, makes him sharp and sly, the most unruly animal there is. That's why he has to be curbed by a great many 'bridles', so to speak. Initially, when he leaves the side of his nurse and mother, and is still young and immature, this will be his tutor's duty, but later on it will devolve on his instructors in the various subjects – subjects which will be an extra discipline in themselves. So far, he will be treated as a young gentleman deserves. However, both the boy and his tutor or teacher must be punished by any passing gentleman who finds either of them misbehaving, and here the child must be treated as though he were a slave.

24. Any passer-by who fails to inflict due punishment, *must for* a start be held in the deepest disgrace, and the Guardian of the Laws who has been put in charge of the 809 young[37] must keep under observation this fellow who has come across miscreants of the kind we mentioned and has either failed to inflict the necessary punishment, or not inflicted it in the approved fashion.

Our sharp-eyed and efficient supervisor of the education of the young must redirect their natural development along the right lines, by always setting them on the paths of goodness as embodied in the legal code.

37. The Minister of Education: see pp. 240–41.

THE LEGISLATOR'S INSTRUCTIONS TO THE MINISTER OF EDUCATION: THE CURRICULUM

But how will the law itself adequately convey its teaching to this Guardian? So far, the instruction he has had from the law has been cursory and obscure, because only a selection of topics has been covered. But nothing, as far as possible, should be omitted; the Guardian should have every point explained to him so that he in turn may enlighten and educate others. Now, the business of choruses has already been dealt with: we've seen what types of song and dance should be selected or revised, and then consecrated. But what type of *prose* works should be put in front of your pupils? How should they be presented? Now here, my dear Director of Youth, is something we've not explained. Of course, we've told you what military skills they must practise and learn, but what about (a) literature, (b) playing the lyre, (c) arithmetic? We stipulated that they must each understand enough of these subjects to fight a war and run a house and administer a state; for the same reasons they must acquire such knowledge about the heavenly bodies in their courses – sun, moon and stars – as will help them with the arrangements that every state is forced to make in this respect. You ask what arrangements we are referring to? We mean that the days must be grouped into months, and the months into years, in such a way that the seasons, along with their various sacrifices and festivals, may each receive proper recognition by being duly observed in their natural sequence. The result will be to keep the state active and alert, to render the gods due honour, and to make men better informed on these matters. All this, my friend, has not yet been adequately explained to you by the legislator. So pay attention to the points which are going to be made next.

We said that you have insufficient information about literature, for a start. Now, what's our complaint against the instructions you were given? It's simply that you've not yet been told whether a *complete* mastery of the subject is necessary before one can become a decent citizen or whether one shouldn't attempt it at all; and similarly in the case of the lyre. Well, we maintain that these subjects do have to be tackled. About three years will be a reasonable time for a child of ten to spend on literature, and a further three years, beginning at 810 the age of thirteen, should be spent on learning the lyre. These times must be neither shortened nor lengthened: neither the child nor its father must be allowed to extend or curtail these periods of study out of enthusiasm for, or distaste of, the curriculum; that will be against the law.

25. Cases of disobedience must be punished by disqualification from the school prizes we shall have to describe a little later.

First, though, you yourself must grasp just what must be taught by the teachers and learnt by the pupils in those periods of time. Well, the children must work at their letters until they are able to read and write, but any whose natural abilities have not developed sufficiently by the end of the prescribed time to make them into quick or polished performers should not be pressed.

LITERATURE

The question now arises of the study of written works which the authors have not set to music. Although some of these works are in metre, others lack any rhythmical pattern at all – they are writings that simply reproduce ordinary speech, unadorned by rhythm and music. Some of the many authors of such works have left us writings that constitute a danger. Now, my splendid Guardians of the Laws, how are you going to deal with these works? What will be the right instructions for the lawgiver to give you about coping with them? I reckon he's going to be very much at a loss.

CLEINIAS: What is the difficulty you're talking about, sir? It looks as if you're faced by a genuine personal problem.

ATHENIAN: Your assumption is quite right, Cleinias. But the two of you are my partners in legislation, and I'm obliged to tell you when I think I anticipate a difficulty and when I do not.

CLEINIAS: Oh? What makes you bring up that aspect of the business at this point? What's the matter?

ATHENIAN: I'll tell you: the idea of contradicting many thousands of voices. That's always difficult.

CLEINIAS: Well, bless my soul! Do you really imagine that your existing legislative proposals flout popular prejudices in just a few tiny details?

ATHENIAN: Yes, that's fair comment. The point you're making, I take it, is that although a lot of people set their face against the path we are following in our discussion, just as many are enthusiastic about it (or even if they *are* fewer in number, they're not inferior in quality) – and you're telling me to rely on the support of the latter and proceed with boldness and resolution along the legislative path opened up for us by our present discussion, and not to hang back.

CLEINIAS: Naturally.

ATHENIAN: Best foot forward, then. Now, what I say is this. We have a great many poets who compose in hexameters and trimeters and all the standard metres; some of these authors try to be serious, while others aim at a comic effect. Over and over again it's claimed that in order to educate young people properly we have to cram their heads full of this stuff; we have to organize recitations of it so that they never stop listening to it and acquire a vast repertoire, getting 811 whole poets off by heart. Another school of thought excerpts the outstanding work of all the poets and compiles a treasury of complete passages, claiming that if the wide knowledge of a fully informed person is to produce a sound and sensible citizen, these extracts must be committed to memory and learnt by rote. I suppose you're now pressing me to be quite frank and show these people where they are right and where they've gone wrong?

CLEINIAS: Of course.

ATHENIAN: Well then, in a nutshell, what sort of estimate will do them all justice? I imagine everybody would agree if I put it rather like this. Each of these authors has produced a lot of fine work, and a lot of rubbish too – but if that's so, I maintain that learning so much of it puts the young at risk.

CLEINIAS: So what recommendation would you give the Guardian of the Laws?

ATHENIAN: What about?

CLEINIAS: The model work that will enable him to decide what material all the children may learn, and what not. Tell us, without any hesitation.

A SET TEXT:
SELECTIONS FROM THE LAWS *OF PLATO*

ATHENIAN: My dear Cleinias, I suspect I've had a bit of luck.

CLEINIAS: How's that?

ATHENIAN: Because I haven't got far to look for a model. You see, when I look back now over this discussion of ours, which has lasted from dawn up till this very moment – a discussion in which I think I sense the inspiration of heaven – well, it's come to look, to my eyes, just like a literary composition. Perhaps not surprisingly, I was overcome by a feeling of immense satisfaction at the sight of my 'collected works', so to speak, because, of all the addresses I have ever learned or listened to, whether in verse or in this kind of free prose style I've been using, it's *these* that have impressed me as being the most eminently acceptable and the most entirely appropriate for the ears of the younger generation. So I could hardly commend a better model than this to the Guardian of the Laws in charge of education. Here's what he must tell the teachers to teach the children, and if he comes across similar and related material while working through prose writings, or the verse of poets, or when listening to unwritten compositions in simple prose that show a family resemblance to our discussion today, he must on no account let them slip through his fingers, but have them committed to writing. His first job will be to compel the teachers to learn this material and speak well of it, and he must not employ as his assistants any teachers who disapprove of it; he should employ only those who endorse his own high opinion, and entrust them with the 812 teaching and education of the children. That, then, is my doctrine on literature and its teachers, so let me finish there.

MUSIC

CLEINIAS: Well, sir, as far as I can judge from our original programme, we've not strayed off the subjects we set out to discuss. But is our general policy the right one, or not? I suspect it would be difficult to say for sure.

ATHENIAN: That, Cleinias, as we have often remarked, is something which will probably become clearer of its own accord when we've completely finished expounding our laws.

CLEINIAS: True enough.

ATHENIAN: After the teacher of literature, surely, we have to address the lyre-master?

CLEINIAS: Of course.

ATHENIAN: Now when we allocate these masters the duties of teaching this instrument and giving instruction in the subject in general, I think we ought to remember the line we took earlier.

CLEINIAS: What line do you mean?

ATHENIAN: We said,[38] I think, that the sixty-year-old singers of Dionysus should be persons who are particularly sensitive to rhythm and the way in which 'harmonies' are constructed,[39] so that when faced with good or vicious musical representations, and the emotions aroused by them, they may be able to select the works based on good representation and reject those based on bad.[40] The former they should present and sing to the community at large, so as to charm the souls of the young people, encouraging each and every one of them to let these representations guide them along the path that leads to virtue.

CLEINIAS: You're absolutely right.

ATHENIAN: With this object in view, here's how the lyre-master and his pupil must employ the notes of their instruments. By exploiting the fact that each string makes a distinct sound, they must produce notes that are identical in pitch to the words being sung. The lyre should not be used to

38. See pp. 102 ff. and 110 ff.   39. See p. 111 and note on p. 85.
40. For art as 'imitation', see pp. 90, 107 and 180.

play an elaborate independent melody: that is, its strings must produce no notes except those of the composer of the melody being played; small intervals should not be combined with large, nor quick tempo with slow, nor low notes with high. Similarly, the rhythms of the music of the lyre must not be tricked out with all sorts of frills and adornments. All this sort of thing must be kept from students who are going to acquire a working knowledge of music in three years, without wasting time. Such conflict and confusion makes learning difficult, whereas the young people should above all be swift learners, because they have a great many important compulsory subjects laid down for them as it is – and in due time, as our discussion progresses, we shall see what these subjects are. But all these musical matters should be controlled, according to his brief, by our official in charge of education. As regards the actual singing, and the words, we have explained earlier[41] what tunes and style of language the chorus-masters must teach: we said – remember? – that these things should be consecrated and each allocated to a suitable festival, so as to benefit society by the welcome pleasure they give.

813

CLEINIAS: Here again you've spoken the truth –

ATHENIAN: – the whole truth and nothing but the truth! So these are the regulations the person appointed as our Director of Music must adopt and enforce: let's wish him the best of luck in his task.

PHYSICAL TRAINING (2)

We, however, must supplement our previous regulations about dancing and the training of the body in general. We've filled in the gaps in our tuition in the case of music, so now let's deal with physical training in the same way. Both boys and girls, of course, must learn to dance and perform physical exercises?

CLEINIAS: Yes.

ATHENIAN: So it won't come amiss if we provide dancing

41. See pp. 285 ff.

masters for the boys and dancing mistresses for the girls, so as to facilitate practice.

CLEINIAS: Agreed.

ATHENIAN: So now let's summon once again the official that has the hardest job of all – the Director of Children. He'll be in charge both of music and of physical training, so he won't get much time off.

CLEINIAS: How then will a man of his advancing years be able to supervise so much?

ATHENIAN: There is no problem here, my friend. The law has already given him permission, which it will not withdraw, to recruit as assistant supervisors any citizens he may wish, of either sex. He will know whom to choose, and a sober respect for his office and a realization of its importance will make him anxious not to choose wrongly, because he'll be well aware that only if the younger generation has received and goes on receiving a correct education shall we find everything is 'plain sailing', whereas if not – well, it would be inappropriate to describe the consequences, and as the state is young we shall refrain from doing so, out of respect for the feelings of the excessively superstitious.[42]

Well then, on these topics too – I mean dances and the entire range of movements involved in physical training – we have already said a great deal.[43] We are establishing gymnasia for all physical exercises of a military kind – archery and deployment of missiles in general, skirmishing, heavy-armed fighting of every variety, tactical manoeuvres, marches of every sort, pitching camp, and also the various disciplines of the cavalryman. In all these subjects there must be public instructors paid out of public funds; their lessons must be attended by the boys and men of the state, and the girls and women as well, because they too have to master all these techniques. While still girls, they must practise every kind of dancing and fighting in armour; when grown women, they must play their part in manoeuvring, getting into battle formation and taking off and putting on weapons, if only to 814

42. That is, simply to mention evil would be regarded as tempting fate.
43. See pp. 279–82.

ensure that if it ever proves necessary for the whole army to leave the state and take the field abroad, so that the children and the rest of the population are left unprotected, the women will at least be able to defend them. On the other hand – and this is one of those things we can't swear is impossible – suppose a large and powerful army, whether Greek or not, were to force a way into the country and make them fight a desperate battle for the very existence of the state. It would be a disaster for their society if its women proved to have been so shockingly ill-educated that they couldn't even rival female birds, who are prepared to run every risk and die for their chicks fighting against the most powerful of wild animals. What if, instead of that, the women promptly made off to temples and thronged every altar and sanctuary, and covered the human race with the disgrace of being by nature the most lily-livered creatures under the sun?

CLEINIAS: By heaven, sir, no state in which that happened could avoid disgrace – quite apart from the damage that would be caused.

ATHENIAN: So let's lay down a law to the effect that women must not neglect to cultivate the techniques of fighting, at any rate to the extent indicated. These are skills which all citizens, male and female, must take care to acquire.

CLEINIAS: That gets my vote, at least.

ATHENIAN: Now for wrestling. We've partly dealt with this already, but we haven't described what in my eyes is its most important feature. But it's not easy to find words to explain it unless at the same time someone gives an actual demonstration with his body. So we'll postpone a decision on this point till we can support our statements with concrete examples and prove, among other points we've mentioned, that of all physical movements, those involved in our kind of wrestling are the most closely related to those demanded in warfare, and in particular that we should practise wrestling for the sake of military efficiency, rather than cultivate the latter in order to be better wrestlers.[44]

CLEINIAS: You're right in that, at least.

44. The point of this remark is less cryptically expressed on p. 292.

DANCING

ATHENIAN: So let's accept what we've said so far as an adequate statement of what wrestling can do for a man. The proper term for most of the other movements that can be executed by the body as a whole is 'dancing'. Two varieties, the decent and the disreputable, have to be distinguished. The first is a representation of the movements of graceful people, and the aim is to create an effect of grandeur; the second imitates the movements of unsightly people and tries to present them in an unattractive light. Both have two subdivisions. The first subdivision of the decent kind represents handsome, courageous soldiers locked in the violent struggles of war; the second portrays a man of temperate character enjoying moderate pleasures in a state of prosperity, and the natural name for this is 'dance of peace'. The dance of war differs 815 fundamentally from the dance of peace, and the correct name for it will be the 'Pyrrhic'.[45] It depicts the motions executed to avoid blows and shots of all kind (dodging, retreating, jumping into the air, crouching); and it also tries to represent[46] the opposite kind of motion, the more aggressive postures adopted when shooting arrows and discharging javelins and delivering various kinds of blows. In these dances, which portray fine physiques and noble characters, the correct posture is maintained if the body is kept erect in a state of vigorous tension, with the limbs extended nearly straight. A posture with the opposite characteristics we reject as *not* correct. As for the dance of peace, the point we have to watch in every chorus-performer is this: how successfully – or how disastrously – does he keep up the fine style of dancing to be expected from men who've been brought up under good laws? This means we'd better distinguish the dubious style of dancing from the style we may accept without question. So can we define the

45. The 'Pyrrhic' (dance) was the technical term for 'war-dance'.
46. In the Greek Plato confuses the motions *imitated* and the motions *performed*, I render what I understand him to have meant, rather than translate the nonsense as it stands.

two? Where should the line be drawn between them? 'Bacchic' dances and the like, which (the dancers allege) are a 'representation' of drunken persons they call Nymphs and Pans and Sileni and Satyrs, and which are performed during 'purifications' and 'initiations', are something of a problem: taken as a group, they cannot be termed either 'dances of peace' or 'dances of war', and indeed they resist all attempts to label them. The best procedure, I think, is to treat them as separate from 'war-dances' and 'dances of peace', and put them in a category of their own which a statesman may ignore as outside his province. That will entitle us to leave them on one side and get back to dances of peace and war, both of which undeniably deserve our attention.

Now, what about the non-combatant Muse? The dances she leads in honour of the gods and children of gods will comprise one broad category of dances performed with a sense of well-being. This is how we shall distinguish between the two forms this feeling may take: (1) the particularly keen pleasure felt by people who have emerged from trouble and danger to a state of happiness; (2) the quieter pleasures of those whose past good fortune has not only continued but increased. Now, take a man in either of these situations. The greater his pleasure the brisker his body's movements; more modest pleasures make his actions correspondingly less brisk. Again, the more composed the man's temperament, and the tougher he has been 816 trained to be, the more deliberate are his movements; on the other hand, if he's a coward and has not been trained to show restraint, his actions are wilder and his postures change more violently. And in general, when a man uses his voice to talk or sing, he finds it very difficult to keep his body still. This is the origin of the whole art of dancing: the gestures that express what one is saying. Some of us make gestures that are invariably in harmony[47] with our words, but some of us fail. In fact, one has only to reflect on many other ancient terms that have come down to us, to see that they should be commended for their aptness and accuracy. One such term

47. The key to the sequence of thought is that 'in harmony' = emmelôs.

describes the dances performed by those who enjoy prosperity and seek only moderate pleasures: it's just the right word, and whoever coined it must have been a real musician. He very sensibly gave all such dances the name 'emmeleiai',[47] and established two categories of approved dancing, the 'war-dance' (which he called 'Pyrrhic') and 'dance of peace' ('emmeleia'), thus giving each its apt and appropriate title. The lawgiver should give an outline of them, and the Guardian of the Laws[48] should see where they are to be found; then, after hunting them out, he must combine the dance-sequences with the other musical elements,[49] and allocate each sacrifice and feast in the calendar the style of dance that is appropriate. After thus consecrating the whole list of dances, he must henceforth refrain from altering any feature either of the dancing or the singing: the same state and the same citizens (who should all be the same sort of people, as far as possible), should enjoy the same pleasures in the same fashion: that is the secret of a happy and a blessed life.

COMEDY AND TRAGEDY

So much for the way men of superior physique and noble character should perform in choruses of the kind we've prescribed. We are now obliged to examine and pronounce on the misshapen bodies and degraded outlook of those performers who have turned to producing ludicrous and comic effects by exploiting the opportunities for humorous mimicry offered by dialogue, song and dance. Now anyone who means to acquire a discerning judgement will find it impossible to understand the serious side of things in isolation from their ridiculous aspect, or indeed appreciate anything at all except in the light of its opposite. But if we intend to acquire virtue, even on a small scale, we can't be serious and comic too, and this is precisely why we must learn to recognize buffoonery, to avoid being trapped by our ignorance of it into doing or saying anything ridiculous when there's no call for it. Such

48. Presumably the Minister of Education.
49. Words and instrumental accompaniment.

mimicry must be left to slaves and hired aliens, and no one must ever take it at all seriously. No citizen or citizeness must be found learning it, and the performances must always contain some new twist.[50] With that law, and that explanation 817 of it, humorous amusements – usually known as 'comedy' – may be dismissed.

But what about our 'serious' poets, as they're called, the tragedians? Suppose some of them were to come forward and ask us some such question as this: 'Gentlemen, may we enter your state and country, or not? And may we bring our work with us? Or what's your policy on this point?' What would be the right reply for us to make to these inspired geniuses? This, I think: 'Most honoured guests, we're tragedians ourselves, and our tragedy is the finest and best we can create. At any rate, our entire state has been constructed so as to be a "representation" of the finest and noblest life – the very thing we maintain is most genuinely a tragedy.[51] So we are poets like yourselves, composing in the same *genre*, and your competitors as artists and actors in the finest drama, which true law alone has the natural power to "produce" to perfection (of that we're quite confident). So don't run away with the idea that we shall ever blithely allow you to set up stage in the market-place and bring on your actors whose fine voices will carry further than ours. Don't think we'll let you declaim to women and children and the general public, and talk about the same practices as we do but treat them differently – indeed, more often than not, so as virtually to contradict us. We should be absolutely daft, and so would any state as a whole, to let you go ahead as we've described before the authorities had decided whether your work was fit to be recited and suitable for public performance or not. So, you sons of the charming Muses, first of all show your songs to the authorities for comparison with ours, and if your doctrines seem the

50. Presumably to prevent familiarity with any one piece from unduly influencing the public. Cf. p. 284.

51. A 'tragedy' did not necessarily have an unhappy ending. In this passage the word means 'straight drama concerned with questions of morality'.

same as or better than our own, we'll let you produce your plays; but if not, friends, that we can never do.'

So as regards chorus performances in general and the question of learning a part in them, custom will march hand in hand with law – dealing with slaves and their masters separately, if you are agreeable.

CLEINIAS: How could we fail to agree, at any rate for the moment?

MATHEMATICS

ATHENIAN: For gentlemen, three related disciplines still remain: (1) computation and the study of numbers; (2) measurements of lines, surfaces and solids; (3) the mutual relationship of the heavenly bodies as they revolve in their courses. None of these subjects must be studied in minute detail by the general public, but only by a chosen few (and who they are, we shall say when the time comes, when our discussion is drawing to a close). But what about the man in the street? It would certainly be a disgrace for him to be ignorant of what people very rightly call the 'indispensable rudiments'; but it will be difficult – impossible, even – for him to make a minute study of the entire subject. However, we can't dispense with the basic necessities,[52] which was probably the point in the mind of the coiner of that saying about God, to the effect that 'not even God will be found at odds with necessity'[53] – presumably divine necessities, because if you interpret the remark as referring to necessities in the mortal realm, as do most people who quote such things, it's by far the most naïve remark that could be made.[54]

52. Here, by a play on the word ἀναγκαῖον, the Athenian seems to pass from the mathematics 'necessary and essential' in ordinary life to the 'necessary and essential' truths involved in them.

53. The sentiment is found in a fragment of the poet Simonides (late sixth and early fifth century), which the Athenian may have in mind here. Cf. p. 210, and see J. M. Edmonds, *Lyra Graeca* (London and New York, 1924; Loeb edition), vol. II, pp. 286–7.

54. That is, although God cannot alter 'necessary' (divine) truths, he is of course above what human beings normally find 'necessary' to their lives. Alternatively, the Athenian may be making a moral point: 'force of circumstance' can always be resisted and should never be adduced as a reason for doing wrong.

CLEINIAS: Well, then, sir, what necessities, divine rather than the other sort, are relevant to these studies?

ATHENIAN: These, I think: the necessities of which at least *some* practical and theoretical knowledge will always be essential for every god, spirit or hero[55] who means to take charge of human beings in a responsible fashion. A man, at any rate, will fall a long way short of such godlike standards if he can't recognize one, two and three, or odd and even numbers in general, or hasn't the faintest notion how to count, or can't reckon up the days and nights, and is ignorant of the revolutions of the sun and moon and the other heavenly bodies. It's downright stupid to expect that anyone who wants to make the slightest progress in the highest branches of knowledge can afford to ignore any of these subjects. But what parts of them should be studied, and how intensively, and when? Which topics should be combined, and which kept separate? How will they be synthesized? These are the first questions we have to answer, and then with these preliminary lessons to guide us we may advance to the remaining studies. This is the natural procedure enforced by the necessity with which we maintain no god contends now, or ever will.

CLEINIAS: Yes, sir, those proposals of yours, put like that, seem natural and correct.

ATHENIAN: They certainly are, Cleinias, but such a preliminary statement of them is difficult to put into legal form. If you like, we'll postpone more precise legislation till later.

CLEINIAS: It looks to us, sir, as if you're deterred by the way our countrymen commonly neglect this sort of subject. But your fears are quite groundless, so try to tell us what you think, without keeping anything back on that account.

819 ATHENIAN: I am indeed deterred, for the reasons you mention, but I am even more appalled at those who have actually undertaken those studies, but in the wrong manner. Total ignorance over an entire field is never dangerous or

55. Eminent benefactors of mankind who have become minor deities after death.

disastrous; much more damage is done when a subject is known intimately and in detail, but has been improperly taught.

CLEINIAS: You're right.

ATHENIAN: So we should insist that gentlemen should study each of these subjects to at least the same level as very many children in Egypt, who acquire such knowledge at the same time as they learn to read and write. First, lessons[56] in calculation have been devised for tiny tots to learn while they are enjoying themselves at play: they divide up a given number of garlands or apples[57] among larger or smaller groups, and arrange boxers or wrestlers in an alternation of 'byes' and 'pairs', or in a sequence of either, and in the various further ways in which 'byes' and 'pairs' naturally succeed each other. Another game the teachers play with them is to jumble up bowls of gold and bronze and silver and so on, or distribute whole sets of one material. In this way, as I indicated, they make the uses of elementary arithmetic an integral part of their pupils' play, so that they get a useful introduction to the art of marshalling, leading and deploying an army, or running a household; and in general they make them more alert and resourceful persons. Next, the teacher puts the children on to measuring lengths, surfaces and solids – a study which rescues them from the deep-rooted ignorance, at once comic and shocking, that all men display in this field.

CLEINIAS: What sort of ignorance do you mean, in particular?

ATHENIAN: My dear Cleinias, even I took a very long time to discover mankind's plight in this business; but when I did, I was amazed, and could scarcely believe that human beings could suffer from such swinish stupidity. I blushed not only for myself, but for Greeks in general.

CLEINIAS: Why so? Go on, sir, tell us what you're getting at.

ATHENIAN: I'll explain – or rather, I'll make my point by

56. The lessons are described very vaguely. For an explanation, see B. Einarson, *Classical Philology*, LIII (1958), 97–8.

57. Or perhaps (toy) 'sheep'.

asking you a few questions. Here's a simple one: you know what's meant by a 'line', I suppose?

CLEINIAS: Of course.

ATHENIAN: Very well. What about 'surface'?

CLEINIAS: Surely.

ATHENIAN: You appreciate that these are two distinct things, and that 'volume' is a third?

CLEINIAS: Naturally.

ATHENIAN: And you regard all these as commensurable?

CLEINIAS: Yes.

ATHENIAN: And one length, I suppose, is essentially expressible in terms of another length, one surface in terms of 820 another surface, and one volume in terms of another volume?

CLEINIAS: Exactly.

ATHENIAN: Well, what if some of these can't be thus expressed, either 'exactly' or approximately? What if some can, and some cannot, in spite of your thinking they *all* can? What do you think of your ideas on the subject now?

CLEINIAS: They're worthless, obviously.

ATHENIAN: What about the relationship of line and surface to volume, or surface and line to each other? Don't all we Greeks regard them as in some sense commensurable?

CLEINIAS: We certainly do.

ATHENIAN: But if, as I put it, 'all we Greeks' believe them to be commensurable when fundamentally they are *in*commensurable, one had better address these people as follows (blushing the while on their behalf): 'Now then, most esteemed among the Greeks, isn't this one of those subjects we said[58] it was disgraceful not to understand – not that a knowledge of the basic essentials was much to be proud of?'

CLEINIAS: Of course.

ATHENIAN: Now there are a number of additional and related topics which are a fertile breeding-ground for mistakes similar to those we've mentioned.

CLEINIAS: What sort of topics?

ATHENIAN: The real relationship between commensurables and incommensurables. We must be very poor specimens

58. See p. 311.

if on inspection we can't tell them apart. These are the problems we ought to keep on putting up to each other, in a competitive spirit, when we've sufficient time to do them justice; and it's a much more civilized pastime for old men than draughts.

CLEINIAS: Perhaps so. Come to think of it, draughts is not radically different from such studies.

ATHENIAN: Well, Cleinias, I maintain that these subjects are what the younger generation should go in for. They do no harm, and are not very difficult: they can be learnt in play, and so far from harming the state, they'll do it some good. But if anyone disagrees, we must listen to his case.

CLEINIAS: Of course.

ATHENIAN: However, although obviously we shall sanction them if that proves to be their effect, we shall reject them if they seem to disappoint our expectations.

CLEINIAS: Obviously indeed. No doubt about it.

ATHENIAN: Well then, sir, so that our legal code shall have no gaps, let's regard these studies as an established but independent part of the desired curriculum – independent, that is, of the rest of the framework of the state, so that they can be 'redeemed' like 'pledges', in case the arrangements fail to work out to the satisfaction of us the depositors or you the pledgees.

CLEINIAS: Yes, that's a fair way to present them.

ASTRONOMY

ATHENIAN: Next, consider astronomy. Would a proposal to teach it to the young meet with your approval, or not?

CLEINIAS: Just tell us what you think.

ATHENIAN: Now here's a very odd thing, that really is quite intolerable. 821

CLEINIAS: What?

ATHENIAN: We generally say that so far as the supreme deity and the universe are concerned, we ought not to bother our heads hunting up explanations, because that is an act of impiety. In fact, precisely the opposite seems to be true.

CLEINIAS: What's your point?

ATHENIAN: My words will surprise you, and you may well think them out of place on the lips of an old man. But it's quite impossible to keep quiet about a study, if one believes it is noble and true, a blessing to society and pleasing in the sight of God.

CLEINIAS: That's reasonable enough, but what astronomy are we going to find of which we can say all that?

ATHENIAN: My dear fellows, at the present day nearly all we Greeks do the great gods – Sun and Moon – an injustice.

CLEINIAS: How so?

ATHENIAN: We say that they, and certain other heavenly bodies with them, never follow the same path. Hence our name for them: 'planets'.[59]

CLEINIAS: Good heavens, sir, that's absolutely right. In the course of my life I've often seen with my own eyes how the Morning and the Evening Star, and a number of others, never describe the same course, but vary from one to another; and we all know that the sun and moon always move like that.

ATHENIAN: Megillus and Cleinias, this is precisely the sort of point about the gods of the heavens that I am insisting our citizens and young men must study, so as to learn enough about them all to avoid blasphemy, and to use reverent language whenever they sacrifice and offer up their pious prayers.

CLEINIAS: Right enough – if it's possible, in the first place, to acquire the knowledge you mention. On the assumption that investigation will enable us to correct any errors in our present statements, I too agree that this subject must be studied, in view of its grandeur and importance. So do your level best to convince us of the case you're making, and we'll try to follow you and take in what you say.

ATHENIAN: My point is not an easy one to appreciate, but it's not unduly difficult either, and won't take up a lot of time, as I'll prove to you by my ability to keep my explanation brief – even though it wasn't so very long ago, when I was no youngster, that I heard of these things. If the subject were

59. Literally, the word 'planet' means 'wanderer'.

difficult, I'd never be able to explain it to you, old men that
we all are.

CLEINIAS: You're right. But what is this subject you say
is so wonderful, so suitable for young men to learn, yet 822
unknown to us? Try to tell us that much about it, at any rate,
as clearly as you can.

ATHENIAN: Yes, try I must. This belief, my dear fellows,
that the moon and sun and other heavenly bodies do in fact
'wander', is incorrect: precisely the opposite is true. Actually,
each of them perpetually describes just one fixed orbit,
although it is true that to all appearances its path is always
changing. Further, the quickest body is wrongly supposed to
be the slowest, and vice versa. So if the facts are as stated,
and we are in error, we're no better than spectators at Olympia
would be, if they said that the fastest horse in the race or the
fastest long-distance runner was the slowest, and the slowest
the fastest, and composed panegyrics and songs extolling the
loser as the winner. I don't suppose the praises showered on
the runners would be at all apt or welcome to them – they're
only men, after all! At Olympia, such a mistake would be
merely ludicrous. But what are we to think of the analogous
theological errors we're committing nowadays? In this field
such mistakes are not funny at all; and it certainly gives the
gods no pleasure to have us spread false rumours about them.

CLEINIAS: Very true – if you're right about the facts.

ATHENIAN: So if we can prove I *am* right, all such topics
as these must be studied to the level indicated,[60] but in the
absence of proof they must be left alone. May we adopt this as
agreed policy?

CLEINIAS: Certainly.

HUNTING: WRITTEN AND UNWRITTEN
RULES AGAIN

ATHENIAN: So it's high time to call a halt to our regulations
about the subjects to be studied in the educational curriculum,
and turn our attention to hunting and all that sort of thing.

60. I.e. to enable people to avoid blasphemy.

Here too we must adopt the same procedure as before, because the legislator's job is not done if he simply lays down laws and gets quit of the business. In addition to his legislation, he must provide something else, which occupies a sort of no-man's land between admonition and law. This is a point, of course, that we've come across often enough as we talked of this and that, as for instance when we dealt with the training of very young children.[61] We hold that although education at that level is certainly the sort of topic on which suggestions are needed, it would be plain silly to think of these suggestions as formal laws. Even when the actual laws and the complete constitution have been thus formally committed to writing, you don't exhaust the praises of a supremely virtuous citizen by saying 'Here's a good man for you, a devoted and utterly obedient servant of the laws'. Your praise will be more comprehensive if you can say 'He's a good man because he has given a lifetime of unswerving obedience to the written words of the legislator, whether they took the form of a law, or simply expressed approval or disapproval'. There is no truer praise of a citizen than that. The real job of the legislator is not only to write his laws, but to blend into them an explanation of what he regards as respectable and what he does not, and the perfect citizen must be bound by these standards no less than by those backed by legal sanctions.

We can cite our present subject as a kind of witness to demonstrate the point more clearly. You know how 'hunting' takes a great many forms, almost all of which are nowadays covered by this one term. There is a variety of ways of hunting water animals, and the same goes for the birds of the air, and the animals that live on land too – and not only the wild ones, either: we also have to take into account the hunting of men, not merely by their enemies in war (such as the raids carried out by robbers and the pursuit of army by army), but by their lovers, who 'pursue' their quarry for many different reasons, some admirable, some execrable.[62] When the legislator comes to lay down his laws about hunting he cannot leave all this

61. Cf. pp. 270–71 and 277–8.
62. This theme is resumed on pp. 334 ff.

unexplained, but neither can he produce a set of menacing regulations by imposing rules and punishments for all cases. So how are we going to tackle this kind of thing? He – the legislator – having asked himself 'Are these suitable exercises and activities for the young, or not?', must then approve or condemn the various forms of hunting. The young men, for their part, must listen to the lawgiver and obey him, without being seduced by the prospect of pleasure or deterred by vigorous effort; and they should pay much more attention to carrying out warm recommendations than to the detailed threats and punishment of the formal law.

With those preliminaries, we may now put in due form our approval or disapproval of the various forms of hunting, commending the kind that is a good influence on the younger generation and censuring the other sort. So let's now follow up with a talk to the young people, and address them in this idealistic vein:

'Friends, we hope you'll never be seized by a desire or passion to fish in the sea or to angle or indeed to hunt water animals at all; and don't resort to creels, which a lazybones will leave to catch his prey whether he's asleep or awake. We hope you never feel any temptation to capture men on the high seas and take to piracy, which will make you into brutal hunters and outlaws; and we hope it never so much as occurs to you to turn thief in town or country. Nor should any young man ever be seduced by a fancy to trap birds – away with such an uncivilized desire! That leaves only land animals for the athletes of our state to hunt and capture. Now sometimes this is done by what is called "night-hunting", when the participants, sluggards that they are, take it in turn to sleep. This sort of hunting is *not* to be recommended, nor is the sort that offers periods of rest from exertion, where the savage strength of the animals is subdued by nets and traps, rather than because a hunter who relishes the fight has got the better of them. All men who wish to cultivate the "divine"[63] courage have only one type of hunting left, which is the best: the capture of four-

824

63. See p. 55.

footed animals with the help of dogs and horses and by your own exertions, when you hunt in person and subdue all your prey by chasing and striking them and hurling weapons at them.'

This address may be taken as an explanation of what we approve and condemn in this entire business. Here's the actual law:

(1) No one should restrain these genuinely 'holy'[64] hunters from taking their hounds where they like and as they like; but the night-trapper, who relies on nets and snares, must not be allowed by anyone, at any time or place, to hunt his prey.

(2) The fowler is not to be restrained on fallow-land or on the mountain side, but any passer-by should chase him off cultivated or holy ground.

(3) The fisherman is to be allowed to fish anywhere except in harbours and sacred rivers, ponds and lakes, provided only that he does not make the water turbid by using noxious juices.

So here's where we have to say that our regulations about education are finally complete.

CLEINIAS: That's good news!

64. See p. 55.

§13. SPORT AND MILITARY TRAINING

The principles and regulations in this section are largely self-explanatory. As we should expect, Plato sees sport as a means to a moral end. Correct physical training ensures that the body functions in perfect harmony with the soul and prevents both from becoming 'slack'. The purpose of military training is not aggrandizement in war, but the preservation of the state.

ARRANGEMENTS FOR FESTIVALS

ATHENIAN: Now then, the next job is to enlist the aid of the oracles reported from Delphi to draw up a programme of festivals to be established by law, and discover what sacrifices the state will find it 'meet and right'[1] to offer and which gods should receive them. It will probably be within our own discretion to decide the number and the occasions.

CLEINIAS: Yes, I dare say the number will be up to us.

ATHENIAN: So let's deal with that first. There are to be no less than three hundred and sixty-five of them, so as to ensure that there is always at least one official sacrificing to some god or spirit on behalf of the state, its citizens and their property. The Expounders, Priests, Priestesses and Prophets are to hold a meeting with the Guardians of the Laws and fill in the details the legislator has inevitably omitted (in fact, this same combined board will also have to spot where such deficiencies exist in the first place). The law will provide for twelve festivals in honour of the twelve gods who give their names to the individual tribes. Every month the citizens should sacrifice to each of these gods and arrange chorus performances and cultural and gymnastic contests, varied according to the deity concerned and appropriate to the changing seasons of the year; and they must divide festivals for women into those that must be celebrated in the absence of men, and those that

1. The Greek here echoes the formula of an oracular response.

need not be. Further, they must not confuse the cult of the gods of the underworld with that of the 'heavenly' gods (as we must style them) and their retinue. They are to keep the two kinds of celebration separate, and put the former by law in the twelfth month, which is sacred to Pluto.[2] Men of battle should feel no horror for such a god as this – on the contrary, they should honour him as a great friend of the human race. The union of body and soul, you see, can never be superior to their separation (and I mean that quite seriously).

MILITARY TRAINING

There's a further point they will have to appreciate if they are going to allocate these events satisfactorily. Although on the score of leisure-time and abundance of all necessities our state has no rivals at the present day, it still has to live the *good* life, just like the individual person; and the first requirement for a happy life is to do yourself no injury nor allow any to be done to you by others. Of course, the first half of the requirement presents no great problem; the difficulty lies in becoming strong enough to be immune to injury – and the one and only thing that brings such immunity is complete virtue. The same applies to a state: if it adopts the ways of virtue, it can live in peace; but if it is wicked, war and civil war will plague it. That's the situation in a nutshell, and it means that each and every citizen must undertake military training in peace-time, and not leave it till war breaks out. So a state that knows its business should reserve at least one day per month (and more than one, if the authorities think fit) for military manoeuvres, to be held without regard for the weather, come rain come shine. Men, women and children should participate, and the authorities will decide from time to time whether to take them out on manoeuvres *en masse* or in sections. They must never fail to mount a programme of wholesome recreation, accompanied by sacrifices; and the programme ought to include 'war-games' which should simulate the conditions of actual fighting as realistically as possible. On each field-day they

2. King of the underworld. The 'twelfth month' is June, when spring, the season of growth, is over.

should distribute prizes and awards of merit, and compose speeches in commendation or reproof of each other according to the conduct of individuals not only in the contests but in daily life too: those who are deemed to have acquitted themselves particularly well should be honoured, while the failures should be censured. But not everyone should produce such compositions. For a start, a composer must be at least fifty years old, and he must not be one of those people who for all their poetical and musical competence have not a single noble or outstanding achievement to their credit. The compositions that ought to be sung (even if in terms of art they leave something to be desired) are those of citizens who have achieved a high standard of conduct and whose personal merits have brought them distinction in the state. The official in charge of education, together with the other Guardians of the Laws, are to select them and grant them alone the privilege of giving their Muses free rein; other people are to be entirely forbidden. No one should dare to sing any unauthorized song, not even if it is sweeter than the hymns of Orpheus or of Thamyras.[3] Our citizens must confine themselves to such pieces as have been given the stamp of approval and consecrated to the gods, and to compositions which on the strength of their authors' reputation are judged to be suitable vehicles for commendation or censure. (I intend the same regulations to apply to men and women alike, both as regards military excursions and freedom to compose unsupervised.)

The legislator should think things over and employ this sort of analogy: 'Let's see, now, once I've organized the state as a whole, what sort of citizen do I want to produce? *Athletes* are what I want – competitors against a million rivals 830 in the most vital struggles of all. Right?' 'Very much so', one would reply, correctly. Well then, if we were training boxers or pankratiasts[4] or competitors in some other similar contest

3. Orpheus' singing was said to be able to charm animals and trees and even rocks. Thamyras was a bard who boasted that not even the Muses could rival his music.

4. The *pankration* was a form of wrestling, in which the contestants were allowed to kick and hit each other.

should we go straight into the ring unprepared by a daily work-out against an opponent? If we were boxers, surely we'd have spent days on end *before* the contest in strenuous practice, learning how to fight, and trying out all those manoeuvres we intended to use when the time came to fight to win? We'd come as close as we could to the real conditions of the contest by putting on practice-gloves instead of thongs,[5] so as to get as much practise as possible in delivering and dodging punches. And if we ran particularly short of sparring partners then we'd go to the trouble of hanging up a lifeless dummy to practise against; and we certainly wouldn't be put off by the idiots who might laugh at us. Come to that, if one day we ran out of sparring partners completely, living or otherwise, and had no one to practise with at all, we'd go so far as to box against our own shadows – shadow-boxing with a vengeance! After all, how else can you describe a practice-session in which you just throw punches at the air?

CLEINIAS: No, sir, there's no other term for it than the one you've just used.

ATHENIAN: Very well. So when the fighting force of our state comes to brace itself to face the most important contest of all – to fight for life and children and property and the entire state – is it really to be after less intensive training than combatants such as these have enjoyed? Is our citizens' legislator going to be so scared that their practice against each other may look silly to some people that he will neglect his duty? I mean his duty of instructing that manoeuvres on a small scale, without arms, should be held every day, if possible (and for this purpose he should arrange teams to compete in every kind of gymnastic exercise), whereas the 'major' exercises, in which arms are carried, should be held not less than once per month. The citizens will compete with each other throughout the entire country, to see who is best at occupying positions and laying ambushes, and they must reproduce the conditions of every kind of battle (that will give them *real* practice, because they will be aiming at the

5. Greek boxers wore thongs to protect their hands.

closest possible approximation to the *real* targets).[6] And they should use missiles that are moderately dangerous: we don't want the competitions they hold against each other to be entirely unalarming, but to inspire them with fear and do something to reveal the brave man and the coward; and the legislator should confer honours or inflict disgrace as appropriate, so as to prepare the whole state to be an efficient 831 fighter in the real struggle that lasts a lifetime. In fact, if anyone is killed in such circumstances, the homicide should be regarded as involuntary, and the legislator should decree that the killer's hands are clean when once he has been purified according to law.[7] After all, the lawgiver will reflect, even if a few people do die, others who are just as good will be produced to replace them, whereas if fear dies (so to speak), he'll not be able to find in all these activities a yardstick to separate the good performers from the bad – and that would be a bigger disaster for the state than the other.

CLEINIAS: Yes, sir, we'd agree that this is the sort of law that every state should pass and observe.

OBSTACLES TO CORRECT MILITARY
TRAINING

ATHENIAN: Now we all know, don't we, the reason why this kind of team-work and competition is not to be found in any state at the present time, except on a very modest scale indeed? I suppose we'd say it was because the masses and their legislators suffer from ignorance?

CLEINIAS: Maybe so.

ATHENIAN: Not a bit of it, my dear Cleinias! We ought to say there are *two* causes, and pretty powerful ones at that.

6. The translation of this parenthesis is something of a paraphrase of some difficult Greek. The point, I take it, is that military exercises are practice not only for ordinary wars but for the *real* 'war' against vice ('the real struggle that lasts a lifetime'); by learning to resist fear in realistic exercises we also learn to resist lust, etc. See the argument at the close of §2, and (for the notion of virtue as a 'target' to be hit by 'weapons'), pp. 160, 176 and 214.

7. Cf. 46A (c), p. 377.

CLEINIAS: What are they?

ATHENIAN: The first is a passion for wealth which makes men unwilling to devote a minute of their time to anything except their own personal property. This is what every single citizen concentrates on with all his heart and soul; his ruling passion is his daily profit and he's quite incapable of worrying about anything else. Everyone is out for himself, and is very quick off the mark indeed to learn any skill and apply himself to any technique that fills his pocket; anything that doesn't do that he treats with complete derision. So we can treat this as one reason why states are not prepared to undertake this[8] or any other praiseworthy activity in a serious spirit, whereas their insatiable desire for gold and silver makes them perfectly willing to slave away at any ways and means, fair or foul, that promise to make them rich. It doesn't matter whether something is sanctioned by heaven, or forbidden and absolutely disgusting – it's all the same to them, and causes not the slightest scruple, provided it enables them to make pigs of themselves by wallowing in all kinds of food and drink and indulging every kind of sexual pleasure.

CLEINIAS: You're quite right.

ATHENIAN: So I've described one cause: let's treat this obsession as the first obstacle that prevents states from following an adequate course of training, either for military or for any other purposes: naturally decent folk are turned into traders or merchant-venturers or just plain servants, and bold fellows are made into robbers and burglars, and become
832 bellicose and overbearing. Quite often, though, they are not naturally corrupt: they're simply unlucky.

CLEINIAS: How do you mean?

ATHENIAN: Well, if you have to live out your life with a continual hunger in your soul, aren't you 'unlucky' to a degree? What other term could I use?

CLEINIAS: Very well, that's one reason. What's your second, sir?

ATHENIAN: Ah, yes, thank you for jogging my memory.

CLEINIAS: According to you, one cause is the insatiable

8. Military exercises.

and lifelong acquisitive urge which obsesses us all and stops us undertaking military training in the proper way. All right – now tell us the second.

ATHENIAN: I dare say it looks as if I'm putting off getting round to it because I don't know what to say?

CLEINIAS: No, but you do seem to be such a 'good hater' of this sort of character that you're berating it more than the subject in hand requires.

ATHENIAN: That's a very proper rebuke, gentlemen. So you're all ready for the next point, it seems.

CLEINIAS: Just tell us, that's all!

ATHENIAN: The cause I want to put forward are those 'non-constitutions' that I've often mentioned earlier[9] in our conversation – democracy, oligarchy and tyranny. None of these is a genuine political system: the best name for them all would be 'party rule', because under none of them do willing rulers govern willing subjects: that is, the rulers are always willing enough, but they never hold power with the consent of the governed. They hold it by constant resort to a degree of force, and they are never prepared to allow any of their subjects to cultivate virtue or acquire wealth or strength or courage – and least of all will they tolerate a man who can fight. So much for the two main roots of pretty nearly all evil, and certainly the main roots of the evils we're discussing. However, the political system which we are now establishing by law has avoided both of them. Our state enjoys unparalleled leisure, the citizens live free of interference from each other, and I reckon these laws of ours are quite unlikely to turn them into money-grubbers. So it's a reasonable and natural supposition that a political system organized along these lines will be unique among contemporary constitutions in finding room for the military training-cum-sport[10] that we've just described – and described in the detail it deserves, too.

CLEINIAS: Splendid.

9. See pp. 170 and 173–4.   10. Cf. pp. 281–2.

RACES

ATHENIAN: The next thing we have to bear in mind about any athletic contest is this: if it helps us to train for war we must go in for it and put up prizes for the winners, but leave it strictly alone if it does not. Isn't that right? It will be better to stipulate from the start the contests we want, and provide for them by law. First, I take it we should arrange races, and contests of speed in general?

CLEINIAS: Yes, we should.

ATHENIAN: At any rate, what makes a man a fine soldier more than anything else is general agility, a ready use of his hands as well as his feet. If he's a good runner, he can make a 833 capture or show a clean pair of heels, and versatile hands will stand him in good stead in tangling with the enemy in close combat, where strength and force are essential.

CLEINIAS: Certainly.

ATHENIAN: But if he hasn't any weapons, neither ability will help him as much as it might.

CLEINIAS: Of course not.

ATHENIAN: So in our contests the first competitor our herald will summon will be (as now) the single-length runner, and he will come forward armed; we shan't put up any prizes for competitors who are *un*armed. So, as I say, the competitor who intends to run one length will come on first, carrying his arms; second will come the runner over two lengths, and third the middle-distance runner; the long-distance man will come on fourth. The fifth competitor we shall call the 'heavy-armed' runner, from his heavier equipment. We shall start by sending him in full armour over a distance of sixty lengths to some temple of Ares and back. His course will be over comparatively level ground, whereas the other runner,[11] an archer in full archer rig, will run a course of 100 lengths over hills and constantly changing terrain to a temple of Apollo and

11. The runner in a sixth race? The passage is confusingly written. (A 'length' = a 'stade' = about 200 yards. 60 lengths = about 7 miles, 100 lengths = about 11½ miles.)

Artemis. While we're waiting for these runners to return, we'll hold the other contests and finally award the prizes to the winners of each event.

CLEINIAS: Fine.

ATHENIAN: Let's arrange these contests in three groups, one for boys, one for youths, and one for men. When youths and boys compete as archers and heavy-armed runners, we shall make the course for youths two-thirds of the full distance and for the boys one-half. As for females, girls below the age of puberty must enter (naked[12]) for the single-length, double-length, middle and long distance races, their competition being confined to the stadium. Girls from thirteen till the marriage-age must enter till they are at least eighteen, but not beyond the age of twenty. (They, however, must put on some suitable clothing[13] before presenting themselves as competitors in these races.)

CONTESTS IN ARMS

So much for men's and women's races; now to deal with trials of strength. Instead of wrestling and other he-man contests that are the fashion nowadays, we'll have our citizens fight each other *armed* – man to man, two a side, and any number per team up to ten. We ought to take our cue from the authorities in charge of wrestling, who have established criteria which will tell you whether a wrestler's performance is good or bad. We must call in the leading exponents of armed combat and ask them to assist us in framing rules about the blows one needs to avoid or inflict to win in this sort of contest, and similarly the points we need to look for to decide 834 the loser. The same set of rules should also apply to the female competitors (who must be below the age of marriage). To replace the *pankration*[14] we shall establish a general contest of light-infantry; the weapons of the competitors are to be bows, light shields, javelins, and stones cast by hand and sling.

12. Or possibly 'unarmed'.
13. Or possibly 'armour' or 'equipment'.
14. For this term see note on p. 323.

Here too we'll lay down rules, and give the honour of victory to the competitor who reaches the highest standard as defined by the regulations.

HORSE-RACING

The next thing for which we must provide rules is horse-racing. In Crete, of course, horses are of rather limited use and you don't find very many of them, so that the comparatively low level of interest in rearing and racing them is inevitable. No one in this country keeps a team of horses for a chariot, nor is ever likely to covet such a thing, so that if we established contests in something so foreign to the local customs, we'd be taken for idiots (and rightly). The way to modify this sport for the local Cretan terrain is to put up prizes for skill in *riding* the animals – as foals, when half-grown, and when fully grown. So our law should provide for contests in which jockeys can compete with each other in these categories; Tribe-Leaders and Cavalry-Commanders should be entrusted with the job of deciding the actual courses and deciding which competitor has won (in full armour, of course: just as in the athletic events, if we established contests for unarmed competitors we'd be failing in our duty as legislators). And since your Cretan is no fool at archery and javelin-throwing in the saddle, people should amuse themselves by competing in this sort of contest too. As for women, there's no point in making it legally compulsory for them to join in all this, but if their previous training has got them into the habit, and girls and young women are in good enough shape to take part without hardship, then they should be permitted to do so and not discouraged.

CONCLUSION

That brings us to the end of our discussion of competitions and the teaching of physical training, and we've seen what strenuous efforts are involved in the contests and the daily sessions with instructors. In fact, we've also dealt pretty thoroughly with the role of the arts, although arrangements about reciters of poetry and similar performers, and the chorus-competitions[15] obligatory at festivals, can wait till the gods and the minor deities have had their days and months and years allocated to them; then we can decide whether festivals should be held at two-year or four-year intervals, or whether the gods suggest some other pattern. On these occasions we 835 must also expect the various categories of competitions in the arts to be held. This is the province of the stewards of the games, the Minister of Education and the Guardians of the Laws, who should all meet as an *ad hoc* committee and produce their own regulations about the date of each chorus-competition and dance, and specify who should compete and who may watch. The original legislator has often enough explained the sort of thing each of these performances should be, and has dealt with the songs, the spoken addresses and the musical styles that accompany the rhythmical movements of the dancers. His successors must emulate his example in their own legislation and match the right contests with the right sacrifices at the right times, and so provide festivals at which the state may make merry.

15. For this and other technical terms in this paragraph, see pp. 84–5.

§14. PROBLEMS OF SEXUAL CONDUCT

Plato devotes a good deal of attention to this topic, for obvious reasons: sex arouses tremendously strong passions that make men difficult to handle and prone to crime. Adultery and paederasty are socially disruptive and spring from base desires, whereas our energies and aspirations should be directed to higher aims.

There are two crucial points in this section, one philosophical and one political. The philosophical point is the insistence on the 'naturalness' of intercourse between man and wife for the purpose of procreation, argued for by (selective) analogy from the practices of animals. This and related arguments from 'nature' have had a long run and in spite of widespread criticism are still common. The political point is the clear distinction between the desirable and the possible. Plato wishes to regulate our lives in the utmost detail, but recognizes that there comes a point when to stay his hand will be wiser than to persist. He apparently thinks there is a chance of suppressing sodomy entirely; but he refuses to make extra-marital relations a formal crime, provided they are kept secret. This is a particularly clear example of the tension between the ideal and the practicable that is present throughout the Laws.

THE PROBLEMS STATED

ATHENIAN: It's not difficult to see how to cast these and similar matters in the form of a law, and making this or that alteration won't help or harm the state very much. But now for something which is not a triviality at all. It's a point on which it is difficult to convince people, and God himself is really the only person to do it – supposing, that is, we could in fact somehow get explicit instructions from him. Since that's impossible, it looks as if we need some intrepid mortal, who values frankness above all, to specify the policy he believes best for the state and its citizens, give a firm 'no' to our most compelling passions, and order his audience of corrupted souls to observe standards of conduct in keeping

with, and implied by, the whole organization of the state. There
will be no one to back him up. He'll walk alone, with reason
alone to guide him.

CLEINIAS: What new topic is this, sir? We don't see what
you're getting at.

ATHENIAN: That's not surprising. Well, I'll try to put the
point more explicitly. When I came to discuss education, I
envisaged young men and women associating with each other
on friendly terms. Naturally enough, I began to feel some
disquiet. I wondered how one would handle a state like this,
with everyone engaged on a life-long round of sacrifices and
festivals and chorus-performances, and the young men and
women well-nourished and free of those demanding and
degrading jobs that damp down lust so effectively. Reason,
which is embodied in law as far as it can be, tells us to avoid
indulging the passions that have ruined so many people. So
how will the members of *our* state avoid them? (Actually,
most desires may well be kept in check by the regulations we
have already framed. If so, we needn't be surprised. After all, 836
the law against excessive wealth will do a great deal to encourage self-control, and the educational curriculum is full of
sound rules designed for the same purpose. The officials too,
who have been rigorously trained to watch this point closely,
and to keep the young people themselves under constant
surveillance, will do something to restrain ordinary passions,
as far as any man can.) But there are *sexual* urges too –
paederasty (of either sex) and heterosexual love among adults.
What precautions should one take against passions which
have had such a powerful effect on public and private life?
What's the remedy that will save us from the dangers of sex in
each? It's a great problem, Cleinias. We're faced with the fact
that though in several other respects Crete in general and
Sparta give us pretty solid help when we frame laws that flout
common custom, in affairs of the heart (there's no one listening, so let's be frank) they are totally opposed to us. Suppose
you follow nature's rule and establish the law that was in force
before the time of Laius.[1] You'd argue that one may have

1. Regarded here as the first homosexual.

333

sexual intercourse with a woman but not with men or boys. As evidence for your view, you'd point to the animal world, where (you'd argue) the males do not have sexual relations with each other, because such a thing is unnatural. But in Crete and Sparta your argument would not go down at all well, and you'd probably persuade nobody. However, another argument is that such practices are incompatible with what in our view should be the constant aim of the legislator – that is, we're always asking 'which of our regulations encourages virtue, and which does not?' Now then, suppose in the present case we agreed to pass a law that such practices are desirable, or not at all *un*desirable – what contribution would they make to virtue? Will the spirit of courage spring to life in the soul of the seduced person? Will the soul of the seducer learn habits of self-control? No one is going to be led astray by that sort of argument – quite the contrary. Everyone will censure the weakling who yields to temptation, and condemn his all-too-effeminate partner who plays the role of the woman. So who on earth will pass a law like that? Hardly anyone, at any rate if he knows what a genuine law really is. Well, how do we show the truth of this? If you want to get these things straight, you have to analyse the nature of
837 friendship and desire and 'love', as people call it. There are two separate categories, plus a third which is a combination of both. But one term covers all three, and that causes no end of muddle and confusion.

CLEINIAS: How's that?

THREE KINDS OF FRIENDSHIP

ATHENIAN: When two people are virtuous and alike, or when they are equals, we say that one is a 'friend' of the other; but we also speak of the poor man's 'friendship' for the man who has grown rich, even though they are poles apart. In either case, when the friendship is particularly ardent, we call it 'love'.

CLEINIAS: Yes, we do.

ATHENIAN: And a violent and stormy friendship it is,

when a man is attracted to someone widely different to himself, and only seldom do we see it reciprocated. When men are alike, however, they show a calm and mutual affection that lasts a lifetime. But there is a third category, compounded of the other two. The first problem here is to discover what this third kind of lover is really after. There is the further difficulty that he himself is confused and torn between two opposing instincts: one tells him to enjoy his beloved, the other forbids him. The lover of the body, hungry for his partner who is ripe to be enjoyed, like a luscious fruit, tells himself to have his fill, without showing any consideration for his beloved's character and disposition. But in another case physical desire will count for very little and the lover will be content to gaze upon his beloved without lusting for him – a mature and genuine desire of soul for soul. That body should sate itself with body he'll think outrageous; his reverence and respect for self-control, courage, high principles and good judgement will make him want to live a life of purity, chaste lover with chaste beloved. This combination of the first two is the 'third' love we enumerated a moment ago.

So there's your list of the various forms love can take: should the law forbid them all, and keep them out of our community? Or isn't it obvious that in our state we'd want to see the virtuous kind spring up – the love that aims to make a young man perfect? It's the other two we'll forbid, if we can. Or what *is* our policy, Megillus, my friend?

MEGILLUS: Indeed, sir, I heartily endorse what you've said on the subject.

ATHENIAN: So it looks as if I've won you over, my dear fellow, as I guessed I would, and there's no call for me to inquire what line the law of Sparta takes on this topic: it is enough to note your assent to my argument. Later on I'll come back to the subject and try to charm Cleinias also into agreeing with me. Let's assume you've both conceded my point, and press on with our laws without delay.

MEGILLUS: Fair enough.

HOW TO DISCOURAGE UNNATURAL
SEXUAL INTERCOURSE

ATHENIAN: I want to put the law on this subject on a firm
838 footing, and at the moment I'm thinking of a method which
is, in a sense, simplicity itself. But from another point of view,
nothing could be harder.

MEGILLUS: What are you getting at?

ATHENIAN: We're aware, of course, that even nowadays
most men, in spite of their general disregard for the law, are
very effectively prevented from having relations with people
they find attractive. And they don't refrain reluctantly, either –
they're more than happy to.

MEGILLUS: What circumstances have you in mind?

ATHENIAN: When it's one's brother or sister whom one
finds attractive. And the same law, unwritten though it is, is
extremely effective in stopping a man sleeping – secretly or
otherwise – with his son or daughter, or making any kind of
amorous approach to them. Most people feel not the faintest
desire for such intercourse.

MEGILLUS: That's perfectly true.

ATHENIAN: So the desire for this sort of pleasure is stifled
by a few words?

MEGILLUS: What words do you mean?

ATHENIAN: The doctrine that 'these acts are absolutely
unholy, an abomination in the sight of the gods, and that
nothing is more revolting'. We refrain from them because we
never hear them spoken of in any other way. From the day of
our birth each of us encounters a complete unanimity of
opinion wherever we go; we find it not only in comedies but
often in the high seriousness of tragedy too, when we see a
Thyestes on the stage, or an Oedipus or a Macareus, the
clandestine lover of his sister.[2] We watch these characters
dying promptly by their own hand as a penalty for their
crimes.

2. Thyestes had intercourse with his own daughter; Oedipus married
his own mother.

MEGILLUS: You're right in this, anyway, that when no one ventures to challenge the law, public opinion works wonders.

ATHENIAN: So we were justified in what we said just now. When the legislator wants to tame one of the desires that dominate mankind so cruelly, it's easy for him to see his method of attack. He must try to make everyone – slave and free, women and children, and the entire state without any exception – believe that this common opinion has the backing of religion. He couldn't put his law on a securer foundation than that.

MEGILLUS: Very true. But how on earth it will ever be possible to produce such spontaneous unanimity –

ATHENIAN: I'm glad you've taken me up on the point. This is just what I was getting at when I said I knew of a way to put into effect this law of ours which permits the sexual act only for its natural purpose, procreation, and forbids not only homosexual relations, in which the human race is deliberately murdered, but also the sowing of seeds on rocks and stone, where it will never take root and mature into a new individual; 839 and we should also have to keep away from any female 'soil' in which we'd be sorry to have the seed develop. At present, however, the law is effective only against intercourse between parent and child, but if it can be put on a permanent footing and made to apply effectively, as it deserves to, in other cases as well, it'll do a power of good. The first point in its favour is that it is a *natural* law. But it also tends to check the raging fury of the sexual instinct that so often leads to adultery; it discourages excesses in food and drink, and inspires men with affection for their own wives. And there are a great many other advantages to be gained, if only one could get this law established.

But suppose some impatient young man were standing here, bursting with seed, and heard us passing this law. He'd probably raise the echoes with his bellows of abuse, and say our rules were stupid and unrealistic. Now this is just the sort of protest I had in mind when I remarked that I knew of a very simple[3] – and yet very difficult – way of putting this law

3. See p. 336.

into effect permanently. It's easy to see that it *can* be done, and easy to see *how*: if the rule is given sufficient religious backing, it will get a grip on every soul and intimidate it into obeying the established laws. But in fact we've reached a point where people still think we'd fail, even granted those conditions. It's just the same with the supposed impossibility of the common meals: people see no prospect of a whole state keeping up the practice permanently. The proven facts of the case in your countries do nothing to convince your compatriots that it would be natural to apply the practice to women. It was this flat disbelief that made me remark on the difficulty of turning either proposal[4] into an established law.

MEGILLUS: You're absolutely right.

ATHENIAN: Even so, I could put up quite a convincing case for supposing that the difficulties are not beyond human powers, and can be overcome. Do you want me to try to explain?

CLEINIAS: Of course.

THE IMPORTANCE OF SELF-CONTROL

ATHENIAN: When will a man find it easier to keep off sex, and do as he's told in a decent and willing spirit? When he's not neglected his training and is in the pink of condition, or when he's in poor shape?

CLEINIAS: He'll find it a great deal easier if he's in training.

ATHENIAN: Now of course we've all heard the story of how Iccus of Tarentum set about winning contests at Olympia and elsewhere. He was so ambitious to win, they say, and his expertise was strengthened by a character of such determination and self-discipline, that he never had a woman or even a boy during the whole time he was under intensive training. In fact, we are told very much the same about Crison, Astylus, Diopompus, and a great many others. And yet, Cleinias, their characters were far less well educated than the citizens you and I have to deal with, and physically they were much lustier.

---

4. (a) common meals for women, (b) the ban on 'unnatural' sexual relations.

CLEINIAS: Yes, you're right – our ancient sources are quite definite that these athletes did in fact do as you say.

ATHENIAN: Well then, they steeled themselves to keep off what most people regard as sheer bliss, simply in order to win wrestling matches and races and so forth. But there's a much nobler contest to be won than that, and I hope the young people of our state aren't going to lack the stamina for it. After all, right from their earliest years we're going to tell them stories and talk to them and sing them songs, so as to charm them, we trust, into believing that this victory is the noblest of all.

CLEINIAS: What victory?

ATHENIAN: The conquest of pleasure. If they win this battle, they'll have a happy life – but so much the worse for them if they lose. That apart, the fear that the act[5] is a ghastly sin will, in the end, enable them to tame the passions that their inferiors have tamed before them.

CLEINIAS: Quite likely.

ATHENIAN: So thanks to the general corruption, that's the predicament we've got into at this point in our consideration of the law about sex. My position, therefore, is that the law must go ahead and insist that our citizens' standards should not be lower than those of birds and many other wild animals which are born into large communities and live chaste and unmarried, without intercourse, until the time comes for them to breed. At the appropriate age they pair off; the male picks a wife, and female chooses a husband, and for ever afterwards they live in a pious and law-abiding way, firmly faithful to the promises they made when they first fell in love. Clearly our citizens ought to reach standards higher than the animals'. But if they are corrupted by seeing and hearing how most other Greeks and non-Greeks go in for 'free' love on a grand scale, they may prove unable to keep themselves in check. In that case, the law-guardians must turn themselves into law-makers and frame a second law for people to observe.

CLEINIAS: So if they find it impossible to enforce the ideal 841 law now proposed, what other law do you advise them to pass?

5. Presumably any forbidden form of sexual intercourse.

ATHENIAN: The second best, Cleinias, obviously.

CLEINIAS: Namely?

ATHENIAN: My point is that the appetite for pleasures, which is very strong and grows by being fed, can be *starved* (you remember[6]) if the body is given plenty of hard work to distract it. We'd get much the same result if we were incapable of having sexual intercourse without feeling ashamed: our shame would lead to infrequent indulgence, and infrequent indulgence would make the desire less compulsive. So in sexual matters our citizens ought to regard privacy – though not complete abstinence – as a decency demanded by usage and unwritten custom, and lack of privacy as disgusting. That will establish a second legal standard of decency and indecency – not the ideal standard but the next to it. People whose characters have been corrupted (they form a single group we call the 'self-inferior'[7]) will be made prisoners of three influences that will compel them not to break the law.

CLEINIAS: What influences do you mean?

ATHENIAN: Respect for religion, the ambition to be honoured, and a mature passion for spiritual rather than physical beauty. 'Pious wishes!' you'll say; 'sheer moonshine!' Perhaps so. But if such wishes were to come true, the world would benefit enormously.

TWO ALTERNATIVE LAWS

However, God willing, perhaps we'll succeed in imposing one or other of two standards of sexual conduct. (1) Ideally, no one will dare to have relations with any respectable citizen woman except his own wedded wife, or sow illegitimate and bastard seed in courtesans, or sterile seed in males in defiance of nature. (2) Alternatively, while suppressing sodomy entirely, we might insist that if a man does have intercourse with any woman (hired or procured in some other way) except the wife he wed in holy marriage with the blessing of the gods, he must do so without any other man or woman getting to know about it. If he fails to keep the affair secret, I

6. See p. 333.   7. See pp. 48 ff.

think we'd be right to exclude him by law from the award of state honours, on the grounds that he's no better than an alien. This law, or 'pair' of laws, as perhaps we should say, should govern our conduct whenever the sexual urge and the passion of love impel us, wisely or unwisely, to have intercourse. **842**

MEGILLUS: Speaking for myself, sir, I'd be very glad to adopt this law of yours. Cleinias must tell us his view on the subject himself.

CLEINIAS: I'll do that later, Megillus, when I think a suitable moment has arrived. For the nonce, let's not stop our friend from going on to the next stage of his legislation.

MEGILLUS: Fair enough.

§15. AGRICULTURE, ECONOMICS AND TRADE

It would be amusing to hear a celestial conversation between Plato and Dr Johnson on the latter's remark that 'there are few ways in which a man is more innocently employed than in getting money'. Plato, it is clear, would disagree violently: the key to this section is his wish, in the interests of morality, to restrict trade to the smallest practicable compass, on the grounds that it tends to encourage a pernicious desire to make as much money as possible. Thus – to state very summarily the economic system of Magnesia – retail trading for profit is to be confined to resident aliens whose consequent moral turpitude will hardly affect the state; the citizen farmers are to sell a fixed part of their crops wholesale to aliens for retail distribution, and buy manufactured goods and services from them in return; even so, the actual selling of the crops must be conducted not by the citizens themselves, but by their slaves as overseers of the farms. The regulations of this section are, so far as they go, self-explanatory, but details are often vague.

THE FOOD SUPPLY (I)

ATHENIAN: Well then, this is the stage we've reached now. We can assume that communal meals have been established (a thing that would be a problem in other countries, we notice, but not in Crete, where no one would think of doing anything else). But how should they be organized? On the Cretan model, or the Spartan? Or is there some third type that would suit us better than either? I don't think this is a difficulty, and there's not much to be gained from settling the point. The arrangements we have made are quite satisfactory as they are.

The next question is the organization of a food-supply in keeping with our communal meals. In other states the sources of supply are many and varied – in fact, at least twice as many as in ours, because most Greeks draw on both the land and the sea for their food, whereas our citizens will use the land alone.

For the legislator, this makes things simpler. It's not just that half the number of laws or even substantially fewer will do, but they'll be more suitable laws for gentlemen to observe. Our state's legislator, you see, need not bother his head very much about the merchant-shipping business, trading, retailing, inn-keeping, customs duties, mining, money-lending and compound interest. Waving aside most of these and a thousand other such details, he'll legislate for farmers, shepherds, bee-keepers, for the protectors of their stock and the supervisors of their equipment. His laws already cover such major topics as marriage and the birth and rearing of children, as well as their education and the appointment of the state's officials, so the next topic to which he must turn in his legislation is their food, and the workers who co-operate in the constant effort to produce it.

AGRICULTURAL LAWS

Let's first specify the 'agricultural' laws, as they're called. The first law – sanctioned by Zeus the Protector of Boundaries – shall run as follows:

No man shall disturb the boundary stones of his neighbour, whether fellow-citizen or foreigner (that is, when a proprietor's land is on the boundary of the state), in the conviction that this would be 'moving the immovable'[1] in the crudest sense. Far better that a man should want to try 843 to move the biggest stone that does not mark a boundary, than a small one separating friend's land from foe's, and established by an oath sworn to the gods. Zeus the God of Kin is witness in the one case, Zeus the Protector of Foreigners in the other. Rouse him in either capacity, and the most terrible wars break out. If a man obeys the law he will escape its penalties, but if he holds it in contempt he is to be liable to two punishments, the first at the hands of the gods, the second under the law. No man, if he can help it, must move the boundary stones of his neighbour's land, but if anyone does move them, any man who wishes should report him to the farmers, who should take him to court.

1. Cf. pp. 130 and 450.

26. If anyone is found guilty of such a charge,
he must be regarded as a man who has tried to reallocate land,
whether clandestinely or by force; and the court must bear
that in mind when assessing what penalty he should suffer
or what fine he should pay.

DUTIES TO NEIGHBOURS

Next we come to those numerous petty injuries done by
neighbour to neighbour. The frequent repetition of such
injuries makes feelings run high, so that relations between
neighbours become intolerably embittered. That's why everyone should do everything he can to avoid offending his
neighbour; above all, he must always go out of his way to
avoid all acts of encroachment. Hurting a man is all too easy,
and we all get the chance to do that; but it's not everyone who
is in a position to do a good turn.

27. If a man oversteps his boundaries and encroaches on his
    neighbour's land,
he should pay for the damage, and also, by way of cure for
such uncivilized and inconsiderate behaviour, give the
injured party a further sum of twice that amount.

In all these and similar cases the Country-Wardens should
act as inspectors, judges and assessors (the entire divisional
company in the graver cases, as indicated earlier,[2] and the
Guards-in-Chief in the more trivial).

28. If a man lets his cattle graze on someone else's land,
these officials must inspect the damage, reach a decision, and
assess the penalty.

29. If anyone takes over another man's bees, by making
    rattling noises to please and attract them, so that he gets
    them for himself,
he must pay for the injury he has done.

30. If anyone burns his own wood without taking sufficient
    precautions to protect his neighbour's,
he must be fined a sum decided by the officials.

2. See p. 235.

31. If when planting trees a man fails to leave a suitable gap
    between them and his neighbour's land,
    the same regulation is to apply.

THE WATER SUPPLY (1)

These are points that many legislators have dealt with perfectly adequately, and we should make use of their work rather than demand that the grand architect of our state should legislate on a mass of trivial details that can be handled by any run-of-the-mill lawgiver. For instance, the water supply for 844 farmers is the subject of some splendid old-established laws – but there's no call to let them overflow into our discussion! It is fundamental that anyone who wants to conduct a supply of water to his own land may do so, provided his source is the public reservoirs and he does not intercept the surface springs of any private person. He may conduct the water by any route he likes, except through houses, temples and tombs, and he must do no damage beyond the actual construction of the conduit. But in some naturally dry districts the soil may fail to retain the moisture when it rains, so that drinking water is in short supply. In that case the owner must dig down to the clay, and if he fails to strike water at that depth he should take from his neighbours sufficient drinking water for each member of his household. If the neighbours too are short of water, he should share the available supply with them and fetch his ration daily, the amount to be fixed by the Country-Wardens. A man may injure the farmer or householder next door on higher ground by blocking the flow of rainwater; on the other hand he may discharge it so carelessly as to damage the man below. If the parties are not prepared to co-operate in this matter, anyone who wishes should report the matter to an official – a City-Warden in the city, and a Country-Warden in the country–and obtain a ruling as to what each side should do. Anyone refusing to abide by the ruling must take the consequences of being a grudging and ill-tempered fellow:

32. if found guilty,
    he should pay twice the value of the damage to the injured party as a penalty for disobeying the officials.

THE HARVEST

Everyone should take his share of the fruit harvest on roughly the following principles. The goddess of the harvest has graciously bestowed two gifts[3] upon us, (a) the fruit which pleases Dionysus so much, but which won't keep, and (b) the produce which nature has made fit to store. So our law about the harvest should run as follows.

33. Anyone who consumes any part of the coarse crop of grapes or figs, whether on his own land or another's, before the rising of Arcturus[4] ushers in the vintage,

must owe

    (a) fifty drachmas, to be presented to Dionysus, if he takes the fruit from his own trees,

    (b) 100 if from his neighbour's, and

    (c) sixty-six and two-thirds drachmas if from anyone else's trees.

If a man wants to gather in the 'dessert' grapes or figs (as they are called nowadays), he may do so whenever and however he likes, provided they come from his own trees; but

34. (a) if he takes them from anyone else's trees, without permission,

he must be punished in accordance with the provisions of the law which forbids the removal of any object except by

845 the depositor.[5]

    (b) If a slave fails to get the landowner's permission before touching any of this kind of fruit,

he must be whipped, the number of lashes to be the same as the number of grapes in the bunch or figs picked off the fig tree.

A resident alien may buy dessert fruit and gather it in as he wishes. If a foreigner on a visit from abroad feels inclined to

3. Dessert fruit for immediate consumption, and coarse fruit for making wine.

4. The autumn equinox.

5. This offence is thus brought under the umbrella of the general law mentioned on p. 343; cf. pp. 450 and 488.

eat some fruit as he travels along the road, he may, if he wishes, take some of the dessert crop *gratis*, for himself and one attendant, as part of our hospitality. But foreigners must be prevented by law from sharing with us the 'coarse' and similar fruits.

35. If a foreigner, master or slave, touches such fruit in ignorance of the law,
  (a) *the slave* is to be punished with a whipping;
  (b) *the free* man is to be dismissed with a warning and told to stick to the crop that is unsuitable to be kept in store in the form of raisins, wine, or dried figs.

There should be nothing to be ashamed of in helping one-self inconspicuously to apples and pears and pomegranates and so on, but

36. (a) if a man under thirty is caught at it,
he should be cuffed and driven off, provided he suffers no actual injury.

A citizen should have no legal redress for such an assault on his person. (A foreigner is to be entitled to a share of these fruits too, on the same terms as he may take some of the dessert grapes and figs.) If a man *above* thirty years of age touches some fruits, consuming them on the spot and taking none away with him, he shall share them all on the same terms as the foreigner, but

  (b) if he disobeys the law,
he should be liable to be disqualified from competing for awards of merit, if anyone draws the attention of the assessors to the facts when the awards are being decided.

THE WATER SUPPLY (2)

Water is the most nourishing food a garden can have, but it's easily fouled, whereas the soil, the sun and the winds, which co-operate with the water in fostering the growth of the plants that spring up out of the ground, are not readily interfered with by being doctored or channelled off or stolen.

But in the nature of the case, water is exposed to all these hazards. That is why it needs the protection of a law, which should run as follows.

If anyone deliberately spoils someone else's water supply, whether spring or reservoir, by poisons or excavations or theft, the injured party should take his case to the City-Wardens and submit his estimate of the damage in writing.

37. Anyone convicted of fouling water by magic poisons *should*, in addition to his fine, purify the spring or reservoir, using whatever method of purification the regulations of the Expounders[6] prescribe as appropriate to the circumstances and the individuals involved.

BRINGING IN CROPS

A man may bring home any crop of his own by any route he
846 pleases, provided he does no one any damage, or, failing that, benefits to at least three times the value of the damage he does his neighbour. The authorities must act as inspectors in this business, as well as in all other cases when someone uses his own property deliberately to inflict violent or surreptitious damage on another man or some piece of his property without his permission. When the damage does not exceed three minas, the injured party must report it to the magistrates and obtain redress; but if he has a larger claim to bring against someone, he must get his redress from the culprit by taking the case to the public courts.

38. If one of the officials is judged to have settled the penalties in a biassed fashion,
he must be liable to the injured person for double the damages.

Offences committed by the authorities in handling any claim should be taken to the public courts by anyone who may wish to do so. (There are thousands of procedural details like this that must be observed before a penalty can be imposed: the complaint has to be lodged, the summonses issued and

6. For these officials, see pp. 232–3.

served in the presence of two witnesses – or whatever the proper number is. All this sort of detail must not be left to look after itself, but it is not important enough for a legislator who is getting on in years. Our younger colleagues must settle these points, using the broad principles laid down by their predecessors as a guide for their own detailed regulations, which they must apply as need arises. They must thus proceed by trial and error until they think they have got a satisfactory set of formalities, and once the process of modification is over, they should finalize their rules of procedure and render them lifelong obedience.)

ARTISANS

As for craftsmen in general, our policy should be this. First, no citizen of our land nor any of his servants should enter the ranks of the workers whose vocation lies in the arts and crafts. A citizen's vocation, which demands a great deal of practice and study, is to establish and maintain good order in the community, and this is not a job for part-timers. Following two trades or two callings efficiently – or even following one and supervising a worker in another – is almost always too difficult for human nature. So in our state this must be a cardinal rule: no metal worker must turn to carpentry and no carpenter must supervise workers in metal instead of practising his own craft. We may, of course, be met with the excuse that supervising large numbers of employees is more sensible – because more profitable – than just 847 following one's own trade. But no! In our state each individual must have one occupation only, and that's how he must earn his bread. The City-Wardens must have the job of enforcing this rule.

39. If a citizen born and bred turns his attention to some craft instead of to the cultivation of virtue,
the City-Wardens must punish him with marks of disgrace and dishonour until they've got him back on the right lines.

40. If a foreigner follows two trades,
the Wardens must punish him by prison or fines or expulsion

from the state, and so force him to play one role, not many.

As for craftsmen's pay, and cases of refusal to take delivery of their work, or any other wrong done to them by other parties or by them to others, the City-Wardens must adjudicate if the sum at issue does not exceed fifty drachmas; if more, the public courts must decide the dispute as the law directs.

IMPORTS AND EXPORTS

In our state no duties will have to be paid by anyone on either imports or exports. No one must import frankincense and similar foreign fragrant stuff used in religious ritual, or purple and similar dyes not native to the country, or materials for any other process which only needs imports from abroad for inessential purposes; nor, on the other hand, is anyone to export anything that it is essential to keep in the state. The twelve Guardians of the Laws next in order of seniority after the five eldest must act as inspectors and supervisors in this entire field. But what about arms and other military equipment? Well, if we ever need, for military purposes, some technique, vegetable product, mineral, binding material or animal that has to be obtained from abroad, the *state* will receive the goods and pay for them, and the Cavalry-Commanders and the Generals are to be in charge of importing them and exporting other goods in exchange. The Guardians of the Laws will lay down suitable and adequate regulations on the subject. Nowhere in the whole country and the whole state are these – or any other[7] – goods to be retailed for profit.

THE FOOD SUPPLY (2)

It looks as if the right way to organize the food supply and distribute agricultural produce will be to adopt something like the regulations in force in Crete. Every citizen must divide each crop into twelve parts corresponding to the

7. The prohibition, as it stands, is over-enthusiastic: Magnesia's economy depends on a small class of retailers. See pp. 352–4 and 458.

twelve periods in which it is consumed. Take wheat or barley, for instance (though the same procedure must be followed for all the other crops too, as well as for any livestock there may be for sale in each district): each twelfth part should be split 848 proportionately into three shares, one for the citizens, one for their slaves, and the third for workmen and foreigners in general (i.e. communities of resident aliens in need of the necessities of life, and occasional visitors on some public or private business). It should be necessary to sell only this third share of all the necessities of life; there should be *no* necessity to sell any part of the other two.[8] So what will be the right way to arrange the division? It's obvious, for a start, that the shares we allocate will in one sense be equal, but in another sense unequal.

CLEINIAS: What do you mean?

ATHENIAN: Well, the land will grow a good crop of one thing and a bad crop of another. That's inevitable, I take it.

CLEINIAS: Of course.

ATHENIAN: None of the three shares – for masters, slaves and foreigners – must be better than the others: when the distribution is made, each group should be treated on an equal footing and get the same share.[9] Each citizen must take his two shares and distribute them at his discretion to the slaves and free persons in his charge (quality and quantity being up to him). The surplus should be distributed by being divided up according to the number of animals that have to be supported by the produce of the soil, and rationed out accordingly.

DWELLING HOUSES

Next, the population should have houses grouped in separate localities. This entails the following arrangements. There should be twelve villages, one in the middle of each of the twelve divisions of the state; in each village the settlers should first select a site for a market-place with its temples for gods

8. The ponderous play on the notion of 'necessity' is reproduced from the Greek.

9. Contrast pp. 214 and 229–30, where 'fair' shares are *un*equal.

and their retinue of spirits. (Local Magnesian gods, and sanctuaries of other ancient deities who are still remembered, must be honoured as they were in earlier generations.) In each division they must establish shrines of Hestia, Zeus, Athena, and the patron deity of the district; after this their first job must be to build houses on the highest ground in a circle round these temples, so as to provide the garrison with the strongest possible position for defence.

Thirteen groups of craftsmen must be formed to provide for all the rest of the territory. One should be settled in the city and distributed all round it on the outskirts, after further division into twelve sub-groups corresponding to the twelve urban districts; and the categories of craftsmen useful to farmers must be established in each village. They must all be under the supervision of the chief Country-Wardens, who must decide the number and type required in each district and say where they should settle in order to prove their full worth to the farmers and cause them as little trouble as possible.
849 Similarly the board of City-Wardens must assume permanent responsibility for the craftsmen in the city.

THE MARKETS

The detailed supervision of the market must naturally be in the hands of the Market-Wardens. Their first job is to ensure that no one does any damage to the temples round the market-place; secondly, to see whether people are conducting their business in an orderly or disorderly fashion, and inflict punishment on anyone who needs it. They must ensure that every commodity the citizens are required to sell[10] to the aliens is sold in the manner prescribed by law. The law will be simply this. On the first day of the month the agents (the foreigners or slaves who act for the citizens) must produce the share that has to be sold to the aliens, beginning with the twelfth part of corn. At this first market an alien must buy corn and related commodities to last him the whole month. On the tenth day the respective parties must buy and sell a whole

10. See p. 351.

month's supply of liquids. The third market should be on the twentieth, when they should hold a sale of the livestock that individuals find they need to buy or sell, and also of all the equipment or goods sold by the farmers, and which aliens cannot get except by purchase – skins, for example, and all clothing, woven material, felt, and all that sort of thing. But these goods (and barley and wheat ground into flour and every other kind of food) should never be bought by, or sold to, a citizen or his slave through *retail* channels. The proper place for 'retail' trading (as it's generally called) in corn and wine is the foreigners' market, where foreigners are to sell these goods to craftsmen and their slaves; and when the butchers have cut up the animals, it is to foreigners, craftsmen and their slaves that they must dispose of the meat. Any foreigner who wishes may buy any kind of firewood wholesale any day from the district agents and sell it to other foreigners whenever he likes and in whatever quantity he pleases.

All other goods and equipment needed by various people should be brought to the general market and put up for sale in the place allotted them. (The Guardians of the Laws and the Market-Wardens, in conjunction with the City-Wardens, will have marked out suitable spaces and decided where each article is to be sold.) Here they must exchange money for goods and goods for money, and never hand over anything without getting something in return; anyone who doesn't bother about this and trusts the other party must grin and bear it whether or not he gets what he's owed, because for such transactions there will be no legal remedy. If the amount 850 or value of the object bought or sold is greater than is allowed by the law which forbids increase or diminution of a man's property above or below a given limit, the excess must immediately be registered with the Guardians of the Laws; but if there is a deficiency, it must be cancelled.[11] The same rules are to apply to the registration of the property of resident aliens.

11. Cf. p. 226. 'Registered' would presumably mean 'confiscated'.

RESIDENT ALIENS

Anyone who wishes may come to live in the state on specified conditions. (a) There will be a community of foreigners open to anyone willing and able to join it. (b) The alien must have a skill and (c) not stay longer than twenty years from the date of registration. (d) He need pay no alien-tax, even a small one (apart from behaving himself), nor any tax on any purchase or sale. (e) When his time has expired, he is to collect his possessions and depart. (f) If during this period he has distinguished himself for some notable service to the state, and is confident he can persuade the council and the assembly to grant his request for an official extension of his stay, either temporarily or for life, he should present himself and make out his case; and he must be allowed to enjoy to the full whatever concessions the state grants him. (g) Children of resident aliens must be craftsmen, and (h) their period of residence must be deemed to have started when they reach the age of fifteen. On these conditions they may stay for twenty years, after which they must depart to whatever destination they like. If they wish to stay longer, they may do so provided they obtain permission as already specified. (i) Before a departing alien leaves he must cancel the entries that he originally made in the records kept in the custody of the officials.

§16. CAPITAL OFFENCES

It now occurs to the Athenian that the presence of alien workmen and traders in the state may lead to serious crime, because foreigners have not enjoyed the benefits of Magnesian education. He therefore passes to a discussion of major crimes such as sacrilege and treason, for which the penalty is death. There are two important points here:

(a) the elaborate and scrupulously fair trials to be held for capital offences: the Athenian criticizes what he considers to be the hit-and-miss methods of Athenian courts;

(b) slaves and foreigners are probably curable, and although their punishment is severe, it falls short of death; but if after education in Magnesia a citizen commits such a crime, he must be hopelessly wicked: he should be reckoned incurable and executed. This prepares us for the discussion, in the next section, of 'cure for injustice' as the aim of punishment, and the attempt to define what 'injustice' really is.

PRELIMINARY DISCUSSION

ATHENIAN: Next, in accordance with the natural arrangement of our legal code, will come the legal proceedings that arise out of all the occupations we have mentioned up till now. To some extent, so far as agricultural affairs and related topics are concerned, we have already listed the acts that should be prosecuted, but the most serious have yet to be specified. Our next task is to enumerate these one by one, mentioning what penalty each should attract and to which court it should be assigned.

CLEINIAS: That's right.

ATHENIAN: The very composition of all these laws we are on the point of framing is, in a way, a disgrace: after all, we're assuming we have a state which will be run along excellent lines and achieve every condition favourable to the practice of virtue. The mere idea that a state of this kind could give birth to a man affected by the worst forms of

wickedness found in other countries, so that the legislator has to anticipate his appearance by threats – this, as I said, is in a way a disgrace. It means we have to lay down laws against these people, to deter them and punish them when they appear, on the assumption that they will certainly do so. However, unlike the ancient legislators, we are not framing laws for heroes and sons of gods. The lawgivers of that age, according to the story told nowadays, were descended from gods and legislated for men of similar stock. But we are human beings, legislating in the world today for the children of humankind, and we shall give no offence by our fear that one of our citizens will turn out to be, so to speak, a 'tough egg', whose character will be so 'hard-boiled' as to resist softening; powerful as our laws are, they may not be able to tame such people, just as heat has no effect on tough beans. For their dismal sake, the first law I shall produce will deal with robbery from temples, in case anyone dares to commit this crime. Now in view of the correct education our citizens will have received, we should hardly want any of them to catch this disease, nor is there much reason to expect that they will. Their slaves, however, as well as foreigners and the slaves of foreigners, may well make frequent attempts at such crimes.
854 For their sake principally – but still with an eye on the general weakness of human nature – I'll spell out the law about robbery from temples, and about all the other similar crimes which are difficult or even impossible to cure.

ROBBERY FROM TEMPLES

Following the practice we agreed earlier, we must first compose preambles, in the briefest possible terms, to stand at the head of all these laws. Take a man who is incited by day and kept awake at night by an evil impulse which drives him to steal some holy object. You might talk to him and exhort him as follows:

'My dear fellow, this evil impulse that at present drives you to go robbing temples comes from a source that is neither human nor divine. It is a sort of frenzied goad,

356

innate in mankind as a result of crimes of long ago that remained unexpiated; it travels around working doom and destruction, and you should make every effort to take precautions against it. Now, take note what these precautions are. When any of these thoughts enters your head, seek the rites that free a man from guilt; seek the shrines of the gods who avert evil, and supplicate them; seek the company of men who have a reputation in your community for being virtuous. Listen to them as they say that every man should honour what is fine and just – try to bring yourself to say it too. But run away from the company of the wicked, with never a backward glance. If by doing this you find that your disease abates somewhat, well and good; if not, then you should look upon death as the preferable alternative, and rid yourself of life.'

These are the overtures we make to those who think of committing all these impious deeds that bring about the ruin of the state. When a man obeys us, we should silently omit the actual law; but in cases of disobedience, we must change our tune after the overture and sing this resounding strain:

41. If a man is caught thieving from a temple and is
    (a) a foreigner or slave,
a brand of his misfortune shall be made on his face and hands, and he shall be whipped, the number of lashes to be decided by his judges. Then he shall be thrown out beyond the boundaries of the land, naked.

(Perhaps paying this penalty will teach him restraint and make him a better man: after all, no penalty imposed by law has an evil purpose, but generally achieves one of two effects: it makes the person who pays the penalty either more virtuous or less wicked.)

    (b) If a citizen is ever shown to be responsible for such a
        crime – to have perpetrated, that is, some great and
        unspeakable offence against the gods or his parents or
        the state,
the penalty is death.

The judge should consider him as already beyond cure; he should bear in mind the kind of education and upbringing the man has enjoyed from his earliest years, and how after all this he has still not abstained from acts of the greatest evil. But the very tiniest of evils will be what the offender suffers;[1] indeed, he will be of service to others, by being a lesson to them when he is ignominiously banished from sight beyond the borders of the state.[2] And if the children and family escape taking on the character of the father, they should be held in honour and win golden opinions for the spirit and persistence with which they have shunned evil and embraced the good.

In a state where the size and number of the farms are to be kept permanently unaltered, it would not be appropriate for the state to confiscate the property of any of these criminals. But if a man commits a crime and is thought to deserve to pay a penalty in money, then provided he possesses a surplus over and above the basic equipment of his farm, he must pay his fine. The Guardians of the Laws must scrutinize the registers and discover the precise facts in these cases, and make an exact report to the court on each occasion, so as to prevent any farm becoming unworked because of a shortage of money. If a man appears to deserve a stiffer fine, and if some of his friends are not prepared to bail him out by contributing the money to set him free, his punishment should take the form of a prolonged period of imprisonment (which should be open to public view), and various humiliations. But no one, no matter what his offence, is ever to be deprived of his citizen rights completely, not even if he has gone into exile beyond our frontiers for it. The penalties we impose will be death, imprisonment, whipping, or various degrading postures (either standing or sitting), or being rusticated and made to stand before temples on the boundaries of the state; and payments of money may be made in certain cases which we have just mentioned, where such a punishment is appropriate.

1. A man should cut his spiritual losses: if he goes on living he will become even more wicked and the ultimate fate of his soul will be even more dreadful. Cf. pp. 191 and 511.

2. See pp. 387 and 390–91.

PROCEDURE IN CAPITAL CASES

In cases involving the death penalty the judges are to be the Guardians of the Laws, sitting in conjunction with the court, whose members are selected by merit from the officials of the previous year. The method of bringing these cases to court, the serving of the summonses and similar procedural details must be the concern of the legislators who succeed us; what *we* have to do is legislate about the voting. The vote should be taken openly, but before this our judges should have ranged themselves according to seniority and sat down close together facing the prosecutor and defendant; all citizens who have some spare time should attend and listen carefully to such trials. First, the prosecutor should deliver a single speech, then the defendant; the most senior judge should follow these addresses by cross-questioning, and continue until he has gone into the arguments in sufficient detail. One by one, the other judges should follow the most senior and work through any points on which either litigant has left him dissatisfied by some kind of error or omission. A judge who feels no such dissatisfaction should hand on the interrogation to his colleague. All the judges should endorse those arguments that appear pertinent by appending their signatures and then depositing the documents on the altar 856 of Hestia. The next day they must reconvene in the same place, and after similar interrogation and examination again append their signatures to the depositions. Having followed this procedure three times, after giving due consideration to the evidence and witnesses, each judge should cast a sacred vote, swearing in the name of Hestia to give, as far as lies in him, a judgement just and true. In this way they should conclude this category of trial.

SUBVERSION

We come next, after these matters of religion, to cases of political subversion. We should treat as the biggest enemy of the entire state the man who makes the laws into slaves, and the state into the servant of a particular interest, by subjecting them to the *diktat* of mere men. This transgressor of the law uses violence in all that he does and stirs up sedition. Second in the scale of wickedness, in our estimation, should come the holder of some high state office, who while not an accessory to any such crimes, nevertheless fails to detect them and exact the vengeance of his fatherland (or, if he does detect them, holds back through cowardice). Every man who is any good at all must denounce the plotter to the authorities and take him to court on a charge of violently and illicitly overthrowing the constitution. The court should consist of the same judges as for robbers from temples, and the procedure of the entire trial should be the same as it was for them, a majority vote being sufficient for the death penalty.

As a rule, penalties and disgrace incurred by a father should not be passed on to any of his children, except where a man's father, grandfather and great-grandfather have all in turn been sentenced to death. The state should deport such cases to the state and city from which their family originally came; and they should take their property with them, apart from all the basic equipment of their farm. Next, sons of citizens who have more than one son over ten years of age should be nominated by their father or grandfather on either the mother's or the father's side. Ten of them should be chosen by lot, and the names of those whom the lot selects should be reported to Delphi. The god's choice should then be installed as heir to the abandoned property – and he, we hope, will have better luck.

CLEINIAS: Splendid.

TREASON

ATHENIAN: The same regulations about the judges that should try the case, and the procedure to be followed at the trial, will apply in yet a third instance, when a man is brought to court on a charge of treason. In the same way, a single 857 law should apply to all three cases and decide whether the children of these criminals (traitor, temple-robber, and the violent wrecker of the laws of the state) should remain in their fatherland or leave it.

§17. THE THEORY OF PUNISHMENT

'*A single law*', then, covers these three capital crimes. But now we learn, rather unexpectedly, that another '*single law*' covers all cases of theft: all thieves are to repay twice the value of what they have stolen. Clearly, thieves will in one sense pay different penalties, because different thieves will have to find different amounts from their own pocket according to the value of their theft. But in another sense, all thieves will pay the '*same*' penalty – twice the value of what they have stolen. Cleinias seizes on the idea that all thieves will suffer the same penalty and protests that on the contrary different thefts require different punishments according to circumstances. Cleinias has to be shown that in fact the penalty for all thieves really ought to be the same, because the object of the punishment is the disposition to rob, which is the same in all thieves. If punishments vary, it should not be according to the amounts stolen, but according to how far the soul of the criminal is infected by the desire to steal. Punishment is concerned with the spiritual state of the criminal, not the gravity of the crime (even though the latter may tell you something about the former).

There then intervenes a rather long-winded section justifying the consideration of such philosophical matters in a conversation devoted to producing a code of law.

After this, the Athenian makes the simple point that merely because the punishments we impose are often disgusting or shameful (for instance, we whip or execute), we are not entitled to say they are unjust and not '*good*', or to think we have blundered into some inconsistency. A punishment may be disgusting as an action, or shameful to the person being punished, but as a punishment it will be just and '*good*'. In short, we may apply contradictory words to the same action, provided we are referring to different '*aspects*' of it. This point becomes vital, as we shall see, for the understanding of the Athenian's penology.

THEFT: SHOULD ALL THEFTS ATTRACT THE SAME PUNISHMENT?

Again, a single law and legal penalty should apply to every thief, no matter whether his theft is great or small:

42. (a) he *must* pay twice the value of the stolen article, if he loses the day and has sufficient surplus property over and above his farm with which to make the repayment.

(b) if he has not,
he *must* be kept in prison until he pays up or persuades the man who has had him convicted to let him off.

43. If a man is convicted of stealing from *public* sources, he *shall* be freed from prison when he has either persuaded the state to let him off or paid back twice the amount involved.

CLEINIAS: How on earth can we be serious, sir, in saying that it makes no odds whether his theft is large or small, or whether it comes from sacred or secular sources? And what about all the other different circumstances of a robbery? Shouldn't a legislator vary the penalties he inflicts, so that he can cope with the various *categories* of theft?

PHILOSOPHICAL LEGISLATION JUSTIFIED

ATHENIAN: That's a good question, Cleinias: I have been walking in my sleep, and you have bumped into me and woken me up. You have reminded me of something that has occurred to me before, that the business of establishing a code of law has never been properly thought out – as we can see from the example that has just cropped up. Now, what am I getting at? It wasn't a bad parallel we made, you know, when we compared all those for whom legislation is produced today to slaves under treatment from slave doctors.[1] Make no mistake about what would happen, if one of those doctors

1. See pp. 181–2.

who are innocent of theory and practise medicine by rule of thumb were ever to come across a gentleman doctor conversing with a gentleman patient. This doctor would be acting almost like a philosopher, engaging in a discussion that ranged over the source of the disease and pushed the inquiry back into the whole nature of the body. But our other doctor would immediately give a tremendous shout of laughter, and his observations would be precisely those that most 'doctors' are always so ready to trot out. 'You ass,' he would say, 'you are not treating the patient, but tutoring him. Anybody would think he wanted to become a doctor rather than get well again.'

CLEINIAS: And wouldn't he be right to say that?

ATHENIAN: Perhaps he would – if he were to bear in mind this further point, that anyone who handles law in the way we are now, *is* tutoring the citizens, not imposing laws on them. Wouldn't it be equally right to say that?

CLEINIAS: Perhaps so.

ATHENIAN: However, at the moment, we are in a fortunate position.

CLEINIAS: How do you mean?

ATHENIAN: I mean the lack of any necessity to legislate. We are simply carrying out our own review of every kind of political system and trying to see how we could put into effect the absolutely ideal kind, as well as the least good sort that would still be acceptable. This is particularly true of our legislation, where it looks as if we have a choice: either we can examine ideal laws, if we want to, or again, if we feel like it, we can look at the minimum standard we are prepared to put up with. So we must choose which course we want to take.

CLEINIAS: This is a ridiculous choice to give ourselves, my friend: it's not as if we were legislators forced by some irresistible necessity to legislate at a minute's notice, without being allowed to put the business off till tomorrow. We, God willing, can do as bricklayers do, or workmen starting some other kind of erection. We can gather our materials in no particular order and then select – and select at leisure –

the items which are appropriate for the forthcoming construction. Our assumption should be, therefore, that we are constructing something, but not under any constraint; we work at our convenience and spend part of the time preparing our material, part of the time fitting it together. So it would be quite fair to describe our penal code as already partially laid down, while other material for it lies ready to hand.

ATHENIAN: At any rate, Cleinias, this will be the more realistic way to conduct our review of legislation. Well then, may we please notice this point that concerns legislators?

CLEINIAS: What point?

ATHENIAN: I suppose literary compositions and written speeches by many other authors are current in our cities, besides those of the legislator?

CLEINIAS: Of course they are.

ATHENIAN: To whose writings ought we to apply ourselves? Are we to read the poets and others who have recorded in prose or verse compositions their advice about how one should live one's life, to the neglect of the compositions of the legislators? Or isn't it precisely the latter that deserve our closest attention?

CLEINIAS: Yes, it certainly is.

ATHENIAN: And I suppose the legislator, alone among writers, is to be denied permission to give advice about virtue and goodness and justice? Is he alone to be prevented from explaining their nature and how they should be reflected in our conduct, if we aim to be happy?

CLEINIAS: No, of course not.

ATHENIAN: Then is it really more scandalous in the case of Homer and Tyrtaeus and the other poets to have composed in writing[2] bad rules for the conduct of life, but less so for Lycurgus and Solon, and all others who have turned legislator and committed their recommendations to writing? The

2. For Tyrtaeus, see note on p. 51. Lycurgus was the traditional founder of the Spartan constitution; for a discussion see W. G. Forrest, *A History of Sparta, 950–192 B.C.* (London, 1968), pp. 40 ff. Solon legislated for Athens in 594 and wrote poems justifying his measures; the surviving fragments can be read in Greek or English in J. M. Edmonds, *Elegy and Iambus* (London and New York, 1931; Loeb edition), 1, pp. 114 ff.

proper view, surely, is this: a city's writings on legal topics should turn out, on being opened, to be the finest and best of all those it has in circulation; the writings of other men should either sound in harmony with them, or provoke 859 ridicule by being out of tune. So what *is* the style in which a state's laws ought to be written, in our opinion? Should the regulations appear in the light of a loving and prudent father and mother? Or should they act the tyrant and the despot, posting their orders and threats on walls and leaving it at that? Clearly, then, at this stage, we must decide whether we are going to try to talk about laws in the right spirit. Succeed or no, we shall at any rate show our good intentions. If we take this course and have to face some difficulties *en route*, then let's face them. Good luck to us, and God willing, we shall succeed.

CLEINIAS: You've put it splendidly. Let's do as you suggest.

ATHENIAN: In the first place, we must continue the attempt we've just made: we must scrutinize our law about robbers of temples, theft in general, and every variety of crime. We should not let it daunt us if in the full spate of our legislation we find that although we have settled some matters, our inquiry into others has still to be completed. We are still aiming at the status of legislators, but we haven't achieved it yet; perhaps eventually we may succeed. So now let's look at these topics I've mentioned – if, that is, you are prepared to look at them in the way I have explained.

CLEINIAS: Certainly we are prepared.

A 'TERMINOLOGICAL INEXACTITUDE'

ATHENIAN: Now, on the whole subject of goodness and justice, we ought to try to see quite clearly just where we agree, and where there are differences of opinion between us. Again, how far do ordinary men agree? What differences are there between *them*? (Naturally, we should claim that we wanted there to be at least a small 'difference between' us and ordinary men!)

CLEINIAS: What sort of 'differences between us' have you in mind when you say that?

ATHENIAN: I'll try to explain. When we talk about justice in general – just men, just actions, just arrangements, we are, after a fashion, unanimous that all these things are 'good'. One might insist that even if just men happen to be shocking in their physical appearance, they are still pre-eminently 'good' because of their supremely just character. No one would think a man was talking nonsense in saying that.

CLEINIAS: Wouldn't that be right?

ATHENIAN: Perhaps. But if everything that has the quality of justice is 'good', we ought to note that we include in that 'everything' even the things done *to* us, which are about as frequent, roughly speaking, as the things *we* do to others.

CLEINIAS: What now, then?

ATHENIAN: Any just action we do has the quality of being 'good' roughly in proportion to the degree to which it has the quality of justice.

CLEINIAS: Indeed.

ATHENIAN: So surely, anything done *to* us, which has the quality of justice, is to that extent agreed to be 'good'? This wouldn't involve our argument in any contradiction.

CLEINIAS: True.

ATHENIAN: If we agree that something done to us is just, but at the same time shocking, the terms 'just' and 'good' will be in conflict with each other – the reason being that we have termed 'just' actions 'most shameful'.

CLEINIAS: What are you getting at?

ATHENIAN: It's not difficult to understand. The injunctions of the laws we laid down a little while ago would seem to be in flat contradiction to what we are saying now.

CLEINIAS: How so?

ATHENIAN: Our ruling was, I think, that the temple-robber and the enemy of properly established laws would suffer a 'just' death. But then, on the brink of establishing a great many such rules, we held back. We saw ourselves becoming involved with penal suffering of infinite variety and on a grand scale. Of all sufferings, these were particularly just; but they were also the particularly shocking ones. Thus, surely, one minute we shall find 'just' and 'good' invariably turning out to be the same, and the next moment discover they are opposites.

CLEINIAS: Likely enough.

ATHENIAN: This is the source of the inconsistency in the language of the ordinary man: he destroys the unity of the terms 'good' and 'just'.

CLEINIAS: That is indeed how it looks, sir.

What follows now is one of the most difficult passages in the Laws; *the argument is far from lucid and the reader should be warned that its interpretation is controversial. I give here my own view.*

The Athenian asserts, as an article of faith, the thesis that 'the wicked man is wicked against his will'. This paradox, attributed in earlier dialogues to Socrates, amounts, baldly stated, to this: it is simply not in the nature of things that a man should choose *evil; if he does wrong, it must be because for some reason he was mistaken or was compelled to do wrong and could not help himself. But as the Athenian points out, this thesis would seem to cut the ground from under a legislator's feet: a legislator provides for punishment of crimes on the assumption that they are voluntary, and that it makes sense to punish a man for choosing to do wrong (except in cases of 'involuntary crimes' committed under compulsion or by accident). Without arguing the truth of his paradox, the Athenian resolutely refuses to accept the customary distinction between voluntary and involuntary crimes.*

A new distinction is put forward to help solve the difficulty. Any crime can be seen under two 'aspects': (a) the actual physical harm or damage done, or the criminal act itself; (b) the 'injustice' which prompted the commission of the crime, and which is a psychological state: against my will, my soul has become 'unjust', and has led me to choose to commit a crime. I have chosen to do a particular (criminal) act, and to that extent my crime is 'voluntary'; but in so far as the psychological state of injustice which led to my committing the crime can never have been chosen by me (according to the Socratic paradox), my crime is 'involuntary'. We can now see the relevance of the preceding discussion about the application of contradictory adjectives to the same object; such an application can make sense only if we see the object under different 'aspects'. At first sight the Socratic paradox ('crime is involuntary') and the popular view ('crime is voluntary') seem to conflict: as the Athenian says (p. 369), 'to suppose that a voluntary act is performed involuntarily makes no sense'. No sense, that is, until we see a crime under two aspects, (a) the (criminal) act itself ('voluntary' – I chose to do this act rather than to refrain); (b) my 'unjust' psychological state ('involuntary').

In the remainder of this section the Athenian first develops his view of the proper purpose of punishment, and then describes what he means by 'injustice' more fully. (1) Punishment. The prime aim is to 'cure' the injustice in the soul, but in addition the criminal must be made to recompense his victim for the damage done. Recompense and cure must be kept distinct. (2) Injustice. This is analysed at some length. The details need not be rehearsed here, but it is worth noting that the three 'causes of crime' range from the purely emotional (anger) to the intellectual (ignorance), with the desire for pleasure coming somewhere in between (see note on p. 373).

Some comments should be made about this ingenious theory. (1) The Athenian does not feel inhibited from producing a penal code constructed in the normal way, with a list of crimes and conventional punishments. But the punishments are to be seen as 'cures for injustice', not as devices for retribution. We have to assume, to judge from his penal code, that the conventional kind of penalty, consisting essentially of the infliction of suffering, happens also to be the best 'cure'. It is quite a large assumption. (2) The distinction between 'voluntary' and 'involuntary' crime is still perfectly in order in the Magnesian code. As in conventional codes, 'involuntary' more or less amounts to 'by accident'; 'voluntary' means 'deliberately chosen, but as a result of involuntary injustice in the soul'. *'Voluntary' crimes in the Magnesian code, as in others, deserve punishment, but punishment is to be seen as 'cure'. (3) This apparently enlightened view of the purpose of punishment should not blind us to some unbelievably barbarous punishments prescribed in the code; the Athenian has to explain that the death penalty is really 'good' for the criminal (pp. 357–8 and 372). (4) The whole theory seems to do away with the notion of free will and to make man a puppet at the mercy of various forces (see pp. 74 and 372); yet from another point of view, it seems to be a resounding vote of confidence in the fundamental soundness of the human will.*

THE ATTACK ON THE DISTINCTION BETWEEN 'VOLUNTARY' AND 'INVOLUNTARY'

ATHENIAN: Now, Cleinias, we ought to examine our own position again. How far is it consistent in this business?

CLEINIAS: Consistent? What consistency do you mean?

ATHENIAN: Earlier in our discussion I think I have said quite categorically – or if I haven't before, assume I'm saying it now – that . . .

CLEINIAS: What?

ATHENIAN: . . . all wicked men are, in all respects, *unwillingly* wicked. This being so, my next argument necessarily follows.

CLEINIAS: What argument?

ATHENIAN: That the unjust man is doubtless wicked; but that the wicked man is in that state only against his will. However, to suppose that a voluntary act is performed involuntarily makes no sense. Therefore, in the eyes of someone who holds the view that injustice is involuntary, a man who acts unjustly would seem to be doing so against his will. Here and now, that is the position *I* have to accept: I allow that no one acts unjustly except against his will. (If anyone with a disputatious disposition or a desire to attract favourable notice says that although there *are* those who are unjust against their will, even so many men do commit unjust acts voluntarily, I would reject his argument and stick to what I said.) Well then, how am I to make my own arguments consistent? Suppose the two of you, Cleinias and Megillus, were to ask me, 'If that's so, sir, what advice have you for us about laying down laws for the city of the Magnesians? Do we legislate, or don't we?' 'Of course we legislate', I'd say, and you'd ask: 'Are you going to make a distinction for the Magnesians between voluntary and involuntary acts of injustice? Shall we

impose stiffer penalties on voluntary wrong-doing and acts
861 of injustice, and smaller penalties on the involuntary? Or
shall we treat them all on an equal footing, on the grounds
that there simply is no such thing as an act of voluntary
injustice?'

CLEINIAS: You are perfectly right, sir. So what use shall
we make of this position we have just taken up?

ATHENIAN: That's a good question. First of all, we shall
make this use of it –

CLEINIAS: What?

ATHENIAN: Let's cast our minds back. A few minutes ago
we were quite right to say that in the matter of justice we were
in a state of great muddle and inconsistency. With that in
mind, we may go back to asking questions of ourselves. 'We
have not yet found a way out of our confusion in these things.
We have not defined the difference between these two categories of wrongs, voluntary and involuntary. In all states,
every lawgiver who has ever appeared treats them as distinct,
and the distinction is reflected in his laws. Now, is the position
we took up a moment ago to overrule all dissent, like a
decision handed down from God? Shall we make just this one
assertion and dismiss the topic, without adducing any reasons
to show that our position is correct?' Impossible. What we
must do, before we legislate, is somehow make clear that there
are two categories, but that the distinction between them is a
different one. Then, when one imposes the penalty on either,
everybody will be able to appreciate the arguments for it, and
make some kind of judgement whether it is the appropriate
penalty to have imposed or not.

CLEINIAS: We think you state the position fairly, sir. We
must do one of two things, either stop insisting that unjust
acts are always involuntary, or, before going any further,
demonstrate its validity by means of a preliminary distinction.

ATHENIAN: The first of the two alternatives, denying the
proposition when I believe it to represent the truth, is
absolutely unacceptable to me. I should be breaking the laws
of both God and man. But if the two things do not differ by
virtue of being 'voluntary' and 'involuntary', how *do* they

differ? What other factor is involved? That is what we have to try, somehow or other, to show.

CLEINIAS: It is surely impossible, sir, to approach the problem in any other way.

THE NEW DISTINCTION, AND THE PURPOSE OF PUNISHMENT

ATHENIAN: So this is what we shall try to do. Look: when citizens come together and associate with each other, they obviously inflict many *injuries*; and to these the terms 'voluntary' and 'involuntary' can be freely applied.

CLEINIAS: Of course.

ATHENIAN: But no one should describe all these injuries as acts of injustice, and conclude that therefore the unjust acts committed in these cases of injury fall into two categories, (a) involuntary (because if we add them all up, you see, the involuntary injuries are no less numerous and no less great than the voluntary ones), and (b) voluntary *as well*. Rather than do that, consider the next step I am going to take in my argu- 862 ment: am I on to something or just drivelling? My position, Cleinias and Megillus, is not that, if someone hurts someone else involuntarily and without intending it, he is acting unjustly but involuntarily. I will not legislate so as to make this an involuntary act of injustice. Ignoring its relative seriousness or triviality, I shall refuse to put down such an injury under the heading of 'injustice' at all. Indeed, if my view is sustained, we shall often say of a benefactor that 'he is committing the injustice of conferring a benefit' – an *improper* benefit. You see, my friends, in effect we should not simply call it 'just' when one man bestows some object on another, nor simply 'unjust' when correspondingly he takes it from him. The description 'just' is applicable only to the benefit conferred or injury inflicted by someone with a just character and outlook. This is the point the lawgiver has to watch; he must keep his eyes on these two things, injustice and injury. He must use the law to exact damages for damage done, as far as he can; he must restore losses, and if anyone has knocked something down, put it back upright again; in place of anything killed or wounded, he must substitute something in a sound condition. And when atonement has been made by compensation, he must try by his laws to make the criminal and the victim, in each separate case of injury, friends instead of enemies.

CLEINIAS: So far, so good.

ATHENIAN: Now to deal with unjust injuries (and gains too, as when one man's unjust act results in a gain for someone else). The cases that are curable we must cure, on the assumption that the soul has been infected by disease. We must, however, state what general policy we pursue in our cure for injustice.

CLEINIAS: What is this policy?

ATHENIAN: This: when anyone commits an act of injustice, serious or trivial, the law will combine instruction and constraint, so that in the future either the criminal will never again dare to commit such a crime voluntarily, or he will do it a very great deal less often; and in addition, he will pay compensation for the damage he has done. This is something we can achieve only by laws of the highest quality. We may take action, or simply talk to the criminal; we may grant him pleasures, or make him suffer; we may honour him, we may disgrace him; we can fine him, or give him gifts. We may use absolutely *any* means to make him hate injustice and embrace true justice – or at any rate not hate it. But suppose the lawgiver finds a man who's beyond cure – what legal penalty will he provide for this case? He will recognize that the best thing for all such people is to cease to live – best even for themselves. By passing on they will help others, too: first, they will constitute a warning against injustice, and secondly they will leave the state free of scoundrels. That is why the lawgiver should prescribe the death penalty in such cases, by way of punishment for their crimes – but in no other case whatever.

CLEINIAS: In one way, what you have said seems eminently reasonable. However, we should be glad to hear a clearer explanation of two points: first, the difference between injustice and injury, and secondly the various senses of 'voluntary' and 'involuntary' that you distinguished so elaborately in the course of your argument.

A FULLER ACCOUNT OF INJUSTICE

ATHENIAN: I must try to meet your request and explain these points. Doubtless in the course of conversation you make at least this point to each other about the soul: one of the constituent elements (whether 'part' or 'state' is not important) to be found in it is 'anger', and this innate impulse, unruly and difficult to fight as it is, causes a good deal of havoc by its irrational force.

CLEINIAS: Yes, indeed.

ATHENIAN: The next point is the distinction we make between 'pleasure' and 'anger'. We say Pleasure wields her power on the basis of an opposite kind of force; she achieves whatever her will desires by persuasive deceit that is irresistibly compelling.[3]

CLEINIAS: Quite right.

ATHENIAN: Thirdly, we would be saying nothing but the truth if we named ignorance as a cause of wrong-doing. The lawgiver would, in fact, do a better job if he divided ignorance into two: (1) 'simple' ignorance, which he would treat as the cause of trivial faults, (2) 'double' ignorance, which is the error of a man who is not only in the grip of ignorance but on top of that is convinced of his own wisdom, believing that he has a thorough knowledge of matters of which, in fact, his ignorance is total. When such ignorance is backed up by strength and power, the lawgiver will treat it as the source of serious and barbarous wrong-doing; but when it lacks power, he will treat the resultant faults as the peccadilloes of children and old men. He will of course regard these deeds as offences, and will legislate against these people as offenders, but the laws will be of the most gentle character, full of understanding.

3. Pleasure (here personified) suggests specious reasons why one should do what one wants to do; desires thus reinforced by reasoning are very difficult to resist.

CLEINIAS: Your proposals are perfectly reasonable.

ATHENIAN: Most of us agree that some people are 'conquerors of' their desire for pleasure and feelings of anger, while others are 'conquered by' them. And that is in fact the situation.

CLEINIAS: It certainly is.

ATHENIAN: But we have never heard anyone say that some people are 'conquerors of' their ignorance, while others are 'conquered by' it.

CLEINIAS: Very true.

ATHENIAN: But we do say that each of these influences often prompts every man to take the opposite course to the one which attracts him and which he *really* wishes to take.

CLEINIAS: Yes, times without number.

ATHENIAN: May I now clearly distinguish for you, without elaboration, what in my view the terms 'just' and 'unjust' mean. My general description of injustice is this: the mastery of the soul by anger, fear, pleasure, pain, envy and desires, 864 whether they lead to any actual damage or not. But no matter how states or individuals think they can achieve the good, it is the conception[4] of what the good is that should govern every man and hold sway in his soul, even if he is a little mistaken. If it does, every action done in accordance with it, and any part of a man's nature that becomes subject to such control, we have to call 'just', and best for the entire life of mankind – and this in spite of the popular belief that damage done in such circumstances is an 'involuntary' injustice. However, we are not engaging now in a captious dispute about terminology. But since it has become clear that there are three kinds of basic faults, we ought first to impress these upon our memory even more firmly. Our first kind is a painful one, and we call it anger and fear.

CLEINIAS: Yes.

ATHENIAN: The second kind consists of pleasures and desires. The third, which is a distinct category, consists of hopes and opinion – a mere shot at the truth about the

4. I.e. the *correct* conception, on my interpretation of this murky paragraph.

supreme good. If we divide this last category twice,[5] we get three types; and that makes, according to our present argument, a total of five in all. We must enact different laws for the five kinds, and we must have two main categories.

CLEINIAS: And what are these?

ATHENIAN: The first category covers every occasion when crimes are committed openly with violence; secondly, we have crimes that take place under cover of darkness, involving secrecy and fraud. Sometimes we find a combination of both methods, in which case our laws will have to be very harsh indeed, if they are going to do their job.

CLEINIAS: Of course.

5. See p. 373: 'ignorance' is divided into a 'simple' and a 'double' form, and then the latter is divided into ignorance 'with power' and 'without power'.

§18. HOMICIDE LAW

Perhaps the most remarkable feature of the homicide regulations is the insistence on scrupulous observance by the homicide of the 'purification' rituals. These rituals, which arose from the belief that the homicide was almost physically 'stained' or 'polluted' and hence a danger to the community, are attested in Athenian law also. Plato seems to go out of his way to inspire the murderer with feelings of intense horror and shame; his insistence on these matters probably goes beyond contemporary Athenian practice. We may note also the careful discussion of murder in anger as midway between voluntary and involuntary murder; this third category is an innovation on Plato's part. If we take this together with §17, we can see Plato's concern with the notions of motivation and responsibility (compare also 'Persons Unfit to Plead' below). Finally, from among many other points too numerous to mention, it is interesting to see how important the status of the victim is in assessing a penalty – killing a parent, for instance, is an indication of extreme injustice in the soul.

PERSONS UNFIT TO PLEAD

ATHENIAN: Now let's go back to the point where we started to digress, and carry on with our enactment of the legal code. Our regulations about those who pillage from the gods, and about traitors, had, I think, already been made; we had also dealt with those who do violence to the laws in order to subvert the existing constitution. A man who commits one of these crimes might be suffering from insanity, or be as good as insane either because of disease, or the effects of advanced senility, or because he is still in the years of childhood.

44. (a) If clear proof of any of these states is ever shown to the judges selected in each case, on the submission of either the criminal or his counsel, and in the opinion of the court the man was in that condition when he committed his crime,

he must pay, without fail, simple recompense for any damage he may have inflicted on anyone, but the other details of the penalty should be waived,

except that

(b) if he has killed someone and his hands are polluted by murder,

he must depart to a place in another country and live there in exile for a year.

45. If he comes back before the legally appointed time, or even puts a foot into any part of his native country,

he must be imprisoned in the public gaol by the Guardians of the Laws for two years, after which he shall be released.

INVOLUNTARY HOMICIDE

The start we have made points the way forward: we need not 865 scruple to lay down a comprehensive set of laws that will cover every category of murder. First we should deal with those committed unintentionally, through force of circumstances:

46 A. If anyone has unintentionally killed a man who is not an enemy

(a) in a contest or public games – whether death occurs immediately, or later as a result of the wounds,

(b) in war similarly,

(c) in military training, whether in javelin-exercises without the protection of armour, or when some weapons are being carried in imitation of wartime usage,

the offender shall be free of pollution when he has been purified in accordance with the relevant law from Delphi.

(d) All doctors, if their patient dies as an unintended result of their treatment,

are to be free of pollution according to law.

B. If one man kills another by his own act, but unintentionally,

(a) by his own hand,

(i) without weapons, or

>   (ii) by tool, weapon, administration of food or drink,
>   application of fire or cold, or deprivation of air,
>   whether
> (β) (i) he does the deed himself, or
>   (ii) through the agency of others,

in all cases it must be reckoned his own act and he must pay
penalties as under:

>   If he kills
>   (a) a slave,

he must indemnify the dead man's master against the damage,
reflecting what the loss would be if his own slave had been
killed.

C. If he fails to indemnify the master,
he must pay a penalty of twice the value of the dead man, the
judges making an estimate of it, and he must resort to
greater and more numerous purifications than those who
have killed in contests; and such expounders as are chosen
by the oracle are to be in charge of these purifications.

B. cont. (b) If he kills a slave of his own,
let him purify himself, and be quit of the murder according
to law.

>   (c) If he kills a free man, inadvertently,

he must undergo the same purifications as the killer of a
slave.

He should not take lightly an old story that comes from our
collection of ancient tales. It runs as follows:

Having lived in the full proud spirit of freedom, the man
murdered by violence, freshly dead, turns his fury on the
person responsible. The dead man is full of fear and loathing
at his own violent sufferings; he abominates the sight of his
own murderer going about localities once familiar to
himself; to the full limit of his powers he visits his own
anguish on the perpetrator of the crime, the man and his
deeds; and his allies are the memories that haunt the
murderer. Therefore

D. (a) *A killer* must keep clear of his victim for all the seasons of an entire year, by staying away from the dead man's usual haunts in the whole of his native country.

    (b) If the deceased is a foreigner,
the killer should keep clear of the foreigner's homeland as well for an identical period.

If a man obeys this law without demur, the deceased's next of kin, who will take note of his compliance with these requirements, will grant him pardon and will be entirely correct to live on peaceable terms with him.

E. If the killer disobeys,

    (a) by daring to enter temples and perform sacrifices, polluted as he is, and then

    (b) by refusing to complete the above-mentioned period abroad,

the deceased's next of kin must prosecute the killer on a charge of murder. In case of conviction, all penalties are to be doubled.

F. If the next of kin does not prosecute the crime,
the pollution must be deemed to have arrived at his own door, owing to the murdered man's supplications for atonement. Anyone who wishes may bring a charge against the next of kin and force him to keep away from his native country for five years, according to law.

G. (a) If a foreigner unintentionally kills a foreigner who is living in the state,
anyone who wishes should prosecute under the same laws.

    (b) If the killer is

        (i) a resident alien,
he must go abroad for a year;

        (ii) a non-resident alien,
he must keep away, for the whole of his life, from the country that lays down these laws, in addition to performing the purifications; this is to apply whether he kills (1) a non-resident alien, (2) a resident alien, or (3) a citizen.

H. If he returns

    (a) illegally,

866

the Guardians of the Laws must punish him by death, and if he has any property, they must present it to his victim's nearest relative;

   (b) unintentionally,

     (i) being shipwrecked on the coast,

he must camp out where the sea washes by his feet and await an opportunity to sail away;

     (ii) being forcibly brought in overland by someone,

the first official of the state that comes across him must set him free and dispatch him unharmed beyond the border.

HOMICIDE IN ANGER

If someone kills a free man by his own hand, but the deed is done in anger, we must first make an internal distinction within this type of crime. Anger is common to (1) those who kill a man by blows or similar means, owing to a sudden impulse: here the action is immediate, there is no previous intention to kill, and regret for the deed follows at once; (2) those who have been stung by insults or opprobrious actions and who pursue their vengeance until, some time later, they kill somebody: they *intend* to kill, and the deed causes no repentance. So it looks as if we have to establish two categories of murder; broadly speaking, both are done in anger, but a proper description would be 'falling somewhere midway between "voluntary" and "involuntary"'; however, each type comes closer to one or other of these extremes. The man who nurses his anger and takes his vengeance later – not suddenly, on the spur of the moment, but with premeditation – approximates to the voluntary murderer. The man whose anger bursts forth uncontrollably, whose action is instant, immediate, and without premeditation, resembles the involuntary killer. Yet even so, he is not an entirely involuntary killer: he only resembles one. It is therefore sometimes difficult to categorize murders done under the influence of anger, and to know whether to treat them in law as voluntary or involuntary. The best course, which corresponds most closely to reality, is to classify them both under what they most resemble, and to distinguish them by the presence or absence of premeditation. We should lay down comparatively severe penalties for those who have killed in anger and with premeditation, and lighter ones for those who have killed on the spur of the moment without previous intent. Something which resembles a greater evil should attract a greater punishment, whereas a lesser penalty should be visited on that which resembles a lesser evil. This, then, is the course our laws should take.

CLEINIAS: Indeed it is.

ATHENIAN: Then let's go back to our subject and carry on as follows:

47 A. If someone kills a free man with his own hand, and the deed is done in a fit of anger, without previous intent,

his penalty should in general be that appropriate to a man who has killed without anger; but in addition he should be obliged to go into exile for two years, by way of a curb for his anger.

B. If a man kills in anger, but with premeditation,

his penalty should in general be that inflicted in the previous instance; but his exile should be for three years as against the other's two, the period of punishment being longer because of the greater violence of his passion.

In such cases, regulations for the return from exile should run as follows. (It is not easy to make hard and fast rules: sometimes the fiercer criminal as defined by the law may turn out easier to manage, whereas the man who is supposedly more manageable may turn out to be a more difficult case, having committed a murder with some savagery; the other, conversely, may have dispatched his victim without brutality. However, my account does describe the cases you'll find are typical.)

The Guardians of the Laws should act as assessors of all these points, and when the period of exile prescribed for either category has come to an end, they should send twelve of their number, as judges, to the borders of the country.

During the time that has elapsed these twelve should have made a still more exact investigation into what the exiles did,[1] so as to decide whether to grant pardon and permission to return; and the exiles are bound to acquiesce in the judgement of these authorities.

868

C. (a) If a returned exile of either category is ever again overcome by anger and commits the same offence,
he must go into exile and never come back.

　(b) If he does come back,
his penalty will be the same as that imposed on the foreigner who returns [46H].

D. (a) If a man kills his own slave,[2]
he must purify himself.

　(b) If he kills another's slave, in anger,
he must pay double damages to the owner.

E. If a killer in any category flouts the law and in his unpurified state pollutes the market-place, the sports stadium, and other holy places,
anyone who wishes should prosecute both the killer and the relative[3] of the dead man who allows the killer to do this, and compel the relative to exact payment of twice the fine and the other expenses;[4] and the prosecutor shall be legally entitled to take for himself the money so paid.

F. (a) If a slave kills his own master, in anger,
the relatives of the deceased shall treat the killer in whatever way they like (except that under no circumstances whatever may they let him go on living), and be free of pollution.

　(b) If a slave murders a free man who is not his master, in anger,
his master shall deliver him up to the relatives of the deceased, who will be obliged to kill him, the manner of the execution being within their discretion.

1. I.e. the circumstances of the murder.
2. Doubtless, in view of 47D(b) and 46B(b) we may add 'in anger'.
3. That is, the relative who has the duty of prosecuting the killer and warning him to keep away from public places.
4. The expenses of the purification rituals, presumably.

G. (This is a rare occurrence, but not unknown.)
  (a) If a father or mother kills a son or daughter in anger
      by beating them or by using some other form of
      violence,
the murderers must undergo the same purifications as apply
in the other cases, and go into exile for three years.
  (b) When they come back, the female killer must be
      separated from her husband and the male from his
      wife, and they must have no more children; and they
      must never again share hearth and home with those
      whom they have robbed of a son or brother, or join
      in religious ceremonies with them.

H. If someone is impious enough to disobey these regu-
    lations,
he shall be liable to a charge of impiety at the hands of
anyone who wishes.

I. (a) If a man kills his wedded wife in a fit of anger, or a
       wife her husband,
they must undergo the same purifications and spend three
years in exile.
  (b) On his return, a person who has done such a deed
      must never join his children in religious ceremonies
      nor eat at the same table with them.

J. If the parent or the child disobeys,
he shall equally be liable to a charge of impiety at the hands
of anyone who wishes.

K. If in anger
  (a) a brother kills a brother or a sister, or
  (b) a sister kills a brother or a sister,
the same purifications and periods of exile as applied to
parents and children should be specified as applying in these
cases too. (That is, they should never share hearth and home
with the brothers whom they have deprived of their fellow-
brothers nor with parents whom they have deprived of
children, nor join in religious ceremonies with them.)

L. If anyone disobeys this law,

869

he will be subject to the relevant law of impiety already laid down, as is only right and proper.

M. If anyone gets into such an ungovernable temper with his parents and begetters that in his insane fury he dares to kill one of them, and

   (a) is let off responsibility for murder by a voluntary statement of the deceased before death,

he must perform the same purifications as those who commit involuntary murder; and when he has followed the rest of the procedure prescribed for those cases, he may be considered purified.

   (b) If he is not let off,

the perpetrator of such a crime will be indictable under many laws. He will be subject to the most swingeing penalties for assault, and likewise for impiety for temple-robbery – he has plundered the shrine that is his parent's body, and deprived it of life. Consequently if one man could die many times, the murderer of his father or mother who has acted in anger would deserve to die the death over and over again. To this one killer no law will allow the plea of self-defence; no law will permit him to kill his father or mother, who brought him into the world. The law will instruct him to put up with all manner of suffering before he does such a thing. But what other penalty than death could the law appropriately lay down for this criminal? The law, then, should run:

   (b) cont.

the penalty for the murderer of a father or mother is to be death.

N. (a) If a brother kills his own brother in a political brawl or some similar circumstances, in self-defence when his victim had struck first,

he should be regarded as free of pollution (as though he had killed an enemy).

   (b) The same applies if

     (i) a citizen kills a citizen, or

     (ii) a foreigner kills a foreigner.

(c) If in self-defence
   (i)   a citizen kills a foreigner, or
   (ii) a foreigner kills a citizen,
the culprit should be in the same position with regard to the freedom from pollution, and likewise if
   (iii) a slave kills a slave.

O. If however a slave, in self-defence, kills a free man, *he should* be subject to the same laws as the parricide [47M].

P. The regulations stated about the acquittal from responsibility for murder granted by a father are to apply to every acquittal in such cases (when, that is, one man voluntarily absolves another of responsibility, on the grounds that the murder has been committed involuntarily):
the criminal must undergo the purifications and spend one year away from the country according to law.

VOLUNTARY HOMICIDE

That will do to describe murders committed unintentionally (through force of circumstances),[5] and in anger. Our next task is to speak of voluntary murders, which are premeditated and spring from sheer injustice – the lack of control over the desire for pleasure and over one's lusts and jealous feelings.[5a]

CLEINIAS: True.

ATHENIAN: First of all, we ought again to make as complete a list as possible of these sources of crime.

The chief cause is lust, which tyrannizes a soul that has gone 870 wild with desire. This lust is most usually for money, the object of most men's strongest and most frequent longing. Because of the innate depravity of men and their misdirected education, money has the power to produce in them a million cravings that are impossible to satisfy – all centring on the endless acquisition of wealth. The cause of this incorrect education is the pernicious praise given to wealth by the public opinion of Greeks and non-Greeks alike. In

5. Or 'with violence'; cf. p. 377.
5a. See the definition of 'injustice' on p. 374.

fact, wealth takes only third place in the scale of goodness;[6] but they make it pre-eminent, to the ruination of posterity and themselves. The best and the noblest policy for all cities to follow is to tell the truth about wealth, namely that it exists to serve the body, just as the body should be the servant of the soul. Although the ends which wealth naturally serves are indeed 'good', wealth itself will take third place, coming after the perfection of the soul and the body. Taking, therefore, this argument as our guide, we shall find that the man who means to be happy should not seek simply to be wealthy, but to be wealthy in a way consistent with justice and self-control. Murders needing still more murders in expiation would not occur in cities that had taken this lesson to heart. But as things are, as we said when we embarked on this topic, we have here one cause, and an extremely prominent cause at that, of the most serious charges of deliberate murder.

Second, an ambitious cast of mind: this breeds feelings of jealousy, which are dangerous companions to live with, particularly for the person who actually feels jealous, but potentially harmful to the leading citizens of the state as well.

In the third place, many a murder has been prompted by the cowardly fears of a guilty man. When a man is committing some crime, or has already committed it, he wants no one to know about it, and if he cannot eliminate a possible informer in any other way, he murders him.

These remarks should constitute the preface applying to all these crimes. In addition, we must tell the story which is so strongly believed by so many people when they hear it from those who have made a serious study of such matters in their mystic ceremonies. It is this:

Vengeance is exacted for these crimes in the after-life, and when a man returns to this world again he is ineluctably obliged to pay the penalty prescribed by the law of nature – to undergo the same treatment as he himself meted out to

6. See the lists on pp. 148–9 and 213.

his victim, and to conclude his earthly existence by encountering a similar fate at the hands of someone else.

If a man obeys and heartily dreads such a penalty after merely hearing the overture, there is no need to play over the relevant law. But in case of disobedience the following law 871 should be stated in writing:

48 A. (a) If a man by his own hand viciously kills a fellow-citizen, with premeditation,

he must be excluded from the places where people usually gather, and not pollute temples or market or harbours or any other common place of assembly, *whether or not* someone makes a proclamation against the culprit in these terms. (The reason is that the law itself makes the proclamation. It makes a permanent and public proclamation on behalf of the whole state, and always will.)

B. If a man fails in his duty to prosecute the culprit or bar him by proclamation, and is a relative (no more distant than a cousin) of the deceased on either the father's side or the mother's,

the pollution, together with the enmity of the gods, should arrive at his own door. (The curse imposed by the law turns the edict of heaven against him.) He must be subject to prosecution at the hands of any man who wishes to take vengeance for the deceased, and the man who thus wishes to take vengeance must scrupulously perform all the appropriate ablutions and all the other ritual details the god[7] prescribes for such cases; and when he has published the proclamation, he must go and make the criminal submit to the imposition of the penalty, under the law.

It is easy for a legislator to demonstrate that all this should be accompanied by a number of prayers and sacrifices to those gods who make it their business to prevent murders occurring in society. The Guardians of the Laws, in association with expounders, soothsayers, and the god,[7] should rule who these gods are to be, and specify the procedure for bringing such cases that would be most in harmony with the requirements of

7. Presumably the Delphic oracle.

religion; they should then follow it themselves in bringing these cases to court, which should be the same as the one given final authority over temple-robbers.[8]

48 A. cont.

 (b) If a man is found guilty,
he must be punished by death and be deprived of burial in the country of his victim. (In this way we can show he has not been forgiven, and avoid impiety.)

C. (a) If the defendant makes off and refuses to submit to trial,
he must remain in exile permanently.

 (b) If such a person sets foot within the country of the murdered man,
the first of the relatives of the deceased who comes across him, or indeed any citizen, should either
  (i) kill him with impunity, or
  (ii) tie him up, and hand him over to the judges who tried the case for them to carry out the execution.

D. When a man undertakes a prosecution, he should immediately demand sureties from the accused. The latter must duly provide his sureties, who must be deemed, in the eyes of the judges who constitute the court in these cases, to be credit-worthy; and these three credit-worthy sureties must pledge themselves to produce the accused at his trial. If a man refuses, or is unable, to produce sureties,
the authorities must arrest him and keep him bound and under guard, so that they can produce him at the hearing of the case.

872 E. If a man does not actually kill with his own hands, but simply plans the murder, and although responsible for it by virtue of plotting arrangements, continues to live in the state with his soul polluted by homicide, his trial for this crime should proceed along the same lines as before, except as regards the bail. If he is convicted,

8. See p. 359.

he may be granted burial in his native land, but the other details of the punishment should conform with the regulations previously laid down for this category.[9]

F. These same regulations about the actual commission and mere plotting of a murder should apply when

  (a) (i)   foreigners prosecute foreigners,
      (ii) citizens prosecute foreigners and foreigners citizens, and
      (iii) slaves prosecute slaves.

  (b) But an exception should be made in the business of the surety. Just as it was said [48D.] that *actual* murderers should provide sureties, the person who proclaims the ban arising from the murder should simultaneously demand sureties in these cases too [48F(a)(i–iii)].

G. If a slave intentionally kills a free man, whether he did the deed himself or planned it, and is convicted,
the public executioner should haul him off in the direction of the deceased's grave to a point from which the culprit can see the tomb. He should then scourge him, giving as many strokes as the successful prosecutor instructs. If the homicide survives the scourging, he is to be executed.

H. If a man kills an innocent slave, fearing that he will inform against his own shocking and disgraceful conduct, or prompted by some similar motive,
he should submit to trial, when a slave has died in these circumstances, precisely as he would have submitted to trial for murder if he had killed a citizen.

Certain crimes, which may occur, make the mere composition of laws for them an unpleasant and distasteful business, but it is impossible to omit them from our code. I mean deliberate and wholly wicked murders of relatives, whether the murderer commits the crime in person or merely plots it. Generally speaking, these killings occur in states that are badly administered or have a defective system of education, but occasionally one of them might crop up even in a country

9. That is, for those who *do* kill with their own hand.

where one would hardly look for it. What we have to do is to repeat our explanation of a moment ago, hoping that anyone who hears it will be more willing and able to avoid committing murders that are absolutely the most detestable in the sight of Heaven. The 'myth', or 'explanation',[10] or whatever the right word is, has come down to us in unambiguous terms from the lips of priests of long ago.

Justice stands on guard to exact vengeance for the spilling of the blood of relatives; she operates through the law we have just mentioned, and her decree is that a man who has done something of this kind is obliged to suffer precisely what he has inflicted. If ever a man has murdered his father, in the course of time he must suffer the same fate from violent treatment at the hands of his children. A matricide, before being reborn, must adopt the female sex, and after being born a woman and bearing children, be dispatched subsequently by them. No other purification is available when common blood has been polluted; the pollution
873 resists cleansing until, murder for murder, the guilty soul has paid the penalty and by this appeasement has soothed the anger of the deceased's entire line.

Thus the fear of such vengeance, exacted by the gods, should hold a man in check. But this is the law the human legislator will lay down in case some people should be overwhelmed by the terrible misfortune of committing such a crime:

I. (a) If they should dare to tear the soul from the body of their father, mother, brothers or children, deliberately and with premeditation,
the proclamations of banishment from places of public resort, and the sureties, should be identical to those detailed in previous cases.

(b) If a man is convicted of such a murder, having killed one of the aforementioned persons,
the court-assistants and the officials shall execute him, and

10. An 'explanation', in Platonic terms, seeks to *prove*, by reason; a 'myth' seeks to *persuade*, to recommend a truth to our feelings, using the language of poetry and mythology.

throw him out, naked, at a specified place where three roads meet outside the city. All the officials, on behalf of the entire state, must take a stone and throw it at the head of the corpse, and thus purify the entire state. After this, they must carry the corpse to the borders of the land and eject it, giving it no burial, as the law instructs.

SUICIDE

But what about the killer of the person who is, above all, his 'nearest and dearest', as the expression is? What penalty ought he to undergo? I am talking about the man who kills *himself*, who (1) uses violence to take his fate out of the hands of destiny, (2) is not acting in obedience to any legal decision of his state, (3) whose hand is not forced by the pressure of some excruciating and unavoidable misfortune, (4) has not fallen into some irremediable disgrace that he cannot live with, and (5) imposes this unjust judgement on himself in a spirit of slothful and abject cowardice. In general, what ritual observances should take place with regard to purification and interment in this case, are matters known to God; the relatives must seek guidance from expounders and the relevant laws, and act in these instances according to their instructions. But

49. (a) People who perish in this way must be buried individually, with no one to share their grave.

(b) They must be buried in disgrace on the boundaries of the twelve territorial divisions, in deserted places that have no name.

(c) The graves must not be identifiable, either by headstone or title.

ANIMALS AND INANIMATE OBJECTS AS KILLERS

50. (a) If a beast of burden or any other animal kills anyone (except when the incident occurs while they are competing in one of the public contests),

(i) *the relatives* must prosecute the killer for murder;

    (ii) *the next of kin* must appoint some Country-Wardens
        (whichever ones he pleases, and as many as he likes),
        and they must try the case;
    (iii) if the animal is found guilty,
        they must kill it and throw it out beyond the frontiers
        of the country.
  (b) If some inanimate object causes loss of human life (but
     not if it is a stroke of lightning or some similar
     weapon wielded by God – it must be one of the other
     things that kill a man by falling on him, or because he
     falls on it),
    (i) *the next of kin* must appoint the nearest neighbour to
874   sit in judgement on the object, and thus effect the
       purification of himself and the deceased's entire line;
    (ii) *the condemned* object must be thrown over the frontiers,
       in the way specified in the case of animals.

MURDER BY PERSONS UNKNOWN

51. If someone is found dead, and the killer is not known and
    cannot be discovered by diligent efforts to trace him,
the proclamations should be the same as laid down in former
cases, being made, however, against 'the murderer': when
the prosecutor has established his case, he must give notice
in the market-place to the killer and convicted murderer of
so-and-so, that he must not enter holy places nor any part
of the country of the deceased; he must threaten that if he
does turn up and is recognized, he will be executed, denied
burial, and his body ejected from the country of his victim.

JUSTIFIABLE HOMICIDE

So much, then, for the law on that sort of murder. In the
following conditions, however, it will be right to regard the
killer as innocent:

  52. (a) If he catches a thief entering his home at night to
      steal his goods, and kills him,
  he shall be innocent.

(b) If he kills a footpad in self-defence,
he shall be innocent.

(c) If anyone sexually violates a free woman or boy,
he may be killed with impunity by the victim of the violence,
or by the victim's father or brothers or sons.

(d) If a husband discovers his wedded wife being raped
and kills the attacker,
the law will regard him as innocent.

(e) If a man kills someone while saving the life of his
father (provided the latter is not committing a
crime), or while rescuing his mother or children or
brothers, or the mother of his children,
he shall be completely innocent.

§19. WOUNDINGS

The next topic that naturally suggests itself after murder is wounding. In the first paragraph, the Athenian's point seems to be that whereas death violates the soul, mere injuries harm only the body. The sections of the code dealing with murder and assault are thus connected, rather oddly to our way of thinking, to the earlier discussions of spiritual and physical education respectively.

PRELIMINARIES

ATHENIAN: Let us assume we have completed our legislation concerning the training and education that the soul needs during a man's life (a life that is worth the living if these needs are met, but not if they are not), and the penalties that should apply in cases of death by violence. We have discussed, too, the training and education of the body, and the related topic in this case is the violent treatment, voluntary or involuntary, of one man by another. So far as we can, we must distinguish the various categories, see how many there are, and say what penalties will be appropriate for each. It looks as if this could properly form the next subject of our legislation.

Even the biggest bungler you could find among would-be legislators will put cases of wounding and mutilation immediately after cases of murder. Woundings ought to be distinguished as murders were: some are inflicted involuntarily, some in anger, some through fear, while others are committed voluntarily and with premeditation. A preliminary address must be given about all these categories as follows:

It is vital that men should lay down laws for themselves and live in obedience to them; otherwise they will be indistinguishable from wild animals of the utmost savagery. The reason is this: no man has sufficient natural gifts *both* to discern what benefits men in their social relationships *and* to be constantly ready and able to put his knowledge to the

875

394

best practical use. The first difficulty is to realize that the proper object of true political skill is not the interest of private individuals but the common good. This is what knits a state together, whereas private interests make it disintegrate. If the public interest is well served, rather than the private, then the individual and the community alike are benefited.

The second difficulty is that even if a man did get an adequate theoretical grasp of the truth of all this, he might then attain a position of absolute control over a state, with no one to call him to account. In these circumstances he would never have the courage of his convictions; he would never devote his life to promoting the welfare of the community as his first concern, making his private interests take second place to the public good. His human nature will always drive him to look to his own advantage and the lining of his own pocket. An irrational avoidance of pain and pursuit of pleasure will dominate his character, so that he will prefer these two aims to better and more righteous paths. Blindness, self-imposed, will ultimately lead the man's whole being, and the entire state, into a morass of evil. But if ever by the grace of God some natural genius were born, and had the chance to assume such power, he would have no need of laws to control him. Knowledge is unsurpassed by any law or regulation; reason, if it is genuine and really enjoys its natural freedom, should have universal power: it is not right that it should be under the control of anything else, as though it were some sort of slave. But as it is, such a character is nowhere to be found, except a hint of it here and there. That is why we need to choose the second alternative, law and regulation, which embody general principles, but cannot provide for every individual case.

THE COURTS' DISCRETION

I have pointed this out because we are now going to settle the penalty or fine to be imposed on someone who has wounded or harmed someone else. Anyone could quite easily and properly take us up on any point and ask: 'What attacker, what wound, what victim do you mean? How was the attack made, and when? The circumstances of these cases differ in a thousand and one different ways.' Now to leave all these details to the judgement of the courts is impracticable, and equally impracticable to leave them none. In every case, however, one point in particular simply must be left to the courts: in each separate instance, they must decide whether the crime did in fact take place, or not. But on the other hand it is hardly feasible to produce laws oneself to cover every case, serious or 876 trivial; one can scarcely leave the courts no discretion at all about the fine or punishment that ought to be imposed on a criminal of this kind.

CLEINIAS: Well, then, where do we go from here?

ATHENIAN: We conclude that some details ought to be left to the courts, but not others; these should be regulated by the legislator.

CLEINIAS: Which points, then, ought to be in the legal code, and which ought to be referred to the judgement of the courts?

ATHENIAN: In this connexion, here's the next thing to notice: sometimes we find in a state that the juries are useless, dumb things; the individual jurymen keep their opinions a mystery known only to themselves and give their decisions by secret ballot. It's even more serious when so far from keeping silent when they hear a case they make a tremendous disturbance as though they were in a theatre, and hurl shouts of applause or disapproval at the speaker on either side in turn. All this puts the state at large into an awkward predicament. It is a wretched business to be forced to lay down laws for courts of that type, but if one is forced, the right thing to do is to hand over to them the assessment of penalties only in very trivial cases, providing for the majority in explicit laws of one's own – if, that is, one ever does legislate for a state organized in this way. But in a country where the regulation of the courts is as satisfactory as can be achieved and the jurymen-to-be have received a good education and been examined by all kinds of tests, it is right and proper to grant them complete discretion on all points to do with the punishments or fines that convicted criminals should suffer. In the present case we cannot be blamed if we leave to their discretion the most frequent and important points that arise, because they are points which even inadequately educated jurymen could grasp and apply when they have to give each individual crime a penalty appropriate both to the damage done and to the wickedness which is at the root of the actual deed. We believe, in fact, that the people for whom we are legislating may well turn out quite conspicuously able judges of these matters, so we should leave most decisions to them. Even so, in enacting earlier parts of our legal code, we mentioned the practice of sketching some examples of penalties – models for the judges to imitate, to stop them exceeding the due limits of justice. We suited the action to the word; it was the right course then and it is the right course now, as I once again resume our legislation.

VOLUNTARY WOUNDING, AND A DIGRESSION ON ADOPTING AN HEIR IN CASES OF CHILDLESSNESS

Our law on wounding, then, should be written in the following terms:

53 A. If a man deliberately intends to kill a fellow citizen (unless the latter is one of those whose death is sanctioned by the law [52(a–e)]), and wounds him without being able to kill him, no pity should be wasted on the man who has inflicted a wound with 877 that sort of intention: he should be treated with no more respect than a killer, and made to stand trial for murder.

But we should have due respect for the luck that has saved him from total ruin, and for his guardian angel too, who in pity for the attacker and the wounded man has stopped the injury of the latter from proving fatal, and prevented the disastrous ill luck of the former from bringing a curse down upon his head. We should duly thank his guardian spirit and not obstruct its wishes:

53 A. cont.
He who has inflicted the wound shall be spared the death penalty, but he must suffer life-long banishment to some neighbouring state, with full freedom to enjoy all the income from his property; he must pay full compensation for whatever injury he has done the wounded man, the sum to be assessed by the court that tries the case. (The court will consist of the same people who would have tried him for murder if his victim had died of the wounds sustained.)

B. If with similar premeditation
   (a) a child wounds his parents, or
   (b) a slave wounds his master,
death is to be the penalty.

C. If similarly
   (a) a brother wounds a brother or a sister, or
   (b) a sister wounds a brother or a sister,
     and is convicted of wounding with premeditation,
death is to be the penalty.

D. If with intent to kill
   (a) a wife wounds her husband, or
   (b) a husband wounds his wife,
he or she must go into permanent exile. If they have sons or daughters who are still in their minority, the trustees must administer their property in trust, and care for the children as though they were orphans. If the offspring are adult, they should themselves take possession of the property, and be under no obligation to support the exile.[1] If anyone who succumbs to such misfortune is childless,[2] the relatives of the exile, as far as the children of the cousins on both the male and female side, must hold a meeting, and in consultation with the Guardians of the Laws appoint an heir for this property, the 5040th in the state.

1. An Athenian was obliged by law to care for his parents in their old age. Cf. pp. 176 and 475–8.
2. The subject of this clause is of course a criminal, not a victim.

(They should look at the matter in the following light: none of the 5040 farms belongs to its occupant or his family in general as much as to the state, which is entitled to it not only as a piece of public property but also as its own private possession; and the state ought to do its best to keep its own properties as holy and prosperous as possible.) Therefore:

54. When one of the properties falls away from this condition of holiness and prosperity to such an extent that the possessor leaves no children to succeed him, being unmarried, or married but childless, and meets his end convicted of

    (a) (i) deliberate murder, or
        (ii) some other crime against gods or citizens for which the death penalty is specifically laid down by law, or if
    (b) someone without male issue goes into permanent exile,

first of all, this property must be cleansed and purified according to law; then the relatives must hold the meeting we mentioned just now, and in consultation with the 878 Guardians of the Laws pick out a family that has the best reputation for virtue of all the families in the state and is at the same time fortunate enough to have produced several children. One of these they must adopt on behalf of the deceased's father and forebears, who will receive him as their son; from them he will take his name, which should be an omen of good fortune. The relatives should pray that as a result of his adoption he will bring them children, and guard the hearth and look after the family affairs, both sacred and secular, with greater success than his adoptive father enjoyed. In this way they should install him, according to law, as heir to the property.

    (c) When such disasters as we have mentioned [54.(a, b)] overwhelm the sinner,

they should let him lie nameless in his grave, childless and deprived of his family estate.

WOUNDINGS INFLICTED IN ANGER

We can see that it is not universally true that one district
extends right up to the boundary of another. In some cases
there is a no man's land in between, which will extend so as to
touch either boundary and occupy an intermediate position
between the two. This, we said,[3] was true of an act done in
anger: it falls somewhere between voluntary and involuntary.
Our regulations concerning wounding inflicted in anger
should therefore run as follows:

55 A. If a man is found guilty, and
   (a) the wound turns out to be curable,
he must pay double damages;
   (b) if it is incurable,
he must pay quadruple damages.
   (c) If he has inflicted a wound which, though curable,
        makes the wounded man feel acutely embarrassed
        and ashamed,
he must pay triple damages.

B. If one man wounds another and injures not only his
   victim but the state, by rendering him unable to defend
   his fatherland against the enemy,

he must, in addition to the other penalties, make restitution
to the state for the loss it has sustained, viz. he must perform
not only his own military service but that of the incapacitated
person as well by serving in the army on his behalf.

C. If he fails so to serve,
he shall be liable under the law to a charge of evading military
service, at the hands of anyone who wishes.

A. cont. The assessment of the damages, double, triple
   or quadruple, must be made by the judges who found
   him guilty.

D. If one relative wounds another in any of these ways,
   the fellow-clansmen and close relatives, male and female, as

3. See p. 380.

far as sons of cousins on both the male and female side, must hold a meeting, and when they have reached their verdict, they must entrust the assessment to the natural parents. If the assessment is challenged, the assessment of the relatives on the male side must be taken as final. If they cannot agree themselves, they must, in the end, hand over the matter to the Guardians of the Laws.

E. When children inflict this kind of wound on their parents, it is essential for the judges to be persons over sixty years of age who have children of their own and not merely adopted ones. If a man is found guilty, *these judges* must decide whether a man who could do such a thing as this should die, or whether the penalty should be something even more severe,[4] or perhaps something a trifle less severe. None of the relations of the culprit should act as a judge, not even if he is of the age required by law. 879

F. (a) If a slave wounds a free man in anger, *the owner* must hand him over to the wounded man, who may treat him in whatever way he likes.

    (b) If the owner fails to hand him over, *he must* remedy the damage himself.

    (c) If anyone alleges that the affair is the result of collusion between the slave and the wounded party,[5] he must contest the point at law. If he does not win the case, *he must* pay triple damages.
If he does win, he must prosecute the author of the collusion with the slave on a charge of kidnapping.

INVOLUNTARY WOUNDINGS

56. If anyone involuntarily wounds someone else, *he must* pay simple damages. (No legislator is capable of regulating the workings of chance.) The judges are to be the same as those appointed to try children who wound their parents; and they will have the duty of assessing the amount of the damages.

4. Such as deprivation of burial.
5. That is, so that the wounded party would acquire a slave for nothing.

§20. ASSAULT

Assault consists of insulting someone by abuse or rough handling without actually causing injury. It is less serious than wounding (§19) but as we should expect, considerations of social status bulk large: slaves and children must be extremely deferential to their masters and parents, though foreigners have a particularly privileged position. But in general Plato's law reinforces the social structure of the state.

In this section, exhortation and law are mingled even more than usual.

ATHENIAN: All the injuries we have so far mentioned involve the use of violence, and so too do the various kinds of assault. In these cases, the point that every man, woman and child should bear in mind is this:

> Age is always very much more highly regarded than youth, and this is so both among the gods and among men, if they intend to live in security and happiness. Therefore, the assault of an older man by a younger in public is a disgusting sight, and the gods hate to see it. No young man who is struck by an old man should ever make a fuss, but put up with his bad temper, and so establish a claim to similar respect when he himself grows old.

Our law, then, should run as follows:

Everyone in our community must show, by his words and actions, respect for his senior. A man should avoid crossing any person (male or female) who is twenty years older than himself, regarding him or her in the same way as he would his father or mother. For the sake of the gods of birth, he must always keep himself from striking anyone old enough to have been his parent. Similarly, he must refrain from striking a foreigner, whether the latter is a long-established resident or a recent immigrant. He must never go so far as to punish such a person by hitting him, either by attacking him first, or in self-defence.

57 A. (a) If he thinks the foreigner is unruly and insolent in an attack on himself, and needs to be punished, he must arrest him and take him, without hitting him, to the court of the City-Wardens, so that the foreigner may learn to banish all thoughts of ever striking a citizen again. The City-Wardens must take the man and interrogate him, with proper respect for the god who is the protector of foreigners. If in fact the foreigner seems to have been in the wrong in striking the citizen,

the City-Wardens must put a stop to this unruliness, so characteristic of a foreigner; they must give him as many strokes of the lash as will equal the number of blows he himself inflicted.

(b) If he is not in the wrong,

they must warn and rebuke the man who made the arrest, and dismiss the pair of them.

B. If one man strikes another who
  (a) is about the same age, or
  (b) is older, but has no children,

whether the attacker is an old man striking an old man, 880 or a young man striking a young man, the man attacked must defend himself by natural means – with his own bare hands, without a weapon. But if a man over forty years of age has the face to fight someone, whether
  (i) he strikes the first blow, or
  (ii) fights in self-defence,

he will get the reputation of being an uncivilized boor with the manners of a slave, and this ignominious punishment will serve him right.

A man who is easily persuaded by these words of exhortation will give us no trouble; but stubborn people, who ignore the preamble, ought to be ready to take more notice of the following regulations:

C. If anyone strikes a man twenty years or more his senior, any bystander, if he is neither of the same age nor younger than the combatants, should separate them, *or be treated* under the law as a wretched coward. If he is of the same age as the person attacked, or younger, he should go to his assistance as if it were his own brother or father being wronged, or some still more senior relative.

D. In addition, the man who dares to strike his senior as defined[1] must stand trial for assault. If he loses the case, *he must* be imprisoned for not less than a year. If the court fixes a longer imprisonment, the period it decides on shall stand.

E. If a foreigner, or a resident alien, strikes a man twenty years or more his senior, the same regulation [57 C] about assistance from passers-by shall be enforced in the same way as before.

   (a) A man found guilty of such a charge, if he is a foreigner not resident in the state,

must pay his penalty by spending two years in prison.

   (b) If it is a resident alien who is in breach of these regulations,

he must go to prison for three years, except that the court may specify a longer period by way of penalty.

F. The passer-by who comes across any of these cases of assault and does not give assistance as required by law *must be* fined: a member of the first property-class 100 drachmas, a member of the second fifty drachmas, a member of the third thirty drachmas, and a member of the fourth twenty drachmas. The court in such cases[2] is to consist of the Generals, Company-Commanders, Tribe-Leaders and Cavalry-Commanders.

Some laws, it seems, are made for the benefit of honest men, to teach them the rules of association that have to be observed if they are to live in friendship; others are made for those who refuse to be instructed and whose naturally tough natures have not been softened enough to stop them turning to absolute vice. It will be they who have prompted the points I am just going to make, and it is for their benefit that the

1. I.e. someone twenty years older.
2. Presumably this refers to *all* cases of assault.

lawgiver will be compelled to produce his laws, although he would wish never to find any occasion to use them. Consider a man who will dare to lay hands on his father or mother or their forebears by way of violent assault. He will fear neither the wrath of the gods above nor the punishments said to await him in the grave; he will hold the ancient and universal 881 tradition in contempt, on the strength of his 'knowledge' in a field where he is in fact a total ignoramus. He will therefore turn criminal, and will stand in need of some extreme deterrent. Death, however, is not an extreme and final penalty; the sufferings said to be in store for these people in the world to come are much more extreme than that. But although the threat of these sufferings is no idle one, it has no deterrent effect at all on souls like these. If it did, we should never have to deal with assaults on mothers, and wicked and presumptuous attacks on other forebears. I conclude, therefore, that the punishments men suffer for these crimes here on earth while they are alive should as far as possible equal the penalties beyond the grave.

Our next enactment, then, should run as follows:

G. If a man who is not in the grip of insanity dares to strike his father or mother, or their father or mother, the first point is that the passer-by must render assistance as provided in former cases.

    (a) (i) If the resident alien renders assistance,
he shall be invited to a front seat at the games;

    (ii) if he does not render assistance,
he must go into permanent exile from the land.

    (b) (i) If the non-resident alien renders assistance,
he shall be commended.

    (ii) If he does not render assistance,
he must be reprimanded.

    (c) (i) If a slave renders assistance,
he shall be set free.

    (ii) If he does not render assistance,
he must receive a hundred strokes of the lash.

If the crime was committed in the market-place, the whipping should be administered by the Market-Wardens;

if in the city but not in the market, by the City-Warden in residence; if somewhere in the countryside, by the chief Country-Wardens.

(d) Everyone of citizen birth who passes by, whether man, woman or child, must shout 'you wicked monster' at the attacker, and repel him. If the passer-by makes no attempt to repel him,

he must be liable under the law to a curse from Zeus, guardian of the family and protector of parents.

H. If a man is convicted of an assault on his parents,
he must be permanently rusticated from the city to some other part of the country, and be banned from all sacred places.

I. (a) If he returns to the city,
he must be punished by death.

(b) If he does not keep away from sacred places,
the Country-Wardens must punish him by a whipping, and by any other method at their discretion.

J. If any free man eats or drinks in company with such a person, or associates with him in some other similar fashion, even by deliberately failing to cut him on meeting,

he must not enter any temple, or market-place, or any part of the city, before he has been purified, bearing in mind that he has come into contact with a misfortune that brings a curse upon a man.

K. If he disobeys the law and in defiance of it pollutes temples and city,
any official who discovers the fact and does not take the man to court will find that this is one of the most serious charges against him at his scrutiny.[3]

882 L. If a slave strikes a free man, foreigner or citizen, the passer-by who does not render assistance
must pay the penalty prescribed for his property-class.

3. At the end of their term officials had to submit to an examination of their conduct in office before being discharged: see p. 495.

M. The passers-by in conjunction with the person attacked must bind the slave and hand him over to his victim; the victim must take him, put him in chains, and give him as many strokes of the whip as he likes, provided he does not diminish the value of the slave to his master; he should then hand him over to the latter's legal ownership. This legal ownership must be subject to the following provision. Any slave who has struck a free man, other than on the orders of the officials,[4] must be tied up; his master must receive him from the assaulted person and not release him before the slave persuades his victim that he deserves to live free of constraint.

The same regulations should apply in all cases (a) as between women, (b) when women prosecute men, and (c) when men prosecute women.

4. Slaves owned by the state might be ordered to inflict corporal punishment on a citizen. See p. 279.

§21. RELIGION

Book Ten deals with philosophical and theological themes rather than social or political, and is probably the best-known part of the Laws. Much ink has flowed from learned pens in attempts to identify which contemporary philosophers Plato was attacking, and to unravel the intricacies of his arguments and the obscurities of his Greek. These are the difficulties of an interpreter; the translator has in addition to render into English a number of key terms for which no precise equivalents exist. Some of these terms I hope to explain below.

The entire book is devoted to refuting three 'heresies': (1) that gods do not exist, (2) that they exist but are unconcerned about the world, (3) that they exist and are concerned, but can be influenced by prayer. From Plato's impassioned denunciations we may fairly assume that all three views were current in his day. It was vital that he should refute them. He believed in the existence of what we would today call 'absolute' moral standards, laid down by some higher power, and perpetually valid. Obviously any of these three heresies could, and doubtless did, afford by themselves arguments for the relativity of moral standards (or at least, in the case of the third heresy, for supposing that these standards are not really absolute if the gods were prepared to waive them).

But there were profounder reasons for opposing the first heresy, that gods do not exist. This (according to Plato) was associated with a pernicious doctrine about the origins and development of the world, and the status of moral terms. The doctrine depended on a distinction between 'soul' (psychē) and 'design' (technē) on the one hand, and 'matter' (sōma), 'chance' (tuchē) and 'nature' (phusis) on the other. It was held that the latter were in some sense basic or primary or fundamental; matter had fallen into certain patterns of arrangement and behaviour by chance and/or its natural constitution and properties; nothing had started or directed the process. 'Art' and 'design' were seen as late and minor influences on a world where life, order, movement and regularity were largely the products of chance, not intelligence. This thesis effectively undermined the position of 'absolute' standards, because it excluded any agency such as gods to establish or enforce them; and law and government were simply matters of human 'design' or convention.

Plato's reply is, in outline, simple. He reverses the order of priority as between matter and soul. Physical motion, he argues, is always produced by some antecedent motion. But what started the process? It can only be soul, the one thing capable of self-generated motion (look at animals, who 'move themselves': we say they are 'alive', that is, they have soul). And soul is presumably intelligent, and imposes movement, order and regularity on the physical world. Individual souls, that drive round the heavenly bodies in an orderly and regular manner, observable here on earth, are gods.

Once Plato has established in this way the existence of gods, the refutation of the two remaining heresies becomes comparatively easy. Neglect of the world, and venality, become vices that could not possibly be attributed to gods, because the regularity and beauty of the movements the gods induce indicate that they are 'good'. (Plato hints mysteriously at a 'bad' soul or souls responsible for irregular motion, and evil.)

Two points may be made about this thesis. (1) It is written at a very high level of generality, which makes it almost impossible to identify as the object of Plato's strictures any particular philosopher or school of thought active at the time. Plato is, in my view, attacking a 'climate of opinion', or an amalgam of several views, rather than a single clear-cut doctrine; but this is still a matter of learned debate, and likely to remain so. (2) Plato's actual 'proof' is philosophically none too rigorous, and depends for any cogency it may have on large assumptions to bridge awkward gaps in the argument. (For instance, the identification of 'soul' with 'god', mentioned above, is possible only if we are prepared, as Cleinias was, to identify without further ado these two vague and exalted notions; only thus can 'priority of soul' be converted into 'existence of gods'.)

It remains to say a few words about the actual law of impiety. It is not an institution peculiar to Plato. Several prosecutions are known of philosophers who held unpopular religious opinions. Precisely how far Plato's law coincides with Athenian law of his day is obscure, apart from two major respects: (1) belief in the venality of the gods was of course widespread and Plato is alone in legislating *against it; (2) committal to prison was not usually used, as far as we know, as a punishment in itself or to facilitate re-education. We may approve in general of Plato's desire to rehabilitate criminals, but his proposal that officials should visit heretics or atheists for five years 'to admonish them and ensure their spiritual salvation' suggests (but does no more than suggest) disturbing modern parallels.*

I have stated Plato's thesis in its barest essentials in order to give the reader a preliminary framework within which he may read this book; reference to fuller discussions may be found in the select bibliography.

THREE SOURCES OF IMPIETY

BK
X
884

ATHENIAN: So much for cases of assault. Now let's state a single comprehensive rule to cover acts of violence. It will run more or less like this. No one may seize or make off with other people's property, nor use any of his neighbour's possessions without getting the permission of the owner. Contempt for this principle has always been (and still is and always will be) the source of all the evils just mentioned. But there are other acts of violence, too, of which the worst are the insolence and outrageous actions of the young. These actions are most serious when they affect sacred objects; and the damage is particularly grave when it is done to sacred property that also belongs to the public, or is held in common by the members of a sub-division of the state, such as a tribe or some similar association. Second, and second in order of gravity, comes wanton damage to sacred objects that are privately owned, particularly tombs; third come attacks (apart from those already dealt with[1]) on parents. A fourth[2] category of outrageous conduct is when someone ignores the wishes of the authorities and seizes or removes or uses something belonging to them without their permission; and any violations of the civil rights of the private citizen which demand legal redress will constitute a fifth class. We have to frame a comprehensive law that will cover each individual case. As for robbery from temples, whether clandestine or open and

1. See pp. 398, 401 and 405.   2. See pp. 488–9.

violent, we have already specified in general terms the appropriate punishment;[3] but our statement of the penalty for offensive remarks about the gods or outrageous actions against their interests should be prefaced by these words of exhortation:

No one who believes in gods as the law directs ever voluntarily commits an unholy act or lets any lawless word pass his lips. If he does, it is because of one of three possible misapprehensions: either, as I said, he believes (1) the gods do not exist, or (2) that they exist but take no thought for the human race, or (3) that they are influenced by sacrifices and supplications and can easily be won over.

CLEINIAS: So what's the right thing for us to do or say to these people?

ATHENIAN: My friend, let's listen to the ridicule and scorn with which I imagine they put their case.

CLEINIAS: What ridicule?

THE CASE OF THE OPPOSITION

ATHENIAN: They'll probably go in for bantering, and address us like this: 'Gentlemen of Athens, of Sparta and of Crete, you are quite right. Some of us are indeed absolute atheists, whereas others do believe in such gods as you describe. So we demand of you what you yourselves demanded of the laws, that before you resort to threats and bullying, you should try to convince us by argument and cogent proofs that gods do exist, and that they are in fact above being seduced by gifts into turning a blind eye to injustice. But you see, it's precisely in these and similar terms that we hear them spoken of by the most highly thought-of poets and orators and prophets and priests and thousands of other people too. That's why most of us make little effort to avoid crime, but commit it first and try to put things right afterwards. So from lawgivers who profess to use the velvet glove rather than the iron fist we claim the right to be tackled by persuasion first. Even if, when you state your case for the existence of gods,

3. See p. 357.

your elegance of expression is only marginally superior to your opponents', persuade us that your argument is a better expression of the *truth*, and then perhaps we'll believe you. Isn't that fair enough? Well then, try to reply to our challenge.'

CLEINIAS: Well sir, don't you think that the gods' existence is an easy truth to explain?

886 ATHENIAN: How?

CLEINIAS: Well, just look at the earth and the sun and the stars and the universe in general; look at the wonderful procession of the seasons and its articulation into years and months! Anyway, you know that all Greeks and all foreigners are unanimous in recognizing the existence of gods.

ATHENIAN: My dear sir, when I think of the contempt these scoundrels will probably feel for us, I'm overcome with embarrassment – no, I withdraw that word: let's say they 'alarm' me – because you don't appreciate the real grounds of their opposition to you. You think it's just because they can't resist temptation and desire that they are attracted to the godless life.

CLEINIAS: What other reason could there be, sir?

ATHENIAN: A reason which you two, living rather off the beaten track as you do, simply wouldn't appreciate. It will have completely passed you by.

CLEINIAS: What are you talking about now?

ATHENIAN: A form of ignorance that causes no end of trouble, but which passes for the height of wisdom.

CLEINIAS: How do you mean?

ATHENIAN: In Athens a number of written works are current which are not found in your states (which are, I understand, too well run to tolerate them). The subject of these writings (some of which are in verse, others in prose) is theology. The most ancient accounts, after relating how the primitive substances – the sky and so on – came into being, pass rapidly on to a description of the birth of the gods and the details of how once born they subsequently treated each other. On some subjects, the antiquity of these works makes them difficult to criticize, whatever their influence – good or bad – on their audience; but when it comes to the respect and

attention due to parents, I for one shall never recommend
them either as a good influence or as a statement of the honest
truth. Still, there's no need to bother with this old material:
we may freely allow it to be arranged and recounted in any
way the gods find amusing. But the principles of our modern
pundits do need to be denounced as a pernicious influence.
Just look at the effects of their arguments! When you and I
present our proofs for the existence of gods and adduce what
you adduced – sun, moon, stars and earth – and argue they
are gods and divine beings, the proselytes of these clever
fellows will say that these things are just earth and stones,
and are incapable of caring for human affairs, however much
our plausible rhetoric has managed to dress them up.

CLEINIAS: Even if it were unique, sir, that theory you've
just described would make trouble. But as similar doctrines in
fact exist in their thousands, the situation is even worse.

ATHENIAN: What now, then? What's our reply? What
must we do? It's as though we were on trial before a bench
of godless judges, defending ourselves on a charge arising
out of our legislation. 'It's monstrous,' they say to us, 'that 887
you should pass laws asserting that gods exist.' Shall we
defend ourselves? Or shall we ignore them and get back to
our legislation, so that the mere preface doesn't turn out
longer than the actual code? You see, if we're going to
postpone passing the appropriate legislation until we've
proved properly to those with a taste for impiety all the points
they insisted we had to cover, so that they feel uneasy and
begin to find their views going sour on them, our explanation
will be anything but brief.

CLEINIAS: Even so, sir, as we've often said in the comparatively short time we've been talking, there's no reason
at the moment to prefer a brief explanation to a full one: after
all, no one's 'breathing down our neck' (as they say). It would
be an awful farce, if we appeared to be putting brevity first
and quality second. It's vital that somehow or other we should
make out a plausible case for supposing that gods do exist,
that they are good, and that they respect justice more than
men do. Such a demonstration would constitute just about

the best and finest preamble our penal code could have. So let's overcome our reluctance and unhurriedly exert what powers of persuasion we have in this field, devoting ourselves wholeheartedly to a full exposition of our case.

ATHENIAN: How keen and insistent you are! I take it you're suggesting we should now offer up a prayer for the success of our exposition, which we certainly can't delay any longer.

ADDRESS TO THE YOUNG HERETIC

Well now, how *can* one argue for the existence of gods without getting angry? You see, one inevitably gets irritable and annoyed with these people who have put us to the trouble, and continue to put us to the trouble, of composing these explanations. If only they believed the stories which they had as babes and sucklings from their nurses and mothers! These almost literally 'charming' stories were told partly for amusement, partly in full earnest; the children heard them related in prayer at sacrifices, and saw acted representations of them – a part of the ceremony a child always loves to see and hear; and they saw their own parents praying with the utmost seriousness for themselves and their families in the firm conviction that their prayers and supplications were addressed to gods who really did exist. At the rising and setting of the sun and moon the children saw and heard Greeks and foreigners, in happiness and misery alike, all prostrate at their devotions; far from supposing gods to be a myth, the worshippers believed their existence to be so sure as to be beyond suspicion. When some people contemptuously brush aside all this evidence without a single good reason to support them (as even 888 a half-wit can see) and oblige us to deliver this address – well, how could one possibly admonish them and at the same time teach them the basic fact about gods, their existence, without using the rough edge of one's tongue? Still, we must make the best of it: we don't want both sides maddened at once, they by their greed for pleasure, we by our anger at their condition. So our address to men with such a depraved outlook should be calm, and run as follows. Let's use honeyed words and abate our anger, and pretend we're addressing just one representative individual.

'Now then, my lad, you're still young, and as time goes on you'll come to adopt opinions diametrically opposed to those you hold now. Why not wait till later on to make up your mind about these important matters? The most important of all, however lightly you take it at the moment, is to get the right ideas about the gods and so live a good life – otherwise you'll live a bad one. In this connexion, I want first to make a crucial and irrefutable point. It's this: you're not unique. Neither you nor your friends are the first to have held this opinion about the gods. It's an illness from which the world is never free, though the number of sufferers varies from time to time. I've met a great many of them, and let me assure you that none of them who have been convinced early in life that gods do not exist have ever retained that belief into old age. However, it is true that some men (but not many) do persist in labouring under the impression either that although the gods exist they are indifferent to human affairs, or alternatively that they are not indifferent but can easily be won over by prayers and sacrifices. Be guided by me: you'll only see this business in its truest light if you wait to gather your information from all sources, particularly the legislator, and then see which theory represents the truth. In the meantime, don't venture any impiety where gods are concerned. You may take it that it will be up to your lawgiver, now and in the future, to try to enlighten you on precisely these topics.'

CLEINIAS: So far, sir, that's very well said.

NATURE AND CHANCE VERSUS DESIGN

ATHENIAN: Certainly, Megillus and Cleinias, but what an amazing doctrine we've got involved in, without noticing it!

CLEINIAS: What doctrine do you mean?

ATHENIAN: I mean the one which many people regard as the highest truth of all.

CLEINIAS: Please be more explicit.

ATHENIAN: Some people, I believe, account for all things which have come to exist, all things which are coming into existence now, and all things which will do so in the future, by attributing them either to nature, art, or chance.

CLEINIAS: Isn't that satisfactory?

ATHENIAN: Oh, I expect they've got it more or less right – they're clever fellows. Still, let's keep track of them, and see what's really implied in the theories of that school of thought.

CLEINIAS: By all means.

ATHENIAN: The facts show – so they claim – that the greatest and finest things in the world are the products of nature and chance, the creations of art being comparatively trivial. The works of nature, they say, are grand and primary, and constitute a ready-made source for all the minor works constructed and fashioned by art – *art*efacts, as they're generally called.

CLEINIAS: How do you mean?

ATHENIAN: I'll put it more precisely. They maintain that fire, water, earth and air owe their existence to nature and chance, and in no case to art, and that it is by means of these entirely inanimate substances[4] that the secondary physical bodies – the earth, sun, moon and stars – have been produced. These substances moved at random, each impelled by virtue of its own inherent properties, which depended on various suitable amalgamations of hot and cold, dry and wet, soft and hard, and all other haphazard combinations that inevitably resulted when the opposites were mixed. This is the process to which all the heavens and everything that is in them owe their birth, and the consequent establishment of the four seasons led to the appearance of all plants and living creatures. The cause of all this, they say, was neither intelligent planning, nor a deity, nor art, but – as we've explained – nature and chance. Art, the brain-child of these living creatures, arose later, the mortal child of mortal beings; it has produced, at a late stage, various amusing trifles that are hardly real at all –

4. Or possibly, 'by these entirely inanimate agencies' (i.e. nature and chance).

mere insubstantial images of the same order as the arts themselves (I mean for instance the productions of the arts of painting and music, and all their ancillary skills). But if there are in fact some techniques that produce worth-while results, they are those that *co-operate* with nature, like medicine and farming and physical training. This school of thought maintains that government, in particular, has very little to do with nature, and is largely a matter of art; similarly legislation is never a natural process but is based on technique, and its enactments are quite artificial.

CLEINIAS: What are you driving at?

ATHENIAN: My dear fellow, the first thing these people say about the gods is that they are artificial concepts corresponding to nothing in nature; they are legal fictions, which moreover vary very widely according to the different conventions people agree on when they produce a legal code. In particular, goodness according to nature and goodness according to the law are two different things, and there is no natural standard of justice at all. On the contrary, men are always wrangling about their moral standards and altering them, and every change introduced becomes binding from the moment it's made, regardless of the fact that it is entirely ⁸⁹⁰ artificial, and based on convention, not nature in the slightest degree. All this, my friends, is the theme of experts – as our young people regard them – who in their prose and poetry maintain that anything one can get away with by force is absolutely justified.[5] This is why we experience outbreaks of impiety among the young, who assume that the kind of gods the law tells them to believe in do not exist; this is why we get treasonable efforts to convert people to the 'true natural life', which is essentially nothing but a life of conquest over others, not one of service to your neighbour as the law enjoins.

CLEINIAS: What a pernicious doctrine you've explained, sir! It must be the ruin of the younger generation, both in the state at large and in private families.

5. Cf. p. 173.

THE DIFFICULTIES OF REFUTING
ATHEISTS

ATHENIAN: That's very true, Cleinias. So what do you think the legislator ought to do, faced with such a long-established thesis as this? Is he simply to stand up in public and threaten all the citizens with punishment if they don't admit the existence of gods and mentally accept the law's description of them? He could make the same threat about their notions of beauty and justice and all such vital concepts, as well as about anything that encourages virtue or vice: he could demand that the citizens' belief and actions should accord with his written instructions, and insist that anyone not showing the proper obedience to the laws must be punished either by death, or by a whipping and imprisonment, deprivation of civic rights, or by being sent into exile a poorer man. But what about *persuading* them? When he establishes a legal code for his people, shouldn't he try to talk them into being as amenable as he can make them?

CLEINIAS: Certainly, sir. If even limited persuasion can be applied in this field, no legislator of even moderate ability should shrink from making the effort. On the contrary, he should argue 'till the cows come home', as the saying is, to back up the old doctrine that the gods exist, and to support the other arguments you ran through just now. In particular, he should defend law itself and art as either part of nature or existing by reason of some no less powerful agency – being in fact, to tell the truth, creations of reason. That, I think, is the point you're making, and I agree.

ATHENIAN: Really, Cleinias, you *are* enthusiastic! But when these themes are presented as you suggest, in addresses composed for a popular audience, aren't they found rather difficult to understand? And don't the addresses tend to go on for ever?

CLEINIAS: Well, sir, we put up with one long discussion, about inebriation in the cause of culture, so surely we can tolerate another, about theology and so forth. And of course this helps intelligent legislation tremendously, because legal instructions, once written down, remain fixed and permanent, 891 ready to stand up to scrutiny for ever. So there's no reason for alarm if at first they make difficult listening, because your slow learner will be able to go back again and again and examine them. Nor does their length, provided they're useful, justify any man in committing what seems to me, at least, an impiety: I mean refusing to facilitate these explanations as best he can.

MEGILLUS: Yes, sir, I entirely approve of what Cleinias says.

ATHENIAN: As well you may, Megillus, and we must do as he suggests. Of course, if this sort of argument had not been disseminated so widely over pretty well the entire human race, there would be no call for arguments to prove the existence of gods. But in present circumstances we've no choice. When the most important laws are being trampled under foot by scoundrels, whose duty is it to rush to their defence, if not the legislator's?

MEGILLUS: Nobody's.

ATHENIAN: Now then, Cleinias, you must take your share in the explanation, so tell me your opinion again. I assume the upholder of this doctrine thinks of fire and water, earth and air as being the first of all substances, and this is precisely what he means by the term 'nature'; soul, he thinks, was derived from them, at a later stage. No, I do more than 'assume': I'd say he argues the point explicitly.

CLEINIAS: True.

ATHENIAN: Now then, by heaven, haven't we discovered the fountain-head, so to speak, of the senseless opinions of all those who have ever undertaken investigation into nature? Scrutinize carefully every stage in their argument, because it will be crucial if we can show that these people who have embraced impious doctrines and lead others on are using fallacious arguments rather than cogent ones – which I think is in fact the case.

CLEINIAS: You're right, but try to explain their error.

ATHENIAN: Well, it looks as if we have to embark on a rather unfamiliar line of argument.

CLEINIAS: Don't hesitate, sir. I realize you think we'll be straying outside legislation if we attempt such an explanation, but if this is the only way to reach agreement that the beings currently described as gods in our law are properly so described, then this, my dear sir, is the kind of explanation we must give.

THE PRIORITY OF SOUL (1)

ATHENIAN: So it looks as if I must now argue along rather unfamiliar lines. Well then, the doctrine which produces an impious soul also 'produces', in a sense, the soul itself, in that it denies the priority of what was in fact the first cause of the birth and destruction of all things, and regards it as a later creation. Conversely, it asserts that what actually came later, came first. That's the source of the mistake these people have made about the real nature of the gods.

892   CLEINIAS: So far, the point escapes me.

ATHENIAN: It's the *soul*, my good friend, that nearly everybody seems to have misunderstood, not realizing its nature and power. Quite apart from the other points about it, people are particularly ignorant about its birth. It is one of the *first* creations, born long before all physical things, and is the chief cause of all their alterations and transformations. Now if that's true, anything closely related to soul will necessarily have been created before material things, won't it, since soul itself is older than matter?

CLEINIAS: Necessarily.

ATHENIAN: Opinion, diligence, reason, art and law will be prior to roughness and smoothness, heaviness and lightness. In particular, the grand and primary works and creations, precisely *because* they come in the category 'primary', will be attributable to art. Natural things, and nature herself – to use the mistaken terminology of our opponents – will be secondary products deriving from art and reason.

CLEINIAS: Why do you say 'mistaken'?

ATHENIAN: When they use the term 'nature', they mean the process by which the primary substances were created. But if it can be shown that soul came first, not fire or air, and that it was one of the first things to be created, it will be quite correct to say that soul is preeminently natural. This is true, provided you can demonstrate that soul is older than matter, but not otherwise.

CLEINIAS: Very true.

ATHENIAN: So this is precisely the point we have to tackle next?

CLEINIAS: Of course.

ATHENIAN: It's an extremely tricky argument, and we old men must be careful not to be taken in by its freshness and novelty, so that it eludes our grasp and makes us look like ridiculous fools whose ambitious ideas lead to failure even in little things. Just consider. Imagine the three of us had to cross a river in spate, and I were the younger and had plenty of experience of currents. Suppose I said, 'I ought to try first on my own account, and leave you two in safety while I see if the river is fordable for you two older men as well, or if not, just how bad it is. If it turns out to be fordable, I'll then call you and put my experience at your disposal in helping you to cross; but if in the event it cannot be crossed by old men like yourselves, then the only risk has been mine.' Wouldn't that strike you as fair enough? The situation is the same now: the argument ahead runs too deep, and men as weak as you will probably get out of your depth. I want to prevent you novices in answering from being dazed and dizzied by a stream of questions, which would put you in an 893 undignified and humiliating position you'd find most unpleasant. So this is what I think I'd better do now: first I'll ask questions of myself, while you listen in safety; then I'll go over the answers again and in this way work through the whole argument until the soul has been thoroughly dealt with and its priority to matter proved.

CLEINIAS: We think that's a splendid idea, sir. Please act on your suggestion.

TEN KINDS OF MOTION

ATHENIAN: Come then, if ever we needed to call upon the help of God, it's now. Let's take it the gods have been most pressingly invoked to assist the proof of their own existence, and let's rely on their help as if it were a rope steadying us as we enter the deep waters of our present theme. Now when I'm under interrogation on this sort of topic, and such questions as the following are put to me, the safest replies seem to be these. Suppose someone asks 'Sir, do all things stand still, and does nothing move? Or is precisely the opposite true? Or do some things move, while others are motionless?' My reply will be 'I suppose some move and others remain at rest.' 'So surely there must be some *space* in which the stationary objects remain at rest, and those in motion move?' 'Of course.' 'Some of them, presumably, will do so in one location, others in several?' 'Do you mean', we shall reply, 'that "moving in one location" is the action of objects which are able to keep their centres immobile? For instance, there are circles which are said to "stay put" even though as a whole they are revolving.' 'Yes.' 'And we appreciate that when a disk revolves like that, points near and far from the centre describe circles of different radii in the same time; their motion varies according to these radii and is proportionately quick or slow. This motion gives rise to all sorts of wonderful phenomena, because these points simultaneously traverse circles of large and small circumference at proportionately high or low speeds – an effect one might have expected to be impossible.' 'You're quite right.' 'When you speak of motion in many locations I suppose you're referring to objects that are always leaving one spot and moving on to another. Sometimes their motion involves only one point of contact with their successive situations, sometimes several, as in rolling.

'From time to time objects meet; a moving one colliding with a stationary one disintegrates, but if it meets other objects travelling in the opposite direction they coalesce into a single intermediate substance, half one and half the other.' 'Yes, I agree to your statement of the case.' 'Further, such combination leads to an increase in bulk, while their separation leads to diminution – so long as the existing states of the objects remain unimpaired; but if either combination or separation entails the abolition of the existing state, the objects concerned are destroyed.

'Now, what conditions are always present when anything 894 is produced? Clearly, an initial impulse grows and reaches the second stage and then the third stage out of the second, finally (at the third stage) presenting percipient beings with something to perceive. This then is the process of change and alteration to which everything owes its birth. A thing exists as such so long as it is stable, but when it changes its essential state it is completely destroyed.'

So, my friends, haven't we now classified and numbered all forms of motion, except two?[6]

CLEINIAS: Which two?

ATHENIAN: My dear chap, they are the two which constitute the real purpose of every question we've asked.

CLEINIAS: Try to be more explicit.

ATHENIAN: What we really had in view was soul, wasn't it?

CLEINIAS: Certainly.

ATHENIAN: The one kind of motion is that which is permanently capable of moving other things but not itself; the other is permanently capable of moving *both* itself *and* other things by processes of combination and separation, increase and diminution, generation and destruction. Let these stand as two further distinct types in our complete list of motions.

CLEINIAS: Agreed.

ATHENIAN: So we shall put ninth the kind which always imparts motion to something else and is itself changed by

6. Transmitted and self-generating – the two fundamental to Plato's argument. The list of the other eight may be compiled in various ways: for details, see the notes *ad loc.* in E. B. England, *The Laws of Plato* (Manchester, 1921).

another thing. Then there's the motion that moves both itself and other things, suitable for all active and passive processes and accurately termed the source of change and motion in all things that exist. I suppose we'll call that the tenth.

CLEINIAS: Certainly.

ATHENIAN: Now which of our (roughly) ten motions should we be justified in singling out as the most powerful and radically effective?

CLEINIAS: We can't resist the conclusion that the motion which can generate itself is infinitely superior, and all the others are inferior to it.

ATHENIAN: Well said! So shouldn't we correct one or two inaccuracies in the points we've just made?

CLEINIAS: What sort of inaccuracy do you mean?

ATHENIAN: It wasn't quite right to call that motion the 'tenth'.

CLEINIAS: Why not?

ATHENIAN: It can be shown to be first, in ancestry as well as in power; the next kind – although oddly enough a moment ago we called it 'ninth' – we'll put second.

CLEINIAS: What are you getting at?

ATHENIAN: This: when we find one thing producing a change in another, and that in turn affecting something else, and so forth, will there ever be, in such a sequence, an original cause of change? How could anything whose motion is transmitted to it from something else be the *first* thing to effect an alteration? It's impossible. In reality, when something which has set itself moving effects an alteration in something, and that in turn effects something else, so that motion is transmitted to thousands upon thousands of things 895 one after another, the entire sequence of their movements must surely spring from some initial principle, which can hardly be anything except the change effected by self-generated motion.

CLEINIAS: You've put it admirably, and your point must be allowed.

ATHENIAN: Now let's put the point in a different way, and once again answer our own questions: 'Suppose the whole universe were somehow to coalesce and come to a standstill – the theory which most of our philosopher-fellows are actually bold enough to maintain – which of the motions we have enumerated would inevitably be the first to arise in it?' 'Self-generating motion, surely, because no antecedent impulse can ever be transmitted from something else in a situation where no antecedent impulse exists. Self-generating motion, then, is the source of all motions, and the primary force in both stationary and moving objects, and we shan't be able to avoid the conclusion that it is the most ancient and the most potent of all changes, whereas the change which is produced by something else and is in turn transmitted to other objects, comes second.'

CLEINIAS: You're absolutely right.

SOUL MOVES ITSELF

ATHENIAN: So now we've reached this point in our discussion, here's another question we should answer.

CLEINIAS: What?

ATHENIAN: If we ever saw this phenomenon – self-generating motion – arise in an object made of earth, water or fire (alone or in combination) how should we describe that object's condition?

CLEINIAS: Of course, what you're really asking me is this: when an object moves itself, are we to say that it is 'alive'?

ATHENIAN: That's right.

CLEINIAS: It emphatically is alive.

ATHENIAN: Well then, when we see that a thing has a soul, the situation is exactly the same, isn't it? We have to admit that it is alive.

CLEINIAS: Yes, exactly the same.

ATHENIAN: Now, for heaven's sake, hold on a minute. I suppose you'd be prepared to recognize three elements in any given thing?

CLEINIAS: What do you mean?

ATHENIAN: The first point is what the object actually *is*, the second is the definition of this, and the third is the name.

And in addition there are two questions to be asked about every existing thing.

CLEINIAS: Two?

ATHENIAN: Sometimes we put forward the mere name and want to know the definition, and sometimes we put forward the definition and ask for the name.

CLEINIAS: I take it the point we want to make at the moment is this.

ATHENIAN: What?

CLEINIAS: In general, things can be divided into two, and this is true of some numbers as well. Such a number has the *name* 'even' and its *definition* is 'a number divisible into two equal parts'.

ATHENIAN: Yes, that's the sort of thing I mean. So surely, in either case – whether we provide the name and ask for the definition or give the definition and ask for the name – we're referring to the same object? When we *call* it 'even' and *define* it as 'a number divisible into two', it's the same thing we're talking about.

CLEINIAS: It certainly is.

ATHENIAN: So what's the definition of the thing we call 896 the soul? Surely we can do nothing but use our formula of a moment ago: 'motion capable of moving itself'.

CLEINIAS: Do you mean that the entity which we all *call* 'soul' is precisely that which is *defined* by the expression 'self-generating motion'?

THE PRIORITY OF SOUL (2)

ATHENIAN: I do. And if this is true, are we still dissatisfied? Haven't we got ourselves a satisfactory proof that soul is identical with the original source of the generation and motion of all past, present and future things and their contraries? After all, it has been shown to be the cause of all change and motion in everything.

CLEINIAS: Dissatisfied? No! On the contrary, it has been proved up to the hilt that soul, being the source of motion, is the most ancient thing there is.

ATHENIAN: But when one thing is put in motion by another, it is never thereby endowed with the power of independent self-movement. Such derived motion will therefore come second, or as far down the list as you fancy relegating it, being a mere change in matter that quite literally 'has no soul'.

CLEINIAS: Correctly argued.

ATHENIAN: So it was an equally correct, final and complete statement of the truth, when we said that soul is prior to matter, and that matter came later and takes second place. Soul is the master, and matter its natural subject.

CLEINIAS: That is indeed absolutely true.

ATHENIAN: The next step is to remember our earlier admission that if soul were shown to be older than matter, the spiritual order of things would be older than the material.

CLEINIAS: Certainly.

ATHENIAN: So habits, customs, will, calculation, right opinion, diligence and memory will be prior creations to material length, breadth, depth and strength, if (as is true) soul is prior to matter.

CLEINIAS: Unavoidably.

ATHENIAN: And the next unavoidable admission, seeing that we are going to posit soul as the cause of *all* things, will be that it is the cause of good and evil, beauty and ugliness, justice and injustice and all the opposites.

CLEINIAS: Of course.

ATHENIAN: And surely it's necessary to assert that as soul resides and keeps control anywhere where anything is moved, it controls the heavens as well.

CLEINIAS: Naturally.

ATHENIAN: One soul, or more than one? I'll answer for you both: more than one. At any rate, we must not assume fewer than two: that which does good, and that which has the opposite capacity.

CLEINIAS: That's absolutely right.

ATHENIAN: Very well, then. So soul, by virtue of its own motions, stirs into movement everything in the heavens and on earth and in the sea. The names of the motions of soul are:

897 wish, reflection, diligence, counsel, opinion true and false, joy and grief, cheerfulness and fear, love and hate. Soul also uses all related or initiating motions which take over the secondary movements of matter and stimulate everything to increase or diminish, separate or combine, with the accompanying heat and cold, heaviness and lightness, roughness and smoothness, white and black, bitter and sweet. These are the instruments soul uses, whether it cleaves to divine reason (soul itself being, if the truth were told, a divinity), and guides everything to an appropriate and successful conclusion, or allies itself with unreason and produces completely opposite results. Shall we agree this is the case, or do we still suspect that the truth may be different?

CLEINIAS: By no means.

SOUL MOVES THE HEAVENLY BODIES

ATHENIAN: Well then, what kind of soul may we say has gained control of the heavens and earth and their entire cycle of movement? Is it the rational and supremely virtuous kind, or that which has neither advantage? Would you like our reply to run like this?

CLEINIAS: How?

ATHENIAN: 'If, my fine fellow' (we should say) 'the whole course and movement of the heavens and all that is in them reflect the motion and revolution and calculation of reason, and operate in a corresponding fashion, then clearly we have to admit that it is the best kind of soul that cares for the entire universe and directs it along the best path.'

CLEINIAS: True.

ATHENIAN: 'If however these things move in an unbalanced and disorganized way, we must say the evil kind of soul is in charge of them.'

CLEINIAS: That too is true.

ATHENIAN: 'So what is the nature of rational motion?' Now this, my friends, is a question to which it is difficult to give an answer that will make sense, so you're justified here in calling me in to help with your reply.

CLEINIAS: Good.

ATHENIAN: Still, in answering this question we mustn't assume that mortal eyes will ever be able to look upon reason and get to know it adequately: let's not produce darkness at noon, so to speak, by looking at the sun direct. We can save our sight by looking at an *image* of the object we're asking about.

CLEINIAS: How do you mean?

ATHENIAN: What about selecting from our list of ten motions the one which reason resembles, and taking that as our image? I'll join you in recalling it, and then we'll give a joint answer to the question.

CLEINIAS: Yes, that's probably your best method of explanation.

ATHENIAN: Do we still remember at any rate this from the list of points we made earlier, that all things are either in motion or at rest?

CLEINIAS: Yes, we do.

ATHENIAN: And some of those in motion move in a single location, others in a succession of locations?

898

CLEINIAS: That is so.

ATHENIAN: Of these two motions, that taking place in a single location necessarily implies continuous revolution round a central point, just like wheels being turned on a lathe; and this kind of motion bears the closest possible affinity and likeness to the cyclical movement of reason.

CLEINIAS: What do you mean?

ATHENIAN: Take reason on the one hand, and motion in a single location on the other. If we were to point out that in both cases the motion was determined by a single plan and procedure and that it was (a) regular, (b) uniform, (c) always at the same point in space, (d) around a fixed centre, (e) in the same position relative to other objects, and were to illustrate both by the example of a sphere being turned on a lathe, then no one could ever show us up for incompetent makers of verbal images.

CLEINIAS: You're quite right.

ATHENIAN: Now consider the motion that is never

uniform or regular or at the same point in space or round the same centre or in the same relative position or in a single location, and is neither planned nor organized nor systematic. Won't that motion be associated with every kind of unreason?

CLEINIAS: Absolutely true, it will.

ATHENIAN: So now there's no difficulty in saying right out that since we find that the entire cycle of events is to be attributed to soul, the heavens that we see revolving must necessarily be driven round – we have to say – because they are arranged and directed *either* by the best kind of soul *or* by the other sort.

CLEINIAS: Well, sir, judging from what has been said, I think it would be rank blasphemy to deny that their revolution is produced by one or more souls blessed with perfect virtue.

ATHENIAN: You've proved a most attentive listener, Cleinias. Now attend to this further point.

CLEINIAS: What?

ATHENIAN: If, in principle, soul drives round the sun, moon and the other heavenly bodies, does it not impel each individually?

CLEINIAS: Of course.

ATHENIAN: Let's take a single example: our results will then obviously apply to all the other heavenly bodies.

CLEINIAS: And your example is ... ?

ATHENIAN: ... the sun. Everyone can see its body, but no one can see its soul – not that you could see the soul of any other creature, living or dying. Nevertheless, there are good grounds for believing that we are in fact held in the embrace of some such thing though it is totally below the level of our bodily senses, and is perceptible by reason alone. So by reason and understanding let's get hold of a new point about the soul.

HOW SOUL MOVES THE HEAVENLY BODIES

CLEINIAS: What?

ATHENIAN: If soul drives the sun, we shan't go far wrong if we say that it operates in one of three ways.

CLEINIAS: And what are they?

ATHENIAN: Either (a) the soul resides within this visible spherical body and carries it wherever it goes, just as *our* soul takes us around from one place to another, or (b) it acquires its own body of fire or air of some kind (as certain people maintain), and impels the sun by the external contact of body with body, or (c) it is entirely immaterial, but guides the sun along its path by virtue of possessing some other prodigious and wonderful powers. 899

CLEINIAS: Yes, it must necessarily be by one of these methods that the soul manages the universe.

ATHENIAN: Now, just wait a minute. Whether we find that it is by stationing itself in the sun and driving it like a chariot, or by moving it from outside, or by some other means, that this soul provides us all with light, every single one of us is bound to regard it as a god. Isn't that right?

CLEINIAS: Yes, one would be absolutely stupid not to.

ATHENIAN: Now consider all the stars and the moon and the years and months and all the seasons: what can we do except repeat the same story? A soul or souls – and perfectly virtuous souls at that – have been shown to be the cause of all these phenomena, and whether it is by their living presence in matter that they direct all the heavens, or by some other means, we shall insist that these souls are gods. Can anybody admit all this and still put up with people who deny that 'everything is full of gods'?[7]

CLEINIAS: No sir, nobody could be so mad.

ATHENIAN: Now then, Megillus and Cleinias, let's delimit the courses of action open to anyone who has so far refused to believe in gods, and get rid of him.

CLEINIAS: You mean . . .

ATHENIAN: . . . *either* he should demonstrate to us that we're wrong to posit soul as the first cause to which everything owes its birth, and that our subsequent deductions were equally mistaken, *or*, if he can't put a better case than ours, he should let himself be persuaded by us and live the rest of his

7. A remark attributed to Thales (*c.* 600 B.C.), traditionally the first philosopher.

life a believer in gods. So let's review the thesis we argued for
the existence of gods against the non-believers: was it cogent
or feeble?

CLEINIAS: Feeble, sir? Not in the least.

ADDRESS TO THE BELIEVER IN THE
INDIFFERENCE OF THE GODS

ATHENIAN: Very well. So far as atheists are concerned, we
may regard our case as complete. Next we have to use some
gentle persuasion on the man who believes in gods but thinks
they are unconcerned about human affairs. 'My splendid
fellow,' we'll say, 'your belief in the existence of gods probably
springs from a kind of family tie between you and the gods
that draws you to your natural kin and makes you honour
them and recognize their existence. What drives you to impiety
is the good fortune of scoundrels and criminals in private and
public life – which in reality is not good fortune at all, although
it is highly admired as such by popular opinion and its mis-
placed enthusiasms: poetry and literature of every kind invest
it with a pernicious glamour. Or perhaps you observe men
reaching the end of their lives, full of years and honour,
900 leaving behind them their children's children, and your present
disquiet is because you've discovered (either from hearsay or
personal observation) a few of the many ghastly acts of impiety
which (you notice) are the very means by which some of these
people have risen from humble beginnings to supreme power
and dictatorships. The result is that although by virtue of your
kinship with the gods you'd clearly be reluctant to lay such
things at their door, your mental confusion and your inability
to find fault with them has brought you to your present
predicament where you believe they exist, but despise and
neglect human affairs. Now, we want to prevent your thoughts
from becoming more impious than they are already: let's see
if argument will ward off the disease while it is still in its early
stages. We must also try to make use of the original thesis we
argued so exhaustively against the absolute atheist, by linking
the next step in the exposition on to it.' So you, Cleinias and

Megillus, must do what you did before: take the young man's place and answer on his behalf. If any difficulty crops up in the argument, I'll take over from you two as I did just now, and conduct you across the river.

CLEINIAS: Good idea. You play your part, and we'll carry out your suggestions to the best of our ability.

PROOF THAT THE GODS CARE
FOR MANKIND

ATHENIAN: Still, perhaps it won't be too difficult to show our friend that gods are just as attentive to details as to important matters – more so, in fact. You see, he was here a moment ago and heard that their special job – an expression of their perfect virtue – is to watch over the universe.

CLEINIAS: Yes, he certainly did hear that said.

ATHENIAN: The next thing is for our opponents to join us in asking this question: what particular virtue have we in mind when we agree that the gods are good? Now then: don't we regard moderation and the possession of reason as a mark of virtue, and their opposites as marks of vice?

CLEINIAS: We do.

ATHENIAN: What about courage and cowardice? Are we agreed they come under virtue and vice respectively?

CLEINIAS: Certainly.

ATHENIAN: And we'll label the one set of qualities 'disgraceful' and the other 'admirable'?

CLEINIAS: Yes, we must.

ATHENIAN: And if the base qualities are characteristic of anyone, they are characteristic of us; the gods, we shall say, are *not* affected by them, either radically or slightly.

CLEINIAS: No one would disagree with that either.

ATHENIAN: Well, then, shall we regard neglect and idleness and riotous living as part of the soul's virtue? Or what's your view?

CLEINIAS: Really!

ATHENIAN: As part of vice, then?

CLEINIAS: Yes.

433

901 ATHENIAN: So it's the opposite qualities that will be ascribed to virtue?

CLEINIAS: Right.

ATHENIAN: Very well then. In our view, all idle and thoughtless *bons vivants* will be just the kind of people the poet said were 'like nothing so much as stingless drones'.[8]

CLEINIAS: Very apt, that.

ATHENIAN: So we mustn't say that God has precisely the sort of character he himself detests, and we mustn't allow any attempt to maintain such a view.

CLEINIAS: Of course not; it would be intolerable.

ATHENIAN: Take someone who has the special job of looking after some particular sphere of action, and who is preoccupied with his major duties to the neglect of the small. Could we possibly commend him, except for reasons that would ring quite hollow? Let's consider the point in this light: doesn't this sort of conduct – divine or human – fall into two categories?

CLEINIAS: Two categories, do we say?

ATHENIAN: *Either* a man thinks it makes no difference to his job as a whole if he neglects the details, *or* important though they are, he nevertheless lives in idleness and self-indulgence and neglects them. Or is there some other possible reason for his neglecting them? (Of course, if it is simply *impossible* to look after everything, and a god or some poor mortal fails to take care of something when he has not the strength and therefore the ability, no question of positive neglect of either major or minor duties will arise.)

CLEINIAS: No, of course not.

ATHENIAN: Now let our two opponents answer the questions of the three of us. They both admit gods exist, but one thinks they can be bought off, the other that they are careless about details. 'First of all, do you both admit that the gods know and see and hear everything, and that nothing within the range of our senses or intellect can escape them? Is this your position, or what?'

CLEINIAS: 'It is.'

8. Hesiod, *Works and Days*, 304.

ATHENIAN: 'And also, that they can do anything which is within the power of mortals and immortals?'

CLEINIAS: Yes, of course they'll agree to that too.

ATHENIAN: Further, the five of us have already agreed that the gods are good – supremely so, in fact.

CLEINIAS: Emphatically.

ATHENIAN: So surely, given they're the sort of beings we've admitted, it's absolutely impossible to agree that they do anything out of sloth and self-indulgence. Among us mortals, you see, laziness springs from cowardice, and sloth from laziness and self-indulgence.

CLEINIAS: That's very true.

ATHENIAN: Then no god neglects anything because of sloth and laziness, because no god, presumably, suffers from cowardice.

CLEINIAS: You're quite right.

ATHENIAN: Now if in fact they do neglect the tiny details 902 of the universe, the remaining possibilities are surely these: *either* they neglect them because they know that no such detail needs their attention, *or* – well, what other explanation could there be, except a lack of knowledge?

CLEINIAS: None.

ATHENIAN: So, my dearest sir, are we to interpret you as saying that the gods are ignorant, and display negligence where it is necessary to be solicitous, because they don't *know*? Or alternatively that they realize the necessity, but do what the most wretched of men are said to do, namely fail in their duty because they are somehow overcome by temptation or pain, even though they know that there are better options than the one they've in fact chosen?

CLEINIAS: Indeed not.

ATHENIAN: Now surely human life has something to do with the world of the soul, and man himself is the most god-fearing of all living creatures, isn't he?

CLEINIAS: I dare say.

ATHENIAN: And we regard all mortal creatures as possessions of gods, like the universe as a whole.

CLEINIAS: Of course.

ATHENIAN: So whether you argue these possessions count for little or much in the sight of the gods, in neither case would it be proper for our owners to neglect us, seeing how very solicitous and good they are. You see, there's another point we ought to consider here.

CLEINIAS: What?

ATHENIAN: It's a point about perception and physical strength. Aren't they essentially at opposite poles, so far as ease and difficulty are concerned?

CLEINIAS: What do you mean?

ATHENIAN: Although little things are more difficult to see or hear than big, they are much easier, when there are only a few of them, to carry or control or look after.

CLEINIAS: Yes, much easier.

ATHENIAN: Take a doctor who has been given the entire body to treat. Will he ever get good results if he neglects the individual limbs and tiny parts, in spite of being willing and able to look after the major organs?

CLEINIAS: No, never.

ATHENIAN: Nor yet will helmsmen or generals or house-holders, nor 'statesmen' or anybody of that ilk, succeed in major day-to-day matters if they neglect occasional details. You know how even masons say the big stones don't lie well without the small ones.

CLEINIAS: Of course.

ATHENIAN: So let's not treat God as less skilled than a mortal craftsman, who applies the same expertise to all the jobs in his own line whether they're big or small, and gets more finished and perfect results the better he is at his work. We must not suppose that God, who is supremely wise, and willing and able to superintend the world, looks to major 903 matters but – like a faint-hearted lazybones who throws up his hands at hard work – neglects the minor, which we established were in fact *easier* to look after.

CLEINIAS: No sir, we should never entertain such notions about gods. It's a point of view that would be absolutely impious and untrue.

ATHENIAN: Well, it looks to me as if we've given a pretty

complete answer to this fellow who's always going on about the negligence of heaven.

CLEINIAS: Yes, we have.

ATHENIAN: At any rate, our thesis has forced him to admit he was wrong. But I still think we need to find a form of words to *charm* him into agreement.[9]

CLEINIAS: Well, my friend, what do you suggest?

THE JUSTICE OF THE GODS, AND THE FATE OF THE SOUL

ATHENIAN: What we say to the young man should serve to convince him of this thesis: 'The supervisor of the universe has arranged everything with an eye to its preservation and excellence, and its individual parts play appropriate active or passive roles according to their various capacities. These parts, down to the smallest details of their active and passive functions, have each been put under the control of ruling powers that have perfected the minutest constituents of the universe. Now then, you perverse fellow, one such part – a mere speck that nevertheless constantly contributes to the good of the whole – is you, you who have forgotten that nothing is created except to provide the entire universe with a life of prosperity. You forget that creation is not for your benefit: *you* exist for the sake of the universe. Every doctor, you see, and every skilled craftsman always works for the sake of some end-product as a whole; he handles his materials so that they will give the best results in general, and makes the parts contribute to the good of the whole, not vice versa. But you're grumbling because you don't appreciate that your position is best not only for the universe but for you too, thanks to your common origin. And since a soul is allied with different bodies at different times, and perpetually undergoes all sorts of changes, either self-imposed or produced by some other soul, the divine draughts-player has nothing else to do except promote a soul with a promising character to a better situation, and relegate one that is deteriorating to an inferior,

9. See pp. 95–6 and 181 ff.

as is appropriate in each case, so that they all meet the fate they deserve.'

CLEINIAS: How do you mean?

ATHENIAN: I think my account explains how easy it could be for gods to control the universe. Suppose that in one's constant efforts to serve its interests one were to mould all that is in it by *transforming* everything (by turning fire into water permeated by soul, for instance), instead of producing variety from a basic unity or unity from variety, then after the first or second 904 or third stage of creation everything would be arranged in an infinite number of perpetually changing patterns.[10] But in fact the supervisor of the universe finds his task remarkably easy.

CLEINIAS: Again, what do you mean?

ATHENIAN: This. Our King saw (a) that all actions are a function of soul and involve a great deal of virtue and a great deal of vice, (b) that the combination of body and soul, while not an eternal creation like the gods sanctioned by law, is nevertheless indestructible[11] (because living beings could never have been created if one of these two constituent factors had been destroyed), (c) that one of them – the good element in soul – is naturally beneficial, while the bad element naturally does harm. Seeing all this he contrived a place for each constituent where it would most easily and effectively ensure the triumph of virtue and the defeat of vice throughout the universe. With this grand purpose in view he has worked out what sort of position, in what regions, should be assigned to a soul to match its changes of character; but he left it to the individual's acts of will to determine the *direction* of these changes. You see, the way we react to particular circumstances is almost invariably determined by our desires and our psychological state.

CLEINIAS: Likely enough.

ATHENIAN: 'So all things that contain soul change, the cause of their change lying within themselves, and as they

10. This sentence is analysed in 'Penology and Eschatology in Plato's *Timaeus* and *Laws*', *Classical Quarterly* 23 (1973), 232–44.

11. Presumably because it persists, in a sense, from generation to generation. The train of thought is none too clear.

change they move according to the ordinance and law of destiny. Small changes in unimportant aspects of character entail small horizontal changes of position in space, while a substantial decline into injustice sets the soul on the path to the depths of the so-called "under"world, which men call "Hades" and similar names, and which haunts and terrifies them both during their lives and when they have been sundered from their bodies. Take a soul that becomes particularly full of vice or virtue as a result of its own acts of will and the powerful influence of social intercourse. If companionship with divine virtue has made it exceptionally divine, it experiences an exceptional change of location, being conducted by a holy path to some superior place elsewhere. Alternatively, opposite characteristics will send it off to live in the opposite region. And in spite of your belief that the gods neglect you, my lad, or rather young man,

"This is the sentence of the gods that dwell upon Olympus"[12]

– to go to join worse souls as you grow worse and better souls as you grow better, and alike in life and all the deaths you suffer[13] to do and be done by according to the standards that birds of a feather naturally apply among themselves. Neither you nor anyone else who has got into trouble will ever be able to run fast enough to boast that he has escaped this sentence – a sentence to which the judges have attached special importance, and which one should take every possible care to avoid.[14] Make yourself ever so small and hide in the depths of the earth, or soar high into the sky: this sentence will be ever at your heels, and either while you're still alive on earth or after you've descended into Hades or been taken to some even more remote place, you'll pay the proper penalty of your crimes. You'll find the same is true of those whom you imagine have emerged from misery to happiness because you've seen them rise from a humble position to high estate by acts of impiety, or some similar wickedness. These actions, it seemed

12. Homer, *Odyssey* XIX, 43.
13. I.e. deaths preceding successive reincarnations, presumably.
14. Cf. p. 191.

to you, were like a mirror which reflected the gods' total lack of concern. But you didn't appreciate how the role of the gods contributes to the total scheme of things. What a bold fellow you must be, if you think you've no need of such knowledge! Yet without it no one will ever catch so much as a glimmer of the truth or be able to offer a reasoned account of happiness or misery in life. So if Cleinias here and this whole group of old men convince you that you don't really understand what you're saying about the gods, then the divine assistance will be with you. But it may be that you need some further explanation, so if you have any sense you'll listen while we address our third opponent.'

Now as far as I'm concerned, we've proved, not too inadequately, that gods exist and care for mankind. However, there remains the view that they can be bought off by the gifts of sinners. No one should ever assent to this thesis, and we must fight to the last ditch to refute it.

CLEINIAS: Well said. Let's do as you suggest.

ATHENIAN: Look – in the name of the gods themselves! – *how* would they be bought off, supposing they ever were? What would they have to be? What sort of being would do this? Well, if they are going to run the entire universe for ever, presumably they'll have to be rulers.

CLEINIAS: True.

ATHENIAN: Now then, what sort of ruler do the gods in fact resemble?[15] Or rather, what rulers resemble them? Let's compare small instances with great, and see what rulers will serve our purpose. What about drivers of competing teams of horses, or steersmen of boats in a race? Would they be suitable parallels? Or we might compare the gods to commanders of armies. Again, it could be that they're analogous to doctors concerned to defend the body in the war against 906 disease, or to farmers anxiously anticipating the seasons that usually discourage the growth of their crops, or to shepherds. Now since we've agreed among ourselves that the universe is full of many good things and many bad as well, and that the

15, The train of thought seems to pick up from the 'ruling' powers on p. 437.

latter outnumber the former, we maintain that the battle we have on our hands is never finished, and demands tremendous vigilance. However, gods and spirits are fighting on our side, the gods and spirits whose chattels we are. What ruins us is injustice and senseless aggression; what protects us is justice and sensible moderation – virtues that are part of the spiritual characteristics of the gods, although one can find them quite clearly residing among us too, albeit on a small scale. Now there are some souls living on earth in possession of ill-gotten gains, who in their obviously brutish way throw themselves before the souls of their guardians (whether watch-dogs, shepherds, or masters of the utmost grandeur)[16] and by wheedling words and winning entreaties try to persuade them of the truth of the line put about by scoundrels – that they have the right to feather their nest with impunity at mankind's expense. But I suppose our view is that this vice we've named – acquisitiveness – is what is called 'disease' when it appears in flesh and blood, and 'plague' when brought by the seasons or at intervals of years; while if it occurs in the state and society, the same vice turns up under yet another name: 'injustice'.[17]

CLEINIAS: Certainly.

ATHENIAN: Thus anyone who argues that gods are always indulgent to the unjust man and the criminal, provided they're given a share in the loot, must in effect be prepared to say that if wolves, for instance, were to give watch-dogs a small part of their prey, the dogs would be appeased by the gift and turn a blind eye to the plundering of the flock. Isn't this what people are really suggesting when they say that gods can be squared?

CLEINIAS: It certainly is.

ATHENIAN: So consider all those guardians we instanced

16. In this parenthesis an illustration (animals trying to escape watch-dogs etc.) and the point to be illustrated (men trying to deceive their masters) are hardly distinguished.

17. Disease, plague and injustice are all thought of as examples of *excess*, the encroachment of one element in the body, etc., on the others. In society this vice appears as the desire to get more than others ('acquisitiveness').

a moment ago. Can one compare gods to any of them, without making oneself ridiculous? What about steersmen who are turned from their course 'by libations and burnt offerings',[18] and wreck both the ship and its crew?

CLEINIAS: Of course not.

ATHENIAN: And presumably they are not to be compared to a charioteer lined up at the starting point who has been bribed by a gift to throw the race and let others win.

CLEINIAS: No sir, to describe the gods like that would be a scandalous comparison.

ATHENIAN: Nor, of course, do they stand comparison with generals or doctors or farmers, or herdsmen, or dogs beguiled by wolves.

CLEINIAS: What blasphemy! The very idea!

ATHENIAN: Now aren't all the gods the most supreme guardians of all, and don't they look after our supreme interests?

CLEINIAS: Very much so.

ATHENIAN: So are we really going to say that these guardians of the most valuable interests, distinguished as they are for their personal skill in guarding, are inferior to dogs, or the mere man in the street, who'll never abandon justice, in spite of the gifts that the unjust immorally press upon him?

CLEINIAS: Of course not. That's an intolerable thing to say. There's no sort of impiety that men won't commit, but anyone who persists in this doctrine bids fair to be condemned – and with every justification – as the worst and most impious of the impious.

TRANSITION TO THE LAW OF IMPIETY

ATHENIAN: Can we now say that our three theses – that the gods exist, that they are concerned for us, and that they are absolutely above being corrupted into flouting justice – have been adequately proved?

CLEINIAS: Certainly, and we endorse these arguments of yours.

18. Homer, *Iliad* IX, 500.

ATHENIAN: Still, I fancy that being so anxious to get the better of these scoundrels, we've put our case rather polemically. But what prompted this desire to come out on top, my dear Cleinias, was a fear that the rogues should think that victory in argument was a licence to do as they please and act on any and every theological belief they happen to hold. Hence our anxiety to speak with some force. However, if we've made even a small contribution to persuading those fellows to hate themselves and cherish the opposite kind of character, then this preface of ours to the law of impiety will have been well worth composing.

CLEINIAS: Well, there is that hope. But even without those results, the lawgiver will not be at fault for having discussed such a topic.

ATHENIAN: Now then, after the preface we'll have a form of words that convey the purpose of our laws – a general promulgation to all the ungodly that they should abandon their present habits in favour of a life of piety. Then in cases of disobedience the following law of impiety should apply:

Anyone who comes across a case of impiety of word or deed should go to the aid of the law by alerting the authorities. The first officials to be notified should bring the matter, in due legal form, before the court appointed to try this category of case.

58. If an official who hears of the incident fails to perform this duty,
   he must himself be liable to a charge of impiety at the hands of anyone who wishes to champion the cause of the laws.

When verdicts of 'guilty' are returned, the court is to assess a separate penalty for each impious act of each offender. Imprisonment is to apply in all cases. (The state will have three prisons: (1) a public one near the market-place for the general run of offenders, where large numbers may be kept in safe custody, (2) one called the 'reform centre' near the place where the Nocturnal Council[19] assembles, and (3) another in the heart of the countryside, in a solitary spot where the

19. See further pp. 502–3 and 515 ff.

terrain is at its wildest; and the title of this prison is somehow to convey the notion of 'punishment'.)

TWO KINDS OF OFFENDERS

Now since impiety has three causes, which we've already described, and each is divided into two kinds, there will be six categories of religious offenders worth distinguishing; and the punishment imposed on each should vary in kind and degree. Consider first a complete atheist: he may have a naturally just character and be the sort of person who hates scoundrels, and because of his loathing of injustice is not tempted to commit it; he may flee the unjust and feel fondness for the just. Alternatively, besides believing that all things are 'empty of' gods,[20] he may be a prey to an uncontrollable urge to experience pleasure and avoid pain, and he may have a retentive memory and be capable of shrewd insights. Both these people suffer from a common failing, atheism, but in terms of the harm they do to others the former is much less dangerous than the latter. The former will talk with a complete lack of inhibition about gods and sacrifices and oaths, and by poking fun at other people will probably, if he continues unpunished, make converts to his own views. The latter holds the same opinions but has what are called 'natural gifts': full of cunning and guile, he's the sort of fellow who'll make a diviner and go in for all sorts of legerdemain; sometimes he'll turn into a dictator or a demagogue or a general, or a plotter in secret rites; and he's the man who invents the tricks of the so-called 'sophists'.[21] So there can be many different types of atheist, but for the purpose of legislation they need to be divided into two groups. The dissembling atheist deserves to die for his sins not just once or twice but many times, whereas the other kind needs simply admonition combined with incarceration. The idea that gods take no notice of the world similarly produces two more categories, and the belief that they can be squared another two. So much for our distinctions.

20. An intentional inversion of the saying on p. 431.
21. Literally, 'wise men'.

THE PUNISHMENT FOR IMPIETY

59. (a) Those who have simply fallen victim to foolishness
and who do not have a bad character and disposition
should be sent to the reform centre by the judge in accordance
with the law for a term of not less than five years, and during 909
this period no citizen must come into contact with them
except the members of the Nocturnal Council, who should
pay visits to admonish them and ensure their spiritual
salvation.

    (b) When his imprisonment is over, a prisoner who
        appears to be enjoying mental health should go and
        live with sensible people; but if appearances turn
        out to have been deceptive, and he is reconvicted
        on a similar charge,
he should be punished by death.

There are others, however, who in addition to not recognizing the existence of gods, or believing they are unconcerned
about the world or can be bought off, become sub-human.
They take everybody for fools, and many a man they delude
during his life; and then by saying after his death that they can
conjure up his spirit, and by promising to influence the gods
through the alleged magic powers of sacrifices and prayers and
charms, they try to wreck completely whole homes and states
for filthy lucre.

60. If one of these people is found guilty,
the court must sentence him to imprisonment as prescribed
by law in the prison in the centre of the country; no
free man is to visit him at any time, and slaves must hand
him his ration of food fixed by the Guardians of the
Laws. When he dies the body must be cast out over the
borders of the state unburied.

61. If any free man lends a hand in burying him,
he must be liable to a charge of impiety at the hands of
anyone who cares to prosecute.

If the prisoner leaves children suitable for citizenship,

the guardians of orphans must look after them too, from the day of their father's conviction, no less than ordinary orphans.

PRIVATE SHRINES

All these offenders must be covered by one general law, which by forbidding illegal religious practices will cause most of them to sin less in word and deed against religion, and which in particular will do something to enlighten them. The following comprehensive law should be enacted to deal with all these cases.

No one is to possess a shrine in his own private home. When a man takes it into his head to offer sacrifice, he is to go to the public shrines in order to do so, and he should hand over his offerings to the priests and priestesses responsible for consecrating them; then he, and anyone else he may wish to participate, should join in the prayers. The grounds for these stipulations are as follows. To establish gods and temples is not easy; it's a job that needs to be very carefully pondered if it is to be done properly. Yet look at what people usually do – all women in particular, invalids of every sort, men in danger or any kind of distress, or conversely when they have just won a measure of prosperity: they dedicate the first thing that comes to hand, they swear to offer sacrifice, and promise to 910 found shrines for gods and spirits and children of gods. And the terror they feel when they see apparitions, either in dreams or awake – a terror which recurs later when they recollect a whole series of visions – drives them to seek a remedy for each individually, with the result that on open spaces or any other spot where such an incident has occurred they found the altars and shrines that fill every home and village. The law now stated must be observed not only for all these reasons but also in order to deter the impious from managing to conduct these activities too in secret, by establishing shrines and altars in private houses, calculating to win the favour of the gods on the quiet by sacrifices and prayers. This would make their wickedness infinitely worse, and bring the reproach of heaven both on themselves and on the virtuous people who tolerate them, so that, by a sort of rough justice, the whole state would catch the infection of their impiety. Still, God won't blame the legislator, because this is the law to be enacted:

The possession of shrines in private houses is forbidden. If a man is proved to possess and worship at shrines other than the public ones, and the injustice committed is not an act of serious impiety (whether the possessor is a man or a woman), anyone who notices the fact must lay information before the Guardians of the Laws, who should give orders for the removal of the private shrines to public temples.

62. (a) If the culprits disobey,
they must be punished until they carry out the removal.

    (b) But if a man is proved guilty of a serious act of impiety typical of an adult, and not just the peccadillo of a child, either by establishing a shrine on private land or by sacrificing on public land to gods not included in the pantheon of the state,

he must be punished by death for sacrificing with impure hands.

The Guardians of the Laws, after deciding whether the crime was a childish peccadillo or not, must then take the matter straight to court, and exact from the culprits the penalty for their impiety.

The Athenian now embarks on a long series of explanations, pre-ambles and laws on a wide variety of topics. At first sight, his exposition is chaotic, but close examination of the sequence of his thought will show that this is simply the result of letting the subject in hand suggest a fresh one. For instance, at the end of §24, in dealing with the respect due to parents, he provides that a slave should be protected from injury in revenge for giving information against someone who has committed a crime. But this almost casual remark reminds him that he has not yet dealt fully with all types of injury, so he launches into a discussion of injuries inflicted by the use of drugs and charms, in order to fill this gap in his legislation. Sometimes he tries, somewhat laboriously, to justify a transition from one subject to another – as for example that from 'Lunacy' to 'Abuse' (p. 482). Such explanations are not simply literary devices to connect disparate subjects, but (I conjecture) the fruit of systematic analysis and classification carried on in the Academy. But some of his changes of subject are abrupt and quite unexplained, and there are passages that look like a mere series of jottings. However, the next three sections form reasonably coherent wholes and I have called them The Law of Property, Commercial Law and Family Law. Thereafter, no single theme appears to predominate, and I have been forced to call §25 'Miscellaneous Legislation'. Yet even this welter of regulations shows signs of being not entirely unplanned. The passage dealing with the Scrutineers, who investigate the conduct of other officials, comes naturally towards the end of the legislation; the discussion of relations with the outside world seems to have been reserved until this late stage in view of its relevance to the philosophical activities of the Nocturnal Council, which as the supreme power in the state is discussed last of all; and the rules for funerals appropriately round off the section and indeed the entire legal code.

§22. THE LAW OF PROPERTY

There is little in this section that needs special comment. It is concerned not with the inalienable estate, which has been dealt with earlier (§9), but with movable property – of which slaves, of course, are one kind (a point of view that was almost universal in the Greek world). The rules about freedmen are tougher than those of Attic law, noticeably in the provision for the summary arrest of a freedman who fails in his duties to his former master; Attic law permitted only a charge of delinquency under ordinary legal procedure. Plato clearly believes that however much a freedman may have deserved his emancipation, he still needs the rigorous treatment he received when a slave.

RESPECT FOR PROPERTY

ATHENIAN: The next subject needing to be reduced to due order will be our transactions with each other. I suppose something like this will serve as a general rule. Ideally, no one should touch my property or tamper with it, unless I have given him some sort of permission; and if I am sensible I shall treat the property of others with the same respect.

REMOVAL OF BURIED TREASURE

Let's take as our first example treasure which someone who was not one of my ancestors stored away for himself and his family. I should never pray to the gods to come across such a thing; and if I do, I must not disturb it nor tell the diviners, as they are called, who (I shall find) can always invent some reason for advising one to remove something deposited in the ground. The financial benefit I'd get from removing it could never rival what I'd gain by way of virtue and moral rectitude by leaving it alone; by preferring to have justice in my soul rather than money in my pocket, I'd get – treasure for treasure – the better bargain, and for a better part of myself, too.

'Hands off immovables'[1] is aptly applied to a great many situations, and this is one of them. And we should put our trust in the traditional view of such conduct – that it injures our descendants. Suppose a man takes no thought for his children and becomes indifferent to the legislator, and removes what neither he himself nor his father nor any of his fathers before him deposited, without the consent of the depositor; suppose he thus undermines the finest law there is, that simple rule of thumb, formulated as it was by a man of great nobility,[2] 'Don't pick up what you didn't put down' – well, when a man treats these *two* legislators[3] so contemptuously and picks up something he had not put down (and sometimes no bagatelle, either, but a huge treasure trove), what penalty should he suffer? God knows the penalty of heaven; but the first person to notice such an occurrence in the city should report it to the City-Wardens; if somewhere in the city's market, to the Market-Wardens; and if in some place in the country, he should inform the Country-Wardens and their Chiefs. On receiving the information the state should send to Delphi and in submission to the oracles of the god do whatever he ordains about the objects and the person who removed them. If the informant is a free man, he should acquire a reputation for virtue, but

914

63. (a) if a free man fails to inform,
he must get a reputation for vice.

If the informant is a slave, then as a reward he will deservedly be presented with freedom by the state, which will give his master what he is worth, but

(b) if a slave fails to inform,
he must be punished by death.

REMOVAL OF PROPERTY IN GENERAL

The natural thing to do next is to apply this same rule to all objects, important or trivial. If a man leaves some piece of his own property somewhere, deliberately or inadvertently, any-

1. Cf. pp. 130 and 343.   2. Solon.
3. Solon and the Magnesian legislator.

one who finds it should let it be, on the assumption that such things are under the protection of the goddess of the wayside, to whom they are consecrated by law.

64. If in defiance of this rule someone picks up an object of no great value and takes it home, and

(a) he is a slave,

he should be soundly beaten by any passer-by who is not less than thirty years of age;

(b) if he is a free man,

in addition to being thought ungentlemanly and lawless, he must pay the person who left the article ten times its value.

If one man accuses another of being in possession of some piece of his own property, whether valuable or not, and the accused person admits he has it but denies that it belongs to the complainant, the latter should – if the object has been registered with the authorities according to law[4] – summon the person in possession of it before the authorities, and the possessor must produce it; then if on being presented for inspection it proves to have been recorded in the registers as the property of one of the disputants, the owner must take it and depart; but if it belongs to some other party not present, then whichever disputant furnishes a credit-worthy guarantor should exercise the absent party's right of removal and take the article away on his behalf for delivery into his possession. If on the other hand the article in dispute has not been registered with the authorities, it must be left with the three oldest officials pending settlement of the case; and if it is an animal that is thus kept in safe custody, the loser of the suit must pay the officials for its keep. The officials are to settle the case within three days.

THE TREATMENT OF SLAVES AND FREEDMEN

Anyone who wishes – provided he's in his right mind – may seize his own slave, and (within the permitted limits) treat

4. See p. 226.

him as he likes. He may also arrest a runaway slave, in order to stop him escaping, on behalf of a relative or friend. If anyone demands the release of someone who is being taken for a slave and arrested, the captor must let him go, but the releaser must furnish three credit-worthy sureties. On these terms and on no other the man may be released.

65. If a man secures a release except on these conditions, he must be liable to a charge of violence and if convicted, *he must* pay to the captor twice the damages claimed in the suit.

915

Freedmen too may be arrested if they fail to perform their services to their manumittor, or perform them inadequately. (The services are these: three times a month a freedman must proceed to the home of his manumittor and offer to do anything lawful and practicable; and as regards marrying he must do whatever his former master thinks right.) He must not grow more wealthy than his manumittor; if he does, the excess must become the property of the master. The freedman must not stay in the state longer than twenty years, but like the other aliens[5] he must then take all his property and leave, unless he has gained permission from the authorities and his manumittor to remain. If a freedman or one of the other aliens acquires property in excess of the limit allowed the third property-class,[6] then within thirty days of this event he must pack up and be off, without any right to ask the authorities to extend his stay.

66. If a freedman disobeys these regulations and is taken to court and convicted, *he must* be punished by death and his property confiscated by the state.

Such cases should be tried in the tribal courts, unless the litigants have previously settled their charges against each other before their neighbours – that is, judges they have chosen themselves.

5. See p. 354.   6. See pp. 214–15 and 226.

§23. COMMERCIAL LAW

Plato's trading regulations are all of a piece with what we have already learned of the economy of Magnesia (§§9, 15). Commerce is to be reduced to the smallest possible compass; credit trading is to be discouraged by the rule that defaulters may not be prosecuted. The purpose of trade should be the redistribution of goods, not the maximization of the trader's profits. It looks as if Plato had at some time been stung by inn-keepers, and his indignant tirade against them sounds like a cri de coeur.

THE LAW OF SALE AND EXCHANGE

If a man formally seizes as his own any animal or some other piece of property of any other man, the person in possession must return it to the warrantor or donor, provided the latter is suable and solvent, or to the person who validly transferred it to him by some other procedure. If he received it from a citizen or a resident alien, he must do so within thirty days; but if he took delivery from a complete alien, he must return it within the five months of which the third shall be the month in which the summer solstice occurs.

When one person makes an exchange with another by buying or selling, the transfer must be made by handing over the article in the appointed part of the market-place (and nowhere else), and by receiving the price on the nail; no payment for delivery later or sale on credit is to be allowed. If a man exchanges one thing for another in any other place or under any other arrangement, trusting to the honesty of the other party to the exchange, he must do so on the understanding that when sales are made other than under the rules now stated the law does not permit him to sue. (Anyone may collect contributions to clubs on a friendly basis, but if some disagreement arises over the collection he must do so on the understanding that in this business no one under any circumstances will be allowed to go to law.)

A seller of an article who receives a price of fifty drachmas or more must be obliged to remain in the state for ten days, 916 and the buyer (in view of the complaints that people are apt to make in this connexion, and so that, if necessary, restitution may be made according to law) must be informed of his address. Here are the rules under which legal restitution may be demanded or refused. If someone sells a slave suffering from consumption or stone or strangury or the so-called 'sacred' disease[1] or some other mental or physical complaint that is chronic and difficult to cure and which the ordinary man could not diagnose, and if the purchase was made by a doctor or trainer, or if the facts were pointed out before the time of sale, the buyer shall have no right to return him to the vendor. But if a layman is sold such a slave by a professional, the purchaser may return him within six months, except in the case of the 'sacred' disease, when the period for restitution is to be extended to a year. The case should be heard before a bench of three doctors appointed by joint nomination of the parties, and if the vendor loses he must pay twice the selling price. If a layman sells to a layman there should be a right of restitution and a hearing as in the previous instance, but the loser should pay only the simple price. If the slave is a murderer, and both buyer and seller are aware of the fact, there shall be no right of restitution for the purchase; but if the buyer acted in ignorance he shall have a right of restitution as soon as he realizes the situation, and the case should be tried before the five youngest Guardians of the Laws; if the vendor is judged to have known the facts, he must purify the house of the buyer under the Expounders' rules and pay him three times the price.

Anyone exchanging money for money or for anything else, animate or inanimate, should always give and receive full value as the law directs. Let's do as we did in other parts of our legislation and allow ourselves a preface dealing with the whole range of crimes that arise in this connexion.

Everyone should think of adulteration as essentially the same sort of thing as lying and deceit – which in fact people

1. Epilepsy.

commonly describe as quite respectable. But they are wrong to defend this sort of conduct as 'frequently justified, on appropriate occasions', because what they mean by the 'appropriate' place and occasion they leave vague and indefinite, and their dictum does nothing but harm both to themselves and to others. Now a legislator cannot afford to leave this vague: he must always lay down precise limits, however wide or narrow they may be. So let's define some limits now: a man must tell no lie, commit no deceit, and do no fraud in word or deed when he calls upon the gods, unless he wants to be thoroughly loathed by them – as 917 anyone is who snaps his fingers at them and swears false oaths, or (though they find this less offensive) tells lies in the presence of his superior. Now the 'superiors' of bad men are the good, and of the young their elders (usually) – which means that parents are the superiors of their offspring, men are (of course) the superiors of women and children, and rulers of their subjects. All these people in positions of authority deserve the respect of us all, and the authorities of the state deserve it in particular. This is in fact what prompted these remarks. Anyone who is so lacking in respect for men and reverence for the gods as to pull off some swindle of the market-place by swearing oaths and calling heaven to witness (even though the rules and warnings of the Market-Wardens stare him in the face), is a liar and a cheat. So in view of the low level of religious purity and holiness most of us generally achieve, let me emphasize what a good habit it is to think twice before taking the names of the gods in vain.

If any cases of disobedience arise, the following law should be invoked: the seller of any article in the market must never name two prices for his goods, but only one, and if he doesn't get it, he will (quite rightly) remove his wares without raising or lowering his price that day; and he must not push anything he has for sale, or take an oath on its quality.

67. If a man disobeys these regulations,
any citizen passing by, provided he is not less than thirty

years of age, should punish the taker of the oath and beat him with impunity.

68. If the passer-by ignores these instructions and disobeys them,
he must be liable to the reproach of having betrayed the laws.

If a man proves to be beyond persuasion by our present address and sells a faulty article, the passer-by who has the knowledge and ability to expose him should prove his case before the authorities, and, if a slave or resident alien, may then take the faulty article for himself; a citizen, however, should dedicate it to the gods of the market-place.

69. If a citizen fails to expose the offender,
he should be pronounced a rogue, as he has cheated the gods.

70. Anyone discovered selling such adulterated merchandise,
apart from being deprived of it, must be whipped (one lash for every drachma of the asking price of the object he was selling), after a herald has announced in the market-place the reason why the culprit is going to be flogged.

The Market-Wardens and the Guardians of the Laws, having ascertained from experts the details of the adulterations and malpractices of sellers, should record in writing rules which specify what vendors must and must not do; these regulations should then be inscribed on a pillar and displayed in front of the Market-Wardens' office for the information of those
918 who transact business in the market-place. (As for the City-Wardens, we have already given an adequate description of their duties,[2] but if it seems some additional rules are needed, the wardens should consult the Guardians of the Laws, write out what they think missing, and record both the new and the old rules of their office on a pillar in front of their quarters.)

RETAIL TRADE

Hard on the heels of tricks of adulteration come the practices of retail trade. First we should give a word of advice on the

2. See pp. 237–8.

whole subject, then lay down legislation for it. The natural function in the state of retail trading in general is not to do harm, but quite the opposite. When goods of any kind are distributed disproportionately and unequally, anyone who makes the distribution equal and even cannot fail to do good. It needs to be stated that this redistribution, in which money too plays an effective role, is precisely the purpose the trader is meant to serve. Hired labourers, inn-keepers and other workmen of varying degrees of respectability all perform the function of satisfying the needs of the community by ensuring an even distribution of goods. Why then is trading thought to be such a low and disreputable occupation? Why has it come to be so abused? Let's see if we can discover the reason, so that we can use our legislation to reform at any rate some branches of commerce, even if not the whole institution. This looks like an important task that calls for exceptional resource.

CLEINIAS: How do you mean?

ATHENIAN: My dear Cleinias, only a small part of mankind – a few highly-educated men of rare natural talent – is able to steel itself to moderation when assailed by various needs and desires; given the chance to get a lot of money, it's a rare bird that's sober enough to prefer a modest competence to wealth. Most people's inclinations are at the opposite pole: their demands are always violent demands, and they brush aside the opportunity of modest gain in favour of insatiable profiteering. That's why all branches of retailing, trade and inn-keeping suffer from abuse and extreme unpopularity. Now here's something I'm determined to mention, ludicrous though it is; it'll never happen, and Heaven help us if it did. But just picture to yourselves some eminently virtuous men forced for a time to go in for inn-keeping or retailing or some similar occupation, or some eminently virtuous women similarly forced by some stroke of fate to take up that kind of life. We'd soon realize how desirable and pleasing each of these trades really is, and if they were carried on according to honest standards we'd value them all as highly as we do our mother or our nurse. But what happens? A man goes off to some remote point on a road running through the middle of

919 nowhere and sets up his establishment to sell provisions; he receives the weary traveller with welcome lodging – peace and quiet for the victim of violent storms, cool refreshment for the sufferer from stifling heat – but then instead of greeting them as friends and offering them in addition to his hospitality some gifts as a token of good-will, he treats them like so many enemy prisoners that have fallen into his hands, and holds them up to ransom for a monstrously steep and iniquitous sum. It's these and similar swindles, which are practised in all branches of the trade, that have given the occupation of helping the worn-out traveller such a bad name, and in every case the legislator has to find a remedy. The old saying is quite right: it's difficult to fight against two enemies, especially when they are fundamentally different (as with diseases, for instance, and there are a lot of other examples). Our present battle is a case in point: it is a battle against two foes, wealth and poverty – wealth that corrupts our souls by luxury, poverty that drives us by distress into losing all sense of shame. So what remedy for this disease will be open to an enlightened community? First, it should keep its trading class as small as possible; second, trade should be made over to a class of people whose corruption will not harm the state unduly; third, some means must be found to prevent those engaging in such activities from slipping too easily into an utterly shameless and small-minded way of life.

After these remarks, our law on the subject should run like this, with Heaven's blessing: God is now re-establishing and re-founding Magnesia, and no inhabitant who holds one of the 5040 hearths must ever, willingly or otherwise, become a retailer or a wholesaler, or perform any service whatever for private individuals who are not his equals in status, with the exception of those services that a free man will naturally render to his father and mother and remoter ancestors, and to all free persons older than himself. Of course, it is not easy to lay down in a law precisely what is consistent with the dignity of a free man and what is not, and the point will have to be determined by those who have won distinctions for their aversion to the latter and devotion to the former. Anyone who by some trick goes in for retail trading in a way forbidden to a gentleman[3] should be indicted by anyone who wishes before a court of judges with a high reputation for virtue, on a charge of disgracing his clan.

71. If he is judged to be sullying his paternal hearth by following an unworthy calling,

he must be imprisoned for a year and so be taught to refrain from such conduct.

72. If he does not then refrain,

he must be imprisoned for two years, and the period of imprisonment must be doubled indefinitely on each subsequent conviction.

Now for a second law: anyone who intends to go in for retail trading must be either a resident alien or a temporary visitor. Thirdly, as a third law, such people must behave with as much virtue and as little vice as possible while they share in the life of the state. To that end, the Guardians of the Laws must not simply be regarded as guardians of those whom it is easy to keep from wickedness and crime thanks to their good birth and education. There are those who do not enjoy such advantages, and need more careful supervision, because they engage in pursuits which are very powerful inducements to vice. So since retail trading is an occupation of great variety and embraces many cognate activities, the Guardians of the Laws must hold a meeting about it, or at any rate about such branches of it as they have concluded are unavoidable and essential to the state, after the others have been eliminated; and just as we ordered in the case of adulteration – a closely connected matter – experts in each branch should be in attendance. The meeting must see what ratio of expenditure to receipts will give the retailer a decent profit, and the ratio arrived at must be recorded in writing, put on display, and then imposed on the various traders by the Market-Wardens, City-Wardens and Country-Wardens. Perhaps thus retail trade will benefit the population at large and do minimum harm to those members of society who engage in it.

3. That is, I take it, a gentleman may sell wholesale to, and buy retail from, a trader; but he may not *be* a retail trader himself.

CONTRACTS

If a man fails to fulfil an agreed contract – unless he had contracted to do something forbidden by law or decree, or gave his consent under some iniquitous pressure, or was involuntarily prevented from fulfilling his contract because of some unlooked-for accident – an action for such an unfulfilled agreement should be brought in the tribal courts, if the parties have not previously been able to reconcile their differences before arbitrators (their neighbours, that is).

DEALINGS WITH CRAFTSMEN

The class of craftsmen who have enriched our lives by their arts and skills will have Athena and Hephaestus as its patrons, while Ares and Athena will be patrons of those who protect the products of these craftsmen by skills of a different order – the techniques of defence. (The consecration of this latter class to these gods is perfectly justified, in that both classes are in the continuous service of land and people, the latter by taking the lead in the struggles of war, the former by producing tools and goods in return for pay.) So if they respect their divine ancestors, they will think it a disgrace to break their word in a professional matter.

921   73. If one of the craftsmen culpably fails to complete his work within the stipulated time, out of disrespect for the god from whom he wins his bread, fondly thinking that he can count on the indulgence of the divinity with whom he has some personal relationship,

(a) *first he* will pay a penalty to the god,
(b) *and secondly*, under the provisions of the law applicable to his case, he must owe the price of the works of which he has cheated his employer, and perform his task all over again within the stipulated period, free of charge.

And the law will give the contractor for a work the same advice as it gave a seller,[4] not to take advantage by setting too

4. See p. 459.

high a price on his services, but to name their actual value without further ado. The contractor has precisely the same duty, because as a craftsman he knows what the job is worth. In a state of gentlemen a workman must never use his craft, which is at bottom accurate and straightforward, to take 'crafty' advantage of laymen, and anyone who is thus imposed upon shall be able to sue the culprit. But if anyone lets a contract to a workman and fails to pay him the price stipulated in a valid legal agreement, and snaps his fingers at those partners in our social framework, Zeus the patron of the state, and Athena, so that his delight at being in pocket wrecks the fundamental bonds of society, then the following law, with the backing of the gods, must reinforce the cohesion of the state:

74. (a) If a man takes delivery of a piece of work and fails to pay for it within the agreed time,

he must be charged double;

    (b) if a whole year elapses,

then notwithstanding the rule that loans in general do not bear interest, he must pay an obol per drachma[5] for every month in arrear.

Actions in these cases should be brought before the tribal courts.

MILITARY 'CRAFTSMEN'

Now that we have broached the subject of craftsmen in general, we ought in all fairness to glance at those whose job it is to keep us safe in war, such as generals and other experts in military techniques. These persons are just as much craftsmen as ordinary workmen, though of a different kind, so when one of them undertakes some public task, voluntarily or under orders, and performs it well, the law will never tire of praising anyone who pays him the honour he deserves – honour being in effect a military man's pay. But if anyone receives the benefit of some splendid military action and fails to pay that price, the law will censure him. For the benefit of the military,

---

5. I.e. 200 per cent per annum. (6 obols = 1 drachma.) Contrast p. 211.

then, let us enact the following regulation-cum-commendation, by way of advising rather than compelling the people at 922 large. Those fine men who safeguard the whole state either by exploits of valour or by military expertise must be accorded honour – but honour of the second rank, because the highest honour should be given first and foremost to those who have proved conspicuously conscientious in respecting the written regulations of the good legislator.

§24. FAMILY LAW

Plato's law of the family is mostly taken from Attic law, with interesting and significant modifications dictated by the peculiar conditions of Magnesia: for a handy summary, see G. R. Morrow, Plato's Cretan City, 120–21, 202–3. The polemic against freedom of testamentary disposition is a good example of Plato's desire to regulate the life of the individual in its most intimate details.

MAKING A WILL

ATHENIAN: We've now pretty well completed our provisions for the most important agreements that men make with each other, with the exception of those relating to orphans and the care and attention due to them from their guardians. So now we've more or less provided for the first topic, here's the next thing on which we are obliged to impose some sort of order. All our regulations must start from two basic facts: (a) people at the point of death like to settle their affairs by a will, (b) sometimes, by chance, they die intestate. What a difficult and contentious business it is, Cleinias! That's what I had in mind when I said we were 'obliged' to deal with it: to leave it unregulated is quite out of the question. If you allow a will unchallengeable validity whatever condition a man near the end of his life may have been in when he drew it up, he might make any number of mutually inconsistent provisions that contradicted not only the spirit of the laws but also the inclinations of those who survive him, and indeed his own earlier intentions before he set out to make his will. After all, most of us, when we think death is at hand, just go to pieces and can't think straight.

CLEINIAS: How do you mean, sir?

ATHENIAN: When a man is about to die, Cleinias, he becomes refractory, and keeps harping on a principle that spreads alarm and despondency among legislators.

CLEINIAS: How's that?

ATHENIAN: In his anxiety for complete authority he's apt to express himself with some warmth.

CLEINIAS: To what effect?

ATHENIAN: 'Ye gods!' says he, 'it's a fine thing if I'm not going to be allowed to give – or not give – my own property to anyone I please! Why shouldn't I give more to one man and less to another depending on whether they have shown themselves good or bad friends to me? My illnesses, my old age and all my other various misfortunes have sorted them out well enough.'

CLEINIAS: Well, sir, don't you think that's well said?

ATHENIAN: Cleinias, my view is that the ancient lawgivers were too easy-going, and legislated on the basis of a superficial and inadequate appreciation of the human condition.

CLEINIAS: How do you mean?

ATHENIAN: My dear fellow, because they feared the line of argument I have mentioned, they passed the law allowing a man to dispose of his own property in his will exactly as he 923 pleases. But when people have come to death's door in your state, you and I will make a rather more appropriate response:

'Friends, you "creatures of a day" in more senses than one, it's difficult for you in your present circumstances to know the truth about your own property and also "know yourselves", as the Delphic inscription puts it. Therefore, I, as legislator, rule that neither you nor this property of yours belongs to yourselves, but to your whole clan, ancestors and descendants alike; and your clan and its property in turn belong, even more absolutely, to the state. That being so, I should be reluctant to tolerate someone worming himself into your good graces when you are smitten with illness or old age, and wheedling you into making a will that is not for the best. I shall legislate with a view to nothing except the interest of your clan and the entire state, relegating (as is only right) that of the individual to second place. So as you go on your journey, which is the way of all flesh, show restraint and goodwill towards us: we will look after your affairs for the future and guard your interests with the utmost care, down to the smallest detail.'

TESTAMENTARY AND INHERITANCE LAW

Let that stand by way of preamble and consolation for both the living and the dying, Cleinias. Here's the actual law:

Anyone who settles his property by writing a will should first, if he has had children, write down the name of that son who in his opinion deserves to be his heir, and he should also record precisely which, if any, of his other children he offers for adoption by someone else. If, however, he is still left with one of his sons not adopted into an estate, who will presumably be dispatched by law to a colony[1], the father should be permitted to present him with as much of his property as he likes, apart from the family estate and all its associated equipment; and if there is more than one son in that position, his father is to distribute his property among them – excluding the estate – in whatever proportion he pleases. But he should not distribute any part of his property to any son who has a home.[2] He should treat a daughter analogously: if she is promised in marriage, he should not let her share his goods, but only if she is not promised. If subsequent to the will one of the sons or daughters is discovered to have come into possession of an estate in Magnesia, he or she should abandon his or her legacy[3] to the testator's heir. If the testator is leaving no male offspring but only female, he should select whichever of his daughters he pleases and in his will provide someone to be a husband for her and a son for himself, and record this person as his heir. And here's another disaster a man should allow for when drawing up his will: if his son (his own or adopted) dies in infancy before he can reach man's estate, the will should specify in writing a child who is to take his place – and who, one hopes, will have better luck. When a man who has no children at all writes a will, he may reserve one tenth of his 924

1. Cf. pp. 201 and 209.
2. I.e. by adoption or by inheriting his father's estate.
3. I.e. of movable property.

acquired[4] property and give it to anyone he wishes; all the rest he should leave to his adopted heir, so that in making him his son with the blessing of the law he gains his goodwill by treating him fairly. When a man's children need guardians, and the deceased has made a will and stated in writing the number of guardians he wants his children to have and who they should be (provided they are ready and willing to undertake the office), the choice of guardians put on record in this way should be binding. But if a man dies absolutely intestate or without selecting guardians, then the two nearest relatives on the father's side and the two nearest on the mother's, together with one of the deceased's friends, must be authorized to act as guardians; and the Guardians of the Laws should appoint them for any orphan who stands in such need. Everything to do with guardianship and orphans should be the concern of the fifteen eldest Guardians of the Laws, who should divide themselves by seniority into groups of three, one group to act one year and another the next, until the five terms of office have been completed in rotation; and so far as possible there should be no gaps in the sequence.

When a man dies absolutely intestate and leaves children in need of guardians, these same laws must be brought into operation to relieve their distress. But if he meets with some unforeseen accident and leaves just daughters, he must forgive the lawgiver for arranging their betrothal with an eye on only two out of three possible considerations: close kinship, and the security of the estate. The third point, which a father would have taken into account – namely to select from among the entire citizen body someone whose character and habits qualify him to be his own son and his daughter's bridegroom – these considerations, I say, will have to be passed over, because it's impracticable to weigh them. So here's how the best law we can manage in such a field should run. If a man fails to make a will, and leaves only daughters, then on his death (a) a brother on his father's side (or, if without an estate of his own, a brother on his mother's side) should take the daughter and the estate of the deceased. (b) If there is a

4. I.e. apart from the estate and its equipment.

brother's son available, but no brother, then if the parties are of a similar age the same procedure is to apply. In the absence of all these, (c) a sister's son is to benefit under the same regulations. (d) Next in line is to be the brother of the deceased's father, next (e) that brother's son, and finally (f) the son of the sister of the deceased's father. And in all cases where a man leaves only female offspring, the succession is to pass through the family according to the same rules of kinship, through brothers and brothers' and sisters' sons, the ₉₂₅ males in any one generation always taking precedence over the females. As for age, the assessor must determine the propriety or otherwise of the marriage by inspection, viewing the males naked and the females stripped down to the navel. If the family suffers from such a dearth of relatives that not even a grandson either of the deceased's brother or of the son of the deceased's grandfather exists, then in consultation with her guardians the girl may single out of her own free choice any other citizen, provided he does not object, who should then become the deceased's heir and the daughter's bridegroom. However, 'flexibility above all': sometimes suitable candidates from within the state itself may be in unusually short supply, so if a girl is hard put to it to find a husband among her compatriots, and has in view someone who has been dispatched to a colony whom she would like to inherit her father's property, then if the man is related to her, he should enter into the estate under the provisions of the law; if he is not of her clan, then provided there are no near kin living in the state, he shall be entitled by virtue of the choice of the daughter of the deceased and that of her guardians to marry her and return to his homeland to take over the establishment of the intestate father.

When a man dies intestate and leaves neither male nor female issue, the situation should in general be met by the foregoing law, and a man and a woman from the clan should 'go in harness' and enter into the deserted establishment with full title to the estate. The order of precedence on the female side is to be: (a) the deceased's sister, (b) his brother's daughter, (c) the sister's son, (d) the sister of the deceased's father, (e) the daughter of the father's brother, and (f) the daughter of the father's sister. A woman from this list should set up home with a man from the other list[5] according to the degrees of kinship and the demands of religion[6] for which we made provision earlier.

HOW TO MITIGATE THE HARSHNESS
OF THE LAW

But let's not forget the severity of such laws. It can sometimes be hard for a near relative of the deceased to be instructed to marry his kinswoman, by a law that to all appearances takes no account of the thousands of social difficulties that deter people from obeying such instructions in a willing spirit, so that they invariably prefer to put up with anything rather than comply – I mean difficulties like physical or mental illnesses or defects in the man or woman one is told to marry. I dare say some people imagine the lawgiver is not bothered about these things at all, but they're wrong. So in the interests of the lawgiver and those for whom he legislates, let's compose a sort of impartial preamble begging those who are subject to the legislator's orders to forgive him if in his concern for the common good he finds it hardly possible to cope with 926 the personal inconvenience experienced by individuals; and the people for whom the lawgiver's regulations are intended should also be forgiven for their occasional understandable inability to carry out the orders which, in all ignorance, he gives them.

CLEINIAS: Well then, sir, what would be the most reasonable way of dealing with such cases?

ATHENIAN: It is essential, Cleinias, to choose people to arbitrate between laws of that sort and the persons affected by their provisions.

CLEINIAS: How do you mean?

ATHENIAN: Sometimes a nephew with a wealthy father might be reluctant to take his uncle's daughter because he fancies his chances and is bent on making a better marriage;

5. See pp. 466–7.   6. See p. 210.

in another case a man would have no choice but to disobey the law because the instructions devised by the lawgiver would lead to untold trouble – as for instance if they tried to compel him to marry someone suffering from lunacy or some other terrible physical or mental defect that would make the life of the partner not worth living. This policy should be embodied in a law with the following provisions:

If in practice people attack the established laws about wills on any point whatever, but especially where a marriage is concerned, and swear that if the legislator were alive and present in person he would never have forced them to either of the courses to which they are in fact being forced (to marry this man or that woman), but one of the relatives or a guardian takes the opposite line, then we must remember that the fifteen Guardians of the Laws[7] have been bequeathed to orphan boys and girls by the legislator to act as their fathers and arbitrate on their behalf; so litigants on any of these matters must go to them to get disputes settled, and carry out their decisions as binding. But if a litigant believes that this is too great an authority to be vested in the Guardians of the Laws, he should take them before the court of the Select Judges and get a decision on the points at issue.

75. If he loses the day,
the lawgiver should visit him with censure and disgrace, a punishment which any sensible person will regard as more severe than a swingeing fine.

THE CARE OF ORPHANS

The effect of this will be to give our orphan children a sort of second birth. We have already described the training and education they should all receive after their first; after this second and parentless birth we have to see that these children who have had the ill luck to be bereaved and made orphans are to be pitied as little as possible for their misfortune. In the first place, the Guardians of the Laws – substitute parents as least as good as the original ones – should lay down rules

7. See p. 466.

for them; in particular, we instruct the three Guardians on duty for the year to look after them as though they were their own children; and for the guidance of these officials and the guardians we shall compose a suitable preamble on the education of orphans. And luckily enough, I fancy, we have described already how after death the souls of the departed enjoy certain powers which they use to take an interest in human affairs.[8] The stories which tell of these things are true, but long, so one should trust to the ancient and widely disseminated common traditions on the point, and also take the legislator's word for it that the doctrine is true – unless, of course, one believes them to be arrant fools. Now if this is really the way of things,

a guardian should fear, in the first place, the gods above, who are aware how deprived orphans are, and secondly the souls of the departed, whose natural instinct is to watch with particular care over their own children, showing benevolence to people who respect them and hostility to those who treat them badly. And he should also fear the reactions of those who, full of years and honour, are still living, because in a state which thrives under good laws their grandchildren will show them glad and tender affection, and old men have sharp eyes and ears for such things: if you do the right thing by an orphan, they'll be kind to you, whereas they'll soon show you their displeasure if you take advantage of an orphan's exposed position, because they regard orphans as a supreme and sacred trust. A guardian or official with even the slightest sense has a duty to give close attention to all these warnings, and take great care over the training and education of orphans, helping them in every possible way, just as if he were contributing to the good of his own self and family.

A man who complies with the preface to the law and refrains from any ill-treatment of an orphan will be spared first-hand experience of the legislator's fury against such actions, but

8. See pp. 378–9.

76. if a man refuses to comply, and harms a child deprived
of its father or mother,

he must pay double the damages that he would have to pay
for a crime committed against a child with both parents
living.

But do we really *need* precise rules to control a guardian's
treatment of an orphan, and an official's supervision of a
guardian? They already possess a pattern of how to bring
up free-born children, in the education they themselves give
to their own, and in the way they manage their private
possessions – and of course the rules they have to guide them
on those matters are pretty exact. If they were not, it would
be reasonable to lay down rules of guardianship as a special
and separate category, and make an orphan's life different from
that of ordinary children by working out a detailed régime of
its own. But in fact in our state being an orphan doesn't
differ very much from living under one's own father, although
in public esteem, and the amount of attention the children
get, orphanhood is usually much less desirable. That is why 928
in dealing with this topic – rules about orphans – the law
has gone to such lengths in encouraging and threatening. And
here's the sort of threat that will come in very handy indeed.
Anyone acting as a guardian of a boy or girl, and any Guardian
of the Laws who supervises that guardian by virtue of being
appointed to control him, must show this child who has had
the misfortune of bereavement no less affection than his own
children, and be just as zealously concerned for his ward's
property as he is for his own – more so, in fact; and everyone
who acts as a guardian will have just that one law to observe
on the subject of orphans. But

77. if this law is contravened in such respects,
   (a) *a guardian* should be punished by his official;[9]
   (b) *an official* should be summoned before the court of
       Select Judges by the guardian and punished by a fine
       of twice the damages as estimated by the court.

9. Presumably the Guardian of the Laws mentioned a few lines earlier.

If a guardian is suspected by the relatives or indeed by any other citizen of neglect or malpractice, he should be summoned before the same court.

78. *He must* be fined four times the sum he is found to have taken, half the fine going to the child and half to the successful prosecutor.

If once he has grown up an orphan concludes that he was badly treated by his guardian, he may bring a suit for incompetent guardianship, provided he does so within five years of its expiry.

79. (a) If a guardian is found guilty,
the court is to estimate what he is to suffer or pay;
    (b) if an official is found guilty of injuring the orphan
      (i) through negligence,
the court must assess how much he is to pay to the child;
      (ii) by criminal conduct,
then in addition to paying the sum assessed, he must be ejected from the office of Guardian of the Laws,
and the government must supply the state and country with a fresh Guardian of the Laws to take his place.

DISINHERITANCE

The bitterness with which fathers quarrel with their children and children with their fathers is often excessive. A father is apt to think that the legislator ought to give him legal authority, if he wishes, to make a public proclamation through a herald that under the provisions of the law his son is his son no longer; for their part, sons believe that if they have a father whose suffering from disease or old age has become a disgrace, they are entitled to prosecute him on a charge of lunacy. Such disputes are usually found where men's characters are irredeemably corrupt, because when the corruption is confined to one party – as when the son is corrupt but not the father, or the other way round – the bad feeling is not sufficient to lead to trouble. Now in any other state a child repudiated by his father would not necessarily find himself a stateless person, but in the case of Magnesia, to which these laws will apply, a man disowned by his father will be obliged to migrate to another country, because the 5040 homes cannot be increased even by one. Consequently before this punishment can be legally inflicted on him, he must be repudiated not only by his father but by the entire clan. Procedure in such cases is to be governed by some such law as this: anyone who has the extreme misfortune to want – justifiably or not – to expel from the clan the child he has fathered and reared, must not be allowed to do so casually and on the spur of the moment. First of all he must assemble all the relatives on his own side and all the relatives of the son on the mother's side, as far as cousins in each case, and accuse his son before them, explaining why he deserves to be drummed out of the clan by its united action. The son shall have the right of reply, to argue that none of these penalties is called for. If the father carries his point, and wins the vote of more than half the relatives (he himself and the mother and the accused son being excluded from the voting, as well as those males and females who are not yet of adult age), then by this procedure and on these terms he shall be entitled to repudiate his son, but in no other way whatever. If some other citizen wishes to adopt the repudiated son, no law is to stop him (a young man's character is by nature bound to change frequently enough in the course of his life), but if after ten years no one has been moved to adopt the disowned person, the supervisors of surplus children intended for the colony[10] must take him too under their wing so that he may be suitably established in the same colony as the others.

SENILITY

Now suppose illness or old age or a cantankerous temper or all three make a man more wayward than old men usually are, unbeknown to all except his immediate circle; and suppose he squanders the family resources on the grounds that he can do as he likes with his own property, so that his son is driven to

10. Cf. pp. 201 and 209.

distraction but hesitates to bring a charge of lunacy. This is the law the son must observe. First of all he must go to the eldest Guardians of the Laws and explain his father's misfortune, and they, after due investigation, must advise him whether to bring the charge or not. If they advise that he should, they must come forward as witnesses for the prosecution and plead on his behalf.

80. If the case is proved,
the father must lose all authority to manage his own affairs, even in trivialities, and be treated like a child for the rest of his days.

DIVORCE AND REMARRIAGE

Whenever a man and his wife find it impossible to get on with each other because of an unfortunate incompatibility of temperament, the case must come under the control of ten men – 930 middle-aged Guardians of the Laws – and ten of the women in charge of marriage, of the same age. Any arrangements they make which reconciles the couple should stand, but if feelings are too exacerbated for that they must do their best to find each some other congenial partner. It's quite likely that the existing partners are people of rough temper, so one should try to fit them in harness with mates of a more phlegmatic and gentle disposition. And when the quarrelling couple have no children or only a few, the procreation of children must be kept in view in the setting up of the new homes; where sufficient children already exist, the divorce and the remarriages should facilitate companionship and mutual help in the evening of life.

DEATH OF A WIFE OR HUSBAND

If a wife dies and leaves male and female children, we'll lay down a law advising, though not compelling, the husband to bring up his existing children without importing a stepmother; but if there are no children, he must be obliged to remarry so as to beget sufficient children for his home and for the state. If the husband dies, leaving an adequate number of children, their mother should remain in her position and bring them up; but if it is judged that she is too young to live unmarried without injuring her health, her relatives should report the facts to the women in charge of marriages and do whatever seems advisable to both sides; and if there have been no children born as yet, they should bear that in mind too. (The minimum acceptable number of children is to be fixed by law as one of each sex.)

CHILDREN OF MIXED STATUS

Whenever there is no dispute about the parentage of a child, but a ruling is required as to which parent it should follow, the offspring of intercourse between a slave woman and a slave or a free man or a freedman should become the absolute property of the woman's owner; if a free woman has intercourse with a slave, the issue should belong to his master. If a free man has a child by his own slave woman, or a free woman by her own slave, and the facts are crystal clear, the female officials are to send the free woman's child along with its father to another country, and the Guardians of the Laws must similarly send away the free man's child with its mother.

RESPECT FOR PARENTS

No god or any man with his wits about him will ever advise anyone to neglect his parents. On the contrary, we should be quick to appreciate how very relevant the following preface on the subject of worshipping gods will be to the respect or disrespect in which we hold our father and mother.

Time-honoured cult observances all over the world fall into two categories. Man exalts some of the gods because he can see them with his own eyes,[11] others[12] he represents, by 931 setting up statues of them, and believes that his worship of these inanimate 'gods' ensures him the abundant gratitude and benevolence of their real and living counterparts. This

11. The heavenly bodies.   12. The traditional deities.

means that no one who has living in his house his father or mother, or their mothers and fathers, treasures old and frail, must ever forget that so long as he possesses such a 'shrine'[13] at his hearth and looks after it properly, no other object of worship will ever be more influential on his behalf.

CLEINIAS: What do you mean by 'properly'?

ATHENIAN: I'll tell you. After all, my friends, such themes are worth a hearing.

CLEINIAS: Tell us, then.

ATHENIAN: Our version of the story of Oedipus is that when he was insulted by his sons he called down a curse on them – and you know how people have never stopped relating how the gods heard and answered his prayer. And Amyntor fell into a rage with his son Phoenix[14] and cursed him; Theseus did the same to Hippolytus,[15] and there are thousands of similar cases, which all go to show that the gods take the parents' side against the children: no man, you'll find, can curse anyone as effectively as a parent can curse his child; and that's absolutely right. So if it is true that the gods listen to the prayers of fathers or mothers who have been wantonly insulted by their children, isn't it reasonable to suppose that when by contrast the respect we show our parents delights them so much that they pray hard to heaven for a blessing on their children, the gods will be just as ready to listen as before, and grant us it? If not, they'd be conferring blessings unjustly – which we maintain is a peculiarly inappropriate thing for a god to do.

CLEINIAS: Very much so.

ATHENIAN: So as we said just now, we must reckon that the most precious object of worship a man can have is his father or grandfather, weak with age, or his mother in a similar condition, because when he honours and respects them God is delighted – if he weren't, he wouldn't listen to their prayers. These 'living shrines', in the shape of our forefathers, affect us far more wonderfully than lifeless ones, because when we

---

13. Cf. p. 384.   14. Homer, *Iliad* IX, 448 ff.
15. See note on p. 134.

look after them they invariably join their prayers to ours, whereas if we insult them, they oppose us. As ordinary statues do neither of these things, a man who treats his father and grandfather and so on as they deserve will have objects of worship that are much more influential than any others in winning him the favour of heaven.

CLEINIAS: Excellently put.

ATHENIAN: Anyone with his wits about him holds the prayers of his parents in fear and respect, knowing that the cases in which such prayers have been brought to pass have been many and frequent. This being the way of things, a good man will regard his elderly forebears as a veritable 932 god-send, right up till they breathe their last; and when they pass on, they will be sorely missed by the next generation, and be a terror to the wicked. Let everyone be convinced by this argument and do their parents all the honour enjoined by law.

But if even so a man gets the reputation of being deaf to such prefaces, then the right law to pass to deal with him will run as follows.

If anyone in this state of ours looks after his parents less diligently than he should and fails to carry out their wishes in all respects with more indulgence than he shows to those of his sons and descendants in general, and indeed to his own desires too, the neglected parent must report the fact, either in person or by messenger, to the three most senior Guardians of the Laws and three of the women in charge of marriages. These officials must take the matter in hand, and provided the offender is still a young man under the age of thirty, chastise him with a whipping and imprisonment. (In the case of a woman, the same chastisement may be inflicted until she is forty.) Older persons, if they persist in neglecting (and perhaps actually ill-treating) their parents, should be summoned before a court consisting of the 101 most elderly citizens of the state.

81. If a man is found guilty,
the court is to assess what penalty or fine is to be exacted,

and absolutely no fine or penalty that a man can pay must be excluded from consideration.

If ill-treatment prevents a parent from complaining, any free man who discovers the situation should alert the authorities.

82. If he does not,

he must be regarded as a scoundrel and be liable to a suit for damage at the hands of anyone who wishes.

If the informant is a slave, he should be given his freedom; if he belongs to the criminal or his victim, he must be released by the authorities; and if he belongs to some other citizen, the public treasury is to see that the owner is reimbursed. Official action must be taken to stop anyone injuring him in revenge for giving information.

§25. MISCELLANEOUS LEGISLATION

*It is difficult to say anything useful about this section as a whole,
though the individual topics are full of interest. (For the structure of
the section, see my discussion on p. 448.) Perhaps the most important
topic is the Scrutineers, who investigate and if necessary punish the
conduct of an official at the end of his term. Scrutineers were known
in the Athenian democracy, but Plato considerably extends the dignity
and powers of the office (see G. R. Morrow, Plato's Cretan City,
219 ff). They form a vital part of his system of constitutional checks
and balances.*

NON-FATAL INJURIES BY DRUGS
AND CHARMS

We have already dealt with *fatal* injuries inflicted by the use
of drugs,[1] but we have not yet discussed any of the less
harmful cases of voluntary and premeditated injury, inflicted
by giving food or drink or by applying ointments. Full
treatment of the question is hindered by the fact that so far
as human beings are concerned, poisoning is of two kinds.
First there is the sort we have just explicitly mentioned: the
injury a body suffers from some physical substance by natural ₉₃₃
processes. The other kind is a matter of spells and charms
and 'enchantments': not only are the victims persuaded that
they are being seriously injured by people with magic
influence, but even the perpetrators themselves are convinced
that it really is in their power to inflict injury by these methods.
It is not easy to know the truth about these and similar
practices, and even if one were to find out, it would be
difficult to convince others; and it is just not worth the
effort to try to persuade people whose heads are full of mutual
suspicion, that even if they do sometimes catch sight of a
moulded waxen figure in a doorway or at a junction of three

1. See p. 378.

roads or on their parent's grave, they should ignore it every time, because they cannot be sure these things work. All this means that our law about drugs must be a double law, reflecting the two methods by which poisoning may be attempted. But first, by entreaty, exhortation and advice, we'll explain that no such thing should ever be attempted, that one should not alarm and terrify the common man, like an impressionable child, and that legislators and judges should not be put to the necessity of curing men of such fears. We shall point out for a start that unless the person who tries to use poison happens to be a diviner or soothsayer, he acts in ignorance of how his spells will turn out, and unless he happens to be an expert in medicine, he acts in ignorance of the effect he will have on the body. So the wording of our law about the use of poisons should be as follows:

83. (a) If a doctor poisons a man without doing either him or any member of his household fatal injury, or injures his cattle or bees (fatally or otherwise), and is found guilty on a charge of poisoning,
he must be punished by death.

(b) If the culprit is a layman,
the court is to decide the proper penalty or fine to be inflicted in his case.

84. (a) If a diviner or soothsayer is deemed to be in effect injuring someone, by spells or incantations or charms or any other poison of that kind whatever,
he must die.

(b) If someone with no knowledge of divination is found guilty of this kind of poisoning,
the same procedure is to be followed as with the other laymen [83.(b)] – that is, the court is to decide what it thinks is the appropriate penalty or fine for him to pay.

THE PURPOSE OF PUNISHMENT

When one man harms another by theft or violence and the damage is extensive, the indemnity he pays to the injured party should be large, but smaller if the damage is comparatively trivial. The cardinal rule should be that in every case the sum is to vary in proportion to the damage done, so that the loss is made good. And each offender is to pay an additional penalty appropriate to his crime, to encourage him to reform. Thus if a man has been led to do wrong by the folly of someone else, being over-persuaded because of his youth or some similar reason, his penalty should tend to be light; but it is to be heavier when his offence is due to his own folly and inability to control his feelings of pleasure and pain – as when he has fallen victim to cowardice and fear, or some deep-rooted jealousy or lust or fury. This additional penalty is to be inflicted not because of the crime (what's done can't be undone), but for the sake of the future: we hope that the offender himself and those that observe his punishment will either be brought to loathe injustice unreservedly or at any rate recover appreciably from this disastrous disease.[2] All these reasons and considerations make it necessary for the law to aim, like a good archer, at a penalty that will both reflect the magnitude of the crime and fully indemnify the victim. The judge has the same aim, and when he is faced by his legal duty of assessing what penalty or fine the defendant must pay, he must follow closely in the legislator's footsteps; and the latter must turn himself into a sort of artist and sketch some specimen measures consistent with his written prescriptions. That, Cleinias and Megillus, is the job to which we must now devote our best efforts; we have to describe what type of penalty is called for in all categories of theft and violence – granted, of course, that the gods and children of gods are prepared to see us legislate in this field.

LUNACY

Lunatics must not be allowed to appear in public; their relations must keep them in custody in private houses by whatever means they can improvise.

2. Cf. p. 357 for the medical terminology.

85. If they fail to do so,
they must pay a fine: 100 drachmas for a member of the
highest property-class (whether it is a slave or a free man
that he fails to keep an eye on), eighty for a member of the
second class, sixty for the third, and forty for the lowest.

ABUSE

There are several kinds of madness, brought on by several
causes. The cases we have just mentioned are the result of
illness, but there are some people with an unfortunate natural
irritability, made worse by poor discipline, who in any trivial
quarrel will shout their heads off in mutual abuse. Such a
thing is highly improper in a well-run state. So this single
law should apply to all cases of defamation: no one is to
defame anybody. If you are having an argument you should
listen to your opponent's case, and put your own to him and
the audience, without making any defamatory remarks at all.
When men take to damning and cursing each other and to
calling one another rude names in the shrill tones of women,
935 these mere words, empty though they are, soon lead to real
hatreds and quarrels of the most serious kind. In gratifying
his ugly emotion, anger, and in thus disgracefully stoking the
fires of his fury, the speaker drives back into primitive
savagery a side of his character that was once civilized by
education, and such a splenetic life makes him no better
than a wild beast; bitter indeed, he finds, are the pleasures of
anger. Besides, on such occasions all men are usually quick to
resort to ridicule of their opponents, and no one who has
indulged that habit has ever acquired the slightest sense of
responsibility or remained faithful to many of his principles.
That is why no one must ever breathe a word of ridicule in a
temple or at a public sacrifice or at the games or in the market-
place or in court or in any public gathering, and the relevant
official must always punish such offences.

86. If he fails to do so,
he must be disqualified from competing for awards of merit,

as being a man who disregards the laws and fails to perform the duties imposed upon him by the legislator.

87. If in other localities someone fails to refrain from abusive language, whether he resorts to it first or by way of reply,

the passer-by, provided he is older than the offender, should lend his support to the law and eject by force this fellow who has shown such indulgence to anger, that bad companion.

88. If the passer-by fails to do so,

he must be liable to the appointed penalty.

THE CENSORSHIP OF COMEDIES

The view we are putting forward now is that when a man is embroiled in a slanging-match he is incapable of carrying on the dispute without trying to make funny remarks, and when such conduct is motivated by anger we censure it. Well then, what does this imply? That we are prepared to tolerate a comedian's eagerness to raise a laugh against people, provided that when he sets about ridiculing our citizens in his comedies, he is not inspired by anger? Or shall we divide comedy into two kinds, according to whether it is *good-natured* or not? Then we could allow the playful comedian to joke about something, without anger, but forbid, as we've indicated, anyone whatever to do so if he is in deadly earnest and shows animosity. We must certainly insist on this stipulation about anger; but we still have to lay down by law who ought to receive permission for ridicule and who not. No composer of comedies, or of songs or iambic verse, must ever be allowed to ridicule either by description or by impersonation any citizen whatever, with or without rancour. Anyone who disobeys this rule must be ejected from the country that same day by the presidents of the games.

89. If the latter fail to take this action, 936

they must be fined 300 drachmas, to be dedicated to the god in whose honour the festival is being held.

Those who have earlier[3] been licensed to compose verse against each other should be allowed to poke fun at people, not in savage earnest, but in a playful spirit and without rancour. The distinction between the two kinds must be left to the minister with overall responsibility for the education of the young; an author may put before the public anything the minister approves of, but if it is censored, the author must not perform it to anyone personally nor be found to have trained someone else to do so, whether a free man or a slave.

90. If he does,
he must get the reputation of being a scoundrel and an enemy of the laws.

BEGGARS

It is not the starving *tout court* or the similarly afflicted who deserve sympathy, but the man who in spite of his moderation or some other virtue or progress towards it, nevertheless experiences some misfortune. That being so, it will be a matter for surprise if a virtuous person, whether slave or free, even if the state and society he lives in is run with only average skill, is ever so grossly neglected as to be reduced to abject poverty. So the legislator will be quite safe if he lays down a law running more or less like this. No one is to go begging in the state. Anyone who attempts to do so, and scrounges a living by never-ending importunities, must be expelled from the market by the Market-Wardens, from the city by the City-Wardens, and from the surrounding country conducted by the Country-Wardens across the border, so that the land may rid itself completely of such a creature.

DAMAGE BY SLAVES

If a slave man or woman damages any piece of someone else's property, then provided the person who suffers the loss was not himself partly to blame because of inexperience or careless conduct, the slave's owner must either make good the damage

3. See p. 310.

in full, or hand over the actual offender. But if the owner counter-claims that the prosecution has been brought as a result of the injured person and the culprit putting their heads together to rob him of his slave, he must sue the allegedly injured party on a charge of collusion. If he wins the day, he is to receive twice the value of the slave as assessed by the court.

91. If he loses,
he must both make good the damage and hand over the slave.

92. If a beast of burden or a horse or dog or some other animal damages a piece of a neighbour's property,
its owner is to pay for the damage on the same basis.

FURTHER RULES OF LEGAL PROCEDURE

If anyone deliberately refuses to appear as a witness, the person who needs his evidence must serve a summons on him; and on being duly summoned the man is to present himself at the trial. If he knows something and is prepared to testify, he should give evidence accordingly; if he claims he knows nothing, he must swear an oath to three gods, Zeus, Apollo and Themis, to the effect that quite definitely he has no information, and thus be dismissed from the proceedings. 937 If a man is summoned to give evidence and fails to answer the summons, he must be liable by law to a suit for damage. No juryman is to vote in a trial in which he has been put up as a witness and given evidence. A free woman is to be allowed to support a case by giving evidence, provided she is over forty years of age, and to bring prosecutions, provided she has no husband; but if she has a husband living, she must be limited to acting as a witness. Slaves (male and female), and children, should be allowed to support a case by giving evidence, but only in a trial for murder and provided a credit-worthy surety is put up to guarantee their appearance at the trial[4] if their evidence is objected to as false. If either

4. Not the murder trial itself, but one held to determine the truth of a witness's evidence when it has been disputed at an earlier hearing of the case.

disputant claims someone has borne false witness, he should enter an objection to all or part of the testimony before a verdict in the case is decided on. The objections, under the seal of both parties, should be placed in official custody and produced at the trial for perjury. If anyone is convicted twice on this charge, he may not be *compelled* under any law to bear witness again; if he is convicted a third time, he must never be *allowed* to be a witness in the future; and if he does have the face to give testimony on a further occasion after a third conviction, anyone who wishes should report him to the authorities, who should haul him before a court.

93. If he is found guilty,
he must be punished by death.

When a court decides to throw out evidence on the ground that the winning side has triumphed because certain witnesses have perjured themselves, and more than half the evidence is condemned, the suit lost on the strength of it should come up for retrial, and after due inquiry a ruling should be given that the false evidence was, or was not, the decisive influence on the verdict; and this ruling, whichever way it goes, will automatically settle the original action.

UNSCRUPULOUS ADVOCACY

Although human life is graced by many fine institutions, most of them have their own evil genius, so to speak, which pollutes and corrupts them. Take justice, for instance, which has civilized so much of our behaviour: how could it fail to be a blessing to human society? And granted justice is a blessing, can advocacy fail to be a blessing too? But valuable though they are, both these institutions have a bad name. There is a certain kind of immoral practice, grandly masquerading as a 'skill', which proceeds on the assumption that a technique exists – itself, in fact – of conducting one's own suits and pleading those of others, which can win the day regardless of the rights and wrongs of the individual case; and that this 938 skill itself and the speeches composed with its help are available free – free, that is, to anyone offering a consideration in return.[5] Now it is absolutely vital that this skill – if it really is a skill, and not just a knack born of casual trial and error – should not be allowed to grow up in our state if we can prevent it. The lawgiver will have nothing to say to those who obey his command that one should either listen to justice and not contradict her, or leave for some other country; but if anyone disobeys him, the law shall pronounce as follows: if anyone seems to be trying to misrepresent to the judges where the course of justice lies, and to enter one plea after another in support of either his own or someone else's case, when equity would call a halt, then anyone who wishes should indict him on a charge of perverse pleading or criminal advocacy. He should be tried in the court of select judges and if he is found guilty the court should decide whether it thinks his motive is avarice or pugnacity.

94. (a) If the court believes his motive is pugnacity,
it must determine how long he must refrain from prosecuting anyone or helping someone else to do so.

    (b) If the motive appears to be avarice,

    (i)   *a foreigner* must leave the country and never return, on pain of death;

    (ii) *a citizen* must die, for letting a love of money become the obsession of his life.

95. If a man is convicted twice of committing such an offence through pugnacity,
he must die.

OFFENCES COMMITTED BY MEMBERS OF DIPLOMATIC MISSIONS

If a man passes himself off as an ambassador or herald of the state and enters into unauthorized negotiations with a foreign power, or, when actually sent on such a mission, delivers a message other than the one with which he was sent – or contrariwise if he is shown to have misreported, in his

5. A sarcastic attack on professional speech-writers.

capacity as an ambassador or herald, the communications which enemy or friendly states have given him, he must be open to prosecution for violating the law by impiety against the pronouncements and instructions of Hermes and Zeus.

96. If he is convicted,
the penalty or fine he must pay will have to be assessed.

THEFT OF PUBLIC PROPERTY

Theft of property is uncivilized, and robbery with violence an act of brazen insolence. The sons of Zeus take no pleasure in fraud and force, and none of them has ever committed either of these crimes. So no one who commits such an offence should be seduced into believing the lies of poets or other story-tellers: the thief or thug mustn't think 'There's no shame in this – after all, the gods do it themselves.' That is neither plausible nor true, and no one who breaks the law by such an act can possibly be a god or child of gods. The lawgiver is in a much better position to understand these things than all the poets in the world. Anyone who is convinced by this doctrine of ours is a happy man, and long may he so continue; but anyone who refuses to listen should have some such law as this to contend with: all theft of public property, great or small, should attract the same punishment. The greed of the pilferer is just as great as any other thief's – it's only his efficiency that's inferior; whereas anyone who makes off with some valuable object he did not deposit[6] indulges his criminal tendencies to the full. In the eyes of the law, the one deserves a lighter penalty than the other not because of the amount of the theft, but because he is probably curable while the other is not. Thus

97. (a) if anyone successfully prosecutes in court a foreigner or slave on a charge of theft of some piece of public property,
a decision must be reached as to the fine or penalty he should pay in view of the fact that he can probably be cured.

6. Cf. pp. 346 and 450.

(b) If a citizen, in spite of the education he will have 942 enjoyed, is convicted of plundering or attacking his fatherland, whether he is caught in the act or not, *he must* be punished by death, as being virtually beyond cure.[7]

MILITARY SERVICE

Military service is a subject on which we need to give a great deal of advice and have a large number of regulations. The vital point is that no one, man or woman, must ever be left without someone in charge of him; nobody must get into the habit of acting alone and independently, either in sham fighting[8] or the real thing, and in peace and war alike we must give our constant attention and obedience to our leader, submitting to his guidance even in tiny details. When the order is given we should stand, march, exercise, wash, feed, stay awake at night on duty as guards or messengers, and even in the midst of dangers not pursue the enemy or yield without a sign from our commander. In short, we must condition ourselves to an instinctive rejection of the very notion of doing anything without our companions; we must live a life in which we never do anything, if possible, except by combined and united action as members of a group. No better or more powerful or efficient weapon exists for ensuring safety and final victory in war, and never will. This is what we must practise in peacetime, right from childhood – the exercise of authority over others and submission to them in turn. Freedom from control must be uncompromisingly eliminated from the life of all men, and of all the animals under their domination.

In particular, all choruses[9] should be calculated to encourage prowess in the field, and for the same reason people must learn to put a brave and cheerful face on it when they have to put up with poor food and drink, extreme cold and heat, and rough bedding. Most importantly, they must not ruin the

7. Cf. pp. 357–8 and 372; contrast p. 362 for the penalty.
8. See pp. 322–5, and especially the 'war-games' on p. 322.
9. On 'choruses' see note on pp. 84–5.

natural powers of head and feet by wrapping them round with artificial protection, so discouraging the spontaneous growth of the cap and shoes that nature provides. When these two extremities are in sound condition they help to keep the whole body at the peak of efficiency, whereas their ruin is its ruin too. The feet are the most willing servants the body has, and the head is the organ of supreme control, the natural seat of all the principal senses of the body.

943   That's the praise of military life that ought, in my view, to ring in a young man's ears. Here are the regulations. When a man is called up, or detailed for some special duty, he is obliged to perform his military service. If he is a coward and fails to present himself, without the permission of his commanders, a prosecution for failure to serve should be brought before the military authorities after return from the field. Such cases must be judged by the soldiers who have fought in the campaign; the various categories (infantry, cavalry and the other branches of the armed forces) should meet separately, infantrymen being brought before infantrymen, cavalrymen before cavalrymen, and the others before their own comrades similarly.

98. If a defendant is found guilty,
    (a) *he must* in future be debarred from
        (i) competing for any kind of military distinction,
        (ii) bringing a charge against anyone else for refusing to perform military service, and
    (b) *the court* must assess the additional penalty or fine he is to pay.

Afterwards, when the charges of refusal to serve have been decided, the commanders must reconvene each arm of the forces and in the presence of the candidates' fellow soldiers seek decisions on those applying for awards of distinction. Supporting statements by eye-witnesses and other evidence adduced by the candidates must not relate to any previous campaign, but only to the one they have just fought. The prize in each case is to be a wreath of olive, which the winner should take to the temple of whichever god of war he pleases and dedicate it, suitably inscribed, as life-long evidence that the first, second or third prize was awarded to him.

If a man does go on active service, but returns home before the commanders withdraw the troops, he should be prosecuted on a charge of desertion before the same court as is concerned with refusal of service.

99. If he is found guilty,
the same penalties should apply as before [98].

ABANDONMENT OF WEAPONS

Naturally, everyone who brings a prosecution ought to be very wary of inflicting an unjustified punishment, whether in cold blood or by accident. Justice is said[10] – and well said – to be the daughter of Respect, and both are the natural scourges of falsehood. So in general we must be careful not to offend against justice, and particularly as regards the abandonment of weapons in the field: we mustn't reproach an enforced abandonment in mistake for an ignominious one, and so inflict penalties as undeserved as the victims are undeserving of them. Although it is by no means easy to tell the two cases apart, a rough and ready distinction must be 944 attempted in the legal code. We can explain the point with the help of a story. If Patroclus had pulled round after being carried to his tent without his weapons (as has happened in thousands of other cases) – the weapons which the poet tells us were presented to Peleus by the gods as a dowry when he married Thetis, and which had been taken by Hector – then it would have been open to all the scoundrels of the time to reproach the son of Menoetius for abandoning his arms.[11] Again, sometimes men have lost their weapons because of being thrown down from a height, or when at sea, or when suddenly caught up by a tremendous onrush of water during their struggles in a storm. There are countless similar circum-

10. Hesiod, *Works and Days*, 254 ff., expresses broadly these sentiments.
11. See Homer, *Iliad* XVI *fin.*, XVII 125 ff., XVIII 78 ff. In the Trojan war, Patroclus, son of Menoetius and companion of Achilles, while wearing the armour of Achilles' father Peleus, was killed by Hector.

stances one could plausibly adduce to excuse and palliate a disaster that positively invites denigration. So we must do our best to distinguish the more serious and reprehensible disasters from the other kind, and in a rough and ready way the distinction can be expressed by varying our expressions of rebuke. Thus 'he *abandoned* his shield' can sometimes be properly replaced by 'he *lost* his weapons'. When you are robbed of your shield with some force, you have not 'abandoned' it in the same way as if you had thrown it away deliberately: the two cases are fundamentally different. The distinction should be written into the legal code in the following terms:

If a man finds the enemy at his heels and instead of turning round and defending himself with the weapons he has, deliberately lets them drop or throws them away, preferring a coward's life of shame to the glorious and blessed death of a hero, then there should certainly be a penalty for losing his weapons by abandonment. But when he has lost his weapons in the other way we've described the judge must not fail to take the fact into account. It is the criminal you need to punish, to reform him, not someone who's simply been unlucky – that's useless. So what will be the right penalty when someone has made good his escape by throwing away the weapons that could have protected him? Unfortunately, it's beyond the power of man to do the opposite of what people say some god did to Caeneus of Thessaly – that is, change him from a woman into a man. If only we could inflict the reverse transformation, from man to woman, that would be, in a sense, the most appropriate punishment for a man who has thrown away his shield. But what we *can* do is to reward him for saving his skin by giving him the closest possible approximation to such a penalty: we can make him spend the rest of his days in utter safety, so that he lives with his ghastly disgrace for as long as possible. Here's the law that will deal with such people:

100. If a man is convicted on a charge of shamefully dropping his weapons of war;

(a) *no general* or any other army officer must employ him as a soldier again, or appoint him to any position 945 whatever;

(b) *and in addition* to being thus permitted, like the natural coward he is, to avoid the risks that only real men can run, the guilty man must also pay a sum of money: 1,000 drachmas if he belongs to the highest property-class, 500 if to the second, 300 if to the third, and 100 if to the lowest.[12]

101. If an officer disobeys and posts the coward again, *the officer's* Scrutineer is to condemn him to pay the same fine: 1,000 drachmas if he belongs to the highest property-class, 500 if to the second, 300 if to the third, and 100 if to the fourth.

THE NEED FOR SCRUTINEERS

Well then, what will be the proper policy for us to adopt on the subject of Scrutineers? So far, we simply have a corps of officials, some appointed for a single year by the luck of the draw, others chosen from a preliminary slate of selected candidates to serve for several years. What if one of them proves so inadequate to the dignity and weight of his office that he gets 'out of true' and does something crooked? Who will be capable of making a man like that go straight again? It is desperately difficult to find someone of high moral standards to exercise authority over the authorities, so to speak, but try we must. So where are our god-like 'straighteners' to be found? The point is this: a state has many crucial parts that prevent it from disintegrating, just as a ship has its stays and bracing ropes and a body its tendons and associated sinews. (Features of this kind are a very widespread phenomenon, and in spite of the many different names we give them in different contexts, they are basically the same sort of thing.) Now the office of Scrutineer is the single most crucial factor determining whether a state survives or disintegrates. If the Scrutineers are better men than the officials they

12. In Plato's text the regulation I have called 100(b) comes *after* 101.

scrutinize, and display irreproachable impartiality and integrity, the entire state and country flourishes and prospers. But if their investigation of the officials is conducted badly, then the sense of justice that unites all the interests in the state is destroyed, with the result that all the officials go their different ways and refuse to pull together any longer; they fragment the state into lots of smaller states by filling it with the party-strife that so speedily wrecks it. That is why it is absolutely vital that the moral standards of the Scrutineers should be exemplary. So let's try to produce these officials by some such procedure as this:

THE ELECTION AND DUTIES OF THE SCRUTINEERS

Every year after the summer solstice the entire state should congregate in a precinct dedicated jointly to Apollo and the Sun, in order to present to the god three out of their number. 946 Each citizen is to propose that person, apart from himself, whom he believes to be perfect in every way; the candidate is to be at least fifty years of age. This preliminary list should be divided into two halves (on the assumption that the total is an even number; if not, the person with the fewest votes should be excluded before the division is made), and the half consisting of those with the most votes should be selected to proceed to the next stage after the other half with fewer votes have been eliminated. If some names receive the same number of votes, so that the selected candidates are too numerous, the excess should be removed by eliminating the youngest candidates. The selected candidates that remain should be voted for again until only three are left, each with a different number of votes. If two of them, or all three, attract equal support, then the decision should be left to chance and the gods of good luck: the first, second and third choices must be determined by lot, crowned with olive and given the rewards of their success. Next, a public proclamation must be made to the effect that the state of the Magnesians, now by the grace of God securely re-established, presents to the Sun-god her three best men; and these, her choicest fruits, in accordance with the law of old, she consecrates for the term of their judicial office as a joint gift to Apollo and the Sun. In the first year twelve such Scrutineers are to be appointed, each to retain office till the age of seventy-five; thereafter three more are to be added every year.

The Scrutineers are to divide all the officials into twelve groups and look into their conduct by making all such inquiries as are consistent with the dignity of a gentleman. During their period of office as Scrutineers they are to live in the precinct of Apollo and the Sun where they were elected. When they have sat in judgement, either privately and individually, or in association with colleagues, on those at the end of their term of office in the service of the state, they must make known, by posting written notice in the market-place, what penalty or fine in their opinion each official ought to pay. Any official who refuses to admit that he has been judged impartially should haul the Scrutineers before the Select Judges, and if he is deemed innocent of the accusations he should accuse the Scrutineers themselves, if he so wishes. But

102. if he is convicted, and

(a) the Scrutineers had decided on death as his penalty, *he must* die (a penalty which in the nature of the case cannot be increased); but

(b) if his penalty is one that it is possible to double, *then double* he must pay.

Now we ought to hear about the scrutiny of the Scrutineers themselves. What will it be, and how will it be organized?

During their lifetime these men, whom the whole state has thought fit to dignify with the highest honours, should sit in 947 the front seat at all the festivals; moreover, when the Greeks assemble to perform sacrifices or see spectacles together, or congregate for other sacred purposes, the leaders of the delegations sent by the state should be chosen from the Scrutineers; and the Scrutineers are to be the only citizens whose heads may be graced by a crown of laurel. They should all be priests of Apollo and the Sun; the chief priesthood should be an annual office, held by the Scrutineer who has come top of the list of those appointed that year – which must be recorded under his name, so as to provide a framework for the calendar for as long as the state endures.

THE FUNERAL OF A SCRUTINEER

After the death of a Scrutineer, his laying-out, his last journey and his tomb must be on a grander scale than for ordinary citizens. All cloth used must be white, dirges and laments must be banned, and a chorus of fifteen girls and another of fifteen youths must stand one on each side of the bier and sing alternately a kind of hymn of praise to the dead priest, celebrating his glory in song throughout the day. As dawn comes up the following day the bier shall be taken to the tomb escorted by 100 of the youths who attend the gymnasia, chosen by the relatives of the dead man. In front must go the young men who are as yet unmarried, each rigged out in his own military equipment; the cavalry should bring their horses, the infantry their weapons, and so on. Around the bier itself, towards the front, will be boys chanting the traditional strains, followed by girls, and women who have finished bearing children. The Priests and Priestesses will bring up the rear; they are of course banned from other funerals, but provided the oracle at Delphi also approves, they shall attend this one, as it will not defile them. The Scrutineer's tomb shall be an oblong crypt built of choice stone of the most indestructible kind obtainable; in this, on benches of stone set side by side, they will lay him who has gone to his reward. On top of the tomb they will pile a circular mound, and plant a sacred grove of trees around it – except on one side, to allow for the indefinite extension of the tomb, where more earth will have to be piled up to cover subsequent burials. Every year the citizens will hold competitions in the Scrutineers' honour, one athletic, one equestrian, and one of the arts. All these honours will be bestowed on Scrutineers whose conduct has borne scrutiny.

PROSECUTIONS OF SCRUTINEERS

If a Scrutineer relies on his election to protect him and goes to
the bad, thus showing he's only too human after all, the law
will order a charge to be brought against him by anyone who
feels inclined to prosecute. The trial should be held in court
according to the following procedure. Guardians of the Laws, 948
and all the Scrutineers, active or retired, must sit in conjunction
with the court of the Select Judges, and the charge brought by the
prosecutor against the defendant must be to the effect that
'so-and-so is a disgrace to his distinctions and his office'.

103. If the defendant is convicted,
he must be ejected from his office, denied the special tomb,
and stripped of the honours he has already received.

104. If the prosecutor fails to win one fifth of the votes,
he must pay a fine of 1200 drachmas if he belongs to the
highest property-class, 800 if to the second, 300 if to the
third, and 200 if to the lowest.

OATHS

Rhadamanthus should be admired for the way in which,
according to report, he decided the suits that came before him.
He realized that his contemporaries were absolutely convinced
of the existence of gods – and not surprisingly, as most people
alive then were actually descended from them, and this is
traditionally true of Rhadamanthus himself. I suppose it was
because he thought that no mere man should be given the task
of judging, but only gods, that he managed to make his
judgements so swift and straightforward. Whatever the subject of dispute, he let the litigants take an oath,[12a] a device
which enabled him to get through his list of cases rapidly and
without making mistakes. Nowadays, however, some people
(as we remarked) don't believe in gods at all, while others
believe they are not concerned about mankind; and there are

12a. One, the guilty, would *decline* it, since gods punish perjurers.

others – the worst and most numerous category – who hold that in return for a miserable sacrifice here and a little flattery there, the gods will help them to steal enormous sums of money and rescue them from all sorts of heavy penalties. So in the modern world the legal procedure used by Rhadamanthus will hardly do. The climate of opinion about the gods has changed, so the law must change too, and a legislator who knows his business ought to abolish the oaths sworn by each side in a law-suit. When a man brings a charge against someone, he should put his accusations in writing without taking an oath; the defendant should similarly write out his denial and hand it to the officials unsworn. It would be dreadful, you see, to know quite well, in view of the frequent law-suits that occur in the state, that although pretty nearly half our citizens[13] have perjured themselves, they go on mixing with each other at common meals and other public and private gatherings without the slightest qualms.

There should therefore be a law requiring a juryman to take an oath before setting about his job. The law should also apply to anyone who votes in the election of officials to public positions: he must do so either under oath or with a ballot-pebble he has obtained from a temple; so too should the judge of a chorus or any other artistic performance, and also the supervisor or umpire of any athletic or equestrian competition – and indeed the judge in any matter where there is nothing to 'gain' (as it seems to human eyes[14]) from perjury. But whenever there is clearly much to be 'gained' from denials and oaths to back them up, then the question at issue between the disputants must be judged at a trial in which oaths are *not* taken.

And more generally, the presiding officials at a trial are not to give a man a hearing if he tries to win belief by swearing oaths, or imprecating himself or his family, or by grovelling appeals for clemency, or effeminate wailing, but only if he states his lawful claims, and listens to those of the other side, with decency and decorum. Otherwise, the officials will

13. Or perhaps 'half the litigants'.
14. I.e. injustice is not really 'gain' at all. Cf. p. 449.

ignore his remarks as irrelevant and instruct him to return to the issue before the court.

However, aliens should be entitled, as at present, to offer and accept binding oaths from each other, if they so wish – after all, they're not going to grow old in the state, nor, as a rule, build a nest in it to produce others entitled to live in the country and behave in the same way as themselves. And whenever an alien prosecutes an alien, the trial should be held under the same rules.[15]

REFUSAL TO CONTRIBUTE TO PUBLIC EXPENSES

Sometimes a free man may defy the state in something not serious enough to deserve a whipping or imprisonment or death – by refusing to take part in a chorus or procession, for instance, or some public ceremony, or to pay some contribution for such communal purposes as a sacrifice in time of peace, or a special levy in war. The first thing to be done in all these cases is to assess the damages; then the culprit is to give a pledge to those officials who have the duty of exacting it under the law of the land. If he still refuses to obey even after the seizure of the pledge, it should be sold and the proceeds confiscated by the state. If a more severe punishment is called for, the official concerned shall impose the appropriate fine on this stubborn fellow and haul him through the courts until he's prepared to do as he's told.

RELATIONS WITH THE OUTSIDE WORLD

A state which does not go in for trading and whose only source of wealth is the soil is obliged to have some settled policy regarding the foreign travel of its own citizens and the admission of aliens from abroad. The legislator, who has to give advice on these problems, must start by being as persuasive as he can.

In the nature of the case, contact between state and state

15. The same general rules as in citizens' trials, I take it.

produces a medley of all sorts of characters, because the
950 unfamiliar customs of the visitors rub off on to their hosts –
and this, in a healthy society living under sound laws, is an
absolute disaster. Most states, however, are not well run at
all, so it makes no difference to them if their citizens fraternize
with foreigners by welcoming them into the state and by going
for trips abroad themselves whenever they feel like it and
wherever their wanderlust takes them, whatever their age. On
the other hand a policy of complete exclusion and complete
refusal to go abroad is just not feasible, and in any case the rest
of the world would think us churlish and uncivilized: we'd
get the reputation of being a truculent and surly people who
have 'Deportations of Aliens', as the term is – and a brutal one
it is, too. Whether the figure you cut in the eyes of others is
good or bad, you should never underestimate its importance.
You see, people in general don't fall so far short of real goodness that they can't recognize virtue and vice when they see it
in others; even wicked people have an uncanny instinct that
usually enables even an absolute villain to understand and
describe accurately enough what distinguishes a good man
from a bad. That is why most states find it an excellent precept
to value their good standing with the rest of the world. But
the soundest and most important rule is this: if you mean to
be perfect, you should seek to live in good repute only if you
are really good in the first place, but not otherwise. And so it
will be entirely right and proper if the state we are now founding in Crete wins among men a brilliant and glorious reputation for virtue, and if things go according to plan there is
every reason to expect that, out of all the states and countries
which look upon the Sun and the other gods, Magnesia will
be one of the few that are well administered.

FOREIGN TRAVEL

So what should we do about the admission of aliens and our
own journeys to places in foreign countries? First of all, no
young person under forty is ever to be allowed to travel
abroad under any circumstances; nor is anyone to be allowed

to go for private reasons, but only on some public business, as a herald or ambassador or as an observer of one sort or another. (Of course, absence abroad on military service in wartime doesn't deserve to be mentioned in the same breath: it's not one of those journeys which are 'for diplomatic reasons'!) We must send representatives to take part in the sacrifices and games held at Delphi in honour of Apollo and at Olympia in honour of Zeus, and to Nemea and the Isthmus;[16] and we must send as many representatives as we can, the finest and noblest of our citizens, who will do credit to our state in these sacred gatherings of peace, and win it renown to 951 match that of her armies on the field of battle. And when they return, they will tell the younger generation that the social and political customs of the rest of the world don't measure up to their own.

THE OBSERVERS

But there are other kinds of observers who should be dispatched, provided the Guardians of the Laws give permission. If any citizen would like to spend rather longer surveying at his leisure the life lived by foreigners, no law should prevent him, because no state will ever be able to live at a properly advanced level of civilization if it keeps itself to itself and never comes into contact with all the vices and virtues of mankind; nor will it be able to preserve its laws intact if it just gets used to them without grasping their *raison d'être*. In the mass of mankind you'll invariably find a number – though only a small number – of geniuses with whom it is worth anything to associate, and they crop up just as often in badly-ruled states as in the well-ruled. So the citizen of a well-run state, provided he's incorruptible, should go out and range over land and sea to track them down, so that he can see to the strengthening of the customs of his country that are soundly based, and the

16. The Athenian names the four major centres at which panhellenic festivals were held. For the site of Delphi, see note on p. 206; Olympia was in Elis in the western Peloponnese; Nemea was a valley in the eastern; the Isthmian games were held near Corinth.

refurbishing of any that are defective. Without this observation and research a state will never stay at the peak of perfection; nor will it if the observers are incompetent.

CLEINIAS: So how can we ensure that both these requirements are met?

ATHENIAN: Like this. In the first place, anyone who goes observing for us in this fashion must be over fifty; and since the Guardians of the Laws are going to send him abroad as a specimen Magnesian, he must be one of those citizens who have gained a good reputation generally, and particularly in war; and on passing sixty he must go off observing no longer. When he has spent as many of his ten years as he pleases making his observations, he should come home and present himself before the council which muses on legislation. This council,[17] which should consist partly of young men and partly of old, must have a strict rule to meet daily from dawn until the sun is well up in the sky. Its membership is to be: (1) those Priests who have won high distinction, (2) the ten Guardians of the Laws who are currently the most senior, (3) the Minister of Education for the time being, together with his predecessors in office. No member should attend alone: each is to bring a young man of his own choice, aged between thirty and forty. The discussion at their meetings must always centre round their own state, the problems of legislation, and any other important point relevant to such topics that they may discover from external sources. They must be particularly concerned with those studies which promise, if pursued, to further their researches by throwing light on legislative problems that would otherwise remain difficult and obscure. Whichever of these studies are sanctioned by the older members should be pursued with all diligence by the younger. If one of the protégés invited to attend is judged to be inadequate, the whole council is to censure the man who invited him; but any that get a good name should be fostered and watched with particular care by the state at large, and if they do what's wanted of them, they are to be specially honoured, but if they turn out worse than most other young

952

17. The 'Nocturnal' council: see pp. 515 ff.

men they should suffer correspondingly worse disgrace. To this council, then, the observer of foreign customs must proceed as soon as he gets back. If he has come across people who were able to give him some information about any problems of legislation or teaching or education, or if he actually comes back with some discoveries of his own, he should make his report to a full meeting of the council. If he seems to be not a whit better or worse for his journey, he should be congratulated at any rate for his energy; if he is thought to have become appreciably better, even higher recognition should be given him during his lifetime, and after his death he must be paid appropriate honours by authority of the assembled council. But if it seems that he has returned corrupted, this self-styled 'expert' must talk to no one, young or old, and provided he obeys the authorities he may live as a private person; but if not, and

105. he is convicted in court of meddling in some educational or legal question,

he must die.

106. If none of the authorities takes him to court when that is what he deserves,

it should count as a black mark against them when distinctions are awarded.

FOREIGN VISITORS

So much for the way foreign travel should be undertaken and the sort of persons who should venture on it. But what about our duty to welcome foreign visitors? There are four categories of them worth discussing. Those in the first turn up every year without fail, usually in summer, with the regularity of migrating birds. Most of them are on business trips in search of profit, and throughout the summer they 'wing' their way like so many birds across the sea to foreign parts. They must be received at trading posts and harbours and in public buildings outside but not far from the state by officials appointed for the purpose, who should (a) take good care that none of this category of visitor introduces any novel custom,

953 (b) handle with proper impartiality the law-suits that affect them, and (c) keep intercourse with them down to the unavoidable minimum. The second type are 'observers' in the most basic sense: they come to see the sights, and to listen, too, at festivals of the arts. All such visitors should be received in hospitable lodgings near temples, by whose priests and custodians they are to be looked after and attended to. Then, when they have stayed for a reasonable length of time, and seen and heard what they came to see and hear, they should take their leave without having inflicted or suffered any harm. If anyone injures them, or they injure anyone else, the Priests are to act as judges, provided no more than fifty drachmas are involved. If the claim is for a greater sum, the trial must be held before the Market-Wardens.

The third type of visitor, who arrives from another country on some matter of state, should be received at public expense, and by no one except Generals, Cavalry-Commanders and Company-Commanders. Together with the executive for the time being, the official by whom he is put up and entertained should have the sole responsibility for him.

Sometimes, though rarely, a fourth kind of visitor arrives. If ever a counterpart to our own observers comes from a foreign country, we shall first of all require that he should be not less than fifty years old, and in addition he should profess to be coming to view something whose excellence surpasses that of anything in the rest of the world, or to report on some such feature to another state. Such a man may dispense with invitations, and present himself at the doors of the wise and rich, because that is the class of man he is himself. In the full confidence that he is the right sort of guest for such a distinguished host, he should go to the home of (say) the Minister of Education, or of someone who has won an award for virtue. He should spend his time in the company of one or other of these, and after an exchange of information take his leave, duly honoured as a friend by friends with fitting presents and tokens of esteem.

These are the laws that should govern the reception of all our visitors from abroad, of either sex, and the dispatch of our own people to other countries. We must show respect for Zeus the God of Strangers, and not keep aliens at arm's length by uncongenial food and offensive sacrifices (like the sons of Old Father Nile[18] do nowadays), or by uncivilized proclamations.

SURETIES

Anyone who stands surety should do so in precise terms, by specifying all the details of the agreement in a written contract, before not less than three witnesses if the sum involved is less than 1,000 drachmas, and not less than five in the case of greater sums. (Also, a warrantor[19] is surety for a vendor who 954 is insolvent or cannot be sued, and is to have the same liability in law.)

SEARCHING A HOUSE

When a man wants to search someone else's premises, he should do so clad in only his tunic, without a belt, and after swearing to the gods specified by law that he really does expect to find what he's looking for. The other party is to open up his home, including all its sealed and unsealed property, to be searched; if he refuses permission to search to anyone requesting it, the party thus hindered must go to law, giving his estimate of the value of the object he is looking for.

107. If the defendant is convicted,
he must pay double the estimated value as damages.

If the owner of the house happens to be away, the residents must make unsealed property available for search; sealed property should be counter-sealed by the searcher, who should then post anyone he likes to guard it for a period of five days. If the householder stays away for longer than that, the other party should fetch the City-Wardens and make the search, opening up sealed property as well and sealing it up

18. Literally 'offspring of the Nile': I take this to be an irreverent circumlocution for 'Egyptians'. Plato shows considerable knowledge of Egypt (cf. pp. 91-2, 313), and it is more than likely that he visited the country and knows what he is talking about.

19. The vendor from whom the vendor bought the object in question.

again afterwards in the same way in the presence of the household and the City-Wardens.

TIME LIMITS FOR DISPUTING TITLE

Now for cases when title is in dispute. After a certain period has elapsed, it must be no longer possible to challenge the rights of the person in possession. In Magnesia, of course, dispute about land or houses is out of the question. But as for other possessions, if a man has used something openly in town or market-place or temple, and no one has tried to recover it and claimed to have been looking for it all the time the other man has obviously made no attempt at concealment, then provided the ownership of the one party and the search of the other have continued for a year, after the expiry of that period no claim for recovery is to be permitted. If a man uses an object openly, not indeed in town or market-place, but in the countryside, and no one confronts him with a claim to it for five years, then on the expiry of that period no one is to be allowed to attempt repossession. If the article is used in a man's town house, the time limit is to be three years; if it is kept in a building in the country, ten years; and if it is used abroad, then there is to be no time limit for recovery at all, however long the claimant may take to find it.

PREVENTION OF ATTENDANCE AT COURT

Sometimes a man may forcibly prevent a litigant or witness from appearing at a trial. If he prevents a slave, his own or another's, the suit should be null and void.

108. If he prevents a free man,

955 *he must* be imprisoned for a year and be liable to a suit for kidnapping at the hands of anyone who cares to prosecute, and the suit will be null in any case.

PREVENTION OF PARTICIPATION
IN CONTESTS

If a man forcibly prevents a rival competitor from participating in an athletic or cultural or any other contest, anyone who wishes should report the fact to the supervisors of the games, who should set the would-be contestant free to enter the competition. If they prove unable to do so, and the man responsible for the competitor's absence wins, the prize should be awarded to the person prevented from competing, and he should be recorded as the winner in any temple he pleases.

109. The person who has hindered him must not be allowed to make any dedication or record relating to that contest, and he must be liable to a prosecution for damages whether he wins or loses.

RECEIVING STOLEN GOODS

110. If a man receives stolen goods, knowing them to be stolen,
he must suffer the same penalty as the thief.

HARBOURING AN EXILE

111. The penalty for harbouring an exile should be death.

WAGING PRIVATE WAR

Everyone is to have the same friends and enemies as the state.

112. (a) If a man makes a private peace or wages private war with anyone without the backing of the state,
he too must be punished by death.

If any sectional interest in the state makes peace or war with any parties on its own account, the Generals must haul those responsible for the affairs before a court.

(b) If the defendants are convicted,
death should be the penalty.

BRIBES

Members of the public service should perform their duties without taking bribes. Such a practice must never be extenuated by an approving reference to maxims like 'One good turn deserves another'. It is not easy for an official to reach his decisions impartially and stick to them, and the safest thing he can do is to listen to the law and obey its command to take no gifts for his services.

113. If a man disobeys and is convicted in court, *the only penalty* permitted is to be death.

TAXATION

Now to deal with payments to the public treasury. For a variety of reasons, an assessment must be made of each man's property, and the members of the tribes must make a written return of the year's produce to the Country-Wardens. The treasury will thus be able to use whichever of the two methods of exacting payment it finds convenient – that is, every year the authorities will decide to levy a proportion *either* of the sum total of the individual assessments *or* of the revenues accruing that particular year. (Payment for the common meals should be excluded from the calculations.)

OFFERINGS TO THE GODS

The offerings a reasonable man makes to the gods should be on a correspondingly reasonable scale. As the earth and every household's hearth are already sacred to all the gods, no one should consecrate them a second time.[20] The gold and silver that you find in temples and private houses in other states 956 encourage jealousy; ivory, taken as it is from a lifeless body, is an unclean offering; and iron and bronze are instruments of war. A man may offer at the public temples any object he likes made of wood or stone, provided that in either case it consists of no more than a single piece; if he offers woven material, it should not exceed what one woman can produce in a month. In general, and particularly in the case of woven material, white is the colour appropriate to the gods; dyes must not be

20. I take it this is a reaffirmation of the rule against private shrines (see pp. 446–7 and G. R. Morrow, *Plato's Cretan City*, 412, note 42).

employed, except for military decorations. The gifts the gods find most acceptable are birds and pictures, provided they do not take a painter more than a single day to complete. All this should serve as a pattern for all our other offerings.

THE THREE GRADES OF COURT

Now that we have described the nature and number of the parts into which the whole state is divided, and done what we can to frame laws for all the most important agreements men make, we're left with the question of legal procedure. The court of first resort will consist of judges – arbitrators, in fact, but 'judges' is really a more appropriate title – chosen by agreement between prosecutor and defendant. If the case is not settled in the first court, the litigants should go and contest it again before the second (composed of villagers and tribesmen, duly divided into twelve groups),[21] but at the risk of an enhanced penalty: if the defendant loses for the second time, he must be mulcted an additional fifth of the penalty previously assessed and recorded. If he is still aggrieved with his judges and wants to fight the case for the third time, he must take it to the Select Judges, and if he is defeated again, he is to pay one and a half times the original penalty. As for the prosecutor, if he is not prepared to lie down under defeat in the first court, and goes before the second, he should be awarded the extra fifth of the penalty if he wins, but be fined that amount if he loses. If the litigants refuse to acquiesce in the earlier decision and go before the third court, and the defendant loses, he must pay one and a half times the penalty as already stated; if the prosecutor loses, he must be fined one half of it.

THE MINOR POINTS OF LEGAL PROCEDURE, AND THE IMPORTANCE OF LEGAL STUDIES

But what about the balloting for jurors, and the procedure for making up the juries? What about the appointment of

21. On this detail and the character of the court, see G. R. Morrow, *Plato's Cretan City*, 260–61.

attendants for the various officials, the fixing of times at which the various formalities should be completed, voting methods, adjournments, and all the other similar inescapable details of legal procedure, such as putting cases early or late in the calendar, the enforcement of attendance and of replies to interrogation, and suchlike? Well, we've made the point before,[22] but the truth is all the better for being stated two or even three times. All these minor rules are perfectly easy to invent, and the senior legislator may skip them and leave it to his young successor to fill in the gaps. But although that will be reasonable enough in the case of the courts that are appointed privately,[23] the common public courts, and those that the various officials need to use in the performance of their duties, need a rather different approach. Sensible people in several states have framed a good many decent regulations which our Guardians of the Laws should adapt for the state that we are now founding. The Guardians should examine them and touch them up after trying them out in practice, until they think they have licked each single one into shape; then they should finalize them, ratify them as immutable, and render them lifelong obedience. Then there is the question of the silence of the judges, and the restraint or otherwise of their language, as well as all the other details in which our standards of justice and goodness and decorum differ from those you find in such variety in other states. We've already had something to say on this topic,[24] and we shall have more to say towards the end. The judge who wants to act with proper judicial impartiality should bear all these points in mind and get hold of books in which to study the subject. The study of laws, provided they are good laws, is unsurpassed for its power to improve the student. (It can't be an accident that the name of this god-given and wonderful institution, law, is so suggestive of reason.[25]) And other compositions, such as eulogies or censures in verse or prose, in the latter case either taking written form or being simply spoken during our day-to-day contacts when we indulge in contentious argument or (some-

957

22. See for example pp. 348–9.   23. See pp. 242 and 509.
24. See pp. 498–9.   25. Cf. p. 171: *nomos* = 'law', *nous* = 'reason'.

times thoughtlessly) express our agreement – all these will be measured against a clear criterion: the writings of the legislator, which the good judge will treasure as a kind of antidote against the others, so as to ensure his own moral health and that of the state. He will confirm and strengthen the virtuous in the paths of righteousness, and do his best to banish ignorance and incontinence and cowardice and indeed every sort of injustice from the hearts of those criminals whose outlook can be cured. However – and this is a point that deserves constant repetition – when a man's soul is unalterably fixed in that condition by decree of fate, our erudite judges and 958 their advisers will deserve the commendation of the whole state if they cure him by imposing the penalty of death.[26]

THE EXECUTION OF JUDGEMENT

When the suits for the year have been finally decided, the following laws must apply to the execution of judgement. First of all, immediately after the voting in each case, and by proclamation of a herald in the hearing of the judges, the official who has pronounced sentence should assign all the property of the convicted party, except the minimum he must retain,[27] to the successful prosecutor. If after the expiry of the month following that in which the case was tried the loser has not settled the business with the victor to the satisfaction of both, the official who gave judgement must at the request of the victorious party hand over the goods of the loser. If the latter lacks the means to pay, and the deficiency amounts to a drachma or more, he must not be allowed to prosecute other people (they however, being entitled to prosecute *him*), until he has paid his debt in full to his opponent. If someone who has received an adverse verdict obstructs the bench that condemned him, the officials thus obstructed should haul him before the court of the Guardians of the Laws.

26. The incorrigible criminal may as well cut his losses: if he stays alive, he will get worse and meet a correspondingly worse fate in the next world. Cf. pp. 191 and 358.
27. The ancestral lot and its equipment.

114. If he is convicted on such a charge,
he must be punished by death,

on the grounds that his conduct is wrecking the entire state
and its laws.

FUNERAL REGULATIONS

Now here's the next point. A man is born and brought up, and
begets and rears his own children in turn; he deals fairly in
his business transactions, paying the penalty if he has done
anyone injury and exacting one if others have wronged him;
and finally, as destiny decrees, after an old age spent in
obedience to the laws, the course of nature will bring him to
the end of his life. So what should we do when a man or
woman has died? First, we must bow to the absolute authority
of the Expounders' instructions about the sacred rites to be
observed in honour of the nether gods and those of this
world. No tomb, whether its mound is large or small, should
be constructed anywhere on land that can be farmed; graves
must take up space only where nature has made the ground
good for nothing except the reception and concealment of the
bodies of the dead with minimum detriment to the living,
because no one, alive or dead, must ever rob the living of any
land which – thanks to the natural fertility of Mother Earth –
will grow food for the human race. The soil must not be piled
higher than five men can manage by working for five days.
Stone slabs must not be made bigger than they need to be to
accommodate a eulogy of the deceased's career of not more
959 than the usual four hexameters. The laying-out at home should
not last longer than is necessary to confirm that the person
really is dead and not just in a faint; in average cases, it will be
reasonable for the body to be taken to the tomb after two days.

We should, of course, trust whatever the legislator tells us,
but especially his doctrine that the soul has an absolute
superiority over the body, and that while I am alive I have
nothing to thank for my individuality except my soul, whereas
my body is just the likeness of myself that I carry round with
me. This means we are quite right when we say a corpse 'looks
like' the deceased. Our real self – our immortal soul, as it is

called – departs, as the ancestral law declares, to the gods below to give an account of itself. To the wicked, this is a terrifying doctrine, but a good man will welcome it. And once he's dead, there's not a great deal we can do to help a man: all his relatives should have helped him while he was still in the land of the living, so that he could have passed his life in all possible justice and holiness; and then after death he could have escaped the penalty visited on evil deeds in the life to come. This all goes to show that we should never squander our last penny, on the fanciful assumption that this lump of flesh being buried really is our own son or brother or whoever it is we mournfully think we are burying. We ought to realize that in fact he has departed in final consummation of his destiny, and that it is our duty to make the best of what we have and spend only a moderate sum on the body, which we may now think of as a kind of altar to the gods below, now deserted by its spirit; and as for what is meant by 'moderate' in this matter, the most respectable ideas will be those of the legislator. The law, then, should specify a reasonable level of expenditure as follows. In the case of a member of the highest property-class, the whole funeral should not cost more than 500 drachmas; 300 may be spent on a member of the second class, 200 on a member of the third, and 100 on a member of the fourth.

The Guardians of the Laws will have to shoulder a great many burdens and responsibilities, but their overriding duty will be to devote their lives to the care of children and adults and indeed persons of all ages. In particular, when a man is nearing his end his household should invite one Guardian to take charge of him, and if the funeral arrangements pass off decorously and without extravagance, this Guardian-in-charge will get the credit, but if not, then the blame will be at his door. The laying-out and other matters should take place according to usage, but usage must be modified by the following directions of our legislator-statesman. 'Tasteless though it is to forbid or instruct people to weep over the dead, dirges 960 should be forbidden; and cries of mourning should be allowed only inside the house. The mourners must not bring the corpse on to the open street nor make their procession a noisy one, and they must be outside the city by day-break.' So much for the regulations on the subject. The person who obeys them will never be punished, but

> 115. if a man disobeys a single Guardian of the Laws,
> *he must* be punished by them all with whatever penalty recommends itself to their united judgement.

The other methods of burying the dead, and the kind of criminals to whom we deny burial, such as parricides, temple-robbers and all similar categories, have already been specified and provided for in the legal code.[28] And that means, I suppose, that we have pretty well come to the end of our legislation.

28. See pp. 176–7, 390–91, 445 and 496.

§26. THE NOCTURNAL COUNCIL

We have seen the Athenian creating a vast number of officials, and we may begin to suspect that in Magnesia the administrators will out-number the administered. Why then does he take the trouble to establish yet another authority?[1] *He does so for three connected reasons.* (1) *The state officials have to administer laws which like all written regulations will need not only to be supplemented but also interpreted and even altered in the light of changing circumstances, or perhaps because the first legislator drafted them badly. The Athenian wishes to ensure that these later amendments are made in the same spirit as the original laws. This suggests a need for a* council of legal studies, *charged with the duty of studying the problems of drafting and clarifying legislation, and studying its relation to the wider issues of jurisprudence.* (2) *As the Athenian remarks on p. 520, a state's legislation will reflect its moral aims. Now if we have no clearly formulated moral aim, we shall tend to think of morality as adherence to a given set of laws; and then if for some reason we change these laws, we may find we have changed our moral standards too. It is not enough to recognize by instinct that this law is good and that bad. We must also know what goodness and badness are in themselves, so as to be able to measure our laws against a real and unchanging moral standard. This is the point of the Athenian's insistence on an ability to understand the nature not only of each of the four individual virtues, but of Virtue itself – or, as he puts it, the sense in which the four are 'one'. This suggests a need for a* council of philosophical studies, *charged with the duty of research into moral standards, so as to have firm criteria for the laws of the state.* (3) *However, such philosophical knowledge is useless if it is not explained and applied, and this suggests a need for a* council of propaganda,

---

1. That the Nocturnal Council is not a last-minute expedient born of a final despair in the constitutional government described in the rest of the *Laws* is shown by a number of anticipatory mentions of it or something like it, e.g. pp. 56, 443 and 445. Nor, of course, should anyone be misled by its somewhat sinister title.

charged with the duty of seeing that the correct moral standards are (however imperfectly) understood in the state at large. These three functions – legal, philosophical and didactic – are combined in the Nocturnal Council. The 'higher education' of the Council also includes theology and cosmology and various other studies relevant to morality. In short, the Council keeps the laws and customs of the state under permanent review; it is a device for the subordination of legislation and government to philosophy.

How, in practice, will the Council carry out its duties? Its course of studies is described somewhat allusively and we cannot be sure of the order in which the various subjects will be taken. The closing pages of the dialogue imply, perhaps, that the Academy would take the infant Council under its wing and arrange a curriculum. But we can get a fairly clear picture of the way in which the Council would perform its other duties. It would receive information about foreign legal codes from the 'observers' (see pp. 502–3), about developments in philosophy from the visiting philosophers to whom its members give hospitality (see p. 504), and about activities and opinions in Magnesia from the young men co-opted (its 'eyes': see p. 524), as well as from its regular members, most of whom hold or have held high office in the state. There is no doubt that the Council would be well informed. And for these reasons it would be well placed to have a pervasive influence on the life of Magnesia. The young men would gain status from their very membership, and would be natural candidates for office later. The other members would belong to various other bodies and would obviously be consulted on matters of policy and the drafting of rules and regulations.

A modern reader will have mixed feelings about the Nocturnal Council. On the one hand he will recognize Plato's wisdom and originality in providing for a permanent body, with few routine responsibilities but not wholly divorced from day-to-day affairs, to review and improve legislation in the light of legal and philosophical research; on the other hand, he will question the fundamental assumption on which the Council is based, namely that there exists fixed moral standards, ascertainable by inquiry and study, which should be reflected in a virtually immutable legal code. Whatever our final judgement on it, the Nocturnal Council must be recognized as one of Plato's most far-reaching and far-sighted institutions.

HOW CAN THE STATE BE PRESERVED INTACT?

ATHENIAN: However, even when you have achieved or gained or founded something, you have never quite finished. Only when you have ensured complete and perpetual security for your creation can you reckon to have done everything that ought to have been done. Until then, it's a case of 'unfinished business'.

CLEINIAS: Well said, sir – but what's the particular point you had in mind in saying that? Could you be a little clearer?

ATHENIAN: Well, you know, Cleinias, a lot of old expressions are extraordinarily apt. I'm thinking particularly of the names of the Fates.

CLEINIAS: What names?

ATHENIAN: Lachesis[2] for the first, Clotho[3] for the second, and Atropos[4] for the third fulfiller of destiny – the last so called from her likeness to a woman making the threads on her spindle irreversible. That is precisely the situation we want to see in our state and its citizens – not merely physical health and soundness, but the rule of law in their souls and (more important than all that) the preservation of the laws themselves. In fact, it seems to me that the service we've still not done for the laws is to discover how to build into them a resistance to being reversed.

CLEINIAS: That's serious, because I don't suppose there's a way of giving anything that sort of property.

ATHENIAN: But there is. I see that quite clearly now.

CLEINIAS: Well then, we mustn't abandon our task till we've achieved this for the legal code we've expounded. It would be silly to waste our labour on something by failing to construct it on a firm foundation.

ATHENIAN: You're right to encourage me, and you'll find me as keen as you are.

CLEINIAS: Splendid! So what is this safety-device for our

2. Literally, 'the Distributor of Lots'.
3. Literally, 'the Spinner'.
4. Literally, 'the Inflexible One'.

political system and legal code going to be, according to you? And how can we construct it?

MEMBERSHIP AND FUNCTIONS OF THE COUNCIL

961 ATHENIAN: We said[5] that we ought to have in the state a council with the following range of membership. The ten Guardians of the Laws who are currently the eldest were to convene together with all persons who had won awards of distinction and the travellers who had gone abroad to see if they could discover any special method of keeping a legal code intact. When these observers got back safe and sound, they were to be accepted as suitable associates of the council, provided they had first passed the scrutiny of its members. In addition, each member had to bring a young man of at least thirty years of age, but only after selecting him as particularly well qualified by natural abilities and education; on these terms the young man was to be introduced to the other members of the council, and if they approved of him, he was to join them; if not, they were not to breathe a word to anyone about the fact that he was considered, least of all to the rejected candidate himself. The council was to meet before dawn, when people are least beset by other business, public or private. That was more or less the description we gave earlier, wasn't it?

CLEINIAS: Certainly it was.

ATHENIAN: So I'm going to resume the subject of this council, and here's the point I want to make about it. I maintain that if one were to lower it as a sort of 'anchor' for the whole state, then provided conditions were suitable, it would keep safe everything we wanted it to.

CLEINIAS: How so?

ATHENIAN: Now at this crucial moment, we must strain every muscle to get things right.

CLEINIAS: That's a fine sentiment. Now do what you have in mind.

5. See pp. 502–3.

ATHENIAN: The question we have to ask about anything, Cleinias, is this: what is it that has the special power of keeping it safe in each of its activities? In a living creature, for instance, this is the natural function of the soul and the head, in particular.

CLEINIAS: Again, what's your point?

ATHENIAN: Well, when these two are functioning satisfactorily, they ensure the animal's safety, don't they?

CLEINIAS: How so?

ATHENIAN: Because no matter what else is true of either, the soul is the seat of reason and the head enjoys the faculties of sight and hearing. In short, the combination of reason with the highest senses constitutes a single faculty that would have every right to be called the salvation of the animal concerned.

CLEINIAS: That's likely enough, I suppose.

ATHENIAN: Of course it is. But *how* do reason and the senses combine to ensure the safety of a ship, in fair weather or foul? Isn't it because captain and crew interpret sense-data by reason, *as embodied in* the expertise captains have, that they keep themselves and the whole ship safe?

CLEINIAS: Naturally.

ATHENIAN: We've no need to multiply examples, but take a general in command of his army, or any doctor tending a human body. What will they each aim at, on the assumption that they intend, as they should, to preserve their charges safe and sound? Won't the general aim at victory and 962 control over the enemy, and won't doctors and their attendants aim to keep the body in a healthy condition?

CLEINIAS: Of course.

ATHENIAN: Now consider a doctor who can't recognize the state of the body we've just called 'health', or a general who doesn't know what's meant by 'victory' and the other terms we reviewed. Could either of them possibly be judged to have a rational knowledge of his field?

CLEINIAS: Of course not.

ATHENIAN: And if the ruler of a *state* were obviously ignorant of the target at which a statesman should aim, would he really deserve his title 'ruler'? Would he be capable of ensuring the safety of an institution whose purpose he entirely failed to appreciate?

CLEINIAS: Certainly not.

ATHENIAN: Well then, in the present circumstances, if our settlement of this territory is to be finished off properly, it looks as if we shall have to provide it with some constituent that understands (a) this target we have mentioned – the target, whatever we find it is, of the statesman, (b) how to hit it, and (c) which laws (above all) and which persons have helpful advice to give and which not. If a state lacks some such constituent, no one will be surprised to see it staggering from one irrational and senseless expedient to another in all its affairs.

CLEINIAS: That's true.

ATHENIAN: So is there any institution or constituent part of our state qualified and prepared to function as an organ of protection? Can we name one?

CLEINIAS: No, sir, not with much assurance, anyway. But if guess I must, I think your remarks point to the Council you said just now had to convene during the night.

ATHENIAN: You've caught my meaning splendidly, Cleinias. As the drift of our present argument shows, that body must possess virtue in all its completeness, which means above all that it will *not* take erratic aim at one target after another but keep its eye on one single target and shoot all its arrows at that.

CLEINIAS: Certainly.

ATHENIAN: Now we can see why it is hardly surprising that rules and regulations fluctuate so much from state to state: it is because legislation has a different aim in each. Nor is it surprising that in most cases you find that some people think of justice as nothing but the subjection of the state to the rule of this or that type of person without regard to their vice or virtue, while others think of it as the opportunity to become rich, no matter whether they are thereby enslaved or not; others again are bent hell for leather on a life of 'freedom'. Some legislators keep both ends in view, and their laws have the dual purpose of securing control over

other states *and* freedom for their own. The cleverest legislators of all (as they like to think of themselves), so far from
aiming at one single end, look not only to these but all others
like them, simply because they cannot identify any supremely
valuable end to which all others ought, in their view, to
contribute.

THE UNITY AND PLURALITY OF VIRTUE

CLEINIAS: Well then, sir, the line we took so long ago was 963
the right one.[6] We said that every detail of our legislation
ought to have a *single* end in view, and the proper name to
call it was, I think we agreed, 'virtue'.

ATHENIAN: Yes.

CLEINIAS: And I think we maintained that the virtues were
four.

ATHENIAN: Indeed we did.

CLEINIAS: The leading one, to which not only the other
three but everything else should be orientated, was reason.

ATHENIAN: You take the point admirably, Cleinias. Now
follow the rest of the argument. As far as the captain, doctor
and general are concerned, we have already indicated that
their intellect aims at some appropriate single end. Now it is
the turn of the statesman's reason to be investigated. Let's
personify it and ask it the following question: 'My good sir,
what aim do *you* have in view? What's your single overriding purpose? The intelligent doctor can identify his
accurately enough, so can't you, with all your superior
wisdom (as I suppose you'd claim), identify yours?' Or can
you two, Cleinias and Megillus, answer for him and tell me
precisely what your notion of his aim is, just as I've often
given you detailed accounts of the notions of many other
people on their behalf?

CLEINIAS: No, sir, we certainly cannot.

ATHENIAN: What about replying, 'I think he should make
every effort to get an overall understanding of his aim, as well
as see it in its various contexts'?

6. See p. 54.

CLEINIAS: What contexts, for example?

ATHENIAN: Well, when we said there were four species of virtue, obviously the very fact that there were four meant that each had to be thought of as somehow distinct from the others.

CLEINIAS: Surely.

ATHENIAN: Yet in fact we call them all by a single name. We say courage is virtue, wisdom is virtue, and the other two similarly, on the ground that really they are not several things but just one – virtue.

CLEINIAS: Very true.

ATHENIAN: It's not hard to explain how these two 'virtues' and the rest *differ* from each other and how each has acquired a different name. The real problem is this: why, precisely, have we described both of them (as well as the others) by this *common* term 'virtue'?

CLEINIAS: What do you mean?

ATHENIAN: My point is perfectly easy to explain. Shall we let one of us ask the questions, and the other answer them?

CLEINIAS: Again, what do you mean?

ATHENIAN: Here's the question for you to put to me: 'Why is it that after calling both by the single term "virtue", in the next breath we speak of two "virtues", courage and wisdom?' I'll tell you why. One of them, courage, copes with fear, and is found in wild animals as well as human beings, notably in the characters of very young children. The soul, you see, becomes courageous by a purely natural process, without the aid of reason. By contrast, in this absence of reason a wise and sensible soul is out of the question. That is true now, has always been true, and always will be true; the two processes are fundamentally different.

CLEINIAS: That's true.

964 ATHENIAN: So there's your explanation of why there are two different virtues. Now it's your turn: you tell me why they are one and the same thing. Your job, you understand, is to tell me why the four of them nevertheless form a unity; and when you have demonstrated that unity, ask me to show you again in what sense they are four.

THE COUNCIL'S DUTY TO TEACH

Next after that we ought to ask ourselves what constitutes adequate knowledge of any object that has a name and a definition: is it enough to know only the name and not the definition? On the contrary, if a man is worth his salt, wouldn't it be a disgrace in him not to understand all these points about a topic so grand and so important?

CLEINIAS: Presumably it would.

ATHENIAN: And as for a giver or guardian of laws, and indeed anyone who thinks of his own virtue as superior to the rest of the world's, and has won awards for his achievement, *is* there anything more important than the qualities we are now discussing, – courage, restraint, justice and wisdom?

CLEINIAS: Of course not.

ATHENIAN: So in such circumstances what role should the expounders, teachers and lawgivers – the guardians of the rest of the community – play when a criminal needs enlightenment and instruction, or perhaps correction and punishment? Should they not prove better than anyone else at giving him a full explanation and description of the effects of virtue and vice? Or is some poet-visitor to the state, or some self-styled 'educationalist', going to put up a better show than the winner of the palm for every kind of virtue? Where there are no efficient and articulate guardians with an adequate understanding of virtue, it will be hardly surprising if the state, precisely because it is unguarded, meets the fate of so many states nowadays.

CLEINIAS: No, hardly surprising at all, I suppose.

ATHENIAN: Well then, shall we carry out these proposals, or what? Shall we make sure our guardians are more highly qualified than the man in the street to explain what virtue is, and to put it into practice? How else could our state function like the head and senses of a wise man, now that it possesses within itself something analogous to protect it?

CLEINIAS: Where is this resemblance, sir? How do we draw such a comparison?

ATHENIAN: Obviously the state itself corresponds to the trunk, and the junior guardians, chosen for their natural gifts and the acuteness of their mental vision, live as it were at the summit and survey the whole state; they store up in their memory all the sensations they receive while on guard, and act as reporters for their elder colleagues of everything 965 that takes place in the state; and the old men – we could compare them to the intellect, for their high wisdom in so many vital questions – take advantage of the assistance and advice of their juniors in debating policy, so that the joint efforts of both ranks effectively ensure the safety of the entire state. Now is this the sort of organization we want to see, or some other? Should the state, in fact, keep all its citizens on the same level, without giving some a more specialized training and education than others?

CLEINIAS: My dear sir! That's quite impracticable.

THE HIGHER EDUCATION OF THE COUNCIL

ATHENIAN: Then we have to pass on to a more advanced education than the one we described earlier.

CLEINIAS: Perhaps so.

ATHENIAN: What about the education we touched on a moment ago?[7] Would that answer our needs?

CLEINIAS: Certainly it would.

ATHENIAN: Didn't we say[8] that a really skilled craftsman or guardian in any field must be able not merely to see the many individual instances of a thing, but also to win through to a knowledge of the single central concept, and when he's understood that, put the various details in their proper place in the overall picture?

CLEINIAS: We did, and rightly.

ATHENIAN: So what better tool can there be for a penetrating investigation of a concept than an ability to look beyond the many dissimilar instances to the single notion?

CLEINIAS: Probably none.

7. See pp. 521–2.   8. Cf. also p. 436.

ATHENIAN: 'Probably!' No, my dear fellow, this is most *certainly* the surest method we can follow, no matter who we are.

CLEINIAS: I trust you, sir, and I agree, so let's carry on with the discussion on that basis.

ATHENIAN: So it looks as if we have to compel the guardians of our divine foundation to get an exact idea of the common element in all the four virtues – that factor which, though single, is to be found in courage, restraint, justice and wisdom, and thus in our view deserves the general title 'virtue'. This element, my friends, if only we have the will, is what we must now cling to like leeches, and we must not relax our grip until we can explain adequately the essence of what we have to contemplate, whether it is a single entity, a composite whole, or both, or whatever. If this point eludes us, can we ever expect to attain virtue – when we can't say whether it comprises a great number of things or just four, or whether it is a unity? Never – not if we believe our own advice, anyway, and we'll have to ensure the growth of virtue in the state by some other means.[9] But if in the circumstances we decide we ought to abandon the attempt entirely, abandon it we must.

CLEINIAS: No, sir, in the name of the gods of hospitality, we must never abandon such a project: you seem to us to be absolutely right. So now then: how is one to tackle the problem?

ATHENIAN: Let's postpone the question of method. The 966 first thing we have to settle and decide among ourselves is whether the attempt should be made at all.

CLEINIAS: Indeed it should, if possible.

ATHENIAN: Well then, do we take the same line about goodness and beauty? Should the guardians know no more than that both these terms are a plurality, or should they understand the senses in which they are unities?

CLEINIAS: It looks as if they are more or less obliged to comprehend that too – how they are unities.

9. By habituation, I take it, rather than by knowledge: cf. p. 528 for the 'ordinary' virtue produced by habituation.

ATHENIAN: But what if they understood the point, but couldn't find the words to demonstrate it?

CLEINIAS: How absurd! That's the condition of a slave.

ATHENIAN: Well then, isn't our doctrine going to be the same about all serious questions? If our guardians are going to be *genuine* guardians of the laws they must have *genuine* knowledge of their real nature; they must be articulate enough to explain the real difference between good actions and bad, and capable of sticking to the distinction in practice.

CLEINIAS: Naturally.

THE IMPORTANCE OF THEOLOGY

ATHENIAN: And surely one of the finest fields of knowledge is theology, on which we've already lavished a great deal of attention. It's supremely important to appreciate – so far as it's given to man to know these things – the existence of the gods and the obvious extent of their power. The man in the street may be forgiven if he simply follows the letter of the law, but if any intended guardian fails to work hard to master every theological proof there is, we must certainly not grant *him* the same indulgence; in other words, we must never choose as a Guardian of the Laws anyone who is not preternaturally gifted or has not worked hard at theology, or allow him to be awarded distinctions for virtue.

CLEINIAS: It's fair enough, as you say, that the idle or incompetent in this business should never be allowed to get anywhere near such honours.

ATHENIAN: Now we know, don't we, that among the arguments we've already discussed, there are two in particular which encourage belief in the gods?

CLEINIAS: Which two are they?

ATHENIAN: One is the point we made about the soul, when we argued that it is far older and far more divine than all those things whose movements have sprung up and provided the impulse which has plunged it into a perpetual stream of existence.[10] Another argument was based on the systematic

10. The translation and interpretation of this mysterious sentence is far from certain.

motion of the heavenly bodies and the other objects under the control of reason, which is responsible for the order in the universe. No one who has contemplated all this with a careful and expert eye has in fact ever degenerated into such ungodliness as to reach the position that most people would expect him to reach. They suppose that if a man goes in for 967 such things as astronomy and the essential associated disciplines, and sees events apparently happening by necessity rather than because they are directed by the intention of a benevolent will, he'll turn into an atheist.

CLEINIAS: Well, what would happen, in fact?

ATHENIAN: Today, as I said, the situation is quite different from the time when thinkers regarded these bodies as inanimate. Even then, men were overcome with wonder at them, and those who studied them really closely got an inkling of the accepted doctrines of today, that such remarkably accurate predictions about their behaviour would never have been possible if they were inanimate, and therefore irrational; and even in those days there were some[11] who had the hardihood to stick their neck out and assert it was reason that imposed regularity and order on the heavens. However, these same thinkers went sadly astray over the soul's natural priority to matter: regarding soul as a recent creation, they turned the universe upside down, so to speak, and their own theories to boot. They concluded from the evidence of their eyes that all the bodies that move across the heavens were mere collections of stone and earth and many other kinds of inanimate matter – inanimate matter which nevertheless initiated a chain of causation responsible for all the order in the universe. Such conclusions led to a variety of atheistic and unpopular doctrines taking hold of these philosophers' minds; poets in particular were inspired to join in the abuse, and among other inanities compared the philosophers to bitches baying at the moon. But today, as I said, the situation is fundamentally different.

CLEINIAS: How so?

11. Presumably Anaxagoras (mid fifth century) in particular. Cf. Plato, *Phaedo*, 97b ff.

ATHENIAN: No mortal can ever attain a truly religious outlook without risk of relapse unless he grasps the two doctrines we're now discussing: first, that the soul is far older than any created thing, and that it is immortal and controls the entire world of matter; and second (a doctrine we've expounded often enough before) that reason is the supreme power among the heavenly bodies. He also has to master the essential preliminary studies, survey with the eye of a philosopher what they have in common, and use them to frame consistent rules of moral action; and finally, when a reasoned 968 explanation is possible, he must be able to provide it. No one who is unable to acquire these insights and rise above the level of the ordinary virtues[12] will ever be good enough to govern an entire state, but only to assist government carried on by others. And that means, Cleinias and Megillus, that we now have to consider whether we are going to add yet another law to the code we've already expounded, to the effect that the Nocturnal Council of the Authorities, duly primed by the course of studies we've described, shall be constituted the legal protector of the safety of the state. Or is there some alternative course for us to take?

CLEINIAS: Oh, but my dear sir, there's no question of refusing to add this law, if we can manage it, even if our success is only partial.

RECRUITMENT OF THE COUNCIL, AND ITS COURSE OF STUDIES

ATHENIAN: Then let's make every effort to win the struggle. I've had a lot of experience of such projects and have studied the field for a long time, so I'll be more than happy to help you – and perhaps I shall find others to join me.

CLEINIAS: Well, sir, we must certainly stick to the path on which – it is hardly an exaggeration to say – God himself is guiding us. But the question to which we need an answer at the moment is this: what will be the correct procedure on our part?

12. Cf. pp. 166 and 522.

ATHENIAN: Megillus and Cleinias, it is impossible to lay down the council's activities until it has been established. Its curriculum must be decided by those who have already mastered the necessary branches of knowledge – and only previous instruction and plenty of intimate discussion will settle successfully such matters as that.[13]

CLEINIAS: How so? How are we supposed to understand *that* remark?

ATHENIAN: First of all, of course, we shall have to compile a list of candidates qualified for the office of guardian by age, intellectual attainments, moral character and way of life. Then there's the question of what they have to learn. It is difficult to find out this for oneself, and it is not easy either to discover somebody else who has already done so and learn from him. Quite apart from that, it will be a waste of time to produce written regulations about the order in which the various subjects should be tackled and how long should be spent on each, because even the students, until they have thoroughly absorbed a subject, won't realize why it comes at just that point in the curriculum. So although it would be a mistake to treat all these details as inviolable secrets, it would be fair to say that they ought not to be divulged beforehand, because advance disclosure throws no light at all on the questions we're discussing.

CLOSING REMARKS

CLEINIAS: Well then, sir, if that's the case, what are we to do?

ATHENIAN: My friends, we must 'chance our arm', as the saying is. If we are prepared to stake the whole constitution on a throw of 'three sixes' or 'three ones', then that's what we'll have to do, and I'll shoulder part of the risk by giving 969 a full explanation of my views on training and education,

13. This opaque speech seems to mean that no rules for the council's studies can be framed except by those already qualified to be members, and they will need to undergo training first and then discuss their task. I have incorporated this view of the passage into the translation. See G. R. Morrow, *Plato's Cretan City*, 513, note 22.

which we've now started to discuss all over again. However, the risk is enormous and unique. So I bid you, Cleinias, take the business in hand: establish the state of the Magnesians (or whatever other name God adopts for it), and if you're successful you'll win enormous fame; at any rate you'll never lose a reputation for courage that will dwarf all your successors'. And if, my good companions, if this wonderful council of ours can be formed, then the state must be entrusted to it, and practically no modern legislator will want to oppose us. We thought of our combined metaphor of head and intellect, which we mentioned a moment ago, as idealistic dreaming[14] – but it will all come true, provided the council members are rigorously selected, properly educated, and after the completion of their studies lodged in the citadel of the country and made into guardians whose powers of protection we have never seen excelled in our lives before.

MEGILLUS: My dear Cleinias, judging from what we've heard said, either we'll have to abandon the project of founding the state or refuse to let our visitor leave us, and by entreaties and every ruse we can think of enrol him as a partner in the foundation of the state.

CLEINIAS: You're quite right, Megillus. That's what I'm going to do. May I enlist your help too?

MEGILLUS: You may indeed.

14. See pp. 519 and 524.

DEPARTURES FROM THE BUDÉ TEXT

Most of these emendations are either to be found in the *apparatus criticus* of the Budé text, or are my own. The sources of the others I give below.

638c5	τυϱούς	863b8	βίαιον
654a3	ἢ δή	864b7	καὶ δόξης, τοῦ ἀληθοῦς
657a7	delete θαϱϱοῦντα		περὶ τὸ ἄϱιστον ἔφεσις, τϱίτον
663c3	ἐναντίῳ for ἐναντίως[1]	871d7	τούτων for που τῶν
712e4	ἀνεϱωτηθείς	877c6	μή
718d2	τοι νυνδή	894c4	insert τε after ἑαυτήν[4]
737d1	ποσούς	903e4	delete μή
751c9	delete τε	914a8	ἀποδιδούσης
751d1	πϱὸς τό for πϱώτους	915d1	αὐτοῦ
759d5	τϱεῖς	932a3	νέοις
769c6	delete εἰς τὸ πϱόσθεν[2]	933e1	αἰστισινοῦν[5]
790e3	βακχείων[3]	933e3	ὧν τῆς
791b6	αὐτοῖς	937e5–6	μηχανήν — εἶναι
807b3	νῦν εἰ		δ'αὐτή — τοῦ τε δικάσασθαι
820b5	ἔφαμεν		καὶ συνδικεῖν ἄλλῳ, νικᾶν
821c5	ταῦτα ἀεί		δυναμένην,
832a11–b3	attributed to Clein-	947d7	πϱοτίμων
832b5–6	ias, not Megillus	954a5	delete ἤ
849b8	τϱίτη	960c9	ἀτϱάκτῳ for τϱί‹τῳ›

1. O. Apelt, *Platons Gesetze* (Leipzig, 1916), p. 234.
2. J. M. Pabon y M. Fernandez-Galiano, *Platon, Las Leyes* (Madrid, 1960), *ad loc*.
3. R. G. Bury, *The Laws of Plato* (London, 1926), *ad loc*.
4. F. Solmsen, in *Studien zur Textgeschichte und Textkritik*, editors H. Dahlmann and R. Merkelbach (Cologne, 1959), p. 268.
5. W. S. Barrett, *Euripides, Hippolytos* (Oxford, 1964), p. 439.

SELECT BIBLIOGRAPHIES

The modern literature on the *Laws* is vast and scattered, and no complete bibliography exists. The most extensive is:

T. J. Saunders, *Bibliography on Plato's Laws 1920–70, with additional citations through May 1975* (New York, 1976). The second edition (New York, 1979) covers 1920–76, and has additional citations through March 1979.

This bibliography has three sections: (a) texts, translations and commentaries; (b) books and articles (arranged under 13 general headings); (c) discussions of individual passages, with a list of selected pre-1920 collections of notes. In addition, the years 1945–55 have been covered by T. G. Rosenmeyer in *Classical Weekly*, 50 (1956–7), 180 and 182, and 1950–57 by H. Cherniss in *Lustrum*, 4 (1959), 103–14; see *ibid.* 8–9 for references to earlier modern bibliographies of Plato. Cherniss's work has been continued down to 1975 by L. Brisson in *Lustrum*, 20 (1977), esp. 42–4, 51, 270–72. See also R. D. McKirahan, Jr., *Plato and Socrates, A Comprehensive Bibliography, 1958–1973* (New York and London, 1978), esp. 115–18, 173–9.

THE TEXT

L. A. Post, *The Vatican Plato and its Relations* (Middletown, Connecticut, 1934)

É. des Places, Introduction (CCVII–CCXVII) to the Budé text below

GREEK TEXTS

J. Burnet (editor), *Platonis Opera*, vol. V (Oxford, 1907) (Oxford Classical Text)

É. des Places and A. Diès, *Platon, Oeuvres Complètes, Tomes XI et XII, Les Lois* (Paris 1951–65) (Budé Text)

COMMENTARY

E. B. England, *The Laws of Plato* (Manchester, 1921; reprinted New York, 1976)

For recent notes by T. J. Saunders, see reference on p. 41 *supra*.

TRANSLATIONS

Since 1870 there have been only four other translations of the *Laws* into English: (a) by B. Jowett (Oxford, 1871, fourth edition revised, 1953); (b) by R. G. Bury (London and Cambridge, Mass., 1926 [Loeb Classical Library]); (c) by A. E. Taylor (London, 1934, reprinted in Everyman's Library, 1960); by T. L. Pangle (New York, 1980)

GENERAL ACCOUNTS

Sir Ernest Barker, *Greek Political Theory* (London, 1918), 292–382

P. Friedländer, *Platon II* (Berlin and Leipzig, 1930), 623–81; second edition, enlarged, 1960, *III*, 360–414; English translation of second edition, with revisions, by H. Meyerhoff (New York, 1969), *III*, 387–444

T. A. Sinclair, *A History of Greek Political Thought* (London, 1951 and 1967), 186–208

A. E. Taylor, *Plato, The Man and His Work* (London, 1926; seventh edition, 1960), 463–97

A. Diès and Louis Gernet, Introduction to the Budé text above

Glenn R. Morrow, *Plato's Cretan City* (Princeton, 1960)

W. K. C. Guthrie, *A History of Greek Philosophy*, vol. V (Cambridge, 1978), chapter 5

THE INTRODUCTION

On Plato's life and thought, see G. C. Field, *Plato and his Contemporaries* (London, 1930)

The three major works in the modern controversy about Plato are: R. H. S. Crossman, *Plato Today* (second edition, London, 1959); K. R. Popper, *The Open Society and its Enemies*, vol. I, *The Spell of Plato* (fifth edition, London, 1966); Ronald B. Levinson, *In Defense of Plato* (Cambridge, Mass., 1953). The controversy is spiritedly continued by Robin Barrow, *Plato, Utilitarianism and Education* (London, 1975)

A useful collection of essays, reviews, etc., may be found in Renford Bambrough (editor), *Plato, Popper and Politics* (Cambridge, 1967). On the role of the utopian see P. H. Partridge, 'Politics, Philosophy, Ideology', in *Political Studies*, vol. IX (Oxford, 1961), reprinted in *Political Philosophy*, editor Anthony Quinton (Oxford,

1967), and H. J. N. Horsburgh, 'The Relevance of the Utopian', *Ethics*, LXVII (1956–7), 127–38. On the possible influence of the *Laws* on political ideas and practice in antiquity see: W. S. Ferguson, *Hellenistic Athens* (London, 1911), pp. 41 ff., C. B. Welles, 'The Greek City', in *Studi in Onore di Aristide Calderini e Roberto Paribeni* I (Milano, 1956), 81–99, and K. von Fritz, *The Theory of the Mixed Constitution in Antiquity* (New York, 1954)

ECONOMICS

A. A. Trever, *A History of Greek Economic Thought* (Chicago, 1916), 22–62

J. Bisinger, *Der Agrarstaat in Platons Gesetzen, Klio*, Beiheft XVII (1925)

S. Lauffer, 'Die Platonische Agrarwirtschaft', *Vierteljahrsschrift für Sozial- und Wirtschaftsgeschichte*, XXIX (1936), 233–69

C. Bradford Welles, 'The Economic background of Plato's Communism', *Journal of Economic History*, Supplement VIII (1948), 101–14

T. J. Saunders, 'The Property Classes and the Value of the ΚΛΗΡΟΣ in Plato's *Laws*', *Eranos*, LIX (1961), 29–39

E. Klingenberg, *Platons ΝΟΜΟΙ ΓΕΩΡΓΙΚΟΙ und das positive griechische Recht* (Berlin, 1976)

SOCIOLOGY

A. W. Gouldner, *Enter Plato* (New York, 1965; London, 1967)

EDUCATION, THE ARTS

G. M. Sargeaunt, 'Two Studies in Plato's *Laws*', *Hibbert Journal*, 21 (1922–3), 493–502 (' "Song and Dance" as a Function of the State'), 669–79 ('Man as God's Playfellow'). (The first item was reprinted as chapter 7 of *Classical Studies* [London, 1929; reprinted Washington and London, 1969])

R. G. Bury, 'The Theory of Education in Plato's *Laws*', *Revue des Études Grecques*, 50 (1937), 304–20

W. Jaeger, *Paideia, The Ideals of Greek Culture* (Oxford, 1945), vol. III, 213–62

H.-I. Marrou, *Histoire de l'Éducation dans l'Antiquité* (Paris, 1948); third edition revised and enlarged, 1955, 99–120; third edition, translated by G. Lamb, *A History of Education in Antiquity* (London, 1956), 61–78; paperback edition (New York, 1964), 95–118

E. W. Schipper, '*Mimesis* in the Arts in Plato's *Laws*', *Journal of Aesthetic and Art Criticism*, 32 (1963), 199–202

W. D. Anderson, *Ethos and Education in Greek Music* (Cambridge, Mass., 1966), 64–110

FAMILY LAW

W. G. Becker, *Platons Gesetze und das griechische Familienrecht* (München, 1932)

W. K. Lacey, *The Family in Classical Greece* (London, 1968), 177–94

HISTORY

R. G. Bury, 'Plato and History', *Classical Quarterly*, XLV (n.s. I) (1951), 86–93

H. van Effenterre, *La Crete et le Monde Grec de Platon à Polybe* (Paris, 1948), 45–74

E. A. Havelock, *The Liberal Temper in Greek Politics* (London, 1957), 44–51

R. Weil, *L' 'Archéologie' de Platon* (Paris, 1959)

M. Piérart, *Platon et la Cité Grecque: Théorie et Réalité dans la Constitution des Lois* (Brussels, 1974)

LAW

G. R. Morrow, *Plato's Law of Slavery in its Relation to Greek Law* (Urbana, Illinois, 1939)

G. R. Morrow, 'Plato and the Rule of Law', *Philosophical Review*, L (1941), 105–26. (Reprinted in *Plato, Popper and Politics* above)

H. Cairns, 'Plato's Theory of Law', *Harvard Law Review*, LVI (1942), 359–87. Reprinted in a revised and enlarged version in *id.*, *Legal Philosophy from Plato to Hegel* (Baltimore, 1949), 29–76; the original version, slightly abridged, appears also in P. Friedländer, *Plato, I*, English translation by H. Meyerhoff (London, 1958), 286–313.

J. P. Maguire, 'Plato's Theory of Natural Law', *Yale Classical Studies*, X (1947), 151–78

PENOLOGY

R. Maschke, *Die Willenslehre im griechischen Recht* (Berlin, 1926; reprinted Darmstadt, 1968), 90–92, 116–33

A. Meremetis, *Verbrecher und Verbrechen: Untersuchungen zum Strafrecht in Platons 'Gesetzen'* (Borna-Leipzig, 1940)

W. Knoch, *Die Strafbestimmungen in Platons Nomoi* (Wiesbaden, 1960)

Morris Davis, 'Monetary Fines and Limitations in Plato's Magnesia', *Classical Philology*, LXIV (1969), 98–101

Philip Schuchman, 'Comments on the Criminal Code of Plato's *Laws*', *Journal of the History of Ideas*, XXIV (1963), 25–40

A. D. Woozley, 'Plato on Killing in Anger', *Philosophical Quarterly*, XXII (1972), 303–17

T. J. Saunders, 'Plato on Killing in Anger: A Reply to Professor Woozley', *Philosophical Quarterly*, XXIII (1973), 350–56

T. J. Saunders, 'Plato's Clockwork Orange', *Durham University Journal*, XXXVII (1975–6), 113–17

T. J. Saunders, 'Protagoras and Plato on Punishment', in G. B. Kerford (ed.), *The Sophists and their Legacy* (Wiesbaden, 1981)

PHILOSOPHY

V. Brochard, 'Les *Lois* de Platon et la Théorie des Idées', in *id. Études de Philosophie Ancienne et de Philosophie Moderne*, ed. V. Delbos (Paris, 1912; new edition, 1926), 151–68

G. Müller, *Studien zu den Platonischen Nomoi* (München, 1951; second edition, 1968)

R. Schaerer, 'L'Itinéraire Dialectique des *Lois* de Platon et sa Signification Philosophique', *Revue Philosophique de France et de l'Étranger*, CXLIII (1953), 379–412

M. Vanhoutte, *La Philosophie Politique de Platon dans les Lois* (Louvain, 1954)

J. Gould, *The Development of Plato's Ethics* (Cambridge, 1957)

H. Görgemanns, *Beitrage zur Interpretation von Platons Nomoi* (München, 1960)

A. W. H. Adkins, *Merit and Responsibility* (Oxford), 1960, especially chapter 14

T. J. Saunders, 'The Socratic Paradoxes in Plato's *Laws*', *Hermes*, 96 (1968), 421–34

THEOLOGY AND RELIGION

F. Solmsen, *Plato's Theology* (New York, 1942), especially 131 ff.

O. Reverdin, *La Réligion de la Cité Platonicienne* (Paris, 1945)

V. Martin, 'Sur la Condemnation des Athées par Platon au X⁰ Livre des Lois', *Studia Philosophica*, XI (1951), 103–54

W. de Mahieu, 'La Doctrine des Athées au X⁰ Livre des Lois de Platon', *Revue Belge de Philologie et d'Histoire*, 41 (1963), 5–24; 42 (1964), 16–47

T. J. Saunders, 'Penology and Eschatology in Plato's *Timaeus* and *Laws*', *Classical Quarterly*, XXIII (1973), 232–44

LIST OF CRIMES

BOOK V

BOOK VI

BOOK VII

BOOK VIII

BOOK IX

APPENDIX: PLATO'S LETTERS

My account of Plato's life and thought, particularly of the Sicilian episodes, is to some extent based on his 'autobiographical' *Seventh Letter*. Unfortunately, at least one of the thirteen letters that have come down to us under Plato's name is spurious, and none of the others can be shown to be certainly genuine; the reasons for asserting their genuineness or falsity are speculative, frequently double-edged and never conclusive. I cannot here go into the details of this highly contentious topic: I merely record my view that *Letters* III, VII and VIII are genuine and may therefore legitimately be used in a reconstruction of Plato's career. This opinion is in accord with the general consensus among scholars in recent years.[1]

How relevant are the *Letters* for our understanding of the *Laws*? There are, I think, two main issues, the first particular and the second general.

(1) It may well be that Plato wrote most of the first four books of the *Laws* with Sicilian conditions in mind. This thesis has been most plausibly argued by L. A. Post.[2] Near the end of the fourth book of the *Laws* the Athenian Stranger refers to the whole of the preceding discussion as 'legislative preamble' (see p. 184). In *Letter* III, written to Dionysius II in the year 357, Plato mentions (316a) that when in Sicily in Dionysius' court in 367 he 'paid some little attention to the preambles to the laws'. Post suggests that this refers in effect to the first four books of the *Laws* and points out that there are many passages in those books which look as if they refer to Sicilian political problems and read like more or less direct advice to Dionysius. The most celebrated of these passages is 709 ff. (pp. 165–6 ff.), where the Stranger asks

1. But see L. Edelstein, *Plato's Seventh Letter* (Leiden, 1966); G. Ryle, *Plato's Progress* (Cambridge, 1966), especially pp. 55–101. For references to other scholarly literature see H. Cherniss, *op. cit.* on p. 533. A good summary of the controversy is J. E. Raven, *Plato's Thought in the Making* (Cambridge, 1965), pp. 19 ff.
2. 'The Preludes to Plato's *Laws*', *Transactions and Proceedings of the American Philological Association*, LX (1929), 5–24.

a legislator what conditions in the state will enable him to run it properly. The legislator replies: 'Give me a state under the absolute control of a dictator, and let the dictator be young, with a good memory, quick to learn, courageous, and with a character of natural elevation.' [He should also be lucky in being] 'the contemporary of a distinguished lawgiver and fortunate enough to come in contact with him. . . .' 'The next best thing would be a pair of such dictators, the third best would be several of them.' For 'dictator' read 'Dionysius', and for 'distinguished lawgiver' read 'Plato'.[3]

I am not bowled over by this seemingly attractive line of argument. Dionysius II was a young man of volatile temper whose taste for philosophy exceeded his ability and whose enthusiasm was greater than his perseverance. Anything more likely than *Laws* I–IV to bore such a man to extinction is difficult to imagine. I prefer to suppose that Plato merely composed, perhaps with Dionysius at his elbow, a number of 'preambles' of the kind he explains in *Laws* 720 ff., which he proposed to prefix to certain laws he was pressing on Dionysius.[4] As for the description of the discussion preceding 722c, as 'preambles', this seems to me to be no more than a slender joke, suggested by the context, to the effect that it is about time the discussion advanced beyond its preliminary stages. The other 'references' to Sicily seem to me so general as to be worthless. But I must admit that I can no more conclusively refute Post's thesis than he can demonstrate it: the only possible verdict is 'not proven'.

(2) On the more general issue I shall be provocative and dogmatic.[5] It is commonly supposed that Plato's disappointments in Sicily marked some sort of turning point in his political thought; that the philosopher-kings of the *Republic* constituted his ideal, which he attempted to realize in the person of Dionysius II, and that after he had learned the impracticability of this ideal he sadly turned to the construction of a more down-to-earth utopia in the *Laws*. This seems to me a distortion. There is not a scrap of evidence to

3. Ryle (*op. cit.* 88–9, 99–100, 180–81, 257) takes for granted the identification of the dictator with Dionysius. For Ryle's views of the composition of the *Laws*, see *op. cit.* pp. 256–9 and my comments in *Revue Belge de Philologie et d'Histoire*, XLV (1967), 496–7.

4. Such 'preamble material' *may* of course have been utilized later at various places in the *Laws*. See Morrow, *op. cit.* below, p. 92, n. 4.

5. Cf. my remarks in the introduction, pp. 27–8.

suggest that Plato ever tried to convert Dionysius or anyone else into a *Republic*-style philosopher-king. Doubtless Plato wanted to give Dionysius some philosophical training, so as to demonstrate the reasons for the code of laws and form of constitution Plato hoped to see him adopt, but that is all. If *Letter* VII is genuine, we have Plato's own word that even in 388 (which is probably earlier and can hardly be later than the composition of the *Republic*), Plato insisted and Dion accepted that the Syracusans ought to live under 'the rule of the best of laws' (324 ab, cf. 334c).[6] This remark, and that of *Letter* III about the preambles, suggest that whatever the advice was that Plato gave in Sicily, it was something more practical than the scheme of the *Republic*. I therefore suggest that although the Sicilian episodes may in one way or another have prompted Plato to commit his practical political programme to writing, they were not the occasion of any fundamental change in his views. Nevertheless, for the student of Plato's political ideas the *Letters* are required reading: they give us an invaluable insight into his character, his reaction to contemporary events, and the lengths he was prepared to go in order to put his theories into practice.

6. See G. R. Morrow, *Plato's Epistles* (second edition, New York, 1962), pp. 148 ff.

INDEX OF NAMES

This index supplements the detailed table of contents (pp. 5–14) and the list of crimes (pp. 539–44); it covers the translation and the more important names in the footnotes, but *not* the Introduction, Appendix or 'signposts'.

MORE ABOUT PENGUINS, PELICANS
AND PUFFINS

For further information about books available from Penguins please write to Dept EP, Penguin Books Ltd, Harmondsworth, Middlesex UB7 0DA.

In the U.S.A.: For a complete list of books available from Penguins in the United States write to Dept DG, Penguin Books, 299 Murray Hill Parkway, East Rutherford, New Jersey 07073.

In Canada: For a complete list of books available from Penguins in Canada write to Penguin Books Canada Ltd, 2801 John Street, Markham, Ontario L3R 1B4.

In Australia: For a complete list of books available from Penguins in Australia write to the Marketing Department, Penguin Books Australia Ltd, P.O. Box 257, Ringwood, Victoria 3134.

In New Zealand: For a complete list of books available from Penguins in New Zealand write to the Marketing Department, Penguin Books (N.Z.) Ltd, P.O. Box 4019, Auckland 10.

In India: For a complete list of books available from Penguins in India write to Penguin Overseas Ltd, 706 Eros Apartments, 56 Nehru Place, New Delhi 110019.

PLATO

THE REPUBLIC

TRANSLATED BY DESMOND LEE

Plato (427–347 B.C.), finally disillusioned by contemporary
politics after the execution of Socrates, showed in his writings
the enormous influence of that great philosopher. *The Republic*,
his treatise on an ideal state, was the first of its kind in
European thought. For Plato, political science was the science
of the soul, and included moral science. *The Republic*'s
emphasis on the right education for rulers, the prevalence
of justice, and harmony between all classes of society, is as
strong as its condemnation of democracy, which Plato
considered encouraged bad leadership.

THE SYMPOSIUM

TRANSLATED BY WALTER HAMILTON

Of all the Greek philosophers, Plato was perhaps the greatest.
The Symposium – a masterpiece of dramatic dialogue – is set at
a dinner party to which are invited several of the literary
celebrities of Athenian society. After dinner it is proposed
that each member of the company should make a speech in
praise of love. A full discussion follows and the dialogue ends
with a brilliant character sketch of Socrates by Alcibiades.
Throughout Plato reveals, as few other authors have done,
the beauty, power, and flexibility of Greek prose.

PLATO

THE LAST DAYS OF SOCRATES

TRANSLATED BY HUGH TREDENNICK

The trial and condemnation of Socrates, on charges of heresy and corrupting the minds of the young, forms one of the most tragic episodes in the history of Athens in decline. In the four works which compose this volume – *Euthyphro*, *The Apology*, *Crito*, and *Phaedo* – Plato, his most devoted disciple, has preserved for us the essence of his teaching and the logical system of question and answer he perfected in order to define the nature of virtue and knowledge. The vindication of Socrates and the pathos of his death are admirably conveyed in Hugh Tredennick's modern translation.

GORGIAS

TRANSLATED BY WALTER HAMILTON

To judge by its bitter tone Plato's *Gorgias* was written shortly after the death of Socrates. Though Gorgias was a Sicilian teacher of oratory, the dialogue is more concerned with ethics than with the art of public speaking. The ability, professed particularly by the Sophists, to make the worse cause appear the better, struck Plato as the source of all corruption. The dialogue's chief interest lies, not in Gorgias' courteous outline of his art, but in the clash between Socrates, the true philosopher, and Callicles, a young Athenian of the stamp of Alcibiades, who brashly maintains that might is right.

PLATO

TIMAEUS AND CRITIAS

TRANSLATED BY DESMOND LEE

The *Timaeus*, in which Plato attempted a scientific explanation
of the universe's origin, is the earliest Greek account of a
divine creation: as such it has significantly influenced European thought, even down to the present day. Yet this dialogue
and, even more, its unfinished sequel, the *Critias*, have latterly
attracted equal attention as the sources of the Atlantis legend.
Plato's exact descriptions of an antediluvian world have
fermented the imaginations of hundreds of writers in this
century and the last, and the translator has now appended
an intriguing survey of Atlantis and of theories (crazy and
plausible) about the vanished continent.

PROTAGORAS AND MENO

TRANSLATED BY W. K. C. GUTHRIE

Plato held that philosophy must be a product of living contact
between mind and mind, and his dialogues afforded him the
means of reaching a wide audience. *Protagoras*, possibly his
dramatic masterpiece, deals, like *Meno*, with the problem of
teaching the art of successful living and good citizenship.
While *Protagoras* keeps to the level of practical common-
sense, *Meno* leads on into the heart of Plato's philosophy, the
immortality of the soul and the doctrine that learning is
knowledge acquired before birth.

Also published:

PHAEDRUS AND LETTERS
VII AND VIII

THE PENGUIN CLASSICS

A selection

THE PSALMS
Translated by Peter Levi

Balzac
SELECTED SHORT STORIES
Translated by Sylvia Raphael

Flaubert
SALAMMBO
Translated by A. J. Krailsheimer

Zola
LA BÊTE HUMAINE
Translated by Leonard Tancock

A NIETZSCHE READER
Translated by R. J. Hollingdale

Cao Xueqin
**THE STORY OF THE STONE VOLUME TWO: THE
CRAB-FLOWER CLUB**
Translated by David Hawkes

Balzac
THE WILD ASS'S SKIN
Translated by H. J. Hunt

Cicero
LETTERS TO ATTICUS
Translated by D. R. Shackleton Bailey